ROVING COMMISSIONS 38

ROYAL CRUISING CLUB
JOURNAL 1997

Edited by PETER CUMBERLIDGE

Editorial Acknowledgements

Our thanks are due to many people for each edition of Roving Commissions: to all the contributors, who put in so much time, thought and effort to write the logs and cruising accounts which form the main content of the book; and also to those who compile the various 'Club Matters' sections at the end.

My grateful thanks to the illustrators: to Maggie Nelson for producing the charts; David Cobb for his sketch on page 2, John Coldrey for the sketches on pages 27, 77 and 171; Henry Franks for the drawing of *Matawa* on page 135; and to Marcia Pirie for the Frisian sketch on page 236.

Jonathan Trafford and Christopher Buckley were our eagle-eyed proof-readers. Grateful thanks also to Sandy Watson for his continued and highly efficient scanning service, which deals with the significant number of contributions that do not arrive on disk.

Finally, thank you to the conscientious staff at Bookcraft and Footnote Graphics, who work hard to ensure that Roving Commissions is produced to a consistently high standard.

ISBN 0 901916 18 8

Typeset by Footnote Graphics. Printed and bound
by Bookcraft, Midsomer Norton 01761 419167

Contents

THE LONG AND THE SHORT OF IT

1997 looks like being a good year for claret and was certainly an exceptional year for contributions to Roving Commissions. More than 50 members have worked hard to produce the extraordinarily diverse chapters packed between these covers. Over 30% more logs than last year found their way onto the editor's desk. Although we have juggled the budget to produce an extra 32 pages, a few good regular authors were still squeezed out of this year's book by sheer pressure of space. We see, on the other hand, some new names in the contents list, which is always a great pleasure.

Among the many notable pieces in Roving Commissions 38, the longest contribution and one of the shortest have a tenuous link through two famous past members. This year's most extensive and far-ranging log is the story of Noël Marshall's circumnavigation with *Sadko*, an account that covers an amazing scope with a brisk pace and light touch. A cruise around the world is a significant and, I always think, almost incredible achievement. Even now, with strong evidence piling up, one still can't be quite sure that the world is really spherical unless you go round and have a look. Theory is all very well, but to arrive back at your starting point by constantly sailing west seems sound empirical evidence.

Sadko's cruise is by no means a 'traditional' circumnavigation, and her wanderings in Micronesia, Japan and Vladivostok make absorbing reading. The end of this chapter is as low-key as the rest has led you to expect, but Noël Marshall's final dedication will strike a chord with many:

"At breakfast time on 17th August we groped our way through driving rain into the Visitors Haven in Falmouth, with three weeks in hand before the Beaulieu Meet. So ended *Sadko*'s First Cruise. The echo is implied homage: for thousands of my generation, it was Arthur Ransome who led us to the sea, in wartime Britain, before many of us had ever seen it. How grateful we are."

One of my favourite short contributions this year, an evocative reminiscence by Richard Coleman, revisits the exploits of another famous early member of the Club, the inimitable Erskine Childers, who shared with Ransome that rare ability to describe what life is really like aboard a small boat at sea. Both writers capture the nub of the whole business, so that you can practically feel the pull of the tiller and catch that unique boaty whiff of sail locker and bilge.

Richard Coleman brings out the fascinating connections between *Dulcibella*'s autumn foray among the German Frisian Islands on a little secret service, and Childers' own eventful cruise with *Vixen* in 1897. It is always intriguing to see those first inspirations for the Riddle of the Sands emerging from the entries in Childers' own manuscript diary, now in the National Maritime Museum.

The memorable description of *Vixen*'s / *Dulcibella*'s headlong dash into Bensersiel in a north-easterly gale makes chilling reading for anyone familiar with the bleak austerity of the German Frisian coast. All the more inspiring to contemplate these exploits from our standpoint of relative decadence, equipped with self-furling sails, diesel engines, electric anchor winches and pinpoint electronic navigation.

It always seems salutary, now and again, to be reminded of the pioneers of cruising under sail and how things were not so very long ago. This is not just for the pleasures of nostalgia, but also to make sure we never lose touch with the essence of cruising or become preoccupied with the technology, of which there is a lot about.

Peter Cumberlidge
February 1998

NORTH TO HVRATSKA

by Christopher Lawrence-Jones

Stretched out in the cockpit under the bimini, I gazed across the inlet from our berth at the Lega Navale and watched the flag hanging limply above the Castello Alfonsino opposite. For two days it had shown that the brisk north wind which had slowed our progress up the Italian coast to Brindisi was unabated. The anticlockwise Adriatic current, enhanced by the north wind, had been running at a relentless two knots. This, combined with unexpectedly steep seas, had resulted in an exciting midnight arrival, with large ferries suddenly appearing from behind the new northern breakwater, unlit that night.

Opposite, the flag was beginning to stir, confirming the forecast for a good south-easterly – ideal for the 100 miles to Dubrovnik. I glanced at Gail who appeared to be reading, but her eyes were closed. I gave her a nudge: 'Time to go north to Hvratska'.

Soon Italy was fading astern, but away to starboard, just over the horizon, lay the baleful coast of Albania. A *frisson* of apprehension under-lay the enjoyment of the sunset, as we recalled stories, suddenly vivid, of high speed launches preying on vulnerable yachts in these waters.

Slipping along under full sail with the crescent moon setting to port, I reflected on the cruise so far. After leaving our winter berth at Cala Galera, near Porto Ercole on the west coast of Italy, there had been some good sailing to and amongst the Pontine islands. At the island of Ventotene, we had planned on anchoring in the Cala Rossano as the old galley port is rather small. As we entered, however, an official looking person beckoned to us and another yacht to go alongside a vacant quay. Just as we had finished making fast, another man arrived:

'Sorry, this is the ferry berth'.

'But we have just been put here!'

'No, no! Sorry, that man is a bad man'.

So, we did anchor after all. Later that evening while walking in the fine old town, I spotted our 'berthing master'.

'You are a very naughty man,' I said. He looked very sheepish but didn't offer to return the *lire* he had received.

At one of the RCC winter dinners, Nicko Franks had told me he knew a member at Naples and would alert him. I soon received a charming note from Captain David Mowlam inviting us to stay as long as we liked at the NATO yacht club at Nisida. It was a new experience to have a Royal Naval Captain in immaculate summer uniform taking our lines and insisting on pulling up muddy mooring ropes – the tradition of Royal Naval hospitality was certainly burning brightly here. David could not have been more helpful, laying on a car for shopping, inviting us to lunch at the NATO HQ and arranging for a brilliant dentist trained in the States to drop all his patients and repair poor Gail's broken tooth, caused by biting over enthusiastically on an olive.

After a day of calm seas off the incomparable Amalfi coast, a bad weather forecast prompted us to make for Salerno. We were berthed alongside the main quay, which was at exactly the same level as our ports. After dusk, when we looked out, it was to find a troop of enormous cockroaches at eye level, assessing us with an unflinching gaze.

We were glad to leave Salerno (and, we hoped, the cockroaches) next day. The wind piped up from the south-west and soon a reefed *Mermerus* was racing across the gulf at seven knots. The 21 miles to Punta Licosa evaporated in three hours, and then we eased sheets for the cape named after the famous pilot Palinuro. *Mermerus* was truly in song as we sped down the coast in brilliant sunshine with the sea to ourselves, until we reached Punta degli Infreschi, 60 miles in eight hours. Just round this point was an entrancing cove, deserted and well sheltered, where we dropped anchor.

Here we had entered the Golfo di Policastro, and the description in the Michelin guide cannot be bettered: 'This magnificent gulf extending from the tip of Infreschi to Praia a Mare is backed by high mountains whose sharp, needle-like peaks soar skywards. The slopes are planted with olive groves and clumps of chestnut trees. A series of small villages succeed one another along this enchanting coast, where green coloured waters lap the charming creeks.'

Our arrival off the Straits of Messina had been timed for neaps and favourable tides, but as a retired Italian captain had told me, the wind matters the most. As we neared the Straits, dark clouds and very uncomfortable short steep seas heralded an increasingly strong south wind. The Straits glowered at us ominously and we remembered how the ancients had feared these waters. It was an easy decision to head for the fishing port of Bagnara Calabra where there was perfect shelter behind a high wall. Made fast alongside a brightly painted fishing vessel, we could study the swordfish boats. They have an enormously high central structure for spotting the swordfish and another projecting forward for harpooning them.

Venice, the finale of a wondrous summer cruise.

Climbing the sea wall next morning it was amazing to see that, after the previous night's storm, the sea was glassy calm and all the swordfish boats were already on the chase. The forecast was still for strong winds from the south, but we could always turn back. The tides were wrong but, as has been remarked in the past, there is a useful inshore eddy off Scilla. To our surprise and delight a north wind then sprang up and we were able to run on through these fascinating waters. The afternoon forecast was for north-westerly F 5-6 so we pressed on to the artificial port of Saline Joniche.

As we approached, there appeared to be a beach just inside the breakwaters, but closer inspection revealed that a sandspit had formed almost right across the entrance, where once large vessels could pass. As no ships can now enter, the harbour had many cruising yachts lying at anchor. The wind arrived around midnight – a howling screeching tempest out of the Straits, with gale force gusts, now from the north, now from the west. No sleep for anyone that night, with lights on and off, chain in and out, and yachts moving to re-anchor or make fast to the harbour wall. It would be 36 hours before the fleet could disperse, which it did with alacrity, anxious to be as far as possible from those waters. Mount Etna looked down with amusement.

My thoughts were interrupted by the dim lights of a vessel converging with us from the east – the Albanian side. The moon had set, leaving the stars even more brilliant than before, and we were continuing to run steadily before the gentle south wind. My pulse quickened as the lights headed straight for us, but then turned slowly away – probably just a lone fishing boat.

Dead ahead and shining in the morning sun, we could make out the walls of Dubrovnik, and by midday we were berthed at Gruz – the port of entry – where formalities were completed with friendliness and courtesy. A few days were spent at the Dubrovnik marina, lying at the head of a magnificent fjord-like inlet, round the corner from the city (where berthing is not allowed). Above the monastery and cypress trees on the east side, a barren wall of rock towered above us – the ancient border and the border once again. The marina was devastated in the war, but now many yachts were back. The damage to Dubrovnik is well on the way to being restored; many roofs have had to be replaced. Everywhere there are the scars left by bullets and shrapnel. Further up the coast, many of the buildings had been systematically shelled, and not all have been rebuilt. The islands, however, were largely spared.

There are said to be over 700 islands stretching up the Dalmatian coast, and for the next month we sailed amongst them, spell-bound by their beauty. Most of the islands are green, with palms and cypresses. There are endless tranquil anchorages; the translucent water is warm and inviting. Ashore there are entrancing villages and ancient walled Venetian towns. Further north, the outer islands are more barren, but it was pure joy to tack *Mermerus* easily among the myriad channels that lie between the astonishing series of ochre coloured cones that are the Kornati.

Eventually, the time came to seek clearance out of Croatia and head across to Venice. Here we knew that our wonderful Honorary Foreign Representative, Dr. Gianpietro Zucchetta, had reserved us a berth. Not only that, but he and his wife Milene would give us a great welcome and take us for a sail round the lagoon in their beautiful yacht *Mattutina*.

To enter the Venetian lagoon on a bright sunny afternoon and follow the winding channel towards the Campanile and Doges' Palace was a sublime experience. Then, after crossing the most famous piece of water in the world amongst gondolas and vaporettos, we berthed in the old harbour on the island of San Georgio, beneath the walls of its great church just opposite the Piazza San Marco: what a finale to a wondrous summer cruise.

Mermerus is a Freedom 38, built in Rhode Island in 1992. She has a single, tall, carbon-fibre unstayed mast and is rigged as a sloop. The mast is fairly well forward and the mainsail, with its large roach, does most of the work. The small jib has an integral camber spar and is self tacking.

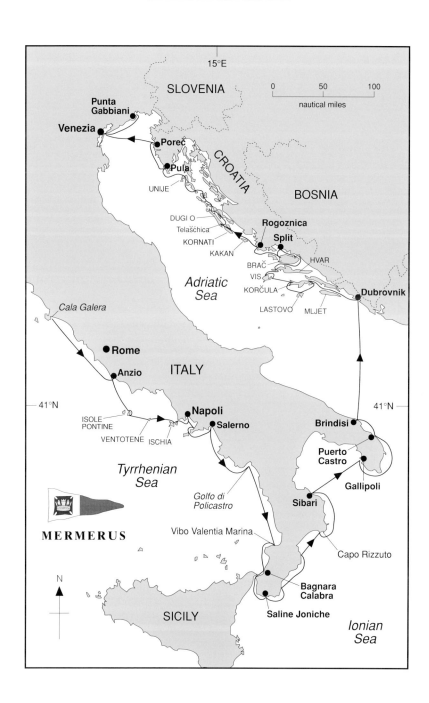

WITH TOPSAIL AND FISHERMAN TO ST KILDA

by Mike Bolton

Mary Bryant is a beautiful 48 foot schooner built in 1981 in Fowey to a design closely modelled upon a traditional New England schooner. Anna Stratton became her owner in 1991 and her try-out cruise was to Iceland and back. Since then she has cruised twice to the Caribbean and on to Nova Scotia to meet and race against sister schooners.

As an Ocean Youth Club skipper for four years, Anna made many friends among her volunteer mates and five of us arranged to sail with her for a ten-day Hebrides cruise starting from Oban in mid-June 1997. The crew was Robert and Erica Hollingdale, Doug and Alison Angus and myself.

Despite a late afternoon start on the first day, a fine NE breeze took us under all plain sail, dining as we went, to anchor in Traigh Gheal Bay on the Ross of Mull. Bright sunshine looked kindly upon a cockpit breakfast next morning as a gentle northwesterly set in. Cooking is on a traditional paraffin stove, toast easily made on the hot plates which tend to make it concave. Getting the anchor under sail, it was time for the crew to be reminded how to set the topsail above the main gaff and the fisherman between the masts. Why is it called a fisherman? It seems that when schooners of this type were fishing, access to the hold was needed for stowing the fish. The fores'l and its spars were lowered and lashed to one side, but a free flying sail – the fisherman – could be set above them.

By mid-morning, as the breeze fell light, it was time to lower the jib and replace it with the genoa and thus the ship had her biggest cloud of canvas aloft; a fine sight which two Minke whales surfaced to admire.

The main objective of the cruise was St. Kilda, and as the long term forecast predicted eventual south-easterlies which were unfavourable for Village Bay, it was decided to set watches and sail straight there. The system selected was one person on the helm for two hours, with a relief on standby below, ready to adjust sails or do anything else as required.

At the end of the spell the relief took over the helm and a new standby came on, so each crew member had six hours off and four hours on. The skipper did not stand a watch and the system worked well.

By midnight the ship was four miles off Barra Head, it still being light enough at midsummer to see dolphins and porpoises cavorting around. It seemed that a quick visit to Mingulay would be in order, as none of the crew had visited before. We anchored in the SW corner of the east-facing bay for a few hours sleep before a cockpit breakfast, during which the midges breakfasted off me. Ashore in bright sunshine, we found only one of the houses occupied, the others in various states of ruin. On the west cliffs, puffins, fulmars and guillemots were nesting.

Towards noon, we motorsailed round the cliffs and geos to see more local birdlife, before setting course for St Kilda under full sail in airs varying between SW and NW. The aquatic admiration society this time comprised two white-beaked dolphins. Towards midnight there was a brilliant sunset and, although we looked for it, there was no green flash.

0500 found *Mary Bryant* beating into Village Bay in gentle airs and sunshine to find four yachts already at anchor. Attempts to anchor under sail were thwarted by a gust which took the ship aback and the engine was needed to be sure we would not foul an anchored yacht. With the expected forecast of SE winds, it was time to breakfast and get ashore to make the best of the day. While we were eating, two great skuas were chasing herring gulls, making them disgorge their breakfasts which then became food for baby skuas. While we cleaned ship after three days at sea, the skipper called on the National Nature Reserve warden to ask if the crew could land on Hirta and pay a courtesy call on the Royal Artillery CO.

All was in order for us to go anywhere ashore, but we were warned to

Western Cliffs, Mingulay

avoid disturbing the great skuas as far as possible as the parents were very defensive of their young. We bought St Kilda T-shirts at the army shop before visiting the museum set up in one of the restored houses. It was a surprise to learn that there had never been a saint called Kilda. The name is thought to be a corruption of the old Norse word 'skildir', meaning shields, a possible reference to the shape of the islands when viewed at a distance from the sea.

It was a hot climb to the hills overlooking the bay to see the long curve of beach backed by the houses and cleits (stone and turf chambers built for the storage of food and fodder). Another surprise was to learn later from the army that the beach upon which the landing craft land their vehicles completely washes away every winter, so, for six months of the year, all communication is by helicopter. Gradually, each spring, the sand builds up again.

Up on the hill we could see female great skuas among the scrub and kept well clear because their chicks would be nearby. But it made no difference, the birds made repeated dives at us, one parent from one direction, the other from the other, so we had continually to be on the defensive, holding rucksacks etc over our heads. The Shetland name for the great skua is "bonxie". Rather appropriate!

Back at the army camp we rather fancied showers, but found that they were not open until late evening. Meanwhile the wind had gone south-easterly with a swell beginning to roll into the bay. With forecast SE 6/7 there was nothing for it but to clear out, the other yachts doing the same. With a reefed main, foresail and jib and a cup of soup inside each of us we sailed for Boreray to see the stacs and cliffs with their thousands of gannets, looking at a distance like teeming white microbes. Hundreds of them circled us, occasionally diving for fish, together with fulmars, razorbills and of course the attendant marauding bonxies. We too dined off fish, but ours was cooked with rice and followed by a delicious baked peach flan. The only complaint was from Robert, at all this dining at sea. We had hardly made a start on the malt whisky and wine so carefully brought aboard.

By midnight, the wind was blowing south-easterly force six, which rushed us at hull speed towards Loch Carloway by 0645. The duty watch comprised Robert, the Skipper and myself, the others remaining blissfully asleep below, not even hearing the cable running out. Mindful of Robert's complaint, I suggested a smidgeon of Black Label to celebrate a fast passage. His face lit up and the Skipper joined us in a hefty dram before we three breakfasted off the remains of the fish and rice.

Dram and breakfast were not enough to drug the Skipper though, because at 1000 we were all awakened by her call. "We're dragging folks!" She had heard the rudder just beginning to bump. The anchor came up bound solidly in a great bundle of weed and we re-anchored, this time pulling the hook in with the engine and with generous extra cable.

Too late for breakfast, too early for lunch, we all brunched off bacon and eggs to give us energy for an expedition to the Carloway Broch, the best preserved example in the west coast and Hebrides. All very impressive and well looked after by Historic Scotland. Then we split into two parties to hitch-hike the six miles to the Standing Stones of Callanish. Robert, Erica and I were fortunate to be picked up by two Swiss lads in their hired car almost immediately and by way of thanks we treated them to tea and cakes in the Callanish visitors' centre. We had all seen the Stones on earlier trips, but the new exhibition in the Centre added more meaning to the visit.

A friendly van driver lifted us back to the ship after we'd walked about half way. Robert spotted a crabber unloading at the pier and rowed over for a bucketful of crabs. He spent an hour cooking and dressing them and they made an excellent first course to the pineapple ham dinner cooked by Anna. He was very happy, as were we all – no restriction on malt whisky and wine! A full night's sleep, with no alarms from a well dug in anchor.

Thursday 19 June dawned sunny and dry with a moderate south-easterly. Setting of all plain sail with two reefs in the main, we were headed for the Butt of Lewis which was abeam mid-afternoon. Decision time – where to go? We chose Loch Laxford, reached in a calm so flat that the fulmars were mirrored in the water as they swooped down over it. Dinner, an excellent ham curry, was still at sea, so no drams or wine – Robert was getting desperate; there was still so much left in the locker.

There was a perfect sunset, but the happiness of seeing it was spoilt as we approached Weavers Bay to find our way barred by masses of mussel buoys and lines. It was too hazardous to try to feel our way past them in the dark and we motored back to another anchorage, Bagh na Airde Bise, to find mussel lines there too; but there was enough clear water to get past them.

The first job in the morning was to motor back to Weavers Bay to see if the anchorage could be used at all, but it could not. The spot marked by an anchor symbol on the chart was free of mussel lines but obstructed by workboat moorings. An inspection of John Ridgeway's adventure school at Ardmore followed. *English Rose* was there but the place was otherwise deserted. By midday we were ghosting round Handa Island looking at cliff ledges resembling white painted high rise flats for the thousands of seabirds nesting there. The most impressive was Great Stack, where *Mary Bryant* was surrounded by rafts of guillemots and razorbills. To get a closer look at the birds, we anchored off nearby Traighe Shourie and walked round to the 'high rise flats'. On our return a warden met us, saying that no landing was allowed; we should have sailed round to Tarbert and paid £6 each on the ferry before walking the approved route

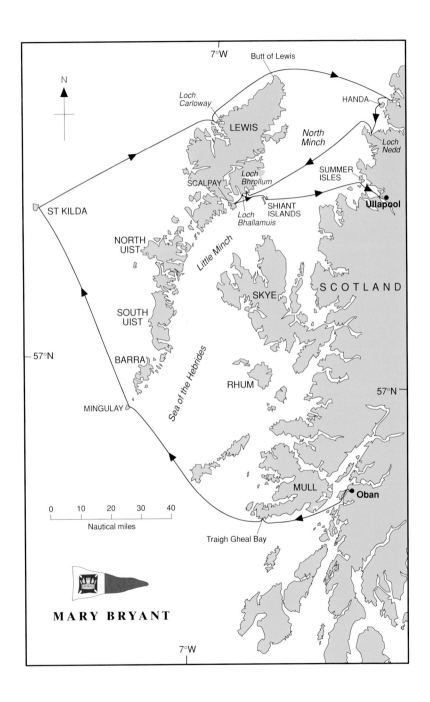

MARY BRYANT

across the island. We had, he said, caused a pair of ring plovers to leave their nest and they had not returned. We apologised but had known nothing of the restrictions. It did seem rather unreasonable to expect sailors to go to Tarbert and use the ferry when they could anchor and access the landing place from their own dinghies.

Variable breezes filled in from the south as we headed for Loch Nedd under plain sail plus the genoa. *Mary Bryant* always enters and leaves an anchorage under sail if possible and I was fortunate to be on the helm at the time. Sometimes it was necessary to spin the wheel to full helm as the wind changed thirty degrees in direction during the gusts, but the schooner was so responsive that it was a delight to be sailing her.

Sailing towards our selected anchoring spot the staysail was lowered, the mainsail hauled flat aft and the peak of the foresail dropped. This allowed a slow approach. As the anchor was lowered and touched bottom, the genoa was backed so that the bow paid off as cable was veered and this sail was then dropped. The foresail was lowered and the still flat mainsail brought the ship neatly head to wind on a tight cable. All excellent seamanship and it was easy to see why Anna so hugely enjoys her schooner! But that sort of manoeuvre needs a crew who know what they are at and we had learned to work together by then.

Doug's sister and her husband had their holiday home nearby and they offered showers to the whole crew despite the late hour.

The morning was overcast, damp and midgy but a breeze from the north-east dispelled the brutes and we made the best of a fair wind to bring the Old Man of Stoer abeam by noon. We enjoyed creaming along as the wind increased but left the fisherman up too long. Attempts to stow it caused it to tear on the masthead as a gust laid the ship on her ear. One reef in the main was not enough and another followed, but not before the bookshelf half emptied itself on to the cabin sole.

We entered Loch Bhrollum in Harris with strong gusts and, for once, the anchor was cast under power at the head of the loch, *Mary Bryant* swinging to squalls off the hills with her rigging singing. A golden eagle circled overhead but we were cold and glad to get below to warming drams and a good dinner.

The continuing cold, overcast, drizzly weather did not enourage early rising and the ladies stayed aboard while the men made a shore expedition to walk, watch birds and sketch. The afternoon cleared sufficiently for a sail round to inspect the newly erected Scalpay bridge, before anchoring in Loch Bhallamuis in a cold, fresh northeaster. Some of us ventured ashore to gather driftwood for the woodburning stove, and what a difference it made! It was almost worth having cold weather so that we could be so cosy down below, yarning away until the small hours.

The Summer Isles beckoned and, after an early cuppa, we got the anchor under reefed canvas with hopes of a visit to the Shiant Isles on the way. Breakfast was somewhat disrupted by bouncy seas in the race off Shiant, and it was soon evident that there was to be no shoregoing. But sailing between the islands there was compensation in seeing magnificent seas surging and foaming through the rock arch with great skuas circling overhead.

We turned into the Summer Isles in a strong, cold northeaster, stowing all sail but the mainsail under which we anchored in the north pool of Tanera Beg in the late afternoon. The first job was to light that woodburner and huddle below for tea and cake. There was a vote to go ashore for more wood, but we had already filled the stowage so, instead, Anna put in an order for a couple of fenders; would we see what we could find? Climbing to the hilltop, we spotted two fishermans' buoys on a beach, one large and one small – they would do very well!

Next day was the last of the cruise and, in a flat calm, all hands set to work. Erica, giving the cooker a housewifely eye, had been longing to clean it and see if the brasswork would polish up. She did and it sparkled. Robert and Doug decided to saw up, split and bag the driftwood deck cargo, while Erica and I repaired the fisherman sail, ironing an adhesive sailcloth patch over the tear with a hot teapot.

Motorsailing to Ullapool, *Mary Bryant* berthed alongside the pier to be met by Doug and Alison's family who had come to collect them. While Anna shopped for stores for the coming week, Robert and Erica scrubbed out the ship and polished the brass. We four then celebrated a happy and successful cruise with dinner ashore.

The Story of Mary Bryant

The schooner *Mary Bryant* is named after a remarkable and resourceful Cornishwoman who survived all sorts of adventures. It was in 1796 that Mary, aged only nineteen and driven to highway robbery by hunger and deprivation, was caught and sentenced to death by hanging at Exeter. Later, the sentence was commuted to transportation for seven years. Up to that date, transportation had been to America but, owing to the war, an alternative destination had to be found. Meanwhile, Mary was imprisoned in appalling conditions with many others in a hulk at Plymouth.

Eventually, Botany Bay in Australia was selected as the site for a prison colony and the transportees were shipped out, again in grim conditions, and it was not long before some began to die. Mary was determined to survive and became the mistress of one of the officers on board, thereby obtaining preferential treatment. A fellow prisoner was Will Bryant, a fisherman. He was unlike most of the transportees, who had no skills or education. Again, with survival in mind, Mary befriended and later married him. Because of his ability to find food for the colony, Will became privileged and he and Mary were able to have their own bothy away from the others. After four years, Mary urged Will and others to steal the governor's cutter, which they had been allowed to use for fishing. They sailed thousands of miles to Timor, but eventually were re-arrested and sent back to England in prison ships where, since she had escaped, Mary could expect her original death sentence to be carried out.

During a further year in prison, James Boswell the diarist, who admired her courage, made numerous appeals for a free pardon for her which eventually succeeded and Mary Bryant was released aged twenty-eight. There is no record of her life thereafter. The early life of this remarkable woman up to her release appears in a book "To Brave Every Danger" by Judith Cook, published by Pan Books in 1993.

Carloway

CHILEAN CHANNELS

by Richard Close-Smith

Those of us tied to a desk from nine to five tend to ration our limited holiday time with particular care, but when I received a fax from Miles Quitmann, a friend from TA days, inviting me to join *Ayesha* cruising the Chilean Channels in late March 1997, I had not a moment's hesitation in faxing back an immediate and enthusiastic acceptance.

Miles, aged 33, left England in September 1995 for a very 'extended cruise' which had already included a 42 day trek on foot across the Pyrenees followed by sailing to the Caribbean, Venezuela, the Panama Canal and the Galapagos. During 50 days hard on the wind from Galapagos to Valdivia in Chile, they lost their mizzen mast, but since November 1996 happier highlights had included getting within 20 miles of the Antarctic Circle and landing on Cape Horn. 'They' consisted of Miles and his cousin Gareth Jones. Gareth had never sailed before this cruise, but turned out to be a natural. Occasionally they'd been joined briefly by friends from England, but for most of their eighteen month cruise they had been double handed.

Ayesha is a standard Biscay 36 ketch. Her seakindly long-keeled hull and well thought through layout had proved excellent, although at times I suspect they would have appreciated a roller headsail. Certainly I had expected to find more evidence of 16,000 sea miles completed and was most impressed by the immaculate condition in which they kept her.

I was due to join the boat in Puerto Chacabuco, which is roughly midway between Santiago and Cape Horn. A veil is best drawn over my journey out, which involved six flights and a three hour bus journey, all of which might have been acceptable if only Aerolineas Argentinas hadn't left my luggage in Madrid!

We could probably have managed without it as I had the whisky, Twiglets and newspapers in my hand luggage, but there were 'red cross parcels' from Miles and Gareth's families which also included some

Chilean Channels

parts for *Ayesha* so we cooled our heels in Puerto Chacabuco for a frustrating thirty hours until the luggage arrived.

The Aisen region is the northern part of the Chilean channels, which must be one of the world's greatest cruising areas – literally hundreds of miles of spectacularly beautiful deep interconnecting fjords and archipelagos, with tree-covered hills in the foreground and a backdrop of the Andes often capped with snow. There is no trace of habitation for days on end and rarely another boat to be seen. Although Miles and Gareth had no need to hurry, they kindly kept the pace up throughout my fortnight cruise, ensuring that I saw as much as possible of this great coastline.

Our first project after Chacabuco was to head due south to Laguna San Rafael. This took two days, one motoring to Puerto Bonito and the second day sailing on a dead run down into the National Park. The main attraction here, apart from the general scenery, is the awesome hanging glacier. For me the sight of my first Bergy Bit, or iceberg as I insisted on calling it, was the prelude to a most memorable day. Miles gently eased *Ayesha* through the ice to within a couple of hundred yards of the glacier, from which bits were regularly calving off with an eerie roar as they hit the sea. Other entertainments included the standard tourist trick of hacking off some glacial ice for one's gin and tonic. Less standard was my insistence on boarding a small ice floe for the camera and then getting some very close attention from a Leopard Seal with a vicious grin who decided I was 'in distress' and therefore a likely meal. The threat of a thwack from a dinghy oar eventually saw him off, but by then I was quite cured of larking around on the ice.

The prevailing wind is northerly, but for the moment it was in the south so we took advantage to retrace our steps to Puerto Bonito, feeling our way into the anchorage in the dusk with the radar. 'Puerto' suggests habitation, but none of our anchorages during this first week had anything apart from wildlife. We saw seals, otters, dolphins and an occasional whale plus albatross and even a condor.

The next three days were largely windless which, though rather boring, enabled us to clock up the miles northwards towards Chiloé, Chile's largest island. The only two villages we passed – Aguirre and Melinka – were both on islands and both charming but primitive. Our visit to Aguirre coincided with my birthday and Rosa, who ran the only restaurant, made a particular effort to proudly produce a fish and chip candlelit birthday dinner, which was much appreciated. Fishing is obviously the main activity hereabouts, but the shellfish business has been hit hard by the 'red tide', a disease which infects mussels etc. To eat an infected mussel can be fatal and sadly the disease continues to move northwards. Happily, crabs are not affected and one passing fisherman was pleased to swop four large Centolla crabs for a half bottle of vodka.

Exploring a bergy bit.

Most of the channels are deep, commonly in excess of 100 metres, but our cruising permit – the *Zarpé* – did not allow us to explore off the agreed route. This restriction cannot be properly policed, but the absence of any soundings on the Chilean charts covering the smaller channels tends to keep you on the principal routes. Our one significant illegal shortcut nearly gave us our come uppance when we found ourselves crossing a sandbar of only 3 metres – a salutary lesson.

Between the Aisen Channels and Chiloé, there are 30 miles of exposed water known as Los Lagos, with nothing to break the huge Pacific swells. We crossed it in balmy conditions, creeping into Punta San Pedro against a foul tide in late evening.

Up until now the tides hadn't been a serious consideration, but around Chiloé the tidal range is five metres and the streams run at four knots off the headlands. Another feature of sailing in Chile is the extraordinary visibility, often in excess of 60 miles providing magnificent panoramas, with the snow-capped volcanoes of the Andes in the background. Our final destination was Castro, roughly half way up the east coast of Chiloé, but off Castro there is yet another collection of small islands occupied by farmers and fishermen. The scenery changes to something more like Devon, with a patchwork of small fields and hedges. One of the most strikingly beautiful characteristics of Chilote architecture are the wooden chapels. Originally built by the Jesuits, they often stand alone on the coast with no nearby human habitation. In the Castro area, shingled houses on stilts stretch out into the lagoons and estuaries. Known as *Palafitos* they enable resident fishermen to 'park' their boats between the stilts at high water.

Ayesha visited a couple of the islands, Quehue and Mechuque, each of which has an almost landlocked lagoon offering perfect shelter. Slightly reminiscent of Sark, neither had any vehicles, the farmers using wooden sleds pulled by horses or bullocks. For some reason electrical power is rationed, so lights come on at 7pm and off again at 10pm. The locals couldn't have been more friendly and, even if they couldn't feed us, there was never a shortage of Pisco, the local brew, which seemed to go to their heads even quicker than it went to ours.

Castro is the capital of Chiloé and felt quite sophisticated after the wilderness we'd enjoyed to date, but even here you realise just how far from civilisation you are when you find it impossible to buy a postcard.

How to sum up this part of the world? Provided you are prepared largely to self cater and can cope with some strong winds, albeit in sheltered waters, the Chilean Channels must be very hard to beat as the ultimate cruising area. Friendly locals are an added bonus – but do make sure that at least one of the crew speaks Spanish.

FAREWELL *FAIR JOANDA*

by Tom Fenwick

Fair Joanda is a Tradewind 33, 'born' into the Club in 1977. She has since sailed about 65,000 miles under the Club burgee. Although Newtown is her home port, *Fair Joanda* has only spent part of one season there since 1981.

Back in April, just home after a visit to Trish's family in Australia, we went on a whim to Holland, just to look at a few aluminium and steel boats – preferably those with a centre-plate and particularly those designed by Koopman. We saw some beautiful hulls, but every time were disappointed by the interiors for long-term living aboard. On the last day, we were persuaded to go out of our way to see a Transworld 41 designed by William Garden, a west coast American whose designs I knew well.

The Transworld had been built in Taiwan, shipped to Holland and fitted out there, so she had all European equipment. We fell for her and within an hour had put in an offer which was accepted. I felt this was a boat that I could exchange for my beloved *Fair Joanda*. Now we had to get *FJ* back to the UK, since I didn't fancy leaving her in some Spanish marina awaiting a buyer. Since we'd been away for nearly three months, she needed tidying up – especially the brightwork – so after six days hard work in the Sevillian sunshine, we were ready to sail.

We came out through the Seville lock at about 1000 on May 15th, and then anchored to wait for high water and the ebb. By 1430 were motoring downriver, continuing until around 2200 when the tide turned against us and we anchored well inshore to keep out of the channel.

On Saturday 17th May, we moved down to fuel up at Chipiona marina, at the entrance to the Guadalquivir. Then we headed out in a light breeze from just west of north, making for Cape St Vincent, 120 miles away. For the next 24 hours we sailed little, motor-sailed a lot and plain motored a fair bit, getting into the middle of a NATO exercise in the evening, among dark silhouettes of frigates and helicopters with

bright lights buzzing around. By daylight we were south and east of Faro harbour, motoring with the tide against us. By 0700, Faro airport tower was abeam.

By mid-morning a slight breeze came up from the south, and by noon we were making 5½ to 6 knots on a reach – at last the wind we wanted, but would it hold round the corner after Cape St Vincent? Well, the wind freshened and as we approached Sagres conditions became uncomfortable – we should have been a mile or two further out. Between Sagres and Cape St Vincent the wind increased from force 4 to 6 as a squall went through, and then it eased for a while leaving us slopping all over the place with a boisterous swell from the west and the backslop from the cliffs. Only one thing to do – get motoring and away from the coast.

As the evening progressed the wind gently picked up from the west and by 2030 we were reaching along nicely – this is one for the book – a free wind going north! As dusk approached we were overtaken by six NATO ships, three on either side. We were to meet them again the next day off the Tagus river.

The first twenty four hours up the Portuguese coast were not comfortable – Trish likened it to being inside a washing machine – three metre swells from the NNW with a persistent sea from the SSW. But the wind continued fair, so what more can you ask? Early evening found us between Berlinga Island and Peniche, in sheltered waters for half an hour. After supper, we headed out into deeper water hoping for less disturbed seas, keeping the speed down to six knots for comfort. By 0300 on Tuesday May 20th, the log notes that we were "swooping along, two reefs still in the main and the genoa rolled in to No 1 mark.".

Heavy rain, then loss of wind around 0700, was followed by the return of a gentle breeze and lessening swells and the day turned into a dream sailing day – force 3 on the beam, sunshine and a much more comfortable motion. By 1600 we were level with Porto, the wind was veering a little to WNW, although we were still able to lay the course with sheets eased slightly. By early in the morning of the 21st we were close-hauled, and that was as good a reason as any to put in to Bayona. We'd had a good run, from the mouth of the Guadalquivir to Bayona in just under four days. In Bayona we encountered a collection of yachts, all with stories of beating all the way from the UK. Would our luck hold?

It was now time to go cruising and for the next ten days we meandered gently up the coast, first having a cracking reach up the Ria de Arosa. Following the 1993 pilot's advice, we made for Puebla del Caramiñal, which turned out to be a great disappointment for it is now the base for a coaster fleet and there is even a sort of marina, completely unprotected, outside the harbour. We anchored well away from the pontoons behind the bluff, as the south-westerly wind was now gusting force 6. Next morning we motored over to Villagarcia to explore the town, and on the following day took the train to Santiago de Compostella, a delightful journey along the estuary and the river before the train climbed up into the hills to this most lovely city, where we joined in the pilgrims' service in the cathedral – very moving.

Well, we'd finished sailing for a bit, as for the next week there was very little wind except under the thunder heads – and we had a spectacular thunderstorm or two. At this stage we were in contact by ham radio with David Pirie aboard *Moongazer*, heading down to the Azores from Plymouth with 'tradewind' conditions. We also raised our Hon. Sec. way up in Scotland.

Rounding Cape Finisterre one morning, in dead calm conditions, we were surprised to see a yacht that had been heading south close inshore, alter course to head directly out towards us. It turned out to be the Bayfields in *Physalian*, who had recognised *Fair Joanda* from afar. We circled each other gently and had a good gam. They'd spent the night in Camariñas, where we had been heading before diverting to Finisterre.

We spent two days at anchor in Lage and then motored to the anchorage inside Islas Sisargas. I had happy memories of having grilled sardines with the lighthouse keeper in 1975 in the old *Joanda* and this time a delightful 24 year old keeper, Sito, invited us to lunch. He spoke good English and we later joined up with him in La Coruña.

All this time that we'd been coming up the coast, the Biscay winds had been north or north-east, taking *Moongazer* so splendidly south. My weatherman was Bill Hall, the Ham net controller, who had the five day charts. He said that the winds were supposed to be going round to the south on Tuesday 3rd June. On the Monday evening we took a breeze over to El Ferrol and anchored in the bay past the forts – always a magical spot for me – and next morning we motored out to try and find the promised south or south-easterly force 3. This didn't materialise and we motored along in a near glassy calm. By 1700 a breeze came up and we managed to sail in varying wind strengths until 0950 next morning, when with a zephyr from the south-west, we succumbed to the engine. That evening the forecast for Biscay was cyclonic, becoming south-easterly force 4–5. Let it come, said we. Meanwhile, whilst motoring on, the alternator belt gave up the ghost. Although the spare had the same part number, it was too small! An hour of rearranging things and we were under way again, and soon we were sailing to a gentle easterly. The gremlins hadn't finished for the throttle lever mechanism, which is in the starboard cockpit locker, became jammed by a tin of paint. An hour later, the Exhaust Guard light and buzzer came on. Nothing serious, but the gremlins were still around!

On our third day out from El Ferrol, dawn broke to a sullen grey day. The barometer, falling gently yesterday, was still falling slowly. No wind came and we motored until 0130 next morning. By 0200 Ar Men and Ile de Sein lights had been identified and soon afterwards Ushant, Les

Pierres Noires and Pointe St Mathieu lights all came up. We reached into the Goulet de Brest, holding close to the southern shore. Once inside the narrows, we decided to continue with the good reaching conditions and pressed on up the northern arm to Le Passage. *Fair Joanda* came to rest on a peaceful mooring, 3 days and 3½ hours out from El Ferrol.

One of the reasons for going into Brest was the forecast the day before, which was giving a nasty depression coming up from the south. A radio ham, sitting on his boat in La Duchess, had said "I'd get in if I were you." At this time, *Moongazer* was under bare poles between the Azores and Spain, and had four or five days of continuous gales from the west.

Fair Joanda

Well, I'd intended that we should continue on the Saturday, with the tide turning to the north at Pointe St Mathieu around 1230. But by 1000 the Goulet was white and those sailing in the local races were well reefed down, so we cancelled and had a good walk instead. Sunday morning wasn't much better, although the forecast seemed to be for an abating wind. It abated too late, as we were already enjoying a good French Sunday lunch at Kerhuon, opposite Le Passage. After lunch there was only one thing to do – have a siesta!

The early shipping forecast on the Monday was giving south-westerly force 3–4, going easterly. I just hoped the latter would hold off. We cast off at noon and managed to sail practically down to Brest before having to motor – the south-west breeze had fallen very light. 1505 at Les Vieux Moines and then up through the Four in rain and no wind, motoring out the other end and carrying our tide until 2230. But then the wind came out of the north-east at about force 3, the chop built up and even motor-sailing progress was poor and uncomfortable. At 0130 I decided to RETIRE!

We were now north of Roscoff, but I had no large-scale chart of that part of the coast, since I had not intended coasting along that part of Brittany. Since I had not been to Roscoff for nearly 20 years, I decided to reach gently back and forth until daylight and we eventually crept cautiously into the Batz channel and dropped anchor at 0715. We slept for most of the day, which was a fairly miserable one. At 2030 I woke to find that the wind had turned south as forecast and persuaded the mate that it was time to move on. We sailed for 1½ hours before the wind died again, and then motored all the way to Guernsey where we refuelled. Catching the last of the tide up to the Casquets, we continued to motor all the way back to the Solent. Two hours after we arrived, a fine westerly set in!

Six days of decommissioning *Fair Joanda* and preparing her for sale, then we were off to Holland to complete the final negotiations on *First Lady*. The case continues.

A USEFUL SHAKE-DOWN CRUISE

by Ian Tew

A couple of years ago I had inspected my dream boat at the Southampton Boat Show, but her price was miles beyond my means. It's amazing how life's fortunes change, and last September I saw her sister ship in Lymington and thought "she is for me."

My Freedom 30, *Freedom Freyja*, had been sold in August and I'd been looking for a suitable Freedom 35, but none had fitted the bill. The only Freedom 39 Pilot House Schooner, the boat I really wanted, was in the States, so I bought her and flew to Boston for the survey at Quincy Massachusetts. A few things were wrong, but there was no time to fiddle around if I was to get south before winter set in. So I flew home on the 22nd September to sell the house and car.

The owner had agreed to deliver her to Annapolis in Chesapeake Bay, but plans went awry (as is usual when you are in a hurry) and I agreed to take over *Independent Freedom* at Sandy Hook, 20 or so miles south of New York. So on 10th October Michael and I flew to Baltimore and drove the 200 miles to Sandy Hook, where we took over the boat and her previous owner took over the car.

I was keen to get south as soon as possible and enter the intracoastal waterway. My idea of fun does not extend to winter in the North Atlantic. My grandfather, Commander R D Graham, had a bad time with a hurricane in his yacht *Emmanuel*, on the way from Canada to Bermuda in November 1934. My elder brother Donald, sailing with Lord Riverdale some 30 years later, was caught by an out-of-season hurricane in March sailing from Charleston to Bermuda. I just felt that the third member of the family cruising this coast had better take the inland waters!

Unfortunately the old cruising licence had expired and I had been summoned to the United States Customs Headquarters in Newark because, technically, the regulations had been violated. We therefore had to sail back north to New York.

It was a stirring and moving sight to sail in bright sunshine goose-winged past the Statue of Liberty to port and the magnificent Manhattan skyline to starboard. To do so in my own yacht exceeded my wildest dreams and the reality is much more impressive than photographs.

Formalities completed, *Independent Freedom* headed back to Sandy Hook, motor-sailing into a headwind. Just before the huge and imposing Verrazano Narrows Bridge, the foresail tore from luff to leech. My heart sank, but the tear was below the first reef so we tucked this in and carried on. We spent the night comfortably at anchor, saving the £40 marina fee.

On Wednesday 15th October we motored out of the bay against the wind in pouring rain, hoisted the sails at the entrance, bore away around Sandy Hook and reached out through the Channel at a good speed. There was much more wind than forecast so we reefed the mainsail, which eased the work of the Autohelm.

We had a swift run down the New Jersey coast to starboard, while to port Europe was thousands of miles away. The yacht was goose-winged under a grey and dismal sky with continuous drizzle. However, it was so exciting to be sailing this fine yacht that the weather didn't matter; between 0900 and 1500 she averaged over seven knots.

St Michael's Lighthouse

We passed Atlantic City, with its bright red lights on the buildings, running fast in the dark and drizzle, when just past midnight a certain amount of chaos ensued. The log notes that:

" . . . the kicking strap on the foresail gave way, Chinese gybe, power off instruments, down sail, eye from main pulled out, maybe batten broken." Always happens at night!

The wind continued to increase, so we put the second reef in the mainsail. At 0430 we rounded up hard onto the wind and beat into Delaware Bay against a vicious, short steep sea – wind against tide, with occasional tugs and huge barges passing. A particularly heavy pound into a sea broke the anchor pin securing the anchor in the bow roller, throwing the anchor on deck. The unstayed carbon fibre masts were bending – an alarming sight to the uninitiated. With occasional bouts of force 7, it was a long hard slog up to the Delaware Chesapeake canal, which we entered under power at 1330. The sun had come out and to see the fall coloured trees lining the banks was very refreshing after the vast expanse of the river.

The night was spent at the wharf marina in Chesapeake City (nearest grocery store seven miles). The 25,000 ton container ships that slid past made less wash than the motor boats.

We spent a lazy Friday morning watching the traffic, phoning the UK for a new sail and finding a repair yard in Chesapeake Bay.

We left in sunshine just after noon and motored out of the canal into the Elk River. We paid for our late departure with a nerve racking hour in the dark dodging the crab pot floats, which are barely visible in daylight let alone by torch light! Rock Hall seemed utterly deserted in the rain, but the restaurant was full.

On Saturday 17th October it rained all day but only lightly. We had a good sail running down the bay, passing under the Chesapeake Bay Bridge which is four miles long with a huge curve at the western end – utilitarian rather than beautiful. At 1340 we luffed up hard onto the wind round No.1 buoy and stormed up the eastern river overtaking boats. *Independent Freedom* was sailing like a witch.

On Sunday 19th October we left historic St Michael's with its museum piece lighthouse in the harbour. The rain was pouring down, with a fresh breeze and gales forecast for southern Chesapeake Bay. The reefed foresail was hoisted and we averaged 5.5 knots, including an hour and a half on the wind, to Cambridge. We entered the harbour that evening ready for repairs on Monday morning. It was still raining, and I swear that American rain drops are larger and wetter than English.

In all, this was a useful shake-down cruise in strange waters with unfamiliar currents. Despite the various gear failures, the trip has given us much confidence in the yacht.

CARDHU TO BANTRY BAY

by Tom Lees

I took *Cardhu* to Bantry during the summer of 1997 for two reasons. The first was because my friends Gimmy and Ellen Nichols, with whom I had sailed in Maine with my wife Faith in 1995, had invited me to join them at a cottage they were renting in Bantry. They had not expected me to come with *Cardhu*.

Nor had they expected me to bring my niece Sheila and my future bride Christine as crew. Well, Christine wasn't that yet, and that was the second reason for the cruise – to test her out! Or rather, to test us both out. Nothing like close quarters on a boat to gauge compatibility. And since Faith died I've been hopelessly lost. I'm glad to say both objectives were successful – Chris has agreed to marry me!

So there we were in Bantry, on a mooring kindly loaned me by the Bantry Sailing Club. I must say what lovely people the Irish are, so welcoming and hospitable. As I was waiting by the slip for Sheila and Chris to return from shopping, I was approached by this old, old man – a total stranger. Did I want to swim? No? Then why was I standing there? What did I want? Nothing? Why not? Did I have everything? I had come off a yacht, had I? Which one? Oh, I was English, was I, and the English would never have won the war if it hadn't been for the Russians. And the Americans.

It was that sort of conversation. He had all the time in the world for me, and at the end of a lively half-hour in which we solved most of the problems in the world without any politicians, he thanked me for the *craic* and carried on his original path.

Then there was the time I left my dinghy at the slip and someone borrowed one of my oars. As I do not have an outboard motor I was rather stuck without a full pair, but one of the sailing club members very kindly lent me a spare, telling me to drop it back when my own oar turned up. Later that same evening my own oar was delivered to the door of the Nichols' house by Mr Denis Collins the postman, who had heard of my loss and had found the oar leaning against the sea wall as he went swimming. Such kindness, where people go out of their way to be helpful, makes one feel so very welcome. I long to return.

DAWDLING IN DONEGAL

by Mike and Hilde Gill

The Irish Cruising Club Sailing Directions, together with the relatively few RCC members who describe their cruises to the north-west coast of Ireland, all make one's mouth water. Here is a host of natural harbours, with magnificent scenery, no crowds and kindness ashore. Yet this spectacular area seems mainly to be visited on the way to somewhere else – round Ireland perhaps, or towards the west coast of Scotland. In many of the Journal logs there is just the hint of rush.

Our first objective, therefore, was to give ourselves enough time to explore: we'd laid *Quicksilver* up the previous winter in Kilrush on the Shannon, but by then we were intrigued enough to want to stay close to the end of the springboard, ready for 1997. The second objective was for the three of us not to be too ambitious, and for Tom (aged ten) to have plenty of time to sail the dinghy in harbour. Around twenty five miles a day seemed agreeable to all. The third was to finish up somewhere further north, possibly on the Clyde, ready for a different cruising area next year.

This was our fourth season in *Quicksilver*, a Nautique Saintonge 44, and the foundations of a proper relationship had begun to be laid. We stole a few days at the end of May and were blessed with easterlies up to Galway and back, allowing us to anchor where we wanted in peace – behind Mutton Island, south of Liscannor Bay and close off Lahinch, normally a fine surfing beach. So it was with high expectations that we slipped from Kilrush on 21st July.

This was our sixth passage to or from Loop Head inside a year, and despite the Shannon Estuary's reputation, it has been easy every time. We anchored on a glorious high pressure evening, ate supper in the cockpit and looked forward to the next four weeks with mounting excitement.

It was fine and easterly when we weighed next morning for Roundstone, but by the time we closed the Inner Passage things started

Quicksilver dawdling in Donegal

to go wrong – cold, wet and westerly. Even St Macdara's island with its little church looked grim and grey. We had to anchor seaward of the bar off Roundstone to wait for enough water; by the time we came to rest it was pelting down.

Next day was no better. We also had a dead battery. The chandler in Galway sixty miles away could supply a replacement, but could not persuade the bus driver to deliver it. I hitched there and back in the rain, trying to look attractive on the kerb in dripping oilskins and with a box of acid I could barely lift. Eventually our *au pair*, who was driving round Ireland with a friend, just happened to be on the right road at the right time, so we sped back to Roundstone. A *ceilidh* in the evening raised spirits, but the Twelve Pins remained invisible until next day, which was clear and gusty.

Quicksilver needed slabs for a lively beat in sunshine down to Slyne Head. All was going well until a huge thunderstorm stole the wind as we closed the head. Eventually we flogged our way round it, noted the popple and what it might become in less clement conditions, and had a brilliant and fast broad reach up to Inishboffin, where we anchored in the main harbour that evening.

We spent the 25th walking the island, watching a wedding, and (for Tom) playing football in the evening with the local kids on a high ground with a fine view at sunset across the rocks and islands. Next day soon became glorious. Having stocked up with crabs' claws and the best bread on the island (from Ann Day's green and gold cottage close to the white beacon), we cleared at noon and found we could lay up to Inishturk and on to Clare Island. The whole coast was looking its best, and Croaghpatrick even bared his top occasionally. The wind was right for the anchorage off Grania Waels Castle, and we scampered ashore in the early evening to soak in the view across to Clew Bay. Another cockpit supper, but alas not enough energy for a *ceilidh*!

On the 27th July we cycled along the island's south coast and clambered up to the old signal tower before slipping away at 1400, chased by a front. We squirted down Clew Bay and won the shelter of Inishgort just as the weather caught up with us. By the time we anchored off Collanmore, even the Glénans Sailing School (who have a base there) was calling it a day, as the last of the fifteen or so dinghies to capsize was rescued. The forecast was for galeforce westerlies by next evening and strong winds thereafter, so we had to balance giving Tom some dinghy sailing against beating out of Clew Bay before it became uncomfortable. We went for the latter, luckily as it turned out.

The second of our four batteries died. I wondered about the others, and how well they had been nursed in the winter.

We could just lay Achill Island next morning, and by the time we were off the Head itself it had become positively hot. The cliffs were shy to show themselves, but going close inside Carrickakin we had a glimpse of these 2,000 foot monsters.

We ran down to Blacksod Bay, a huge indentation protected by the Mullet peninsula, with the gale now forecast force 9/10 south to south-east, and the depression causing it said to be 970 millibars. We had a look at Saleen Bay but it seemed shallower than charted, so we turned back to Elly Bay next door. We now discovered that battery number three had died. This was potentially serious. We now faced a choice between being able to start the engine on the 12 volt circuit *or* being able to use the 24 volt anchor winch. If we had to move anchorage in anger during the night, we would need both. After anchoring in Elly Bay we managed to raise Michael Lavelle, the local garage owner, on the mobile phone. Within twenty minutes a brand new engine battery was being carried across the strand, and all was well. The gale did arrive that night. *Quicksilver* didn't budge – thank God for heavy ground tackle, and thank Mike Lavelle for his kindness.

It had cleared and moderated enough to allow Hilde and Tom to hitch to Belmullet for supplies next day, but it blew harder again that night – 48 knots recorded at Belmullet. Much scrabble, canasta and natter filled the next day, for it was blowing too hard even to launch a dinghy. The following morning I rashly talked about going to sea. Hilde wisely gave me an old fashioned look. A local fisherman delivered another battery on the beach, and then took me to the Atlantic side of the peninsula, only fifty yards from our shelter. The fury of a major Atlantic disturbance spoke, no roared, for itself. He had measured sixty knots off Achill the day before. To limit harbour rot we made the momentous three-mile passage down to Blacksod quay under a tiny staysail, travelling rather quickly in the murk. In a really bad south-easterly the fisherman tuck behind the quay in Saleen Bay, but for all its bleakness in these conditions, Elly Bay was an outstanding anchorage.

Imagine the excitement, after three days galebound, when the forecast referred to an incipient ridge. We were off next morning in wind much too gentle to push us through the swell we might have predicted, but uplifted by the sight of Achill's huge cliffs. Eventually we could lay the passage inside the Inishkea Islands. We stopped for lunch off the ruined village, deserted since 1927 after the loss of many of its menfolk in a freak storm. The sun reappeared, but our experience of the previous three days kept alive an image of what winter must be like hereabouts.

We shot up inside all the islands, including Eagle. With the glass rising, the sky becoming blue and the entrance to Broadhaven looking lovely, we forgave Blacksod, anchoring inside the lifeboat on a still and beautiful evening, having conveniently filled with water from the jetty.

The coast immediately east of Broadhaven is spectacular, which made up for having no wind at all for the fifty odd miles across Donegal Bay. Off Rathlin O'Birne, we decided to poke our nose into Malin Beg Bay (a tiny inlet with three pillars of rock) and also into White Strand Bay next door, but the swell made anchorage for the night in either place rather marginal, so we slipped past the massive cliffs of Slieve League and anchored in Teelin, a gem. As we went ashore in the evening, we couldn't understand why there were so many people standing around on the quay, saying nothing and looking glum, until we saw the Rescue Boat and shortly afterwards a hearse. A local man had jumped off Slieve League.

Teelin has no shop nearby, but hitching to Carrick village for supplies was little trouble. My old friend Kevin Esmonde was supposed to join us the next day for a few days from Cork, but in the end it was after midnight when he appeared, leaving behind him some vicious weather further south. He proved a mascot and the next few days were magical. A splendid beat in a north-easterly brought us on August 4th to the entrance of the Southern Sound off Aranmore, fortunately with enough rise of tide to make the last bit to Rutland 'harbour' off Burtonport. We'd seen less than half a dozen yachts at sea since joining, so discovering we had to share an anchorage with one other came as something of a shock. A line ashore pulls you out of the fairway, clear of the Aranmore ferry. All

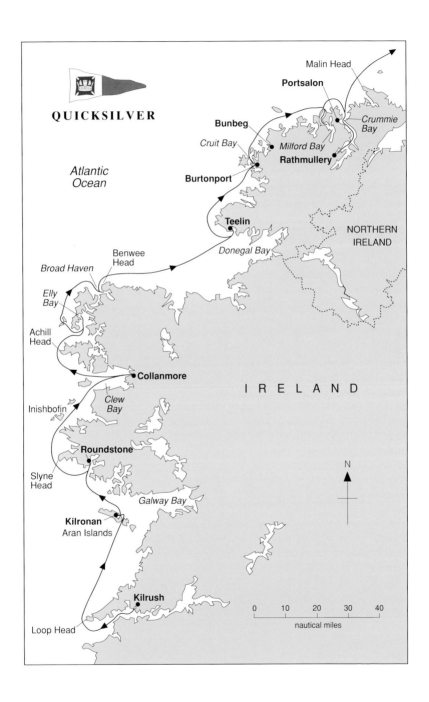

QUICKSILVER

Atlantic
Ocean

Malin Head

Portsalon

Crummie
Bay

Bunbeg

Cruit Bay

Milford Bay

Rathmullery

Burtonport

Teelin

Donegal Bay

NORTHERN
IRELAND

Benwee
Head

Broad Haven

Elly
Bay

Achill
Head

Collanmore

I R E L A N D

Clew
Bay

Inishbofin

Roundstone

Slyne
Head

Galway Bay

N

Kilronan
Aran Islands

Kilrush

Loop Head

0   10   20   30   40

nautical miles

who come to this spot wax lyrical about its safety and beauty. In addition we had the finest sunset of the cruise, lighting up Aranmore.

We went into Burtonport near high water next morning, tied alongside one of the fishing boats (who seem to have fallen on hard times), and leapt ashore for a rather indifferent shop, apart from a huge slab of smoked salmon, for which Hilde somehow knew whom to ask. Then we headed north, beat outside Owey Island and sped into Cruit Bay, anchoring among the lobster *viviers* in perfect surroundings behind Odd Island. This part of Donegal, the Rosses, combines the red rock sculptures of North Brittany with miles of beautifully contoured beaches, mountains behind, with trees – and pubs – in between. To one of these, Iggy's Bar, we walked by the side of the estuary in torrid midday heat, and ate as good a seafood lunch as anywhere. A gentle swim in the low water channels, surrounded by red rock and empty strands, made for a tolerable afternoon, followed by another cockpit supper.

On August 6th we beat slowly up to South Sound in Gola Island three miles away, having the whole place to ourselves. The island has not been permanently inhabited since 1967, but we met a man born on the island doing up one of the houses. Gola is a lovely island to walk, with fine cliffs on its north coast. We anchored off the little pier for the night, rocks very red, and the white of Mount Errigal looking grand over them in the distance.

After a still night we motored over to Bo Island to arrive off the bar marking the entrance to Gweedore Harbour an hour before high water. This was just as well: we had plenty of water over the bar, but the 'deep water' channel is now much closer to Carrickbullog than suggested in the Sailing Directions (50 metres, not 150 metres!), so we had an unplanned opportunity for some hydrography from the dinghy. Bunbeg, the main quay, is very full, and it was springs, so the delightful anchorage south-west of the inlet was not possible. We anchored on the edge of the tide-scoured pool, 10 metres from Yellow Rocks (the recommended 5.5 metres distance prevented a safe swing, especially past a little rocky ledge towards their south-west end, invisible above half tide). Like Cruit Bay, the vast expanses of pure sand, the islands, cliffs and shelter make this a very special spot. We had our own little beach near low water, and the afternoon slipped quickly through our fingers, before a memorable dinner inland at Annagary (on a wise tip from Wallace Clark and Georgina Nixon).

Kevin had to leave next morning, allowing us to set off at the top of the tide, but he took the fine weather with him. Everything clamped down and we never saw Bloody Foreland, but as we closed Tory Island, there was a hint of lift. Although the wind had backed and Camusmore Bay offered only partial protection, it was all fairly gentle, and we only wanted a few hours there anyway. We walked over to Port Doon, noting how even the little spots of heather huddle on the lee side of clumps.

They are building an all-weather harbour wall at Camusmore. The photographs of winter storms on the walls of the community club make it plain why.

We shot off in the afternoon to ogle at the Torrs on the island's north-east corner, before a fast run down to Mulroy River. In the dark winter evenings we'd been much taken by the pictures of this huge inlet in the Sailing Directions. Apart from the rain, it did not disappoint. Once over the bar this is a protected trip up a beautiful winding expanse of water through rolling farmland, with some interesting pilotage, extraordinary ranges of depth, and great peace. It was near the head of this river that *Tzu Hang* wintered in 1958. There is little ashore at Milford Quay, but with the large-scale chart this is a very worthwhile stop. Next day was still drizzly, and it was rather a damp beat round to the entrance of Lough Swilly (lough of shadows). We soon lost the wind and had to motor up to Rathmullen. Repeated attempts over the previous few days to leave messages on mobile phones had failed to connect us with Winky Nixon's brother James and his wife Catherine, but there they were, sauntering in the murk down the beach as we arrived, as if planned to the minute. We had a great evening with them ashore, and on Sunday August 10th next day climbed a mountain together before inveigling James to drift down to Portsalon Bay with us in baking heat.

That night a south-easterly set in, and was forecast to increase, so a heavily rolled jib took us across to perfect shelter in Crummie Bay. We found our own little rocky cove well out of the wind for swimming, and had a great walk up to the fort on Dunree Head on a very blue day.

We now had six days left and had hoped to see a little more of Ireland before heading north, but the south-easterlies promised to continue, so on August 12th we decided to make for Islay. We romped up to Inishtrahull, expecting a fast passage, but were then headed. Portrush seemed on the cards again after all, but after two more hours and several more wind changes, we could eventually lay Islay.

This was my first landfall in Scotland. The Rhinns and the Mull of Oa came and went in the clouds, breathing promise. We eventually came to rest on a fine evening in Port Ellen, after three fascinating weeks in Ireland. As if to mark the break I managed that night to drop some of the riding light, a much travelled heirloom, in the oggin.

We slid through the mist up to Plod Sgeirean next day. The peace and natural beauty of that anchorage among the skerries gripped us as it has gripped others. Tom made friends with the seals whenever he swam. The sun and fog vied with each other all evening, spraying the spot with incredible colours.

We motored round to the anchorage by Kildalton House (no longer a hotel) next day and walked up to Kildalton Cross, a fine stone cross in very good repair, before screeching across to Gigha on a broad reach in the afternoon. To be surrounded by so many boats again came as something of a shock. Several headed down to the Mull of Kintyre with us on the 15th, much of it in calm. So we went close in, enjoying the tidal shove and the brilliant sun and purple heather. But not for long. As we began to turn north the fog rolled in and visibility dropped to 50 metres. The GPS confirmed we were past the worst of the tide and I set a course accordingly. Soon we found ourselves inside the Arranman Barrels buoy, touching something fortunately well coated in seaweed, and in a calm sea but fierce tidal set. We slid off, chastened, and found our way with the aid of GPS up to Campbeltown. The second disaster was when I discovered that evening that my wallet had walked. The third was when a boat careered into the harbour at high speed in the dark and, as though transfixed by our (replacement) riding light, made a convincing assault on our pulpit. Not a good day.

On the 16th we achieved close to hull speed in the lee of Arran as we sped up to Loch Ranza for lunch, before a more sedate run up to Tarbert for the night. The sun obliged for our last sail on Sunday 17th through the Kyles of Bute and round to a mooring at Rhu. Five days of cruising in relatively protected water surrounded by mountains was more than enough to coil us up like springs for next year. Meanwhile we had enjoyed a surfeit of Ar(r)ans (sic), a huge range of weather, and expanses of cruising area that remain almost empty: we saw only three yachts at sea north of Achill, until reaching Islay. We'd also succeeded in not rushing – twenty odd miles a day turned out to be just right.

Quicksilver is a Nautic-Saintonge 44, designed by Brenneur and built in 1984. She is sloop rigged and since the summer of 1997 has several new batteries and a new riding light.

HAIGRI IN THE AEGEAN

by Simon Butler

This is the cruise for which the Royal Cork Yacht Club Vase was awarded.

We arrived in Skiathos in the Northern Sporades on 13th July, exactly three months after leaving Warsash. Our route had taken us through the French waterways, south via Corsica and Sardinia to Sicily. Then across to Greece where we went through the Corinth canal and north between Evia and the mainland. We'd covered 2,300 miles and *Haigri*, our 20 year old Rival 38, had looked after us well.

In Skiathos we much enjoyed a week's rest and the company of my nieces Emily and Frances and my mother Rosalind who had flown out to meet us. My mother had last visited Skiathos with my father when we sailed *Dorothy Jane*, his 38 foot David Hillyard, to Istanbul in 1967. Part of our motivation for this year's cruise was to contrast our experiences with those of 30 years ago when I was only thirteen.

We now had the Dardanelles in our sights and made two quick night passages to Canakkale, stopping at Limnos *en route*. With our two young daughters Alice (4) and Lucy (2) on board, my wife, Catherine, and I have found this a good system of covering the ground and allowing us all time ashore during the day. We had the calmest sea and brightest moon you could wish for as we motored past Ormos Moudhrou on the south side of Limnos. It was sad and eerie to reflect on the huge number of Allied troops that set off from here for the Gallipoli campaign, never to return. In the morning, despite a fine breeze and keeping close inshore, we made slow progress against the current through the Dardanelles and past the daunting British and Turkish war memorials.

In Canakkale, our first Turkish port, I spent most of the day obtaining our transit log, visiting and revisiting charming and courteous officials in different parts of the town who all pressed tea or coffee on me while the necessary ledgers and forms were completed. Next day we met Louisa Hawker and her two children Jack (8) and Constance (6) in Gelibolu.

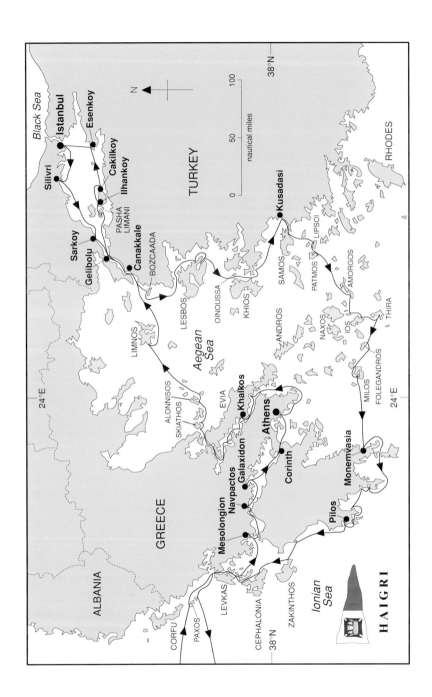

There was just room for us in the little harbour amongst the fishing boats moored in front of the restaurant where we ate delicious sardines. At this same restaurant in 1967, we'd had a strange encounter with a solitary diner who passed notes to my father which read:

'I learn English at Izmir deaf and dumb school; you must find address a girl in 24 or 25 old to me. I want to write a English dumb girl, I am liking the English dumb girls very much; I am always your darling well as ever, Rustem'.

In 1997 we had no such meeting, but I began to realise the Turks thought I had four children and two wives and so began a week of often hilarious confusion.

One of the most memorable places we visited thirty years ago was the island of Pasa Limani at the entrance to the sea of Marmara. The small rural village and the tiny mosque with its squat minaret look over the bay. Ashore, we found it unchanged and a cart pulled by two oxen was making its way along the foreshore. In the tiny shop I brought out some photographs we'd taken thirty years ago of two families we had met there. Sadly it seemed that they'd either died or moved away, but suddenly there was a lot of interest in one of the girls in the photograph and it appeared that she was here on holiday. We were befriended by a couple who ran a boutique in Istanbul but whose family came from the island. They gave us strong tea and coconut cake while the girl in the photo was located. She had no recollection of the incident, but was as delighted as we were to have the reunion and to see pictures from her childhood.

We should have been warned by the threatening sky that built up during the afternoon, but foolishly we went ashore for supper at a little café perched on stilts above the beach. The menu for the first course was simple – 'fish or shish with chippies' – but there was no time to think about pudding. The wind started howling from the north and the sea was already getting up. We piled into the dinghy and had a wet, uncomfortable and anxious ride back to *Haigri* and found her tossing and heaving safely at her anchor.

This storm heralded the start of strong winds that were with us for much of the next eight weeks as the *meltemi* built up. A couple of days later we were stuck in Chakilkoy, a large fishing harbour, because of poor weather. All the berths were taken by substantial fishing boats, so we anchored behind the breakwater and swam for the first time in the Sea of Marmara untroubled by jellyfish. Ashore we were surprised at the poor living conditions, but the warmth and generosity of the people was overwhelming. In the back streets, the local women and their daughters were sitting in front of their houses in traditional clothes, spinning, knitting or sewing. They insisted we sat with them and gave us glasses of fresh yoghurt drink. As we left they gave us parcels of delicious olives, bread, tomatoes and onions.

We'd hoped to reach Istanbul with the sun rising over the city, but were disappointed – as we had been thirty years ago. A thick mist developed with the dawn as we sailed past the Princes Islands, but slowly the domes and minarets appeared through the haze. We joined the throng of traffic and proceeded up the Bosphorus passing Leander's Tower to starboard, up to the first bridge, before turning back and past the Golden Horn. We sailed close under Topkapi Palace, with a light north wind taking us past a unique skyline dominated by the Blue Mosque in the foreground and behind it Aya Sofia. In all directions minarets rose into the sky. Making our way to Atakoy Marina, we were thrilled by the bustle of shipping, large and small ferries going in all directions and merchant ships ploughing steadily to and from the Black Sea.

Louisa left us in Istanbul and Alice and Lucy were sad to say farewell to Jack and Constance; we had met few families sailing and they missed the company of their own age terribly. After three hot days sightseeing, we turned for home and made long day sails back through the Sea of Marmara and the Dardanelles to the Turkish island of Bozcaada, staying a couple of days to let some particularly strong north winds blow through. This was no hardship as the town is charming with an impressive castle to explore. Bozcaada is still a military zone, but restrictions are much relaxed now. In 1967 we had not been allowed ashore, but the obliging harbour master had done our shopping.

We were enjoying some good downwind sailing now, but under disappointingly cloudy and threatening skies. The wind remained strong day and night, so we were selective in our overnight anchorages. After three stops on the island of Lesbos we sailed across to Nisos Oinoussa. Here, in 1967, we'd been turned away by two swimmers who indicated that we would be shot at from the radio station at the summit of the hill. This year we found Mandraki harbour very smart and welcoming.

We crossed back into Turkish waters and anchored in Sarpdere Limani. The wind shrieked off the surrounding hills into this large bay, but the anchor held fast in soft golden mud. At the head of the bay is a small development of villas and, rather intriguingly, an area of the beach cordoned off with screens. We discovered that fundamentalist Muslims from Istanbul had developed the bay for their holidays and the screened off area was for women and children to swim in. The perimeter was fenced and guarded, but not well enough to prevent a large herd of goats from getting in, wandering across the gardens and beach munching vines as they went, pursued by the fundamentalist holidaymakers throwing stones.

Thirty years ago we had anchored in the next bay east and had dragged out of the anchorage in the middle of the night. Mindful of this I laid a kedge at sunset as the wind moderated, and by midnight the wind was gusting 35 knots and continued to do so until morning. I was not looking forward to a forty mile passage to Kusadasi in this amount of

Haigri off Amorgos

Alice (L) and Lucy (R) entering Turkish waters.

wind, but once we were offshore the wind moderated and we ended up motoring in a flat calm. The two highlights of our stay in Kusadasi were our visit to the magnificent ruins of Ephesus and Alice taking her first unaided strokes in the marina swimming pool. We promised her a pink bikini when she could swim ten metres and for the next few weeks we were lucky to find safe harbours with nearby clean beaches where she could practise and we could all cool off. Such is the joy of sailing in the Greek islands and thus started a slow idle through the Dodecanese and Southern Cyclades.

We'd left England in company with our friends James and Linda Bowen and their two sons Ben (4) and Sam (1) aboard *Freyja of Salthouse*, a Moody 34. Travelling together for some of the way, we then separated and met up again every couple of weeks. Now we met up on the tiny island of Lipsi, and all four children were delighted to have friends to play with again.

The beauty and serenity of Patmos was most appealing. We enjoyed visiting the monastery, high on the spur, that dominates the town physically and spiritually. Halfway down the hill is the cave, now a chapel, where St John wrote the Apocalypse. I was able to buy a new steering compass in the town as, despite two attempts to change the liquid in our original binnacle, the liquid would cloud over and the card become invisible after a couple of weeks. The new compass eased the task of steering considerably and made us reflect how lucky we were to have so many electronic aids compared to my father, who had only an echo sounder, Walker log and compass to guide his navigation.

After the prolonged period of north-westerlies, we anticipated an uncomfortable ride for the 50 miles from Patmos to Amorgos. A large swell was running as we rounded the south of the island, but we had a fine sail under reduced canvas in the sort of weather *Haigri* enjoys.

My father had spent three days storm bound here and had walked across the island to the monastery of Hozoviotissus, carved out of the rock face high on the cliffs on the south of the island. We took a bus, but were delighted to find this intriguing and remote monastery still offering the same hospitality to its visitors. The piece of loukoumi and thimbleful of sweet liqueur were most welcome after the hot climb up steep steps cut into the cliffs.

In 1967 we were taken up to the monastery of Patmos on donkeys. This year we had our chance of donkey rides in Santorini. Sailing into this island is awe-inspiring, as you are entering the crater of the volcano that erupted almost 3,500 years ago. The sheer cliffs are black burnt rock that plunge far down into the sea bed making anchoring almost impossible. The pilot book was gloomy about the safety of the small quay, owing to the wash from passing tripper boats. By chance we arrived in the early evening as these boats were tying up for the night and we had an undisturbed visit. No sooner had we moored than Dimitri appeared with donkeys and mules, so we set off at a cracking pace up the 700 feet of almost vertical cliff face to the busy tourist town in time to watch the spectacular sunset.

Milos is also a volcanic island with a large natural harbour. Like many of the Cyclades, the main town is situated above the port and was well worth visiting. We caught an early bus up the hill and from here had a superb view of the bay. As we wandered around the dazzlingly white streets waiting for a *taverna* to open for breakfast, an old man picked handfuls of delicious figs for us from the enormous tree in his garden.

Sadly this was our last Aegean island before setting course for the Byzantine town of Monemvasia on the east coast of the Peloponnese. The 70 mile night passage under a beautifully clear sky, with a smooth phosphorescent sea and dolphins for company, was a perfect end to our tour of the Aegean. Alice enjoyed steering in the evening and looking up at the heavens as the stars slowly revealed themselves. By the time the Milky Way stretched across the sky she was ready for her bunk. Catherine and I wondered if in the future this cruise might inspire Alice and Lucy to revisit this magical cruising ground, perhaps in thirty years time.

We had diverged from my father's route by cutting across the Cyclades. He had gone south to Crete before wintering in Malta. However we spent three weeks exploring the Peloponnese and Ionian islands before crossing to Sicily and then Malta before finally reaching Monastir in Tunisia for the winter. By then we'd been away for six months and covered 4,200 miles, visiting 111 ports.

I hope my father would have approved of our wanderings. He certainly would have been amused by the similarities of our experiences – the warmth and generosity of everyone we met; the infuriating short steep seas that made many simple passages uncomfortable; the pleasure of rolling downwind with the sun and breeze on your back. Above all the joy of exploring new places in your own boat. Next year we hope to bring *Haigri* home.

Haigri is a Rival 38 designed by Peter Brett and built in 1977. She is cutter rigged and has made a comfortable, safe cruising home for a family of four to explore the Mediterranean.

DETOUR TO TAHITI

by Francis Hawkings

This is the cruise for which the Romola Cup was awarded.

There seem to be two types of cruiser: those who dream of places like Chile and those who dream of places like Tahiti. I have always been in the Chile camp myself – its channels, islands, glaciers, mountains, wildlife and wilderness have made it, for many years, the focus of my goal for some 'really serious cruising'. However, ten years of living and sailing in southern California teach one the attractions of sailing in sun and warm weather. Your foul weather gear is forgotten in a locker, and if things get really bad you put on a sweater. Enough to give me doubts, and to convert Marilyn firmly to the Tahiti camp.

After a dozen or so years of rather hard work and a lot of travel, we made our opportunity in 1997 to do the kind of cruising we'd been aiming for – a change of career and pace of life, and a slow move back to the UK from California. In three frantic months we took the irrevocable steps – jobs and house given up, furniture in storage, cars gone, cats dispatched to quarantine and our lives reduced to a sailing boat and a mailing address.

Our ultimate destination for 1997 was Chile. But starting from California, the problem is how to get there. If you head straight down the coast you have nature against you – a windless region west of the Mexican mainland and central America, and then, south of Panama, headwinds and contrary current for 2,500 miles down the south American coast. An alternative is to head further west, to Easter Island. But this is a long trip, a short stopover at best, and the dates are problematic. Leaving early enough to clear the Mexican hurricane season by June means arriving too early in the Chilean winter.

So we decided to head further west still – to make a passage to the Marquesas during the northern spring, spend a couple of months in French Polynesia, then continue to Chile late enough to arrive there at

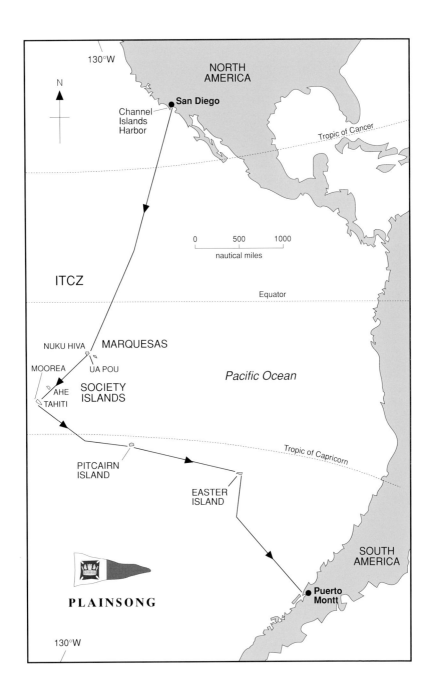

the end of their winter. More miles, but reasonably favourable wind directions and the added bonus of having to kill time in the south seas. And we no longer had to choose between the dream of Chile and the dream of Tahiti.

We join Plainsong in the sunny Marquesas

Murray Longmore flew back to England and Marilyn flew out from Los Angeles in the first week of June and *Plainsong* was ready for some island hopping. We had two months to spend in French Polynesia before our planned departure for Chile in early August. We decided to visit fewer places, each in more depth, rather than attempt to go everywhere.

Geology is the starting point for the Polynesian scene. Volcanoes created the three groups of islands which now constitute most of French Polynesia: the Marquesas, Tuamotus and the Societies, from north-east to south-west. Coral reefs tend to form around volcanic islands in the Pacific, and the islands themselves erode and sink. So today each island group is different. The Marquesas, the youngsters, are all mountain and no coral. The Tuamotus are the opposite, their volcanic cores all gone leaving atolls with lagoons in the middle. Tahiti and the other Societies combine the best of both: beautiful mountainous islands with fringing coral reefs.

The Marquesas are truly magnificent, both for a landfall and for a prolonged cruise. Rising sheer to 3,000 feet from a deep ocean, they have craggy cliffs, mysterious peaks and sheltered, indented bays. The hillsides are lush and green and each island collects its hat of clouds, which brings welcome relief from the sun and refreshing showers which are not worth covering up for. The islands have abundant fruit and wild goats, and the way of life is simple, although the simplicity hides a startling level of prosperity thanks to French subsidy.

The beaten track for cruisers in Nuku Hiva leads from Taiohae to Daniel's Bay (Baie Tai Oa), an exceptionally beautiful anchorage surrounded by steep mountains with a gentle valley sloping away at the head of the bay. You can hike up a nearby valley to a spectacular waterfall, and the whole is presided over by a charming idiosyncratic Marquesan called Daniel and his wife Antoinette. Kind and engaging, they dispense water, help and advice to cruisers and maintain a fascinating visitors' book of yachts for many years past.

To the south of Nuku Hiva is Ua Pou, mountainous again with volcanic spires and spikes rising improbably to nowhere. Searching for some solitude by now, we anchored in a tiny cove and hiked over a rough track to a remote village, to barter tea for an enormous bunch of bananas which saw us all the way to Tahiti.

Then on to the Tuamotus on the full moon, an unexpectedly rough five-night passage as a trough lay across our south sea paradise. We stopped for a week in Ahe, one of the north-western atolls, and a more striking contrast with the Marquesas could not be found: no mountains here, indeed nothing higher than a palm tree. The coral reef keeps the ocean at bay and inside the lagoon are clear turquoise water and brilliant tropical fish. The wind swishes through the coconut palms and the surf breaks distantly on the reef outside. The sounds of ukulele and guitar waft out from the village.

It was a strange sort of peace – restful and soothing, yet so close to danger. The islands are a major navigational hazard, low-lying and hard to see, the danger compounded by unpredictable currents. The land grows next to nothing and barely supports life. Supplies come twice a month – more rarely on smaller atolls – aboard a rickety inter-island trader.

But pearl farming has created an important source of income in some of the Tuamotus, including Ahe. The Polynesian oyster is black-lipped and produces a 'black' pearl, really many shades of grey and cream. They are on everyone's finger, ear, neck and wrist in Tahiti, and very attractive they are too.

At the end of June we did the two further nights on to Tahiti, mainly calm, but blustery as we approached the island in the early evening. I was looking for the lighthouse on Pointe Venus, where Cook observed the transit of the planet in 1769. Suddenly the sky above Papeete exploded with circles, flashes and stars – the fireworks marking the beginning of *Heiva*, Tahiti's three weeks of traditional culture and celebration in July.

We spent a month in Tahiti and its beautiful sister island, Moorea – a month of variety and interest, with island tours, many cultural events of singing and dancing, the Gauguin museum, the Botanical Gardens and much else, along with socializing, boat jobs and some good old-fashioned time-wasting.

We were, we'll admit it, captivated by Tahiti's magic. Both Tahiti and Moorea are gentle, abundant, beautiful and comforting, and their magic is rather sensuous. At the same time, the impressions of downtown Papeete are almost overwhelming after two months of simple life at sea. Not a big city really, Papeete is nevertheless cosmopolitan and European, but also relaxed and Polynesian. Chic Paris fashions coexist with the more informal local style – quite literally from high heels to bare feet in the same shops and restaurants. There was also a great gathering of cruising boats crowding every berth and anchorage.

France's approach to colonial government in Polynesia is very different from America's treatment of Hawaii, Tahiti's northern hemisphere counterpart. In Hawaii, being American amounts to a free rein for commerce. The French, by contrast, have taken a more *dirigiste* approach and kept tourist and other development to a tiny scale in their part of Polynesia. They support the economy by artificially high wages in the large government sector, which primes the pump for the rest of the economy. With government subsidy and fruit growing on trees, there is no real need for commerce. The price is dependency, and of course the nuking of a couple of atolls. In fact the entire south-eastern portion of the Tuamotus can be cruised only with special permission, partly because of continuing fallout from Mururoa.

In Tahiti we learned to use and benefit from the radio, the cruising community's telephone and public address system. We've had VHF and SSB on board for a while, but I'd always regarded them as an intrusion, a last resort if you couldn't figure things out for yourself. Now I learned how useful radio could be for sharing weather and other information, for informal cruising in (radio) company, and for the socializing and friendships that form amongst the boats. After overcoming my reticence, I was soon 'Roger That-ing' with the best of them.

Tahiti was hard to leave, especially as Marilyn was staying on another month while *Plainsong* made her way towards Chile. The island peaks looked stunning as we sailed down the western shore on Friday 8th August, and it was rather a relief when this paradise had disappeared the next morning.

My shipmate for this leg was Chris Chan, a Canadian I'd met through a bulletin board for crew on the Internet (http://www.cruisingworld.

Plainsong peacefully at anchor.

com; I also recommend http://www.ualberta.ca/~sjones/ for a useful index of sailing web sites). It was gutsy of Chris to come, since he was joining an unknown boat for a long and potentially difficult passage. But everything worked out wonderfully, and as well as being a terrific sailor and shipmate he has left a legacy of Chinese flavour in *Plainsong*'s galley repertoire.

The weather tactics for this leg were important. At 17°S, Tahiti lies in the belt of south-east trades. South of Tahiti, from about 25° to 35°S, is an area of variable winds in which no particular direction predominates. Then south of 35°S, or thereabouts, the westerlies begin to prevail. For obvious reasons, knowledgeable opinion says head straight south until you pick up westerlies, and then head due east or so to Chile. But both Pitcairn and Easter Island lie temptingly east and north of this track. While we acknowledged the logic of the preferred route, Chris and I had agreed to try and reach Easter Island on the way. If we were defeated by headwinds, then we simply fall back on the normal strategy further east. I also had some slim reasons for unusual optimism. Cruisers coming out from Panama were complaining about the weakness of the trades this year, and the local forecasts all summer had been giving winds with a surprising amount of west in them for Rapa, the southernmost part of French Polynesia (which is also at about 27°S). Since this was an *El Niño* year, perhaps conventional bets were off.

In our first week we found more southerlies than south-easterlies. Not wishing to head west of south on the port tack, we were pushed south-east on the starboard tack. After a week we were approaching the latitude of Pitcairn, able to head either due east for Pitcairn or south-east for our destination in Chile. It wasn't a hard decision, so off we went to the east.

Almost immediately, a nasty shock – a truly horrendous weather forecast from Mahina Radio in Tahiti, giving strong gales and gusts up to 100 knots for Rapa, downgraded next day to a modest 60–70 knots. We could conceivably have run for shelter in the Gambiers, at that time only 60 miles to the north, but it seemed – even to my conservative instincts – too speculative amidst the welter of coordinates and times, and we thought there was a good chance that we'd be far enough north and east to avoid the worst of this low.

We pressed on and were 20 miles north of Pitcairn at dawn on the morning of Thursday 21st August. As we turned south to run towards the island, the wind backed sharply to the west and the front arrived. It blew hard and visibility was poor. No sign of the island, so it was comforting when a cheery voice responded, 'Pitcairn here, good morning *Plainsong*', to our VHF call. At six miles off, still no island, and we were down to storm jib to slow ourselves in the hope of a clearance. At four miles off, excitement! A tiny, battered-looking island, indistinct through a veil of mist. At three miles, we lost it again in a blast of rain that felt like hail. But eventually, as we closed the land, the squalls relented enough

Pacific Paradise.

that we could see the island clearly, with its houses clinging to the hillside. No chance of landing, we thought, because Pitcairn doesn't have a sheltered anchorage. In fact there was another yacht at anchor off Adamstown, but its rolling and rearing didn't make us want to change our minds.

So it was a sail-by only. After a botched tack by me rather close to the breakers, we gybed away to the south and east and were on our way, having delivered by radio a message from some youngsters on a yacht we had met in Tahiti to their friends on Pitcairn.

But we did make a remarkable discovery. While talking on VHF, it turned out that the pastor to Pitcairn's 40 inhabitants, John Chan, and his wife Yvonne, were both childhood friends of Chris whom he had not seen in 30 years. All the more disappointment that we couldn't land, but they chatted at length on VHF.

It was blowing hard by now and we were running fairly dead downwind. Our Monitor self-steering likes these conditions, but when I emerged after lunch and found the Monitor sailing us rock-steady with 6.7 knots on the speed indicator and 41 knots on the wind indicator it was a little rich for my taste. So we took in the rest of the heavily-reefed main and ran under storm jib for two days. Good progress to the east, but the sea built and built until eventually we were pooped. No serious damage, although the Monitor's windvane was sheared off by the wave. I could replace it with a spare, but it was an unwarranted indignity for our Most Valuable Player.

Our luck with wind direction generally held and we made the 1,100 miles from Pitcairn to Easter Island through a mix of weather with only a spell of easterlies, through the worst of which we hove-to. We arrived at Rapa Nui (Easter Island's Polynesian name) on Monday 1st September, feeling exhilarated to have achieved our intermediate goal.

The stop proved a wonderful interlude, another highpoint amongst highpoints in our Polynesian detour. We spent our first morning dealing with the officials, which when you are excited enough about your destination can be part of the fun. From their log we counted 22 boats signed into Rapa Nui in 1997, including *Plainsong*. Signed in just ahead of us, by two weeks, was Tim Trafford aboard *Ardevora of Roseland*.

We spent four days at Rapa Nui. The island is notorious for sudden shifts of wind which oblige yachts to change anchorage. During our stay the weather was blustery and exceptionally wet, but the rain was a small penalty to pay for wind from the east. This enabled us to anchor off the main town of Hanga Roa with the wind off the land and easy access through the surf to the harbour. We took it in turns to rent a car and tour the island.

My own day ashore was almost too intense for one 24-hour period. On a morning of execrable weather, I was nervous about leaving the boat because there was a threat of windshift to the south-west in the weather forecast. Paralyzed by indecision, I hovered in the museum in Hanga Roa, waiting for the rain to clear and glancing furtively out of the window across the bay to *Plainsong*. Eventually plucking up courage to venture out of VHF range, I found myself lost on the outskirts of Hanga Roa (a place so small you wouldn't think it *possible* to get lost) inadvertently worked my way inside the airport perimeter.

The airport on Rapa Nui is an outsize affair, enlarged by the Americans as a possible emergency landing site for the space shuttle. In my attempt to extricate myself I followed a track literally across the runway (I did look both ways first) and eventually found myself the wrong side of customs and immigration amongst the disembarkation ladders for passengers on foot. Contemplating several weeks in jail at least by now – my handheld VHF was bound to raise additional suspicion – I was becoming desperate for an exit and finally managed to bolt out through the LAN-Chile cargo yard in my conspicuous bright red jeep.

The day was back on track and I was still a free man, but I'd frittered away valuable time. I headed east through wind and rain along the dirt roads to the quarry at Rano Raraku, where the famous statues, the *moai*, were carved. This is an astonishing and haunting place, with scores of *moai* abandoned in the quarry around the end of the 17th century. They seemed to me beautiful and dignified, bearers of the unfathomable thoughts and fears of people who had lived rich lives on this incredibly isolated island. There was almost no-one about and you could wander among the monuments with an immediacy like that at Stonehenge in the old days.

The weather was starting to clear now, but there was no change in wind direction. *Plainsong* would be safe in the anchorage off Hanga Roa for the afternoon at least, so there was time to continue round the island and visit the pretty cove at Anakena. Of course a day is woefully little to spend somewhere that certainly makes it onto my list of the world's great places, along with the likes of the Grand Canyon, Venice and the rice terraces of south-east Asia. But it was all we could allow ourselves, and what a memorable day.

We also had fun ashore with the locals during our stay at Rapa Nui. In *The Happy Isles of Oceania*, Paul Theroux found the Rapa Nui people 'by turns both giggly and gloomy', putting this down to inbreeding. We must have met our tiny cross-section in a giggly week, because we found them outgoing, informal and, in a couple of cases, just slightly and endearingly whacko.

But they didn't seem to like their Chilean governors. Life was harder on Rapa Nui than on the other Polynesian islands we were familiar with – especially after Tahiti, pampered by nature and underwritten by Paris. On Rapa Nui the houses were small, disposable dollars were scarce and our foul-weather gear was fingered a little enviously. The arm of the military was more in evidence than the purse of the exchequer. If Hawaii is a playground for American capital and French Polynesia a prisoner of France's nuclear programme, then Rapa Nui seemed more like an expression of unaffordable territorial ambition on the part of Chile.

Off to sea again for our final leg on another Friday (5th September) – I just can't find it in myself to take the Friday superstition seriously. We were now headed for Puerto Montt at the northern end of the Chilean channels, about 2,000 miles to the south-east. We found headwinds. A large high was established over the south-east Pacific, about ten degrees further south. We couldn't skirt it clockwise to the north, because that would probably mean contrary winds all the way. So we held a long port tack due south for seven days, until at last the isobars began to bend and we could shape a more easterly course. Finally, at about 38° S, we steered for Puerto Montt with sheets eased a little and *Plainsong* began to fly. The Tradewind 35 is really a 33-footer with an extended bow and stern, so she has long overhangs and a short waterline (25ft 10in) which constrains her speed. But on a beam reach she stretches out, and in our second week we recorded over 1,000 miles, with daily runs over 150 miles – a personal best for *Plainsong*.

Now the high had become our friend, extending a ridge towards the mainland to help us carry the reaching breeze for longer. We steered slightly further north than our rhumbline course, to use the high pressure centre as protection against lows approaching from the west.

We could literally feel the miles rolling by. The weather was fine though getting colder – it was winter, after all, and we were almost down to 40° S. A time to adjust to cooler places after ten wimpy years in California, and a time to start thinking about *Plainsong*'s programme for 1998 and 1999. Mulling this over on night watches, I managed to articulate the cruising philosophy I'd like to aspire to: *Ambitious plans, cautiously carried out.* But of course everything's relative – to one's boat, one's experience and so on – and what's still ambitious to me is a mere bagatelle to many others.

The high did its job well and although we had two brief low pressure systems come over us, they brought nothing more troublesome than rather damp conditions down below. By way of counter-measures Chris, now mercifully in full control of the galley, began to excel himself: two hot meals a day, with such cunning use of a single pot there was hardly any washing-up.

Once these lows had blown over, we were back to wonderful crisp reaching weather for our final days to landfall, now with the wind from the south. On Tuesday 23rd September, an unmistakable scent of land hung in the air – then a change of sea colour during the morning, and in the early afternoon that exciting first sight of a strange coast. We arrived at Punta Corona, the northern entrance to the channels, just after dark, and crept round the point to anchor for the night in, appropriately enough, Puerto Inglés.

A landfall brings everything to a close so suddenly and a night-time arrival has the additional thrill that at first light next morning – there it all is. And there indeed it was, a pastoral scene rich in greens and the yellow of gorse. We were 4,500 miles and 42 days at sea from Tahiti, 8,000 miles and five months from Channel Islands Harbor.

As we sailed to Puerto Montt over the next two days, escorted by dolphins, we realized how wonderful this cruising ground was going to be – islands, bays and estuaries in the foreground, and behind them snow-capped volcanic mountains to the north of Puerto Montt. To the east and south, we saw a rim of snow along the jagged, shark's tooth peaks of the Andes.

It was early in the spring. *Plainsong* was the first boat to arrive in Puerto Montt that season, with four months of coastal exploration in Chile ahead of us. Chris said to me that it must be exciting to be at the beginning of the fulfillment of a twenty-year dream to cruise these waters. To which, now, there was only one possible reply: 'Roger That.'

Plainsong is a Tradewind 35, designed by John Rock and built in 1992 by Tideway Boat Construction in Salcombe, Devon. She is fitted out with long-distance cruising and a small crew in mind.

SOMNAMBULISM IN FRANCE

by Jonathan Virden

Twayblade took a different sort of cruise in 1997. The main object was to visit some French friends at their holiday house on Ile de Ré near La Rochelle. A secondary purpose was to enjoy some sunshine with as little trouble as possible. Joseph (16), his friend Allen and I took *Twayblade* from her mooring at Cargreen to Plymouth for a day of victualling and a scrub of the bottom alongside the wall at Alec Blagdon's yard. My sister Sue joined us there, and we spent the night of 22nd July at Barn Pool to taste the last good beer for nearly four weeks.

From Barn Pool we motored to the Raz de Sein, taking 30 hours because there was no wind. There we could set the spinnaker and we anchored at St Evette (Audierne) three hours later. The noise of the engine and calmness of the sea had made everyone sleepy; I hoped that a night would cure this . . . but not so!

In order to get Sue and Allen to a train for their return to UK on Saturday, we sailed early from Ste Evette, on a reach, almost to Les Sables d'Olonne. This took a day and a night; the boys were on watch for the first eight hours while I slept and Sue snoozed in the cockpit. During the afternoon the motion began to affect Sue and Joseph so they retired to sleep for 12 and 15 hours respectively, and Allen was deeply out too. I kept watch while *Twayblade* sailed herself peacefully under genoa only. The breeze gradually rose to 25 knots and then fell away to nothing.

During that night I was single-handing a combination of hearse, with three corpses in the bunks, and Indian railway carriage stuffed with bags of gear. *Twayblade* has very small stowage volume, so with a crew of four the bags spill over into the remaining space. When the wind failed, we motored into the marina at Les Sables d'Olonne.

During the whole cruise of four weeks we only used the anchor seven times. We sailed overnight three times and were in a marina for all the other nights. This is very unusual for us and it was most interesting to see another style of boating. I was first in these parts in 1974 and there were

The bustling wet basin at St Martin-de-Ré

almost no marinas. Now every inlet has one or two boat-parks and several
towns have created giant marinas on the foreshore (e.g. Pornichet). I was
amazed at the way Republican France has made yachting a mass
occupation and how anonymous it was, and how extraordinarily con-
vergent are the designs of yachts today. However there were some elegant
older yachts, mostly wooden, if one could detect them among the glare of
GRP.

At Les Sables d'Olonne there was plenty of room. The ferry which
plies between the marina and the town was very noisy every 20 minutes
all day until 2000 hrs. We gathered an unauthorised crew of tiny silent
mosquitoes which travelled with us for the next three weeks.

There is a big *Intermarché* and most other normal facilities nearby. The
town is on the east side of the river and has a splendid market on
Saturday mornings. I met *Squander* RCC and had a brief exchange of
news about anchorages in West Brittany.

Sue and Allen took the train to Nantes, Paris and home on Saturday as
planned, leaving Joseph and me to go on to La Rochelle. As there was no
wind we motored all the way, mostly avoiding the heavy clumps of weed
which float below the surface. At the giant *Port de Minimes* marina the
reception was well organised for visitors, as were all the marinas we
visited. They were not particularly cheap – on average, about 150 francs
per night would cover a berth for 10 metres overall and showers for
three.

Joy arrived from home by train, via the Chunnel and Paris, a few minutes ahead of the itinerary. After a day in La Rochelle (20 minutes walk or a 12 franc ferry ride from the marina) we motored to St Martin de Ré, finding a berth in a trot with four feet depth at low water (the lock gate leaked, but the bottom was extremely soft mud). Here, we were immediately taken over by my friends. For two days we were with them for lunch and dinner and to explore the island. They have a small, secluded bungalow with extra room for children and grandchildren. The island has a resident population of 11,000, but at the peak of the summer season there are more than 300,000 on the island. Most of the visitors camp, and most go about on bicycles as the land is flat and there are many dedicated cycle tracks. We went to the principal towns and had a pleasant picnic and beach party at Baleines at the north-west tip of the island. The local wine is good and the aperitif better; the brandy is most respectable. It was hot, humid and windless.

From St Martin we returned to *Minimes* and on 1st August we sailed slowly to the entrance of the *Charente* river and then motored ten miles with the last of the flood up to Rochefort. After a small delay the lock opened and we went to a berth in the inner basin. This was a mistake because the nearest restaurant had outdoor live music set to wake the dead as well as those who would rather sleep; perhaps Saturday nights only. Rochefort is a pleasant and extremely interesting town with much to see, as it was purpose-built as a naval base and shipyard on a grand scale. It was hot in Rochefort and humid, so we slowed down even more.

Rochefort was furthest south for us this year. Coming home we motored, with occasional patches of sailing, to Sables d'Olonne through some heavy rain; then to Pornichet motoring all day, and on to Ile aux Moines in the Gulf of Morbihan. Whenever we were at sea an extraordinary desire to sleep overtook all of us, particularly Joseph. This partly came from heat and noise and from having little to do other than look out for the ubiquitous dan-flags of fishing gear.

The tide had been flooding for four hours as we approached the Morbihan and the turbulent currents at the entrance were spectacular. Ile aux Moines has all the usual village shops and many small hostelries for visitors who arrive in large ferries in the morning and depart in the early evening. Outside visitor hours Moines is a delightful place, reminiscent of the Isles of Scilly. After two nights we moved to a peaceful anchorage south-east of Ile d'Ars and next day went on to Vannes, which is a city with everything the visitor may want. There was enough room for a remarkable number of yachts in the enclosed dock within the lock. A guide meets everyone and allocates a berth according to the beam of the yacht. We met Brian and Onora Lynch of *Ionion* from Galway for an evening's natter.

From Vannes we motored out of the Morbihan into a thunderstorm, some lightning (much too close for comfort) and very heavy rain for a short while. We hoped that the accompanying wind would hold until we'd cleared the tip of Presqu'Ile de Quiberon, but no such luck; we motored, again, to Ile de Groix. For an overnight anchorage, *Anse de Melite*, the bay on the north side of the north-east tip of Groix, was excellent, remarkably free of swell and tide. We fetched up about 1½ cables from the beach in approximately three metres (LWS), over gravel and weed patches. Some charts show a group of rocks off the beach in the western part of the bay; but we saw no sign of them. Next day was almost all motor-sailing to Concarneau, for the final purchase of stores. The supermarket trolleys were used to good effect, although the shop is about a kilometre from the pontoons.

We sailed most of the ten miles to Bénodet, anchored in Anse du Trez and some of the crew went swimming. Next day we motored for four hours round Pointe de Penmarc'h and then sailed gently to St Evette for the night.

To catch the start of the north-going tide at the Raz de Sein, we left the Ste Evette anchorage as dawn was breaking and mist was pouring out of the river valley. We motored all the way to Plymouth, which took 28 hours. Our tan coloured mainsail was hoisted when fog rolled over the sea as we approached the Chenal du Four, although the iron genoa was making almost all of the breeze. I retreated to the navigation table with the remote control and steered among the buoys and beacon towers using the GPS. Meanwhile the others looked out for more mobile troubles. The fog lifted to show that our position was exactly as expected on the four knot tide, which improved my confidence in the system. Fog came again twice, but all cleared away by the evening in time for a magnificent sunset. Although it was becoming cooler our persistent sleepiness continued.

Our cruise ended on 16th August at Cargreen on *Twayblade*'s own mooring and at a splendid club dinner party in the Cargreen Yacht Club. Over the whole cruise we had sailed for 20 hours and motored for 110 hours.

Twayblade was built in 1961 by Harry King at Pin Mill to the classic design of Alan Buchanan. She is a wooden masthead sloop, 32ft long, just under 9ft beam, draws 6ft and sleeps 4 in reasonable comfort. We bought her in 1981and she was much rebuilt in 1982, making her simpler and more durable.

SADKO'S FIRST CRUISE

by Noël Marshall

This is the cruise for which the Challenge Cup was awarded.

As soon as I retired in July 1993 I intended to do some full-time sailing. I rather fancied the idea of starting life afloat by sailing to New Jersey, USA, for the Alumni Weekend at the end of April 1994, marking the 40th Anniversary of my year as an exchange student at Lawrenceville School. It might just be feasible.

Although I had done much cruising and racing, including on oceans, I had never owned anything grander than half a Fireball. There was much to learn, starting with the fact that serious cruising yachts did not seem to be plentiful. I eventually found my boat in Holland in October 1993. She is a Hallberg-Rassy 38′ centre-cockpit sloop and I renamed her *Sadko* after the legendary adventurer from Novgorod. Drawing on friends and through the good offices of the CA Crewing Service, a team was assembled (an arrangement which continued, with some single-handed gaps, for the duration of the cruise). The early winter was spent at Hamble Point hastily re-fitting for ocean voyaging, including brief sailing trials in a chilly Solent. A false start took us as far as Weymouth, where it snowed, and on to Plymouth for more refitting, including a new alternator and regulation circuit.

The Atlantic

On 28th February 1994 we finally set out to cross the Bay of Biscay and were blessed with a brisk northerly wind. I had told friends and relations only that I was going 'initially on the Atlantic circuit'; but I stowed planning charts reaching as far as the North Pacific. We arrived in Antigua, via Madeira, on 6th April without incident of note.

Insufficient time remained to make a landfall in the United States as far north as New Jersey itself so we settled for the 1,250-mile passage to

Beaufort, North Carolina. Despite getting caught on a fish-trap line and having to limp into Virgin Gorda to disentangle the float from *Sadko's* rudder, we made it with two days to spare: enough time to park the boat, hire a car and drive north, dropping the First Mate with relations in Annapolis. The Lawrenceville celebrations were spiced by receiving the bottles of champagne awarded to the alumnus who had travelled the longest distance to attend.

The rest of the summer of 1994 was spent cruising up the Intra-coastal Waterway and the Chesapeake Bay and from there, with a relay of friends from England, going north as far as Shelburne in Nova Scotia. The Maine coast offered cruising ground of the choicest kind: interesting scenery, few people and adequate facilities. In October, a flawless New England fall was spent on Cape Cod, attending to various repairs and improvements in an old-fashioned family-run boatyard.

Hoping to take advantage of what appeared to be a good weather window for the passage to Bermuda, I left Block Island on 11th November, with a young American couple as crew. Soon after we had crossed the dreaded Gulf Stream serenely, we were caught in savage weather between an Atlantic High and the unseasonable tropical depression 'Gordon' off the US coast. We reached Bermuda safely, but it took eight days and resulted in a broken Aerogen mounting and other minor damage. Also my crew deserted. Not wanting to spend the winter in Bermuda, I continued single-handed to St Lucia, arriving on Christmas Eve.

This was my first real solo passage and was tedious because most of the two weeks were to windward, but there were no alarums worse than being lassoed off Martinique by another fishing float. There was also a memorable encounter. Believing that gentlemen do not motor across oceans just to get to the other side, I was patiently sitting out a calm patch when a minkie whale spent an hour sniffing round the boat. I found myself trembling with awe and vague apprehension, although I managed to get a photograph of the creature just under the keel.

The Caribbean

A young Australian and his partner joined ship for a few days. Leaving St Lucia on New Year's day, we savoured the *pina colada* belt as far as Grenada. With two new crew who were unfortunately short of time we made a rather perfunctory cruise along the Venezuelan coast. The undoubted highlight was the almost uninhabited island group *Los Testigos*. From Puerto Cabello we went to Central America with brief visits to Bonaire and Jamaica. The passage between those two islands across strong north-east trade winds remains *Sadko's* record run: 600 miles in just under four days. I had a lady transplant surgeon as crew. Fortunately her services were not needed. The boat was at Maya Landings near Belize City for a month while I spent part of the time with friends in Belmopan, making excursions to the interior and to the imposing Mayan city of Tikal in the Guatemalan jungle.

Southwards down the coast we made a diversion to the gorge of the Rio Dulce in Guatemala. The trip through the Panama canal on 4th-5th March was unique, although something should be done about the mind-numbing bureaucracy involved.

Pacific Crossing

The passage to the Galapagos was slow – fourteen days for under 1000 miles – but undoubtedly worth the effort. Until recently the islands have had a bad press as the result of numerous reports of obstruction and extortion on the part of the local authorities. In 1995 things were improving; we were allowed to stay five days and charged reasonable, published fees. Yachts must remain in one of two designated anchorages. In order to see the sights we went on two organized day excursions by bus and launch. We had literally to step our way through carpets of basking seals and sea lions; blue-footed boobies displayed within yards of us and the unique land and sea iguanas were happy to be photographed close-up. Giant turtles stared out of the long grass.

The next leg turned into something of an endurance test. Leaving on

Sadko in Guam

27th April, the 4,400-mile leg from Puerto Ayora to Hawaii took David Park and myself 64 days, on some of which we covered less than 20 miles. Concern about our supplies led us to keep open for several weeks the option of diverting to the Marquesas. But in the end we picked up the north-east trade winds and reached Hilo in good order at the end of June. We had learned much, including about the reliance to be placed on pilot charts. We also identified a belt of counter-current around 2°S between 117° and 125°W which averaged 0.8 knots against us for nearly a week. This is about 8° south of any charted counter-current.

In a marina wedged between a tropical beach and the high-rise jungle of Waikiki, *Sadko* was hauled out and I spent over two months re-fitting and taking a break. On 2nd September, at the Pacific Memorial Cemetery in the amphitheatre overlooking Pearl Harbour, I attended the moving ceremony marking the 50th anniversary of the end of the Second World War, which was addressed by President Clinton.

Micronesia I – The Line and Marshall Islands

The next goal was the Russian Far East. The area appealed to me as a Russia hand from Diplomatic Service days and because it is little known as a cruising destination. For practical reasons, among them the need to obtain Russian visas, the approach would be through Japan, and for weather reasons this would not be before the spring of 1996. We spent the intervening time in Micronesia.

Chris Powell joined ship and on 25th September we left Hawaii for Christmas Island, 1,100 miles to the SSE. Once clear of the notorious seas around the Hawaiian islands we made a relatively painless 400 miles in the first three days. With an SSB now working properly we began to learn our way round the various cruising-yacht 'nets'. *Sadko* continued to slip on at well over 100 miles per day, although as we came nearer to the equator we experienced, as expected, more variable and sometimes unfriendly weather. There was no hurricane danger, but much rain and many sudden squalls requiring rapid sail-shortening.

Fanning (03° 1.5′N 159° 21.6′ W), reached on 6th October, was a delight. On a narrow strip of atoll encircling a lagoon about ten miles across, a thousand Kiribati people pursue subsistence life based on fishing, coconuts, taro and other local produce. The government provides an administrator, a nurse, a small agricultural station and a school. An enterprising American living alone in a lagoon-side hut runs a business processing sea cucumbers and shark fins for export to China and Japan. The airstrip was disused, but flights were supposed to resume to bring sport fishermen when the small bungalow-type hotel then under construction was completed.

Meanwhile a few yachts and the occasional cruise ship visit each year. This was one of many places where we used our battered folding bikes to go exploring. Our five-day stay coincided with the funeral of a local dignitary. We were able to see the procession and watch the whole community gathered in their impressive *maneaba*. Every Kiribati village, even a small settlement, has one of these—an open-sided structure with a high thatched roof. They were the traditional places of discussion and government. Nowadays they seem to serve more as social centres – particularly we noticed for the showing of bloodthirsty video films, with little electric generators chattering away under the palm trees.

After a wet and windy three-day run to the north-west, we reached Palmyra atoll on the evening of 10th October. There are no navigation marks and getting into the lagoon involves mustering at a precise GPS position just outside the reef (which is about half a mile south of its charted position) and then following a narrow passage with compass, depth sounder and some unclear landmarks onshore. We had made radio contact with Roger Lextrait, the 'manager' of Palmyra Island, who attempted to guide us in the gathering dark, but it was clear that the operation, if possible, was unseamanlike. We decided to stand off for the night enjoying a bottle of wine and a sing-song with the guitar.

Entry in the morning proved hardly less hair-raising, because one could see the coral heads waiting to gouge holes in the hull a few feet below the surface. Two or three wrecks underscore the hazards, but we eventually made it into the lagoon and anchored, along with two other visiting yachts, at 05° 53.2′ N 162° 05.3′W.

Asked to nominate a single highlight from the cruise, it has to be Palmyra. It is the archetype of the palm-fringed tropical isle, but distinctive because of a combination of its remoteness, unspoilt condition and the profusion of nature. Boobies, fairy terns and many other species of birds abound. Millions of sooty terns have adopted the abandoned airstrip as a breeding ground. In the season (autumn) the carpet of fussing birds stretches to the horizon. The noise they make and their aggression when disturbed outdo Alfred Hitchcock's film. A Manta Ray patrols the landing bay. The sea is teeming with fish and when we went snorkelling the whole reef was a quivering kaleidoscope.

The atoll is American territory, privately owned by a company in Hawaii and falling under the seemingly loose supervision of the US Department of the Interior. There is no resident population apart from Roger Lextrait and a French yachtsman who is the company's representative.

During the Second World War Palmyra was a naval refuelling base and 6,000 US servicemen were stationed there. Such of their installations as have not been reclaimed by the jungle constitute some of the *curiosités* of the place but do not intrude – a sea-plane landing ramp, an underground hospital, a colossal water cistern which among other things supplies a yellow enamel bath standing on the jungle floor and a few huts. An unsuccessful attempt was made in the sixties to start a plantation and some sheds remain from that time.

A fishing vessel with a concession in the area visits periodically with supplies for Roger. A dozen or two yachts visit in the course of a year. Apart from water and coconuts there are no supplies available for visitors, and no facilities of any kind. But hurry: the owners have plans to develop the place for tourism, starting with beach cottages to which sport fishermen would be flown in small planes via Christmas Island. Even if the 747s are some years away, the magic of the place will be broken,

Tearing ourselves away with difficulty, we set out westwards on 23rd October to head for Tarawa (Kiribati) where Chris could catch a flight to Fiji and New Zealand. Benefitting from at least one knot of current and with wind up to force 5, we averaged 120 miles for the next few days. We watched stars and flying fish, listened to the screech of sooty terns and caught the occasional fish for supper – and played Scrabble.

On a broad reach with the genoa drawing well, we were working a few degrees south of our course. Secretly this suited us well because we wanted to sneak in a visit to Howland island. A small alteration of course on 29th October brought us there the following day and provided the second remarkable experience in two weeks. Unlike Palmyra, Howland – at 00° 48.5′ N, 176° 37.3′ W – is a flat slab covered with scrub grass and a few bushes, run as a nature reserve by the US Fish and Wildlife Service. Howland is uninhabited and visitors – if any – are not allowed beyond the beach area. A stubby unmarked beacon commemorates the

A fishing houseboat at Palawan in the Philippines.

American pioneer aviator Amelia Erhart, who disappeared *en route* to Howland in 1937. There is no fresh water. The place is desolate, eery and beautiful.

A certain tension attended our landing. We wanted to go ashore but had visions of the anchor dislodging itself so that *Sadko* would be whisked out to sea by the strong wind leaving us to a disagreeable fate. We decided to take a kedge ashore with a long line. This was easier said than done. There was more surf than appeared from offshore and the line, despite buoys at various points, snagged on the coral. Inquisitive sharks prowled round Chris's knees when she waded to free it. We succeeded in wedging the anchor in some rocks on the beach and went for a unique nature ramble, trying to keep an eye on the yacht's mast. But we came back along the beach to re-launch the dinghy with a powerful sense of relief.

After Palmyra and Howland, Tarawa could hardly compete. Crossing the International Date Line on 1st November we arrived off the harbour at Betio five days later after running most of the way under twin headsails. Tarawa (01° 21.9′ N 172° 55.8′ E) can provide a useful pit-stop. The situation is delightful but, apart from some decaying relics of WW II, points of interest are few and tourist facilities minimal. The general impression was of a local culture fast disappearing under a thin layer of western-style life supported by aid donors. Perhaps North Tarawa and some of the outer islands may better enable the visitor to rediscover the romance of the Gilbert Islands captured by Sir Arthur Grimble in *A Pattern of Islands*.

Having got Chris safely onto a plane towards a family reunion in New Zealand, I spent a few more days in Tarawa, looking around and tending to practical matters such as laundry and fresh food. Most of the latter is imported and supplies were no more than adequate. On 14th November the meteorological station assured me that none of the dreaded westerlies was in prospect and I left single-handed for Majuro in the Marshall islands.

The 350 mile passage was mostly a fast broad reach, interrupted by sail changes in response to numerous squalls. On the third day I was fortunate to get through the only passage into Majuro lagoon just before dark; especially as I found that the buoyage had been changed from IALA system B to system A after my (current) chart went to press and was then engulfed in a squall which blotted out everything. As I approached the port at Uliga in the dark I was hailed on the VHF by friendly American voices. Gary and Lisa on *Almitra* had spotted my lights and directed me into the anchorage (at 07° 06.2′ N 171° 22.5′ E). Later we were to cruise together.

Apart from an interesting but tiny museum and some good-quality handicrafts – including reproductions of the intriguing 'stick charts' used by the traditional Pacific navigators – Majuro has little for visitors.

My month's stay there was strictly a utility stop during which I had some spare parts shipped out and did some boat-work. But the best news was that Chris was able to re-join ship and would arrive on 15th December. Majuro was moving into full seasonal festivities with *Joy to the World* crooning from loudspeakers in every bank and supermarket. We decided that it was no place in which to spend Christmas. We also knew that if we wanted to have a truer impression of the Marshall Islands we should visit one of the outer islands. A chance conversation led us to Ebon Atoll, for which a chartlet was drawn for us on the back of a shop receipt.

The advice was inspired. We covered the 200-odd miles to the southwest in a brisk two days of somewhat moody weather and arrived on 22nd December (04° 34.3' N 168° 41.3' E). The village of Ebon is sprinkled along the lagoon shore of the principal island and contains about 500 people. There are no vehicles but surprisingly there is half-a-mile of main street with graded-surface and stones along the kerbs, apparently a relic of the period of German occupation. Also from that time is a splendid Gothic church in wood which was to be central to our visit.

There is a government representative, a school and a 'reverend' (unidentified Protestant) but the person who really counted was evidently the *Iroij* or traditional leader. It was he who presided over the day-long Christmas celebrations. The reverend had ruled that, since Christmas Eve was a Sunday it would be wrong to spend it doing all the necessary preparations. Christmas would therefore be postponed until the 26th. This suited us since it meant we were able to use the time to explore the island and also meet the rest of the unexpected European community: an American archeologist and his assistant, and Torbjorn and Sidsel, a young Norwegian couple who were living in a hut somewhere as part of a year savouring the Pacific outback.

The deferred Christmas Day was memorable. The church pews had been cleared to the sides, leaving a large arena in which for over seven hours groups from the various villages put on displays of a kind of formation dancing, the women in bright uniform dresses of varying degrees of elaboration. The dances were led by young men with referee's whistles and accompanied by music which seemed to combine local elements, the missionary heritage and modern pop, some of it recorded and some provided by guitars and singing. Accompanying sideshows included offerings to collection baskets, the throwing of necklaces of sweets to the children and one or two dances depicting scenes of village life. It was easy to believe that the dancers had been practising for weeks. Notwithstanding the modern influences and the battery-powered loudspeakers, this was genuine folk culture and fascinating.

At the lunch break the visitors were invited to the pastor's house for a feast of breadfruit, taro, buns fried in coconut cream, tuna fish fried in coconut oil, rice and small bananas. It was authentically local, and surely nutritious, if not the most appetizing of Christmas dinners. But we were genuinely grateful for the hospitality. Towards the end of the resumed festivities we were each presented with elegant pieces of shell-decorated basket and this provided an opportunity to say publicly a few words of thanks, which were translated and perhaps audible above the gathering excitement.

Next day at 1400 we set out for Kosrae, the most easterly of the States of the Micronesian Federation, 400 miles to the west. However, this was not quite the end of our dealings with the Marshall Islands. Two days out, *Sadko* became the first British yacht to be apprehended by the Marshallese 'navy'. At about 1800 we came upon a small patrol vessel which was evidently in the process of stopping a foreign (Korean) fishing boat. As we sailed by, monitoring the proceedings on VHF, we were surprised to be called, told to heave to and await a boarding party. An inflatable duly arrived and two young officers in heavy boots clambered aboard. Since they admitted that they had never intercepted a yacht before and were evidently unsure what to do, we settled for them inspecting the ship's papers and signing the visitors' book. The Australians have equipped and trained the proto-navy of the Marshall islands and I half-suspect there was a hidden Australian adviser chuckling away on the patrol boat.

Micronesia II – The Federated States

We reached Kosrae on New Year's Eve and celebrated aboard *Almitra* with Gary and Lisa who had sailed direct from Majuro. Kosrae is a true micro-state: a pleasant tropical island of 8,000 inhabitants, a subsistence economy with a trickle of tourists coming mainly for the diving and to see the remains of the mediaeval city of Insaru. We stayed longer than intended because Chris had the extraordinary mischance to break a rib – falling in the galley at anchor! Although kindly treated by a Filipino doctor at the hospital, there was little to do beyond pain relievers. Chris bravely decided against being 'medivacced' and by 23rd January she reckoned she was fit enough to move on, although fortunately we had crew reinforcements in the shape of the Norwegians we had met at Christmas.

The 300-mile trip towards Pohnpei started badly with a severe squall, during which the mainsail tore when a reefing line slipped. The wind eased, but the first twenty-four hours were lively and poor Sidsel, who had little experience of sailing, succumbed to sea-sickness from which she didn't recover until we took a break at the tiny island of Pingalap, exactly half-way to Pohnpei (06°12.3′ N, 160°42.0′ E). It was a worthwhile stop. The locals were friendly and showed us around, but

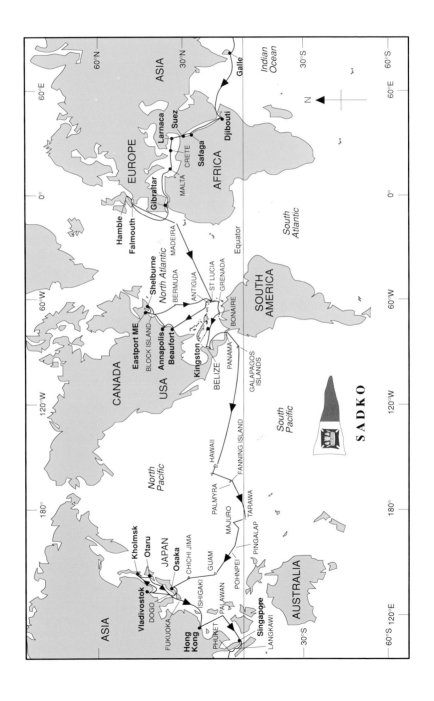

explained that life was very difficult because there was no economic base and the young people were all leaving. We saw an unusual communal taro pit a hundred yards or more across in which each family apparently had its own patch.

Another day and a half of fast sailing, punctuated by catching our first wahoo, took us into Pohnpei on 27 January (06°58.7′N, 158°12.1′E). Pohnpei provides the capital of the Federated States of Micronesia at Palikir. For the visitor, apart from the normal facilities of a tropical island, Pohnpei has a major historic site at Nan Madol. To explore it we rented a pick-up truck with two other boats and took dinghies and outboards. The ruins of the mediaeval city are built of big basalt blocks over an area of several square miles. The seven of us were almost the only visitors that day. If the place were in Europe or North America it would be visited by hundreds of thousands annually.

From Pohnpei our route lay towards Guam, 900 miles to the WNW, with one more stop in the Federated States of Micronesia. We left on 8th February in loose company with *Almitra* and reached Oroluk early on the 10th (07°36.6′ N, 155°09.7′E). Oroluk island is a tiny spot of land in the corner of a lagoon about 15 miles across and is inhabited by one family of seven. They are Polynesians and part of the displaced community from Kapingamarangi, the southernmost island of the FSM, many of whom are settled in part of Pohnpei. By arrangement on the radio, we carried stores for them from their people in Pohnpei and various gifts.

In return they showered us with lobsters, fish, palm syrup, coconuts and bananas, took us on spectacular snorkelling excursions among the reefs and entertained us in their home. It made one pause to think. Here in 1996 was a family living off the produce around them. They import only rice, clothing and a few domestic items such as needles and cooking pots. They pay for this with bags of air-dried copra which is collected by a steamer once or twice a year. A few yachts bring them goodies, including magazines. No discos, no soft drinks, no videos. Among the few concessions to 20th century amenities is a simple SSB set, powered by a second-hand solar panel, with which they keep in touch with Pohnpei. They are not entirely isolated and have all been to school. They know about the outside the world, but they prefer Oroluk.

Of course we pondered whether we too would not be happy in this ideal spot. But in our hearts we knew that to those reared in western civilization the charm of such a place is ephemeral. The trick is to move on with the seductive memories before the realities of remoteness and the implications of true self-reliance close in. And move on we did, sadly parting company with *Almitra*, and reached Guam on 23rd February. We covered the 700 miles in five occasionally boisterous days and arrived at Apra in a near-gale.

Guam is the only serious place for a pit-stop between Hawaii and Japan. A dozen or two yachts arrive early each year before moving north in March-April or going west to the Philippines. The Marianas Yacht Club is welcoming and most American facilities are available if you hunt for them in the enfuriatingly scattered town. The island has become a boom centre for Japanese tourists who come on very short visits, many of them to get married. The sights do not extend much beyond a modest waterfall and a monument to Magellan, who was the first western visitor in 1521.

A busy two months was spent in Guam working on the boat and joining in a little local activity. Chris Powell left and Ann Fraser arrived. After a laborious victualling (following the advice that food would be prohibitively expensive in Japan and scarce in Russia – wrong on both counts) *Sadko* finally left on 1st May. We headed for Kyushu, 1,400 miles to the NNE, but with the option of diverting to the island of Chichi Jima to the east or towards Okinawa to the west if the weather so determined.

Eastern Japan

We made generally good progress with the north-east trades and were soon out of the tropical conditions and into jersey and oilskins. By deliberately keeping up to windward we were edging towards Chichi Jima. But early on 10th May we got warning of a typhoon which the Guam weather centre thought might turn east of Japan and that clinched the decision to put in to Chichi Jima. It is not in fact a very secure hurricane hole and if the eye of the storm had come through we could have been in danger. In the event, the typhoon passed about 100 miles west but we spent one apprehensive night while *Sadko* was ground against a quay in the inner harbour, protected by the heavy lines and chain that we had prepared for a threatened typhoon in Guam and held off the harbour wall by a mass of fenders, pile boards and motor tyres.

However, this enforced stop on a low-key tourist island was otherwise an agreeable introduction to many aspects of Japan, including the friendly hospitality, the frustrations of language, unfamiliar shopping and, unexpectedly, poor telephone communications.

When the weather improved we made the remaining 700 miles to Osaka in a week. During the last part of the crossing the wind went light and we had to motor hard across the Kurosio current which was sweeping us north at several knots. We had our first taste of the dizzying amount of shipping in Japanese waters and of winkling information out of the Japanese Small Craft Guides. These slim pilot books cover every navigable nook and cranny of the coast. Unfortunately they are only available in Japanese. As they include no coordinates, places have to be identified by shape, but the guides are nevertheless invaluable for their immaculate chartlets, with numerous enlargements.

Once recovered from the shock of the metropolis of Osaka, our prime business there was to obtain visas for Russia. This was surprisingly painless. When the Consulate officials saw our invitation from the Sailing Federation in Vladivostok it was a matter of filling in a few forms and waiting a week. Joined by Sally Humphreys, an academic friend who managed to combine the trip with attending a seminar in Osaka and giving a lecture in Tokyo, we spent the intervening time on a day trip to see the wonders of Kyoto and on the first part of the passage westwards through the Inland Sea as far as Ushimado. The route offered everything from the industrial region around Kobe to the beautiful mediaeval castle towering over the town of Himeji. Between Honshu and the Awaji islands we passed below the construction work on the longest suspension bridge in the world, which will have a central span two kilometres long. Everywhere the density of shipping and fishing boats was heavier than the Dover Strait on a bad day. It was easy to see why night sailing was not recommended.

By 14th June we had our Russian visas and we completed our transit of the Inland Sea in six day-stages, stopping wherever we could find a suitable corner, as we would in Europe. Japanese sailors do not appear to do this and foreign craft are supposed to visit only approved harbours and to check at each stop with the authorities. In view of our imprecise destination the Ushimado official gave us a sealed envelope addressed to the customs 'at the next port of call', but when we reached Ube nobody asked where we'd been for nearly a week.

Two days in Ube sufficed for provisioning, checking out and having some farewell *sushi* and *tempora*. On 22nd June we successfully negotiated the tide through the Kanmon Kaikyo and set out across the Japan Sea. As promised in the pilot chart, during the week it took to sail the 550 miles to Vladivostok the wind blew from every direction between north-east and north-west but was predominantly moderate and favourable with patches of rain, calm and fog. We might have been in the English Channel.

Russia

At midday on 29th June, *Sadko* emerged from thick fog into Vladivostok harbour. Nobody paid any attention to a foreign yacht. After some civil but unproductive dialogue by VHF with the harbour authorities, friendly Russians in a launch escorted us to the Yacht Club, which is in fact the sailing centre of the Merchant Marine Academy. We were smuggled ashore for a sauna, which was additionally welcome because it was by then blowing force 6 or so and pouring with rain.

The authorities, led by a smart young woman officer, eventually appeared the following day and were pleasant and correct, although they omitted to remind us that we had to check in with the police within three days. This caused us some bother and a fine. As we discovered when it came to extending our visas, the procedures for handling foreigners still date from Soviet times and are wearisome. What had changed, however, was the attitude of many officials. Instead of hostility they tended to convey, and occasionally say, "sorry about all this nonsense".

It was fascinating to see the historic city emerging from seventy-odd years of isolation and to make friends with Russians and with the small expatriate community, both trying to come to terms with the realities of the post-Soviet order. No country has previously attempted the transformation from a total state economy back to capitalism, from totalitarian order to relative personal freedom. I found the process intriguing and far from re-assuring. We also fitted in a busman's holiday to Irkutsk, where we chartered a boat and sailed round Lake Baikal, returning to Vladivostok by trans-Siberian railway.

Ann had to return to England. On 20th August with Sergei (a young Russian) as crew, *Sadko* left for Sakhalin island 550 miles further north. Even with an invitation from the Sakhalin sailing federation it had taken much time and intervention from the yacht club to extract permission for this passage from the Border Guards. But during the trip there was none of the hassle about which our Russian friends had warned us. On the contrary, at more than one of the coastguard stations which called us to identify ourselves on the VHF, the officer of the watch was delighted with the opportunity to chatter with a western yachtsman. Sergei explained that they would be national servicemen posted to the edge of the world and bored to death. We averaged eighty miles a day and arrived off Kholmsk (47°03′N, 142°03′E) on 27th August to be escorted in by the flagship of the local yacht club. I stayed two weeks, during which I made an excursion by train and bus to Alexandrovsk, the old capital. It has a museum in the house where the author Chekov lived in 1891 while preparing his exposé of the Tsarist regime of exile and forced labour.

Despite its forests and attractive coastline, the present face of Sakhalin is no less sad than its grisly past. The island has not found a role in the new economic order and was in visible decline. In the difficult circumstances the yacht club – in practice a recreational arm of the Sakhalin shipping company – was struggling in the dilapidated harbour with two or three cruising yachts, a few class racing boats and some Optimists for teaching the children. But the sailing community seemed delighted to welcome *Sadko*, which they said was the first European yacht to visit, and entertained her skipper as only the Russians know how. He even warranted a full-page interview in the local newspaper. With all the gloom, Sakhalin was the place where I had caviar for breakfast and where friendly people wandered on and off the boat clutching vodka and offering help. I left on 14th September, single-handed.

Western Japan

Kholmsk was the turning point of the voyage. From now on *Sadko* was heading for home. In accordance with conventional advice I planned to leave southern Japan for Hong Kong towards the end of November and reach Suez by the end of April. But first there were nearly 2,000 miles of the Japan Sea and the Nansei Shoto to negiotiate. My Russian friends were concerned that it was getting late in the year and I didn't have to wait long for autumn to show her hand. Apart from one genuine gale, the pressure remained relatively high, dipping briefly from say 1020 to 1015 millibars as small sharp fronts went through. These systems were usually too local to feature in the forecasts from Guam or the faxes from Tokyo, but they brought nasty short seas.

I was glad to reach Otaru safely on 18th September. *Sadko* was the guest of the marina, and thus of the city, since it was a municipal enterprise. As everywhere in Japan, but particularly when single-handing, her skipper was royally received by the sailing community. Japanese hospitality was frequently embarrassing in its generosity. I tried to understand that the Japanese really enjoy spoiling visitors and I hoped this was adequately recognized with souvenirs – when available – or sometimes whisky. But it was impossible to repay them: when I invited people back on board Sadko they would turn up with lavish boxes of sweetmeats or whole crates of beer! From Otaru I also made an excursion to Sapporo by train and thence to the Shikotsu-Toya National Park, surprising myself by doing an 11 kilometre walk to the top of a mountain.

It was delightful country but time to move south. Unfortunately the English barrister friend who was due to join me was sent off on a case by

Accompanied by pilot whales in the Bay of Biscay.

his clerk and I was left alone on 1st October to cruise the 600 miles to Fukuoka, a striking offshore leg the length of the mountain chain of Honshu. Apart from dodging fishing boats – one night forty floodlights surrounded *Sadko* – there were one or two interruptions. On the first night out an inadequately controlled gybe resulted in multiple tears in the ancient mainsail. I then discovered that during two years lotus-eating in tropical waters, the flapping of lines on the mast had bent the trysail track so that the sail would not hoist. I continued under jib and changed to the spare mainsail in daylight when conditions eased. Further down the coast a hang-glider manufacturer reconstructed the mainsail and it lived to bring us home from the Mediterranean when the other mainsail fell victim to a *melteme*.

I made three stops en route. At Akita and at Hagi, a fascinating and well preserved historic city, there were large new marinas. I was hosted by local yachtsmen, including my introduction to the Japanese bath, and interviewed on radio and television. At the charming island of Dogo I simply took a place in the commercial harbour and was befriended by an English-speaking engineer who was working there on a project.

Sadko arrived in Fukuoka on 29th October, a week ahead of Bob and Ruth Heeley who were to be crew for most of the rest of the journey. There was much to do, including ordering spares and charts to be shipped from the US, but we managed to fit in some tourism in the historic but large modern city before leaving on 13th November. We stopped in Nagasaki, as impressive for what is to be seen of its historic links with the outside world as for the terrible testimony of nuclear war. We took a short break at Awami-O-shima and had a pleasant unscheduled stop at Miyako island when heavy weather from a massive high pressure system over China impelled us to seek refuge after a very disagreeable 24 hours. Our last stop in Japan was at Ishigaki, the most southerly point at which one can check out. We left on 9th December and sailed in distant company with our Australian friends on *Jawarra*, whom we had last seen in Vladivostok. *Sadko* reached Hong Kong after a fast but very bumpy six-day ride across the South China Sea.

Homeward passage

From here we were following a well-trodden route. With an eye to the 'gate' at Suez, our cruise tended toward passage-making but was nevertheless an interesting and rewarding run. We left Hong Kong on 6th January 1997 and rode the north-east monsoon across the South China Sea to the Philippines. There were no pirates, but enough heavy weather for the crew to be glad of the remote peace of Palawan island after 740 miles in six days (11°10.6′N, 119°23.6′E). The next stop was at Nat Steel Marine in Singapore, which emerged from radio consultations as the best place to deal with some scrapes on the keel acquired from a grounding when manoeuvring in a Philippine harbour. The damage was slight but it was a good opportunity to have the anti-fouling renewed. Like almost everything in Singapore, the service was impeccable but not cheap.

Thereafter the north-east monsoon seemed often to be hiding somewhere in south-east Asia and in the 18 days it took to transit the Malacca Straits and reach Galle in Sri Lanka (excluding stops in Langkawi, Malaysia and Phuket, Thailand) we had to motor for 120 hours, probably a third of the 1,500 miles. From Galle we took a week's holiday and visited friends of Bob and Ruth in the Church of South India. We then crossed the Arabian sea, not picking up any consistent wind until we were well west of the Maldives. The Red Sea lived up to its reputation for adverse winds and square seas. The 1,400 miles from Djibouti to Suez took forty days, although that included time out for a visit to the Valley of the Kings from Safaga. We later went to Cairo where an hour or so with the Tutenkamun treasures did much to compensate for the travails of getting there.

By the time we made the Suez Canal transit on 22nd-23rd May, conditions were still tolerable. Behind us was a sprinkling of the fleet of nearly 300 yachts which made the Red Sea transit during the season, with many of whom we had been in regular contact on the 'Si-oui' and 'Big Fish' radio nets. We called at Cyprus and enjoyed our first taste of Europe with great relish. About 200 miles west of Cyprus we weathered a disagreeable *melteme* but eventually arrived in Aghios Nikolaos, Crete, in benign conditions. Here there was a crew change and the last three legs of the journey (with stops in Malta and Gibraltar) were less eventful, although we had the trysail in use for a night in the Strait of Gibraltar and had to motor half the way across the Bay of Biscay. At 0532 on 13th August, at a point some eighty miles north of Cape Finisterre, *Sadko* crossed her outward track of 4th March 1994 and so completed a circumnavigation. Happily, David Park, who had been on that first leg as well as in the Pacific, had joined ship in Malta – this time with his wife Helen – and was there to tackle the bottle of champagne hidden away by the skipper for just such an occasion.

At breakfast time on 17th August we groped our way through driving rain into the Visitors Haven in Falmouth, with three weeks in hand before the Beaulieu Meet. So ended Sadko's First Cruise. The echo is implied homage: for thousands of my generation, it was Arthur Ransome who led us to the sea, in wartime Britain, before many of us had ever seen it. How grateful we are.

Sadko is a Hallberg-Rassy 38, which has gradually been fitted out, improved and adapted for long-distance, short-handed cruising. She served me well on this circumnavigation, but has now been sold while I think about my next ideal boat.

A MATTER OF ILLUMINATION

by Michael Gilkes

Several decades ago, when *Foggy Dew* still had pretensions to being an ocean racer, we had some interesting experiences relating to her electrics, including expiring navigation lights and other failures. That these arose from the false economy of using Government surplus Nife alkaline batteries is neither here nor there.

Suffice it to say that, after a prolonged calm in mid-Channel with failing lights and crowded steamer lanes, on the occasion of a visit to the local chandler my gaze fell on a trio of classic ships paraffin navigation lamps which had obviously been in stock for some years. Their price reflected this and I emerged from the shop their proud owner, certain that *Foggy Dew* would be the only vessel in the ocean racing fleet so superbly equipped.

Halfway through our next Channel Race, our battery again failed and expeditiously the lamps were raised from their lair and ranged for lighting on the cabin sole. One should add that they were of the very best pattern, complete with separate coned burners.

They lit readily but every attempt to move them to their lamp irons led to flickering and rapid extinction. Each member of the crew, convinced of the incompetence of his fellows, went through the procedure to meet an identical failure. At last came dawn and we could apply ourselves, with little success, to the serious business of racing.

During the subsequent post-mortems it seemed clear that the actual lamps could hardly be at fault. After all, the design had been unchanged since long before the days of electrics. It had been used by the great figures of the past – McGregor, Worth, Childers and probably Hiscock. One must refer to the scriptures (dare one even say Gospels).

These revealed interesting references to 'train oil, colza' and other substances which enquiry disclosed were no longer even remotely available. Interrogation of fellow yachtsmen laid bare an unsurprising lack of acquaintance with paraffin navigation lamps, Tilleys and the like.

At the close of the year the mystery remained and at the Boat Show we produced the lamps at the stand of the very long-standing and much respected manufacturers. They listened to the saga with interest and concern at the problems with their product, and offered to take them away for test. They were clear that generations of such lamps had been demonstrated as completely storm and motion proof.

Two days later the lamps were available for collection. They had been held out of the car window on their journey through the night and had duly failed to stay alight, but I could now be confident that they would work perfectly. And so they did, and have done without fail for the past thirty years even though, I am glad to say, the battery situation is now much less fraught.

On enquiry the nature of the remedy was revealed. The lamps had gone to the dessicator in the factory safe in which all wicks are stored until their lamps are sent out. If the wicks are at all damp the fuel will not permeate properly. My lamps had been on the shelf for some while without fuel in them and had soaked up moisture. Hence their waywardness. On the whole, once the wicks have been exposed to paraffin, there will be no problems – but, see below!

I was regaling the Hon Secretary with this saga, adding that I was sure that past members of the Club were probably fully aware of this little quirk, when he revealed that he had been having similar problems with his paraffin riding light – also of a proven wind and motion-proof design.

In brief it transpired that the lamp, with fuel, had been in store for quite some while. On investigation the fuel had absorbed a large percentage of water and the wick could no longer feed. Yes, paraffin *is* hygroscopic.

Finally a coda. I told this saga again, emulating the Ancient Mariner, as we do in Scotland, to Ann Thomas while standing outside her shop in Tarbert. "Funny," she said "When my copier paper gets damp it won't copy."

Doubtless the traditionalists are well aware of these things, but it seems to me that this is perhaps just another piece of that infinity of lost knowledge on the shoulders of which we stand and which we have a duty to share.

And *Foggy Dew* flaunts her navigation lamp irons with a certain insouciance and even pride. "Lang may their lums reek."

WHY ENVY THE IMMORTAL GODS?

by Ewen Southby-Tailyour

This is the cruise which won both the Cruising Club Bowl and the Goldsmith Exploration Award.

> When one has good wine,
> A graceful boat,
> A maiden's love,
> Why envy the immortal gods?

. . . so wrote the Chinese poet Li T'ai Po in the seventh century AD. Despite the maiden's absence I envied nobody this summer – not even the gods – for the truth is I fell in love again, this time with another set of islands, in another hemisphere, but with the same capricious weather.

Black Velvet, a twelve-ton gaff cutter, usually plies her trade carrying environmentalists to places they would not, otherwise, be able to reach, but for nine glorious weeks she took my son Hamish and me to Iceland's uninhabited Vestfirdir – a round journey of about 3,500 miles.

We started this odyssey from Plymouth, in forty knots of wind, on 7th June by taking part in the Reykjavik Yacht Club/Royal Western Yacht Club's two-handed Iceland race. *Black Velvet* carried, as she is designed to do, a two and a half ton weight penalty made up of crampons, pulks, skis, 250 man-days of food and duty-frees, plus an astounding seventeen pairs of climbing boots.

Three friends of ours, for whom we had agreed to supply the 'terminal' transport and logistic base, intended to climb peaks inland from Depotfjord on the east Greenland coast at about 66°07'N, 35°55'W. Neither the peaks nor the fjord had been, knowingly, visited before, and as the only chart is suspiciously free of soundings until 20 miles offshore (and, anyway, is on a scale of 1:400,000) the chances for what I call 'impact hydrography' were real.

The seventeen day 'first leg' northwards included drifting around the

Black Velvet entering Jokulfjordhur.

Fastnet before running south-westerly for thirty hours streaming warps and rolling like blazes:

11 June, 0615: Wet and windy. NE F7. Occasional sea across deck. 0700: F6-8. Handed jib to deck – wind too strong for furling gear . . . 1000: Sea increasing. Tried to set storm jib but not possible unless in stops. Wind gusting F9. Towing warps. 1200: Noon to noon 149′ in wrong direction. Now under bare poles as enough windage with 600 yards of rigging!

12 June, 0415 . . . We are not going to win this race. **13 June**: Heading for Bantry Bay to wait favourable winds. The aim is to get to Reykjavik with no damage and ready for the next, more difficult, phase of the operation.

We failed to land on Rockall to pay our respects to its temporary inhabitants from Greenpeace and finally motored the last 300 miles in a flat calm, to arrive at a deserted Reykjavik Yacht Club in the pouring rain. This enforced use of the engine was to get us in before the climbers' aeroplane, but we had already (unwittingly) disqualified ourselves from the race by embarking bananas and two bottles of stout in Bantry Bay.

The day before the mountaineers arrived in Reykjavik, the meteorological office produced their latest ice charts showing between 6 and 8/10ths of ice to within 60 miles of Iceland's north-west corner, with nothing less than 6/10ths south of Angmassalik – and from there to Cape

Farewell as much as 9/10ths. We always knew it was an optimistic hope that the ice would clear early this year, but now there were distinct signs that it would not clear at all, at least not down to 3 or 4/10ths, the thickest I was prepared to attempt.

With the climbers aboard and accepting that Depotfjord by sea was 'out', we adjourned to the nearby, very Irish pub to agree that, as we now had a week 'free', it would be better to spend it sailing; if not to Depotfjord then at least as far as the ice to take some shots alongside a floe or two. After that the climbers would fly to Kulusuk (Angmassalik's nearest airport) and thence to the icecap by helicopter. We took our departure for the Arctic Circle and the pack ice at 0800 on 3rd July, sailing in a wonderful quartering sea towards Snæfullsness Peninsula.

But soon the wind veered to the north-west – our course – and increased beneath an angry and lowering cloud base pierced by the very tip of the silhouetted Stapafell volcano. Two of the three climbers succumbed, and the third, a doctor who did not wish to climb alone, asked that we find some shelter – preferably about five-hundred miles up a fjord. While I silently debated this request the scene reminded me, chillingly, of a Hitchcock film. Everything – sea, sky, land – was painted in some variation of the colour grey.

I chose Grindavik, east of the notorious Reykjanes headland, despite no charts on a scale less than 1:300,000 and the knowledge that the port was closed except one hour either side of high water because of dredging. We turned and ran downhill, rolling hideously, which seemed to suit the mountaineers who now began calling for soup, then, encouragingly, for brandy. As we approached to one and a half miles off Reykjanes' rocks in an onshore near-gale, the linkage 'twixt wheel and rudder came adrift: at least that's what Hamish, on watch at the time, assumed. He woke me with the quiet but urgent news that, "Don't tell the climbers but I think we have a bit of a situation."

The doctor, sharing the watch, looked on while Hamish rigged the emergency tiller as though this was a minor, dog-watch evolution. With rather less tranquillity, I scrabbled around a seldom-visited portion of the bilges behind the engine with a torch in my teeth trying to see what had happened and, once established, looking for the absent nut and washer.

The dreaded cape missed its opportunity and shortly afterwards we were able to enter the marvellous bolt-hole under the precise guidance of the harbourmaster on the foreshore with his handheld VHF. The Blue Lagoon's sulphurous waters, two monkfish bartered for three cans of Tesco's beer and one day of enforced idleness while the winds moderated, had even the climbers itching for action. We still had days to use up, so the next Time Passing Measure was a visit to Hvalfjördhur – Whale Fjord – where the World War II base HMS *Baldur III* (for the forming of Arctic convoys) can still be seen at Hvitness. We lay to seventy feet of cable off Hvammsvik's north-western beach, drinking whisky through a still, almost sunlit, midnight.

By 0600 the wind had turned through 180° and was now onshore. While we still had plenty of water, soundings suggested we should sail before the ebbing half tide. I hoisted the Blue Peter for the shore party to return. Two further defects now manifested themselves; the gear box would not engage 'ahead' and the windlass jammed. Neither was a serious problem for we had a light breeze and five pairs of strong arms. Once out into the main fjord the wind, as perverse as ever, changed again, forcing us to beat the 25 or so miles. In fact, with the propeller trailing at about three knots, the gear box did engage and we were able to make our ETA. Hamish mended the windlass – better than before – by drilling a deeper recess for a retaining pin (clearly a design fault). Thanks to an obliging insurance company, a spare part for the gearbox was flown in the next day from Germany.

We arrived back at Reykjavik Yacht Club on 8th July; the climbers flew the next day and, after repairs, the two of us were free to set off once more for the pack ice. By the 12th we had just 10 days before meeting the shore party down from their Greenland hills, exchanging their kit, putting them on an aeroplane home and re-stowing for our journey to the Faeroes. This was not long to achieve the new aim which was to sail to the ice-edge 'for trials' before accepting the challenge offered in the RCC Pilot: "There are six fjords to the east of Skutulsfjördhur, shown without soundings . . . They might make interesting exploring . . . "

At midnight we again approached the Snæfullssness ice-cap, magnificent in the last of the dying sun's rays (or was it the first of the rising sun?) and soft breezes. To port and starboard whales breached amid pink and white depth-charges of spray. Next day we were becalmed and, while supposedly in a hurry, it was too beautiful a day to allow 'Mr Perkins' to disturb it. So Hamish fished for cod; we had steaks for lunch, fish cakes for supper and paté until Reykjavik! That evening (Sunday 13th July) we were again crashing along in a force 4 north-easter which (apart from the fine drizzle) was perfect for the nearest reported ice north-west of Vestfirdir. Now the wind-chill factor crept below freezing for the first time. As we approached the line at 24° 50′W, I briefed King Neptune on his latest recruit, lying off-watch below. At the precise moment (1723) Hamish was woken by the fog horn. He leapt to the hatch to find nobody in the cockpit, but a bearded and bedraggled (more than was intended) monarch of the Arctic seas, climbing up from the bobstay clutching a bottle of rum and a scroll – unfortunately the trident didn't make it onto the foredeck.

After His Majesty's departure, we agreed that *Black Velvet* should continue towards the ice. Obligingly, a wonderful example of ice-blink now lined the western horizon with three, up-side-down icebergs suspended in it. Beautiful though this was, it was clear it would still take considerable time to reach and with a beat back this meant less time for exploring. The unsurveyed fjords beckoned more strongly and we tacked round for Isafjardhardjup (66°15'N, 23°15'W).

The wind-chill had dropped to –20°C but we had the right clothes while we kept the cabin at the outside, ambient temperature. Only when peacefully at anchor would we have any form of artificial heating to warm the cabin – and we were better off for that ruling (see 'Arctic Notebook' in Roving Commissions 1988).

Isafjardhardjup is easy to enter and with such beguiling beauty not so easy to leave. Beyond the safe, twelve-miles wide entrance exists a variety of scenery, a glacier, a spotless town for provisions, wild flowers in great profusion, seals, swans and red phalarope. Isafjardhardjup is sometimes iced-up in winter (a few years ago, a hungry polar bear walked ashore here) and has nine and a half uncharted fjords leading off it, including those mentioned in the pilot .

All around, mist-shrouded mountains of great grandeur towered over their fjords, benign looking but capricious, while Æolus rejoiced with us as we set five fair-weather sails to catch the zephyrs towards Isafjardhardjup's northern shore in blazing sunshine. The south-eastern fjords mentioned in the pilot had taken second place to those leading off Jökulfirdhir, itself an offshoot of Isafjardhardjup. We were bound instead for Leirufjördhur and the Drangajökull glacier, before attempting to

Alongside at Grindavik.

survey Hrafnsfjördhur, Lonafjördhur and the upper reaches of Veioileysufjördhur. As we headed for Leirufjödhur's entrance, the water turned milky from Drangajökull's melt-waters, reducing underwater visibility to nil. This was a pity for the entrance is guarded by a terminal moraine along which (as we now know) are dotted huge rocks.

Although preferring to anchor, we picked up one of two mooring buoys to see if they were suitable; by their size and well-kept appearance they were. That evening Hamish walked ashore to the western edge of the Drangajökull – a longer walk than he anticipated – and returned after midnight clean from a shower beneath a fall of melt-water. Later we were told that the glacier has advanced 800 metres in the last three years – global warming has yet to reach Vestfirdir.

The next day we sailed first for Lonafjördhur (66°16′N, 22°33′W), for no other reason than it has the prettiest shape. Safely across the bar on a three-part transit chosen from the chart, we continued on this course until just short of the Lonanupur peninsula. With no soundings to guide us we initiated a routine for the future. Hamish sat at the chart table with the radar's 'distance off' cursor switched on, the echo sounder calibrated to the waterline, the tide tables for Reykjavik, a matrix of tidal differences and a blank piece of paper. Out on deck, I moved *Black Velvet* forward in a series of short, slow bursts with one of the two dinghies alongside loaded with the armed lead line and a ten-foot sounding pole. The mains'l was hoisted with two reefs, regardless of how little wind there might be, to allow for any sudden williwaw and the jib was ready for instant furling on the modern Wykham-Martin with an endless line.

About one hundred soundings later, we had circumnavigated the fjord as close as we could to its edges (even closer in the dinghy) and established five good-looking anchorages. It was the end of a wonderful, fulfilling day as we headed back down our transit into Leirufjödhur. The reason for returning rather than staying at anchor elsewhere was an attractive German girl (plus her boyfriend and kayak) to whom we had promised to act as safety craft while they explored the fields of flowers before lifting them to Hesteyrarfjördhur (66°20′N, 22°49′W), the summer foot ferry to Isafjördhur and their motor car.

Next morning we sailed for the upper reaches of Veioileysufjördhur (66°20′N, 22°40′W) to find two useful anchorages before giving Hrafnsfjördhur (66° 15′N, 22° 26′W) the same treatment. Ironically we did not survey our base fjord as carefully, for on our fourth pass and with three feet below the keel registering on the echo sounder, we hit a rock in the entrance.

An unexpected mist had, within about 30 seconds, obscured the transit marks on our approach and, coupled with an almost certain (but previously untabulated) magnetic anomaly on the moraine, we had swung, unknowingly, in a gentle arc to starboard. As soon as were off, by swinging out to port on the end of the boom, Hamish took the dinghy ahead, and over, the obstruction with a sounding pole. When the mist cleared it was obvious that we were about one cable off the transit but not quite as far to the east as the rock marked on the chart. All this indicates that the deepest part of the bar is very narrow, probably further west. Like the back of a dragon, the bar has peaks and troughs along much of its length, and a certain amount of luck is needed to pass over a trough!

Hrafnsfjördhur was another unknown quantity which we had entered against a cold, easterly wind, lowering visibility and occasional driving, freezing drizzle. It was also very late in a long day of close navigation. We were both tired and perhaps should not have entered the fjord at all, although the sail out was most exhilarating. Apart from the enticing lack of charted soundings, it is not really an interesting fjord.

An abiding impression was the lack of jetsam and only the occasional piece of flotsam – usually at the tops of the fjords where a tree trunk might be beached. Also memorable were the thousands of ice patches across the fields and mountains, representing every possible shape – many beautiful, some erotic, others accurate in their impression of a country or a well-known figure (Paddington Bear was particularly life-like!).

Having dropped the kayakers to a lament on the pipes at Hesteryi, we reluctantly sailed for the south, calling first at the dying village of Flatyeyri (66°02′N, 23°31′W) in Önundarfjödhir for fresh water. Hamish (whose second name is Patrick) had his 24th birthday on 21st July, so we pushed on quickly to Patreksfjördhur to celebrate there. On our way in, well after midnight, we stuck our nose into Vatneyri's inner harbour and were quickly driven out by the smell. In a flat calm, we motored to the very head of the fjord (Osafjördhur), passing beautiful sand dunes to starboard, where we lay to our anchor in, without doubt, the most stunning haven of them all.

The next morning, after Hamish's birthday shower beneath the seven-stepped waterfall, we held our noses and re-fuelled in Vatneyri while I baked my first (and last) chocolate cake. Having telephoned home we managed, quite without planning, to exchange one litre bottle of duty-free whisky for 138 litres of diesel using only my four Icelandic words – Tak (thank you), Nei (no), Jao (yes) and Whisky (let's have a party). Quite who lost out I'm not sure: we achieved an amazing bargain, the tanker driver was ecstatic and the amount of fuel was less than his monthly spillage allowance!

Making, sadly, for Reykjavik, we sailed into the thickest of fogs off Blakknes and an increasing southerly wind. By the time we were 'on finals' next day, the approach was out of the question and we sought a perfect spot off the hamlet of Alfsnes (66°11′N, 22°46′W) where we anchored at 0140 (23th July) to both the Admiralty Pattern and CQR anchors, with the wind gusting to 55 knots.

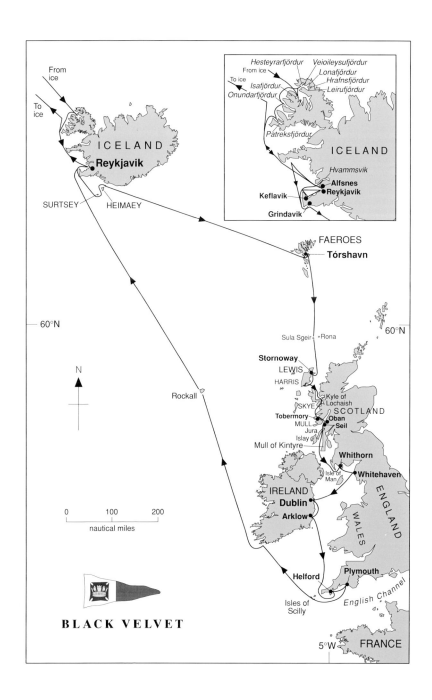

By 2000 the wind had moderated a little, allowing us to enjoy a cracking sail into Reykjavik harbour where we moored, for the last time, among the RYC's friendly yachts. My part was now over and on 26th July I left *Black Velvet* in Hamish's hands, happy that he would look after her impeccably. He did and to drive the point home arrived in Plymouth at the precise hour we'd agreed; without a blemish and in time for the next crew of whale-watchers the following day.

I said at the beginning that I envied nobody, but during my last evening in Reykjavik two maidens (plus two men) had joined *Black Velvet*. Before them lay the Vestmannaeyjar Islands in glorious sunshine, the Faeroes in mist, a landing on Sula Sgeir in the fog, Corryvreckan, drying out alongside in Whitehaven to offload the climbing boots, Howth and the Helford. As I left at 0400 to catch my flight home I envied them all.

ENVIOUS? NOT I

by Hamish Southby-Tailyour

This is the cruise which was awarded the Sea Laughter Trophy.

So the old man flew home. I said good bye and returned to my bunk in the yacht club shower. One of the maidens is a great friend of mine and with the new arrivals there was no space on board for the both of us. The day started like most to follow, the crew being coaxed out of their bunks with offers of caffeine and nicotine. An interesting bunch showed their faces: Steve Sleight, an old friend and experienced all round sailor; Ben Harrison, a good friend and excellent hand; Seonaid Murray (pro-nounced Shona), Ben's maiden whom I had only met once before; and Sammie Coryton, a wonderful friend with much experience on Black Velvet. All but one of the new crew had sailed Black Velvet before so they knew the ropes, literally. As for Seonaid she wouldn't know anything different – this was her first time afloat.

The day was not wasted as the boat was stowed with all the new gear and I looked on trying to get used to all this new company. By the evening we had hired a car and early next morning we set off to see a tiny inland portion of this beautiful island.

I will not even attempt to describe the majesty and untouched wonder of the interior, but just to cruise Iceland by boat would be a great waste.

The ice caps and runoff rivers with their waterfalls, the exploding geysers and hot pools, the volcanic craters and their lava plains; all set in a pure summer cloak of flowers and covered in a changing, often dramatic sky. A special day and we returned to the boat exhausted by what we had experienced.

The next day we left Reykjavik after a night of true Icelandic hospitality. Icelandic schnapps seriously impairs your ability to have a bad time. Thanks to a local architect and friend who fed and watered us well into the early hours, we were ready. *Black Velvet* slipped from the yacht club pontoon at 1800. We made a good passage to Keflavik 25 miles to the west. Conditions had been squally, which resulted in a simple shake down for the new crew.

Heimaey in the Vestmannaeyjar was the next planned port of call. With the wind fresh north-easterly we had a lively sail out and around the Reykjanes peninsula. As we came on track for Surtsey, the wind died leaving an uncomfortable sea. We motored on through the night.

A grey day greeted the morning watch and, shortly afterwards, Surtsey loomed out of the mist and the weather started to clear. *Black Velvet* arrived in Heimaey after a magnificent motor sail through this archipelago of old volcanoes, with the puffin and dolphin in almost constant company. She had brought with her the sun and a crew longing for a drink.

The entrance to Heimaey is straightforward but impressive to any visitor, with sheer and polished cliffs to starboard and the lava flow from the 1973 volcanic eruption to port. We found a berth at the southern end in the most western basin. There is a convenient fuel station across the road and water nearby at a pontoon in the corner of the basin.

The next morning after a quiet night of sorts (one of the crew had produced the schnapps and some ice from the fish factory) a gentleman approached me on the quay. He asked whether the yacht was 'Black Velvet' and if so was I Hamish! As he pulled out a newspaper from his jacket I was ready to deny anything. Unfortunately we'd been busted. Ten days earlier, father and I had left Flateyri in Önundarfjördhur very early. My bagpipes were in full working order for the quiet, still morning and I was practising. Obviously it had been too early and we were now in the national press; names, picture and all!

We left the Vestmannaeyjar and headed east towards the Faeroes. The wind set in at a steady force 4 from the west and stayed with us all the way. Steve and I had been poring over the only two charts we had of these fast approaching islands and trying to collect as much supplementary information as possible on the tides – Katharine Thornhill's article in Roving Commissions 37 was a great help here.

On our approach the weather closed in, so plan B was brought into action. Plan A had been to sail around the north of the islands to see the magnificent sea cliffs and then on to the Hebrides without stopping. We decided, however, to enter through Skopen Fjord as this was the widest and the most direct route to Tórshavn. Once there we would rest for twelve hours before continuing south.

We entered the fjord with one hour of foul tide to run. As the sea began to boil and large areas exploded all around us we realised this was a mistake. The cockpit was flooded twice and Sammie and I were drenched. With very poor visibility, entry was only made possible with Steve's competent use of both GPS and radar. Ben and Seonaid were asleep in the focs'l and never even stirred. We eventually reached the back eddy, having experienced some interesting moments. The sun came out and we sailed north to Tórshavn. The stop-over was brief but served as a good recce for the future. We all left with fond memories. Two days out of Tórshavn more adventures were waiting.

Only half a mile away, silent and floating in the slight Atlantic swell, Sula Sgeir rose out of the fog. Creeping slowly into the protection of a tiny cove, under the watchful eyes of the resident seals, we anchored in 20 metres and took a kedge ashore. Having inspected the stone huts and been attacked by the fast moulting chicks, we returned to Steve and the boat not a moment to soon. We had been allowed a brief and precious moment to land, but it doesn't pay to overstay your welcome in such a remote and exposed location. A new and increasing tidal set on the beam had begun. If we had only been lying to the main anchor, without the kedge, we would have swung onto the once protective islet behind.

Leaving was not going to be easy. The vital kedge was buoyed in advance and its warp led forward on a continuous line from the stern. Still holding the stern to the current it was slowly released as the main anchor was hauled. As soon as the main anchor broke the kedge's stern lead was dropped. We now swung to the kedge from the bow, away from the islet but towards the shore on the other side. In the middle of our swing the engine was engaged and the kedge dropped with the already buoyed line. With Steve now at the helm I rowed ashore to collect the kedge. The flukes told of the tensions they had been under. With the crew now working well together, a potential problem developed into nothing more than a good experience. Then, for the first time during our brief visit, the fog cleared totally and the whole island was bathed in sunshine.

Having cleared customs in Stornoway, and armed with some excellent advice from Bill Speirs, a well known RCC member to anyone cruising these parts, we went exploring. Now we were back in coastal waters, Ben, Sammie and Seonaid took over the running of the boat. Each day one would be skipper and another navigator, with the roles reversing daily for the rest of the trip. This gave everybody the opportunity to learn the skills involved in running a boat on passage and handling a heavy displacement, traditionally rigged yacht under power and sail.

Lochs Flodabay and Scadabay on Harris provided some interesting safe anchorages. The height of the new bridge to Scalpay was deter-

Leaving the sheltered anchorage of Scadabay.

The skipper after a very near soaking.

mined using relative sextant angles and various less used forms of navigation were practised for the benefit of all. A memorable moment was spent watching a sea otter bringing its breakfast ashore in Flodabay.

After a delightful two days we headed round Skye and through the Sound of Sleat towards Tobermory. By now we were motoring in light winds, but enjoyed a cracking sail in a warm wind down the Sound of Sleat and another from north of Ardnamurchan Point to Tobermory.

Our plans called for a stop in Whitehaven on the Cumbrian coast. *Black Velvet* had a rendezvous to drop off all the climbing gear we'd had on board since Iceland, so we were soon on our way through the Sound of Mull to arrive in the glorious collection of anchorages near Seil. We dropped the hook at 1800 to wait for the fair tide south.

We left the Seil anchorage under a dramatic sunset and continued our journey south. This was a non-stop passage, through the sound of Jura at nearly ten knots over the ground, and round the Mulls of Kintyre and Galloway, motoring in fog for most of the way to Whitehaven.

A quick 12 hour stop dried out alongside one of the Whitehaven fish quays was the result of some excellent boat handling by the duty skipper and his crew. We off-loaded the climbing gear in front of a suspicious local crowd, checked the hull for damage sustained in Iceland and had an evening in the pub. This is a rarely visited quay (south once inside the entrance) as most yachts enter the marina in the north-east corner. The fishermen were very friendly and we left with a large bag of prawns from the morning's catch. A lock is being built in this well protected harbour so drying out will not be possible in the future.

As we left Whitehaven, the prospect of another passage under power was becoming inevitable. However Howth was our next port of call and the prospect of a two day stopover in Dublin was good tonic for the skipper and crew. It was on this 24-four hour passage that the duties of skipper were stretched to new levels. Ben and Seonaid were on watch, each accompanied by a colourful tequila hangover. I was down below. At 1642 the announcement of their engagement to be married filtered down to the chart table. Not really knowing how to respond to this serious development in their relationship, I continued looking at the chart of the Irish sea. We duly arrived in Howth, but not without a date for the wedding having been arranged! After an excellent evening in Dublin, we picked up a great friend and sculptor Hamish Mackie. He was to join us for the final passage back to Plymouth.

The weather stayed much the same as it had been since leaving the Faeroes. We left Howth, after a sunny two days in Dublin, amongst the national fleet of Mirrors. Heading south again there was little prospect of quality sailing. Six hours after leaving and having spent the fair tide, we called into the very friendly harbour of Arklow. Having tied up alongside a fishing boat the Harbour Master arrived. He asked for the sum of seven pounds, which was reasonable as there were no facilities on hand.

However he went on to explain that this was a year's fee and we could use the heads in the RNLI building. At £0.0005p. per foot per night, this was very reasonable!

With the fair tide in the morning we started a miserable three and a half day passage to the Helford River, motor-sailing into a light to moderate wind that stayed stubbornly in the south-east. The Helford was our last night together and next morning we slipped our mooring bound for Plymouth.

The marriage had been set for this, our last day at sea, and after breakfast preparations were well under way. Hamish and I set about making the rings from twisted mousing wire and braided copper. The cake was prepared and the champagne cooled. Ben, although groom, was also the bride's hairdresser. Hamish, by invitation, was best man and photographer. Sammie was the lady in waiting and captured the whole ceremony on film. I, as skipper, was master of ceremonies and Steve was to give the bride away, albeit reluctantly. Although I could only find guidelines for 'burials at sea' in the ships library, all went without a hitch. The vows were exchanged on the foredeck two miles south-west of Rame Head. We drank the couple's health and cake was cut and eaten.

It was a serious ceremony, although the bride and groom were not dressed according to convention, whatever that is these days. As for the legality of the marriage, well there were enough witnesses!

Our final day had us motoring again in poor visibility and a flat calm from the Helford to Plymouth, but the warmth of the welcome from assembled families waiting at Queen Anne's Battery more than made up for it. *Black Velvet* was home again after two and a half months away with many new and different experiences now under the keel. As for envy, it never had a chance.

Postscript

The Faeroese tidal atlas recommended by the Admiralty Pilot is a must for navigating around the islands. It doesn't bother with conventional tidal arrows and numbered rates, but shows where the races are, and where you definitely don't want to be, for each hour. Highly graphical strokes of red show the severity and extent of each race. When we saw a copy in Stornoway and checked the time we'd sailed through Skopen Fjord, the message was clear – it was not the place to be.

Black Velvet of Tamar is a Tradewind 35 with a traditional gaff rig. Built in Lymington, she was launched in 1993 and she has been cruising and working ever since.

MURPHY AND THE DOLPHINS

by John Power

Several years ago I wrote in these pages of Murphy, a creature of revolting habits who does his best to thwart us from achieving our annual objectives for our cruise. In *Kataree*'s saloon there are two silver dolphins glued onto the ledges each side of the bookcase. These dolphins were the last things which we removed from the cabin of our previous boat, *Pennyroyal*, after her loss on a Bahamian reef in 1981. From time to time the glue fails, and one or other of the dolphins falls off, but hitherto I have always glued it up again before the other one falls.

During our transatlantic passage in 1997, both dolphins fell off the day after we left Falmouth. The significance of this was lost to me at the time, but it was not until a week after our arrival in Manchester, Massachusetts, that I had time to refix them. Only then did things begin to go right. I now know with absolute certainty that it is the dolphins which form our only protection from Murphy's mischief, and only when they are both in place do we stand a chance of gaining the upper hand.

The purpose of this year's voyage was to take part in the Cruising Club of America's 75th Anniversary cruise in company in Maine, taking in, if possible the Ocean Cruising Club Maine rally which preceded it. Both of these objectives were achieved, and to that extent we won the battle with Murphy. But the cost of our victory you must judge for yourself.

Five of us left Falmouth in *Kataree* on the afternoon of 2nd June, bound for Ponta Delgada in the Azores, full of the usual idiot optimism for a fast and effortless passage, and encouraged by an easterly that had been blowing for weeks and seemed set to go on doing so. That night the tricolour light at the masthead failed, but we have bow lights as well and switched them on instead. The following morning the loo was found to be blocked, the pump which empties the galley sink broken and the Pinta autopilot failed. The loo was quickly, if messily, unblocked, and that afternoon a long session with the galley pump resulted in a makeshift repair, using a large galvanised coach bolt. The autopilot defeated us, however, and we persuaded ourselves that it was peripheral to our needs. Next day Murphy tormented us in a different way. For long voyages *Kataree* is fitted with two flexible water tanks which are installed in the forepeak. Although both had been filled in Falmouth, Murphy had got at one of the plumbing joints and emptied them both. Fortunately on this leg of the voyage we had sufficient water in the main tank, but it would be essential to deal with the problem before tackling the leg from the Azores to the USA. Apart from this, Murphy amused himself by jamming the engine stop control in the stop position and immobilising the barograph.

By now we were three days out from Falmouth. Although we had no barograph, the records of previous barometer readings showed a steady decline and it was clear that we were in for a blow. That evening the wind was up to force 6 from the south and it was raining. Two reefs were put in the main and No.2 yankee and the small staysail set. The barometer dropped 15 millibars, and we slogged on into a rising wind, with a heavy sea developing. Murphy took pity on us and by the following afternoon we were shaking out the reefs. This was too much for him: his next step was to ruin the GPS, the face of which first became anaemic and then locked into a rigid grimace, giving position only, before finally giving up the ghost and dying.

The saving grace was that, having stayed on the starboard tack during the previous blow, we were well to the east of the rhumb line and could lay the course, a cause for considerable jubilation. And even Murphy could not stop the weather from getting warmer as we worked further south. From a low of 995 millibars, the glass was now steadily rising. Predictably, as we approached the Azores high, the wind left us, leaving a foul sea. So we motored when necessary until Murphy got at the engine, and for a whole day it would not start, while we slatted around and tried to find the reason. A clamp had come loose from the starter battery, not so loose that it cut off all current to the starter motor (in which case we would have quickly diagnosed the fault), but loose enough to prevent it turning over the engine. Once found the problem was solved.

After another rough night, the high land of São Miguel appeared above the horizon and we arrived at Ponta Delgada 11 days out from Falmouth, praising the Lord but aware of a defect list of daunting proportions and the need to deal with it quickly if we were to stand a chance of getting across the Atlantic in time for out appointments in Maine.

With the welcoming smile of Carlos Garoupa, the club's representative in Ponta Delgada, problems fell like ninepins. Everyone worked like beavers, and on the evening of the second day after our arrival we'd got the job list down to containable proportions and were planning a departure the following day for Horta.

The voyage to Horta took 26 hours, much of it under power. Two members of the crew, having made the mistake of demonstrating artistic talent, set about painting a record of our visit on the jetty. It took them all day in very hot sunshine and the contribution made by the rest of us was limited to quick expeditions from the cool safety of the marina bar to encourage them from time to time. The tricolour light at the main masthead was repaired, and on one day we hired a car and drove up to the crater and round the island. I had not been in Horta since 1970 and was astonished to find that I was recognised and greeted after 27 years by Peter Azavedo like a long-lost brother. But perhaps his memory of my previous visit was not all that surprising, involving as it did a night in the cells for one of our crew and an interview with the chief of police over which a veil had better be drawn. One afternoon I took the ferry over to Madalena on Pico, and of course we went alongside the fuelling dock and filled with diesel every can we had. Murphy, unbeknown to us, took part in this operation.

By 20th June we were ready to sail, but that day was a Friday and we felt that in our state of open warfare with Murphy we needed all the luck we could get. So it was not until early on the morning of 21st June that we motored out of Horta and set course due west, the plan being to follow Carlos' advice and keep in the latitude of the Azores until we were north of Bermuda. After a few hours in a fine southerly, the wind fell light as expected and we began motoring. It was not until the third day out that Murphy struck again, this time with a double whammy to the navigation lights. We had repaired the masthead tricolour in Horta, where it apparently worked perfectly. Now it failed again, and with it also the bow lights. We made a note in the log to get one or other of them working in the morning, but next morning we were busy with other things. At 0300 the automatic electric bilge pump failed, apparently blocked. Now readers of this Journal will know that I will defend to the death the virtues of wooden boats over all alternative methods of construction, but it has to be admitted that an efficient automatic electric bilge pump is of much greater value to most wooden boats than to GRP ones. So throughout the forenoon I was head down in the bilge, dismantling every section of the pipe-work and pump to try to find the trouble. It was eventually traced to the non-return valve between the pump and the discharge line, in which Murphy had caused the ball to stick, but it was not until 1500 that the bilge pump was working again.

While motoring that day a fearful rattle from the fridge compressor caused us to conclude that Murphy, busy while we were trying to deal with the bilge pump, had turned his attentions to that department, so the fridge was not used for the rest of the voyage, resulting in the menus for the next few meals including all the frozen food we'd embarked at Horta. This, however, later turned out to be one of Murphy's feints. Weeks later an American refrigeration engineer declared the refrigerator faultless.

That night, with both sets of navigation lights still out of action, I was on watch alone and saw the lights of a yacht approaching on a reciprocal course. Presumably on her radar she must have known we were approaching, because she turned on her deck lights and later a very bright searchlight that totally blinded me. I altered course further and further off the wind to avoid her, but she did the same. I had left it too late to go below to get our own big torch to indicate that we had seen her, and eventually did not dare to leave the wheel long enough to go below to wake up another member of the crew to help. My relief came on watch to find the other yacht about twenty yards away, shining his searchlight on us for all he was worth.

I handed over the wheel and went below to apologise on the VHF and explain why we were sailing without lights, to be greeted by an efficient-sounding American voice telling me that she was on passage from Bermuda to the Azores, and did we know that we were running into a 'big storm'. Although the barograph was now working again, it seemed reasonably steady, but quite soon afterwards it began to fall sharply and we reduced sail to No.1 Yankee, working staysail and mizzen. Next day a front went through, giving us winds up to about force 7, but the worst effect was a very lumpy sea and torrential rain, which soon meant that everything below decks became soaked. On 26th June I caught Murphy in the act and managed to beat him. *Kataree*'s Aries vane gear steers her by means of steering lines to a drum on the wheel which are secured to

After the boom broke.

the gear itself with stopper knots. Once in a blue moon, the lines chafe through above the stopper knot and the job of re-reeving is long, fiddly and uncomfortable, involving a brass fairlead stuck painfully in the belly. I happened to be admiring the way the gear was working when I noticed that the line was all but chafed through: it was the work of a moment to make a new knot an inch further up the line.

The wind again increased from ahead as another front went through, accompanied as usual by violent squalls and torrential rain, but we were making good if uncomfortable progress. After the second front the sun came out at last and we were able to dry some of the bedding and clothes. That night the bow lights, which we had managed to get working, failed again, and early the following morning the genoa staysail tore across. It owed us little, but we were sorry to lose it as it pulls well in light winds. We were even sorrier that in lowering its remains the staysail halyard was lost, so we were left with no means of setting another staysail. However an hour later the working staysail was set on the spinnaker halyard. The weather was now very hot and humid, and that afternoon the wind was up to force 7 from dead ahead. There was a perfectly foul sea and heavy rain and we had to keep changing sails to give enough power to make headway over the sea.

On 30th June there was a loud bang and we realised that the hook joining the windward main runner to its Highfield Lever had broken. This hook was marked 1500kg and had been in use since 1989, giving no trouble. Murphy clearly decided that we needed livening up and was not content to allow us simply to replace the hook with a shackle. Within five minutes of doing so there was another loud bang from the same runner. This time the bolt forming the axle of the runner block had sheared. To be fair to Murphy – a thing I find hard to do because he is never fair to me – in replacing the hook with the shackle I'd had to re-adjust the tension on the runner and I set it up a good deal tighter than before. This was, I'm sure, the cause of the second failure, and demonstrated the enormous rigging loading in a heavy sea. Fortunately we had a spare block with which we were able to replace the broken one. Next day the log records 'Runner trouble again'. By now we had got so used to misfortune that I cannot remember what was wrong, and can only assume we cured it.

On 1st July, taking advantage of an unusual calm, we decided to refill the diesel tank. For this purpose we had, on George Pulver's advice, bought an electric pump, which was a godsend. I unscrewed the cap of one of the two 12 gallon drums which we had bought in Ponta Delgada and filled, we thought, in Horta. To my astonishment, shame and anger I found it was completely empty. I was convinced that Murphy had made a hole in the bottom, but I am now certain that when we filled the tanks, cans and drums he distracted me and I missed this one out. At about the same time we dipped the luboil in the engine sump and there followed a search lasting a good two hours for the can of oil which I was certain was on board. Eventually we found it, hidden by Murphy in a nearly inaccessible part of the starboard after locker.

Thursday 3rd July was an eventful day. At breakfast time everything seemed to be going impossibly well: after weeks of waiting we had a fair wind at last, and the spinnaker, and later the mizzen staysail went up. The sun came out and the wind settled into the south at force 4. *Kataree* stormed along on course and all was right with the world. Too right, indeed, for Murphy's liking. At 1400 the spinnaker, which, to be fair, was of considerable antiquity, split across. Within ten minutes, while we were up forward getting its remains into the bag, Murphy was busy aft and there was an almighty bang, followed by more flapping. This time the windward mizzen runner and, strangely, the mizzen boom had broken, and both mizzen and mizzen staysail had to come in. These little diversions all took place in the middle of lunch and before the meal was ended, just to maintain variety, two whales surfaced close alongside us.

Looking back, we were very lucky that it was the mizzen boom and not the mizzen mast that was lost, as the runner, which takes a great deal of weight when the mizzen staysail is set, undoubtedly broke before the boom did. The day ended with the glass falling, the wind rising and heading us, the sky clouding over and we were back to the old routine of water in our bunks and oilskins on watch. At about this time the bilge pump failed again. Hard on the wind and in that sea we were in no position to spend another four hours dismantling the system, so settled down to the hand bilge pump. From now on this was a major chore, but the strange thing was the enormous variation in the number of strokes needed to keep the bilge dry. In fact the reason for this did not become apparent until months later: the gland on the rudder stock was leaking. When going fast, or in a following sea, the bilges filled. When on an even keel or sailing slowly the gland would be above water level. Meanwhile, Murphy turned his attention to the Brooks and Gatehouse log and dropped the impeller from the transducer into 3,000 metres of ocean.

Up to now, Murphy had been only joking. Fortunately the forenoon of 5th July was calm and we were under power, because it was then that Murphy got serious. At 1150 the helmsman smelled smoke and I immediately stopped the engine, as on a previous occasion shortly before the voyage began the fridge drive coupling had slipped, causing burning of the rubber in the coupling. Within seconds it became clear that this was not the cause of the smell, and thin smoke could now be seen from the back of the VHF set, which I disconnected. The smoke became very rapidly thicker and in not more than five seconds the cabin was so full of black, choking smoke that it was impossible to see across it.

It was now obvious that the source of the smoke was the electrical compartment in the chart room, which is behind a plywood panel, usually screwed in position. By the grace of God I had fixed it with only

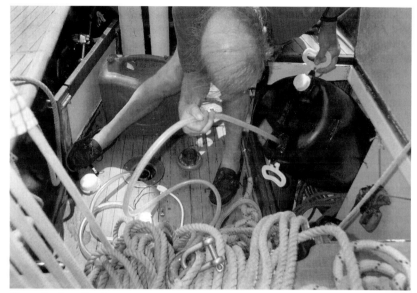

Transferring diesel at sea

one screw and it could be quickly removed to reveal flames licking up into the switch panel above it. Realising the seriousness of the situation, but still hoping to avoid the mess from a dry powder extinguisher, I shouted to someone in the doghouse to pass me the Halon extinguisher which is housed there. I pulled the trigger and nothing happened. Reaching for the extinguisher in the galley, I fired it at the flames which were instantly put out. I suppose that from first smelling the fire to putting it out had taken about 45 seconds and there is not much doubt that if it had not occurred in calm weather and at a time when we were all awake the damage would have been very much greater. As it was, all the wiring to the fuse boards, and the fuse boards themselves, were destroyed.

We disconnected the batteries and, after isolating the area where the fire had occurred, connected them up again. With bated breath, I restarted the engine. Much to our surprise, the alternator was charging. We began to test lights and found that apart from a very few cabin lights, all were lost. Don, one of the crew, now spent hours rigging a jury set up in which he restored the compass lights, bow lights, the galley light and one or two others, while all the time we had to keep up the routine of bilge pumping.

There now began a long period of calm during which we did a great deal of motoring and our twin preoccupations became bilge pumping and concern about whether we had enough fuel. By 6th July we had altered course up towards Cape Cod, and the following day, still with no wind, it became apparent that we had insufficient fuel to reach Manchester and we therefore planned to call at Nantucket for more diesel. On 7th July, however, we saw a fishing boat, the *Diligence of Fairhaven* (Mass) and motored over to her.

'Would she,' we radioed 'be prepared to sell us 10 gallons of diesel for $50?'

'Nope,' came back the reply 'But you can have as much as you want for nothing.'

Forty minutes later, when he had hauled his nets, we were alongside and fish buckets lined with bin liners and full of wonderful diesel oil were being passed down to us. More than that, he insisted on refilling our own spare diesel cans and for good measure threw down a couple of lobsters and a box of scallops. A warmer welcome to New England we could not have imagined.

Of the rest of the voyage there is little to tell. Now having plenty of fuel, we motored all the way to Manchester. Two remarkable things happened as we crossed Massachusetts Bay. The first, for those who know the area, would have been predictable: the appearance of masses of huge hump-backed whales, some within 15 feet of the boat. The second was much rarer: in the mist we saw what could only be an eighteenth century warship. She was about five miles off, and as we watched she began to set sail – first a jib and then a fore-topsail. By now we could make out her gun ports and there could be no doubt about what we were seeing. Later, after we arrived at Manchester, we heard that the USS *Constitution* had that day gone to sea and set sail for the first time in 110 years.

At lunchtime on 8th July we motored into Manchester and experienced the wonderful welcome for which Americans are world-renowned. We were taken into the bosom of the Walker family, lent a car by Flo Perkins and *Kataree*'s wounds were bound up by Crocker's boatyard. It was not until 16th July, now rather late for the OCC rally in Maine, that we left Manchester with a new mizzen boom, new fuse boards and wiring, new genoa staysail and replacement spinnaker. As we motored out of the harbour preparatory to a night passage to Maine, I saw the engine temperature gauge rise suddenly and realised that Murphy had got at the alternator belt. A yard launch towed us to a mooring, but within half an hour I had fitted a replacement which we carried as a spare. You see, while we'd been at Manchester I had refixed the two dolphins in the saloon.

Kataree is an Arthur Robb designed wooden yawl built in Hamble in 1959. Despite the few technical mishaps this summer, she is a comfortable, powerful 42ft cruising boat and something of an Atlantic veteran. Kataree now never sets to sea without her two dolphins firmly in place.

BALAENA GOES SOUTH

by Andrew O'Grady

This is the cruise which was awarded the Founder's Cup.

Before leaving New Zealand to start ocean cruising again, Bette and I wanted to visit Fiordland, both for its own attractions and as a trial run for cruising in higher latitudes like Patagonia. The weather was kind to us in late January, with easterly winds to see us around North Cape and Cape Reinga at the northern tip of New Zealand. Easterlies and clear skies lasted all the way to Fiordland, making it a very pleasant passage. The sailing was fairly rough, as we were well off the West Coast, so we limited our speed for comfort.

Five days out, the rising sun silhouetted the Southern Alps against the eastern sky. Even from 80 miles offshore this was an impressive sight. Next morning, despite the mountains being shrouded in cloud, we successfully identified Milford Sound. Going up or down the coast was just a matter of counting the inlets as they passed by. If you miscount you may well land up in the wrong Sound. The charts are based on an 1853 survey by HMS *Acheron*. They did a wonderful job to chart 14 sounds in less than two months, but it was interesting to be using charts that have some very significant errors; Sutherland Sound did not appear at all.

At the entrance to George Sound, our 15 knot breeze became 40 knots as the wind tore down the mountainside. The main came down rapidly and we carried on under genoa. We were able to sail 12 miles inland and after several turns found ourselves tucked into the anchorage at Alice Falls. A more tranquil spot would be hard to imagine. We were surrounded by 4,000 foot mountains; there was hardly a breath of wind, no swell and the water was clear, almost fresh and surprisingly warm.

Next day, at the head of Emelius Arm in Charles Sound, we found a tiny bay sheltered from the sea breeze that had sprung up when we entered the Sound. Here we anchored and pulled our stern into the shore to reach perfect shelter. In the afternoon we rowed six miles up the

Irene River and back. The dark bush and overhanging peaks embraced us, a land untouched by the hand of man. We came upon a small tributary fed by a high waterfall dropping from the mountain above and had a short stroll around its base. There were many huge trees sunk in the stream; in places they lay one upon the other, like the wreckage of some titanic sea battle.

On 4th February we traced our way back down the sounds (we were 18 miles from the sea) as far as Acheron Passage that links Breaksea and Dusky Sounds. Sailing was difficult as the wind kept shifting and was very light. When we reached Dusky Sound we were surprised by the difference from the more northerly Sounds. Dusky is much broader; the mountains are just as high but stand back further from the water. The effect is one of wide open spaces all perfectly sheltered. On all sides the timber grows tall and cataracts run to the sea. We chose to anchor in Sportsman's Cove on Cooper Island. To reach the cove we had to run through a passage only 20 metres wide.

8 February: The forecast was for a small front to bring north-westerly 35 knots and showers, not too bad for heading south. (Typical British weather, I told Bette.) We set out well prepared, all battened down and two reefs in the main. Apart from poor visibility the run down to Cape Providence was simple enough. We kept an accurate dead reckoning that saved our skins at the Cape, where the wind rose to 45 knots with heavy williwaws from the land. The rain had been continuous but was now

Balaena in Snug Cove, Doubtful Sound.

seriously obscuring visibility. We set a course to pass the huge reef to the south of the cape and clawed into the shelter of Chalky inlet.

The chart from 1853 was rather sketchy, so the whole process was extremely nerve racking. Eventually we made our way into the inlet and reached the millpond of North Port. What a difference this was from the raging sea just outside. Once securely anchored, we lit the pot-belly stove and stripped off our wet clothes. *Balaena* dried out quickly. Along with insect netting, a good cabin heater is essential in these waters.

On 12th February, after beating around Puyseger, we were able to lay our course and had a delightful sail to Codfish Island off the north-west coast of Stewart Island. We anchored off the white sands of Sealers Bay, a breeding reserve for the almost extinct flightless bird the Kakapo. The birdlife was prolific – we could hear kiwis all night long and were able to watch a yellow eyed penguin sunning herself on the rocks alongside.

13th February was another day with cloudless sky and light winds. We slowly beat down the deserted west coast of Stewart Island, a dramatic scene with white sandy beaches and bold rocky headlands. We spent the night in Murderers' Cove on Big South Cape Island. We would never have found this little gap in the rocks without the wonderful Mana Cruising Club Guide to Stewart Island. Indeed the fisherman who joined us at dusk was most surprised that anyone should have found their way in here.

We set off before dawn in order to get round the Southern tip of Stewart Island with a favourable tide. With only 25 knots of westerly breeze and a three metre southern swell, the seas off the Point were said to be calm. However, we found them suitably impressive. It was only a short hop into the smooth waters of Port Pegasus. What a wonderful harbour, with several dozen secure anchorages. We went to the east arm of Evening Cove, one of the World's ultimate hurricane holes – totally protected from the sea (if you had not navigated in you'd have difficulty finding your way out) and surrounded by interesting rock formations and lush bush.

From here we cruised slowly towards Half Moon Bay, the only community on the island, where we met my mother, Sue, who flew in from Scotland. As she'd had a tiring journey we decided to take it easy for a few days. This fitted well with the weather, which had now turned to unsettled westerlies and we wanted a more settled pattern before setting off for Fiordland.

We decided to leave during the night of 22nd February, as soon as the fronts had passed, and we departed at 3 am. Unfortunately this was just before the passage of the final front and we found ourselves beating into 45 knots. As the front passed through very rapidly we went from full sail to staysail alone and back to working sail all in a few hours. In the rain and incredibly steep seas this was exhausting. Foveaux Strait certainly lived up to its reputation as a very rough place indeed. By morning the wind

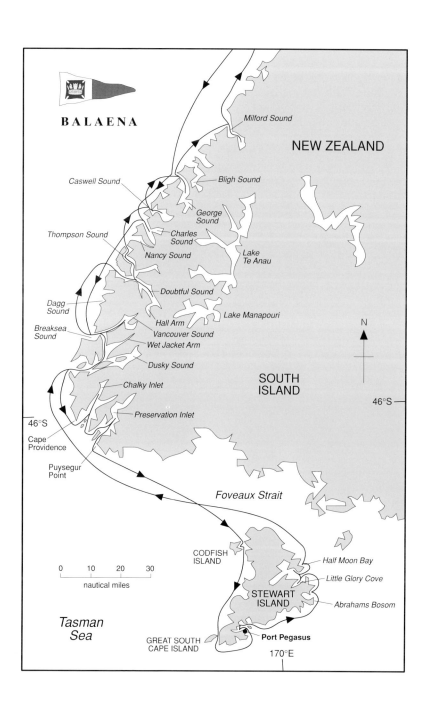

BALAENA

Milford Sound

NEW ZEALAND

Caswell Sound

Bligh Sound

George
Sound

Thompson Sound

Charles
Sound

Nancy Sound

Lake
Te Anau

Doubtful Sound

Dagg
Sound

Lake Manapouri

Breaksea
Sound

Hall Arm

Vancouver Sound

Wet Jacket Arm

Dusky Sound

SOUTH
ISLAND

Chalky Inlet

N

46°S

Preservation Inlet

46°S

Cape
Providence

Puysegur
Point

Foveaux Strait

0   10   20   30

CODFISH
ISLAND

Half Moon Bay

nautical miles

Little Glory Cove

STEWART
ISLAND

Abrahams Bosom

Tasman
Sea

GREAT SOUTH
CAPE ISLAND

Port Pegasus

170°E

had moderated and swung to south-west in the wake of the front. We had an easy sail along to Puyseger Point. There was no need for speed as we planned to arrive at Dusky Sound at daybreak. Unfortunately Sue was laid low by seasickness for the whole of this trip and it was not really long enough for Bette and I to retrieve our sea legs.

24 February: A slow night sail in brilliant moonlight brought us to Dusky Sound. We arrived at Pickersgill Harbour soon after dawn and promptly went to bed in order to recover from what had been a hard little passage. There were a few breakages and we spent the afternoon on repairs and maintenance. The wisdom of our choice of departure time was rapidly apparent as the wind veered to north-west and the barograph started to drop almost as soon as we were at anchor. The anchorage was a little unsettled in the building gale, so we moved a few miles further up the sound to Cascade Cove. Here we had perfect shelter as the front passed over.

25 February: After gathering mussels for our next few meals, we set off under fores'l alone to make our way slowly up Dusky Sound, Acheron Passage and Wet Jacket Arm to a tiny nook totally sheltered from north-east to south-east which we named Rainbow cove. It was a lovely day with occasional rain squalls and long sunny spells. We saw at least 100 waterfalls gushing down the steep mountainsides – Fiordland at its very best.

The next front brought hurricane force winds at sea, so we were exceedingly glad to be tucked away behind a mountain virtually over-hung by the forest. Looking out we could see only rock and trees. The rain was torrential but the wind flew away overhead – we could hear it in the treetops but hardly feel it at all.

The gale blew by and left a glorious sunny day with fair winds. We had a magnificent run up to Doubtful Sound where we anchored in exquisite Snug Cove. This was surrounded by high peaks and totally sheltered (though reputed to be subject to williwaws in strong winds). That night we watched a seal fishing all around us and were able to see the constellations as clearly in the smooth dark water as in the sky.

On 2nd March we met Tom Fenwick off the bus and took him back to *Balaena* at Deep Cove. Tom had come from the South of Spain via Australia and was delighted to be plunged into such a wilderness. We visited precipitous Hall Arm and found a snug anchorage right at the end. *Balaena* was almost under the canopy of beech trees. Here the mountains loomed above us in a spectacular array. It is a feature of this area that the stormy seas are contrasted with the most sheltered anchorages imaginable.

Very large bottlenosed dolphins escorted us down Hall Arm and in the clear water could be seen perfectly. A day of gentle sailing brought us to Neck Cove at the mouth of Thompson Sound. Here we had a short bush walk and for the first time found a multitude of the tiny Easter Orchid

Looking up Hall Arm.

scenting the air with a sweet vanilla perfume. They grow in profusion on the mossy branches of beech trees.

We weighed anchor rapidly in the early morning as a hard breeze started to blow onshore. A brisk little beat up the coast took us to Caswell Sound. Again the scenery was superb and was subtly different from other sounds. In parts it has gentler slopes and denser vegetation, yet there are still the spectacular mountain vistas and dramatic waterfalls.

5th March: As the winds were now offshore, we expected a blow at the entrance to George Sound. At first we had violent williwaws of maybe 55 knots off the south entrance point. In the entrance the wind was steadily blowing 40–45 knots and the sea was white. Very slowly we clawed our way into the sound, tacking under sail and using the motor to ensure we didn't miss stays. Eventually the wind started to ease and we were able to sail again. It took 3 hours to make 6 miles to the first anchorage. Anchorage Cove was a lovely spot where we tucked behind a tiny island and tied to a fishing boat in complete shelter. Again we enjoyed the good company of the fishermen, most of whom are young and full of enthusiasm for their profession. The wind kept us in here for two days, with good walking and the best fishing yet.

Once the wind had dropped we motored back down the sound in a fraction of the time it had taken to go up it. Off the coast there was little swell and perfect visibility with not a cloud in sight. Nearing Milford Sound the breeze picked up and we enjoyed a smooth reach for the rest of the trip. We ran up the sound in idyllic conditions with superb views of the 5–6,000 foot peaks looming above. The evening sun cast shadows that showed up every facet of the rock faces. At Stirling falls we saw several rainbows in the cascade and were able to sail right into the spray. Then a large group of dolphins picked us up and escorted us to our anchorage at Harrison Cove. Here we were overhung by the glacier on Mount Pembroke which seemed so close but, such is the scale of the Sound, was really three miles away.

9th March: In the afternoon, we dropped Tom and Sue at the tour boat dock. Bette and I were once again on our own and had a calm and pleasant evening back at Harrison Cove.

10th March: The forecast was for moderate south-westerlies so, despite a tropical cyclone approaching North Cape, we set off. Hopefully the cyclone would have moved away to the east by the time we arrived in the north.

12th March: According to the forecast it was blowing 65 knots only 150 miles north-east of us. However, we were almost becalmed and, apart from a few hours motoring to recharge the batteries, sailed along at two knots. We didn't want to get any closer to the cyclone, which seemed to be slow in moving off. We baked, played cards and backgammon, and read in the sunshine. At home they had floods and 50 knot winds.

15th March: Eventually the wind returned, a gentle south-westerly allowing us to lay a course for Cape Reinga. We arrived at the Cape during the night and had a gentle sail along the North coast. The wind stayed steady until the next evening and carried us south to the Cavallis before dark. We arrived in the Bay of Islands just after dusk and sailed directly to our mooring. Rowing ashore to visit my cousin Martyn, we found much of the family there to greet us.

Balaena is a 42 ft gaff cutter, designed by Denis Brown and built in wood and epoxy by her owner. She was launched in 1988.

META URSA INCOGNITA

by Pete Hill

This cruise was awarded Juno's Cup.

Annie and I crossed the Atlantic to the West Indies for the winter in 1996 and sailed up to Nova Scotia from the Virgin Islands the following April. When we arrived in early May, we were a little surprised to find it frosty and that all the local yachts were still laid up. After visiting friends, we cruised up the Eastern Shore of Nova Scotia and then through the beautiful Bras d'Or lakes.

Our plan for the summer was to cruise up the Labrador coast in July, and then to cross the Hudson Strait to Frobisher Bay in August, before beating a retreat to the Azores in the autumn. These plans were totally dependent on the ice conditions. The previous year, the Strait of Belle Isle (separating Newfoundland from the Labrador) had been closed by ice until very late summer.

Most of the coast in the northern section of the Labrador has not been surveyed and often there is just a thin line of soundings along the 'recommended track.' The shoreline and most of the islands are shown taken from aerial surveys, but there is no shortage of exploring to do. When we sailed into a likely-looking bay at the south-east corner of Green Island, we were rewarded with finding a well-sheltered bay and 18 feet of water in which to drop the anchor (57°39′N, 61°46′W). A walk ashore the next morning revealed three caribou who, far from startled, wandered close to us to investigate and then went down to the beach to sniff at our dinghy. We sailed out in a light breeze and fine, sunny weather and had a look in the harbour at the north end of the island (57°40′N, 61°48′W) where *Aratapu* (RCC) had anchored, four years previously.

The wind disappeared and we motored for a while to catch the tide through Mugford Tickle. The Kaumajet mountains rise sheer on either hand as you pass through the tickle, with the cliffs 1,000 feet high. We were fortunate to have gentle, clear weather for the passage. Once round the corner, there is a good view of the Bishop's Mitre, a 4,000 foot peak which is split by a deep ravine, looking (in fact) just like a bishop's mitre. The breeze remained light and after another spell of motoring, we anchored in Three Mountain Harbour (57°58′N 62°08′W) at ten o'clock that evening. The next day was Annie's birthday and our original intention to spend the day at anchor was modified by the squalls that were assaulting *Badger* in the anchorage. We scrambled to the top of the hill above the bay so that Annie could build her standing man – a new craze – and after collecting some driftwood on the beach, we decided to go and look for a more tranquil spot.

As we left the bay there appeared to be a clear, deep channel between Sturman Island and the mainland. Sailing through, we were a little alarmed to see the bottom come up quickly to 12 feet with an underwater rock nearby, but fortunately the soundings increased again and we sailed north in the fresh breeze to Finger Hill Island. We lost the wind in its lee and it never came back with any strength. We eventually found a tiny cove in Napartokk Bay, (58°01′N, 62°19′W) where we could enjoy the mandatory birthday feast and had a peaceful night.

As we approached Hebron (58°12′N 62°37′W) the following after-noon, word had obviously got out that there was a free show in store. A helicopter landed and a small group of people gathered to watch *Badger* enter. The Pilot led us to believe that we could anchor off the settlement, although the Mate was somewhat dubious, but as we approached the shore under power, we went aground. Putting the engine astern pulled us off, but as we turned around, we went aground on another rocky shoal. This time we stuck fast. It was just on low water, but as we had an audience, who were obviously getting their money's worth, I thought it would look better to try and pull ourselves off, rather than waiting for the tide to do the work. I duly rowed out an anchor and we were soon off. We retreated with our tail between our legs to a deeper anchorage, further out. When the fun was over, the helicopter took off again. This struck us as a rather extreme case of Sod's Law that states if you make a mess of things there will always be someone there to watch you do it.

Hebron was a Moravian Mission station, which was abandoned about 1960. Many of the buildings are falling down, such as the Hudson Bay trading post, but the church and mission, similar in style to the one at Hopedale, is still intact. It has been recognized as an historic building and attempts have been made by the Government to stabilize its condition. But unless more effort is put in, it will soon start to deteriorate quickly, as several of the outside doors could not be closed and the roof cladding had gone from a large area. We were glad that the helicopter had disappeared, as the setting of these buildings, on a beautiful site, had to be appreciated in solitude.

A falling glass brought a freshening breeze, which soon sent us round

Iceberg off Labrador.

to Saglek Fjord. A radar station perched on the edge of a high cliff guards the entrance, presumably put there to keep us safe in our beds, or maybe just to give us four minutes warning that we weren't. There is no all-weather anchorage in this Fjord: St John's Harbour is open to the north and East Harbour (58°32′N 62°46′W), next to Big Island, is open to the south-east. We chose the latter, as the wind was south-westerly and looked as though it might shift to the north. The entrance is wide, but there are a couple of submerged reefs to avoid. This area was surveyed by the US Navy in the 1950s in anticipation of the radar station (which is part of the DEW line). The wind increased all afternoon and the woollies were so bad that we put out a second anchor – after which they died away. In the evening, I rowed ashore and scrambled to the top of the island next to us. The chart showed the top end of the harbour as drying out, yet from my vantage point it looked to be reasonably deep. Sounding with the lead from the dinghy revealed that much of the area had a minimum depth of 10 feet and it was possible for a yacht to tuck behind the western end of Big Island in a perfect landlocked harbour – quite a find.

The wind eased off the next morning and after lunch we checked out the top end of the harbour in *Badger* and then sailed over to St John's Harbour (58°27′N, 62°48′W), the breeze dying away. At the head of the inlet, two small ships were moored together – as we approached, an open boat came over and asked us to raft up alongside and have dinner with them. It seemed churlish to refuse and we were soon tied up to the Michael J Symonds and the Newfoundland Tradition. Rex Symonds, the owner of the two vessels, made us welcome and gave us the ten cent tour. Newfoundland Tradition was a new fishing boat, which spent the summer catching turbot off Baffin Land and the Michael J Symonds was a converted trawler which took the catch back to Newfoundland. The crew were having a mid-season break at home and the two vessels were moored here awaiting their return. A chartered aeroplane was using the airstrip at the radar base to transfer the crew. Rex had brought some friends with him from St Antony's to look after the fishing boat and make a holiday of it.

Word travels fast in the North and they knew all about our grounding in Hebron. The helicopter belonged to a diamond prospecting party, based at a cabin ashore. After a meal on board, several of the crew came over to *Badger* for the rest of the evening. We were told a fascinating tale about an RAF bomber that crash-landed on the site of the future airstrip, in November 1944. The plane was flying from Greenland to Goose Bay in Labrador, when it became lost in bad weather. The crew survived the landing and eventually the navigator worked out where they were – only 20 miles from Hebron, which was then inhabited. The weather and lack of suitable clothing prevented them from travelling overland, so two of the crew tried to reach Hebron in their inflatable boat, but disappeared in the attempt. The rest of the crew starved to death the following

The abandoned Moravian Mission church, Hebron, Labrador.

January. Two months later, a hunting party from Hebron discovered the wreck and found the pilot's diary.

Next morning, we walked along the roadway, built for the DEW line station and then abandoned, and later called at the cabin to have a chat with the prospectors' cook, Mr Blake. When we left, he presented us with four enormous T-bone steaks. We had hoped to sail up to the top of Saglek Fjord, which reaches into the heart of the Torngat mountains, but there was just too little wind to contemplate going up. Progress up the coast had been much slower than expected owing to the light breezes, but making the best use of the winds given is the essence of cruising under sail, and any temptation to use the motor to keep up a high average speed must be resisted, or much of the satisfaction of the sport will be lost. We did, however, sometimes use our engine – often at the end of the day to get to an anchorage for the night. *Badger*'s diesel engine is air-cooled and somewhat noisy. Our usual cruising speed is 2½ knots, which is economical and not too loud – after all, we'd be happy sailing at 2½ knots, if there were any wind.

The weather was generally wonderful, with sunshine and good visibility, so we could appreciate the barren, mountainous landscape as we slowly sailed north. We had a lay day at Bib Cove (59°51′N 64°05′W), as there was little wind. Annie spent the morning washing, while I fetched water from the nearby stream and sawed up some driftwood ashore. We seemed to have left the mozzies behind, or perhaps it was getting too late in the summer for them, so we were able to have a barbecue ashore at lunchtime.

It was 16th August when we anchored in Clarke Harbour (60°14′N 64°23′W) at the top of the Labrador. On the way in, we passed quite a large tented camp and, as the anchor rattled down, two open boats came by to see us. It was late and they soon left, but asked us to visit them the next morning. We walked over and there was quite some excitement as we arrived. Had we seen Nanuk? One had approached their camp that morning and most of them had never seen a polar bear before. Several families had come up from George River in Ungava Bay for their summer holiday, cruising along the coast in their fishing boat, camping at various places along the way to fish for Arctic char and hunt for seals. The bell tents all had smoking chimneys poking through (with many scorch holes in the canvas) and a few sealskins were pegged out on the ground to dry. Sammy was very friendly and forthcoming and we had a long talk with him about the Inuit way of life in George River. Whilst obviously embracing much of the 'western' way of life, he was keen to remember his heritage; travelling each summer and winter in the land was very important to him. He was very optimistic for the future of the Inuit and when Annie asked him if the thought that he had a good life, his face beamed:

'Yes, I have,' he replied, spreading his arms and gesturing to all around him, 'I have my freedom.'

The northern end of Labrador forms the southern entrance to the Hudson Strait and the tides here are fearsome. Our plan was to cross the Straits and have a look at Frobisher Bay in Baffin Land, but first we wanted to visit the Button Islands, at the very tip of the Labrador. Unfortunately the tides were approaching springs, but we had no time to wait for neaps, as it was already 17th August and the summer was nearly over. We set out in a light breeze just after lunch to catch the favourable tide. The wind soon died, so we motored past Cape Chidley and then a force three easterly sprang up as we entered the Grey Strait. *Badger* crabbed across the channel with a five knot current pushing her sideways, the light wind making the overfalls no more than a popple. The chart showed an unnamed inlet on Lawson Island, which looked as though it might provide an anchorage, but of course there were no soundings. The wind died again and we motored against the last of the flood and tried to enter the inlet before dark. We just made it and now kept our fingers crossed that there would be suitable depths, especially as the tidal range was some 26 feet. Luckily, we found a shelf with 30 feet over it and just enough room to swing. The shores were littered with stranded growlers (60°36′N, 64°41′W).

I awoke in the dim dawn to hear a piece of ice tapping against the hull and thought it wise to go and fend it off. Sleepily looking over the side, I was amazed to see a polar bear alongside. I dashed below to wake Annie and as we came back again, we saw the bear swimming for the shore. He climbed out and with a quick backward glance, disappeared over a rocky ridge. He was obviously as surprised as we were.

After breakfast and with no sign of the polar bear, we rowed ashore to take a picture of the anchorage. From the top of the cliff above the anchorage, we could see the polar bear just around the headland, swimming towards us. The thrill of seeing the bear again was somewhat tempered in my case, by the thought of being trapped ashore. We scrambled down towards the dinghy, but before we reached it, we saw the bear swimming towards us and didn't have time to get into the dinghy before he arrived. Annie, who is good with animals, suggested to me, who am not, that we stand up and shout fearlessly at him, to make him a little wary and give us time to get into the dinghy. We shouted, and I hope that it sounded fearless – I was quaking in my wellingtons. If nothing else, we probably confused him and he veered off while we dashed down the rocks and into the dinghy.

We were soon aboard and the dinghy on deck. After sniffing around our scent ashore, the polar bear swam out to *Badger* and then slowly swam around the boat. What a privilege to watch this magnificent animal at such close quarters! We were both euphoric at the encounter and certainly, for my part, it was in no small measure due to the contrast with the close shave ashore. After forty minutes or so, he lost interest and swam away. We pulled up the anchor and headed out to cross over to

Frobisher Bay. Just before passing the end of the Button Islands, we passed another polar bear swimming nonchalantly across the straits in the strong tide.

It took us three days to cross the Hudson Strait, with 127 miles made good. Light winds and the spring tides accounted for the very slow progress. The current was up to seven knots around Resolution Island, at the north side of the Strait, and we always seemed to be in the wrong place when the tide turned. Resolution Island has the reputation of being the foggiest place in the world – on average it is foggy one day in two. We were very fortunate in that respect as the weather stayed remarkably clear, with amazing mirages on the horizon. It was on 21st August that we at last anchored off the Meta Incognita Peninsula, in Baffin Land. There is some uncertainty about the meaning of 'Meta Incognita', the name that Martin Frobisher gave to this peninsula. One theory is that 'meta' means the turning post in a chariot race and that Frobisher is referring to the turning point of his voyage to unknown lands. It is perhaps also a nod to the classical scholarship of Queen Elizabeth I.

This area of Frobisher Bay looked the most interesting, with mountains, glaciers and an almost totally uncharted coastline. After finding an anchorage in a well-sheltered bay (61° 59′N, 66° 05′W), we were keen to get ashore. We were now cautious about polar bears being around, but having read our Tristan Jones we went ashore well prepared with our Very pistol (don't fire until you can see his tonsils). There were many caribou antlers on the ground, but no sign of bears. A walk to the top of

Meta ursa incognita

the hill gave a good view over the Kendall Strait, Annie built her standing man and we both rolled boulders. The next day saw us sailing and drifting up the Kendall Strait in bright sunshine. The tide was with us, and often the many pieces of ice would overtake us as the wind faltered.

The Pilot has little to say about the Strait, except to comment that the north end is encumbered by shoals and rocks. We had a few frights as the bottom came up to meet us, but there was always enough water and the tide was making. Ashore we spotted a polar bear with two cubs, and from now on we saw several each day, including one on an iceberg, looking just like the advert for Fox's Glacier Mints. This rather curtailed any thoughts of long walks ashore. The bay that was earmarked to provide our night's anchorage (62°10′N 59°58′W) obliged, with suitable depths and a handy stream for replenishing our water.

Continuing north-east, we sailed into another unnamed bay (62°18′N, 66°10′W), near Halford Island. A fresh breeze was blowing in, but otherwise the place would have been a good anchorage. A polar bear and her two cubs watched us from the shore. The next bay north would have given us shelter from the wind, but unfortunately there was a drying reef across the entrance. We continued on to Jackman Sound and found a snug anchorage by Buerger Point (66°20′N, 66°15′W). After dropping the hook, I commented that it made a change to be in a harbour where there was no polar bear. Annie wordlessly pointed to a nearby islet, on top of which a lone white bear lazed in the evening sun.

We sailed further up Jackman Sound, with the sun shining on the Tierra Nivea icecap and the many streams running down from it turning the water a cloudy green. Our last anchorage in Frobisher Bay was at the north-west corner of Jackman Sound (62°20′N 66°29′W) and here we dropped the hook in a landlocked basin next to a waterfall. Unfortunately, our time was now up and that was as far as we went. The arctic summer is very short, but perhaps that is part of the attraction and it had certainly been worthwhile travelling the long distance to experience it.

We set out from Jackman Sound on 27th August. The weather had broken and it was blowing force five from the north, with rain and mist. As we beat out, a Canadian Coastguard helicopter flew past and circled us; we gave them a cheery wave. We planned to sail to the Azores. With luck, we would be too late in the year to get hit by a hurricane and too early to have the autumn gales setting in. The weather cleared up as we passed Resolution Island – still no fog there – and we had several days of light southerly winds and clear weather, with spectacular Northern Lights. The skies then clouded over and the wind increased to force 4–5, but the sea that got up was out of all proportion to the wind. It was vilely uncomfortable as we crashed and bashed our way south.

One night, the main halliard block broke and the sail banged down into the topping lifts. To cover such an eventuality, we have a large spare block at the masthead, with the flag halliard rove through it. It was a

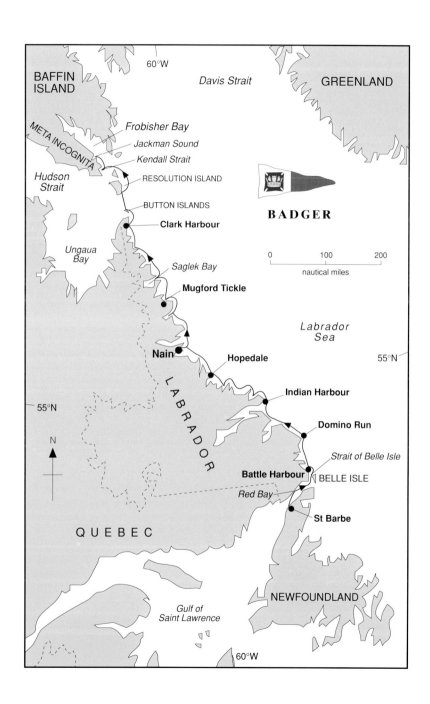

Annie's birthday 'standing man', 3 Mountain Harbour, Labrador.

quick job to pass the main halliard through this block and be underway
again. Two days later, the halliard jammed in the block when it jumped
off the sheave. After a bit of head scratching, we managed to release it
and haul up another block to the spare one. Then the halliard parted.
More head scratching and then, using the burgee halliard, we hauled up
yet another block on a rolling hitch. All was now reasonably well, but the
rolling hitch very slowly slid down, so that by the time we arrived in the
Azores, we had two reefs permanently in the mainsail.

We had two blows that just reached gale force, through which we were
hove-to. As they passed, *Badger* plodded her way south-east, still with a
very rough sea and contrary wind. As we approached the Azores, the
weather improved and the wind freed, but the moderate breeze made us
miss the two panels of main that we couldn't set. We ended the passage
in Terceira, at Angra do Heroísmo, having been 27 days at sea to cover
the 2,260 miles. We were back once again in the land of fresh fruit,
vegetables and wine, to find that had we arrived much sooner we would
have experienced hurricane Erica – perhaps proving that it's an ill wind
that blows nobody good.

*Badger is a 34ft, junk-rigged dory built by Pete and Annie Hill in 1983. She
is schooner rigged and her two junk sails are easy to handle in heavy
weather. Over several years she was to be found in high latitudes but has
been seen wintering in warmer climes more recently.*

UPSHOT TO PANAMA AND ISLANDS WEST

by Jeremy Swetenham

Leaving Home

"Having worked our fingers to the bone at the marina in Poole, with frequent but welcome interruptions from friends with bottles and enquiries as to our departure date, Sandrine finally snapped. On 9th August 1995 I found her clearing the pontoon around us (which for two weeks had looked like a car boot sale) and throwing everything on board.

'But Sandrine we're not read . . . '

'We'll never be ready! We're leaving now' . . . "

And they did.

From Poole, Jeremy and Sandrine cruised to northern Spain via Guernsey and the Biscay coast of France. After a short sojourn in Portugal, Upshot set off for Porto Santo before joining the 1995 ARC fleet in Las Palmas, Gran Canaria. Three weeks at sea took them to St Lucia, and thence via the Grenadines and other Caribbean islands to Panama.

We left Panama on 2 April with a favourable wind and headed, as advised, south-west to catch the current out of the Gulf of Panama and make some southing before meeting the prevailing wind between Panama and the Galapagos. The current was superb, but dawn next day revealed other passengers hitching a ride south – large amounts of driftwood, bamboo and trees – yes, trees, up to forty feet long and three to four feet in diameter. We helmed most of the day to avoid as much as we could, but since we continuously had small debris rattling along the hull we decided to step off the moving walkway and head directly for the Galapagos.

We crossed The Line at dawn on 10th April and sailed along it for a while playing "guess the hemisphere" every so often. Next morning at

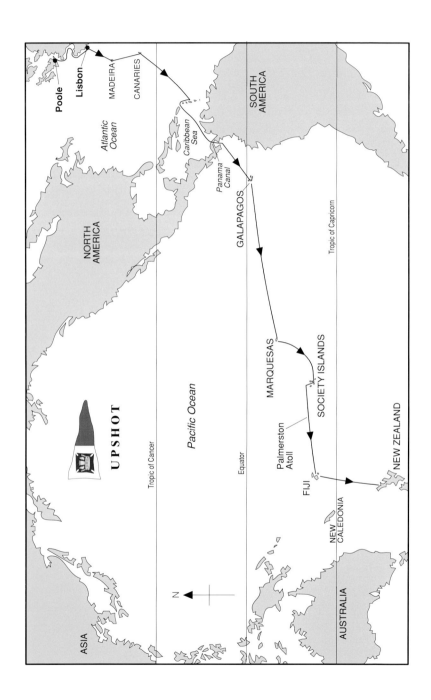

dawn we crept into Academy Bay on Santa Cruz. Thankfully the charges were much less than we had feared and during our stay we didn't even need to go to the bank – unbelievable! Tempting as it was to hang around for a while, we wanted to press on and so used every available moment of our five day stay. We visited the research station, rode through the pampas with a local farmer to see the giant tortoises (refreshing ourselves from wild orange, guava and passion fruit trees) and, best of all, we took the dinghy out to a small island at the mouth of the bay and swam with the young sea-lions. They were as inquisitive as they were playful and got very excited if you dived down and swam one way and then the other, playing follow my leader and then skimming past you as you doubled back on yourself – a very special afternoon.

We left early on the morning of 16th April and stopped briefly at Post Office Bay on Santa Maria, hoping to leave something in the barrel used years ago by passing whaling ships. Sadly there was an official tour in the bay and we were reminded, very politely, that we were not allowed ashore without a guide. Well there are plenty more islands in the sea, so we set off to try one in the Marquesas, 3,000 miles away.

The first couple of days were rather quiet, followed by five days of continuous torrential rain and squalls. The squalls were not too violent but I have never seen so much rain and we became convinced in the end that some of it must have recirculated and fallen on us at least twice! At this point our 'waterproof', nitrogen filled, hand-held GPS, which we had been using since the main GPS gave up in Panama, became only slightly damp (unavoidable) and decided to expire. We dried some desiccator bags in the oven, sealed them in a plastic carton with the GPS to draw out the moisture and pulled out the sextant. We reasoned that, with 2,000 miles to go, if we hadn't remembered how to navigate by the sun and stars before approaching the nearest land, then we didn't deserve to be here in the first place. By the time we had the GPS working again two days later, we had our position accurate to ten miles which, for the swell and hurried sights through thinner patches in the cloud, seemed acceptable. We certainly couldn't have asked for more sea room.

Halfway across and 1,500 miles from anywhere, we sighted a yacht that had berthed next to us in Panama. As we drew closer, there ensued a gratuitous photo session. We sailed in company without even trying for three days, each watching the other disappear and then reappear behind the long, vast swell. After that the winds became good and stiff and we made good progress.

After breakfast on 6th May, 20 days out of the Galapagos, we sighted a distant speck of land and tried to tune in to the local radio. Suddenly *Upshot* was filled with the sound of ukuleles and Polynesian singers. As the mountains of the Marquesas Islands opened their arms to us we danced and sang the rest of the way. Two-handed, we had taken a day

"Got it."

less to cover about 300 miles more than our Atlantic crossing, and we had arrived in a true South Sea island paradise.

Polynesian Beauties

Picture the most rugged peaks and razor sharp ridges of Scotland around 3,500 feet high, cover this with tropical vegetation and that is what the Marquesas look like. The natives, though initimidatingly over-sized, really were friendly. Not effusive, but very ready to smile and never appearing on their guard or suspicious as with many in the Caribbean. They were also very generous, always offering fruit or fish, seldom wanting anything in return though occasionally asking for whisky – but at £20 for a bottle of spirits, *Upshot* was a dry boat for the majority of our stay in the colonial islands of French Polynesia!

The friendliness of Polynesians can have little to do with lack of contact with cruising yachts, since every major port on each island is packed with boats that are disappointed with not being the only one there. However, a little exploring around the coasts in the Marquesas revealed quite a few valleys covered in coconut plantations and anchorages that were reasonably well protected. Even in these places, if there was a village, the locals were not surprised to see a yacht even if we had the place to ourselves.

The most remarkable discovery was that these out of the way valleys, inhabited or not, were strewn with the stone ruins of a very large civilisation. Wide areas now overgrown had the remains of foundations for houses and temples that were home to a population ten times the size of that living there now. The huge boulders used in the construction reminded Sandrine of the Inca buildings, though not fitting together so perfectly. The surrounding landscape was as dramatic as Glencoe and provided enough rain to fill our water tanks several times over.

After some unseasonal strong winds we had a four day sail to Raroia, one of the easternmost Tuamotu atolls halfway up this vast chain, and where Kon Tiki finally came to rest. It should have taken us a day less, but if you wait for a drop in the wind you always end up with nothing. These atolls can only be approached from the side with palmed islands on the reef, since the windward side is normally just under the surface with no landmarks other than the occasional wreck. The ocean washes over the reef into the huge lagoons (Raroia is about seven by ten miles across), and the narrow entrance passage make for some exciting arrivals and departures if you don't get the tides right. It's best to pass through with a little counter-current for manoeuvrability, but we managed to get it wrong both times and so were sucked in, or on leaving – spat out!

Raroia is about medium size, but the lagoon still seemed huge compared with what we had imagined. The atolls are formed by the erosion and subsidence of ancient islands which then leave behind their fringing reef that grows fast enough to hold its own against the sea. We carefully picked our way between the coral heads (that rise from depths of up to fifty metres) across to the windward side of the lagoon to shelter behind a line of *motus* – small, thin, flat, coral and sand islands covered in coconut palms and scrub. There we relaxed for several days working on *Upshot*, hunting for crabs, searching for lobsters on the reef at night (without success) and accompanying some friends spear fishing. There were a lot of Black Tip sharks around all of the time which seemed only inquisitive, but if there was blood in the water we got out quickly. We also collected a huge colony of Remora (sucker fish) under the boat that shot out to investigate any scraps that were thrown overboard. They did a remarkably good job of cleaning our bottom and one even attached itself to our sailing dinghy with just his tail flowing out behind.

We had hoped to visit a couple more of the atolls as we crossed the main chain on our way to Tahiti, but a large swell was running into the only available passes. So, making good time, we decided to explore behind the reef, along the less populated south coast of Tahiti. Most yachts are drawn directly to the bright lights of Papeete in the north-west corner, so we had this other stretch of the islands almost all to ourselves.

By contrast, Papeete is like a suburb of a Mediterranean city, but it still has its charm and the locals are no less friendly, just richer – and they need to be! The cost of living is astronomical in French Polynesia, but in Papeete it is a joke – a chicken, for example, costs about £14. Our budget was blown out of the water, but since Papeete is the only place to get certain things done, we just had to close our eyes and hand over the cash. In the end we were very lucky to find work on another yacht which softened the blow. The French Polynesian cultural festival was in full swing during the same period, with a spectacular costumed parade and evenings of the most fantastic dancing.

Cruising the Societies

After ten days of city life we managed to escape to the peace of Moorea, Tahiti's neighbour and one of the fairytale Society Islands. There we found a tiny cove at the head of one of Moorea's deep bays, where we could take a stern line to a palm tree and almost step ashore. The shops were out of harm's way and we spent a week on our own job list. The cove belongs to Mari Mari, a lady whose American parents bought the valley at auction in the 1920's after it had been confiscated from the Germans. They arrived by yacht, built the colonial style house in which Mari Mari was born and then set up a plantation.

Mari Mari had spent some time restoring many of the archaeological sites throughout French Polynesia. She also introduced us to an eccentric English artist friend of hers who had been there twenty years, since she was stranded by being unable to return to Beirut where she was living at the time. We too were stranded for a while when a six metre swell came up from the south and poured over the normally protective reefs of all of the Societies and Tuamotus, washing away houses and hotels and throwing beaches a hundred yards inland. The oldest locals had seen nothing like it, even during a hurricane when the reef offers a fair amount of protection. In the north we felt nothing, but looking across the lagoon to the east it looked as if rolling hills were migrating north. We went to help one of Mari Mari's friends (another Moorean born American lady who lives alone) whose house – a series of traditional huts on stilts – stands on the southern most isthmus of the island. These huts, roofed with palm leaves, were partially protected from the force of the waves by a huge ancient coral platform on the tip of the isthmus. She had sat the whole thing out in her loft as the sea swept through her kitchen. We spent the day there removing the marine life from her garden, now more like a beach, and clearing paths through the huge coral heads that had been swept off the sides of the platform and lay strewn everywhere as if giants had been playing marbles.

By this time we were getting very excited because Neil Lumsden, a great friend and best man at our wedding, had decided to take his whole year's holiday to join us for a month. We re-stowed *Upshot* to free the quarter berth for him, and fitted a new hatch opening into the cockpit, to make the berth habitable in the tropics. The difference was amazing – light, airy and far less claustrophobic. Once Neil arrived we spent a few more days in a reef anchorage so that he could recover from the flight and see a little of the island. In fact, he saw quite a lot when we took him on our second climb out of the vast volcanic crater that holds Moorea's two bays. Up and up we climbed, right to the rim from where you can see both north and south coasts of the island.

Then on to Bora Bora, an island that really lives up to its reputation for beauty. We had to tear ourselves away after two weeks, having been mesmerised by the snorkelling and anchorages on the less accessible south east corner. There we anchored in only three metres of clear water, where the fine sand was the colour that swimming pool designers strive for.

Our next stop was Tahaa, just to the north of another island Raiatea, but enclosed by the same reef. Neil's last day with us was memorable, as we sailed the entire length of Raiatea under spinnaker, picking our way

Upshot off Bora Bora.

through the narrow passages between the island and the reef. Sandrine had discovered there was some informal local dancing in the school gymnasium, which turned out to be extremely good, though only attended by a few locals and no tourists – well, three of us. The last stage of such an evening is for the dancers to pick partners from the audience and then these couples take it in turn to do their thing whilst everyone watches. The lead dancer was refused by a local man sitting next to me (probably owing to a heart condition – risky things at these events) and so I ended up centre stage. Neil received the same treatment and Sandrine was in tears wishing she could have photographed the looks on our faces.

A World in an Atoll

Neil's departure left us very low; our enjoyment of the islands had been more than doubled by being able to share the experience with him and catch up with news from home at the same time. Pulling ourselves together we tried to focus on the next leg ahead, there being only two months left before the start of the hurricane season and a wealth of island groups between us and the safety of New Zealand. We decided to head straight for the Vava'u Group of Tonga (ten days away) to save time, and would only stop *en route* if the wind deserted us within motoring distance of one of the Cook Islands.

In the end, halfway to Tonga, we had to put in to Palmerston Atoll. Passing this remote outpost we'd been horrified to discover that sea water had siphoned into the engine cylinders during the sail and had also mixed with the oil. The pass into Palmerston's lagoon is too shallow for the keel of a yacht and we were a little worried about hanging off a precipitous coral reef. As we ran down the lee side of the atoll towards the largest *motu*, we tried calling on the radio and were immediately answered by a New Zealand/Polynesian accent: 'Hello *Upshot*, this is Palmerston Radio, there'll be a boat out in a moment to show you where to anchor . . . by the way welcome to Palmerston, my name is Melbourne Marsters.'

At that moment an open boat roared up from behind us and a little boy jumped onto our deck.

'Hi, I'm Lihai Marsters and that's Ned Marsters in the boat, follow him.'

Soon afterwards, another boat was alongside:

'Welcome to Palmerston, I'm Bob . . . '

'Marsters?' we interrupted.

'Yep, we're all Marsters here.'

'How many?'

'Sixty.'

In 1862, Lancashireman William Marsters arrived on this isolated speck in the Pacific to set up a coconut plantation. He brought with him three Cook Island sisters, married all three and had 26 children. He divided the main *motu* and remainder of the atoll between the three branches of the family (now numbering hundreds, spread through the Cooks and New Zealand) and established strict rules about inter-marriage. These rules have undoubtedly worked and all the islanders we met were particularly astute.

Nowhere on our travels has the hospitality compared with that we received over the next day and a half. Bob stood by to ferry us back and forth whenever we requested it, and if we didn't eat ashore because we were working on the engine, then food was brought out to us. The following day was a Sunday and a strictly observed day of rest. I will never forget dressing up for one of the three services, where the shadows of palms and breadfruit trees played against the walls inside the little church and we were lifted by the shrill harmonies of the English and Cook Islands Maori hymns.

After more prayers in one of the very basic houses, we joined one of the three families for Sunday lunch. And what a lunch! Outside a house, and stretching the whole length of it, was a table totally covered in dishes of food. Up until now the only produce we had seen from an atoll were coconuts or fish and Palmerston was lucky if a supply ship arrived more than three times in a year. In front of us were roast chickens and pork, all manner of fish, potatoes, bananas, papaya, taro root, bread fruit and far more that we couldn't name. A well needed leg stretch around the *motu* after lunch revealed the secret.

Over the last hundred years, the Marsters families had dug down into the coral and sand to build impressively sized artificial hills and valleys. The thin soil from under the trees and scrub had been scraped into these areas where rain would collect and the result was an area as abundant with food as the most fertile plains of Tahiti. The hills also provided a place of refuge during the hurricanes that had occasionally sent waves over the rest of the *motu*.

Palmerston is too remote to receive television or radio broadcasts and they have no satellite TV or telephones as is the case with French Polynesia. If it were not for their short wave radio, videos and historical bond with England, then their unique generosity and way of life could just as well belong to another world.

Missionaries and Kings

That evening the wind picked up and stories of wrecks on the reef forced us on towards the island of Tonga. Tonga is a Kingdom, and if Kings chosen by God are omnipotent then it stands to reason that Tonga can defy the rules of science and bend the International Date Line.

Bear with me: Tonga lies east of 180 degrees from Greenwich, but their day of the week is the same as that to the west (for example, Fiji or New Zealand) or one day ahead of everywhere further north, south or east. If you are confused, then feel sorry for the Christian and Mormon missionaries on a Saturday . . . or is it Sunday? Consequently, the Tongans are the first in the world to welcome each day and plans are already being made for welcoming in the year 2,000. Cruise ships will start to party in these islands and then sail across to Samoa in time to party all over again. We sailed through this time warp at midnight on Thursday 12th September and, popping out the other side on Saturday 14th, had by the skin of our teeth avoided Friday 13th altogether.

The Vava'u Group in the north of the Kingdom's chain of islands sits on the edge of the deepest part of the ocean. At over six miles deep in places, it makes the volcanic seamounts, which break the surface and then eerily disappear, well above the height of Everest. The remainder of the islands were forced up by collision of tectonic plates, so the Polynesians had a good grip of the geology when they recount how the gods had fished the group from the sea.

We enjoyed some of our best sailing in this enchanted archipelago with good breezes, calm water and a yellow fin tuna welcoming us from the end of our line as we sailed in. A brief two weeks was spent darting between the multitude of anchorages, scouring the isolated beaches for shells and exploring the caves. One of these caves can only be entered by swimming through an underwater entrance that also allows in just enough light to see the spectacle. Once inside, your gasps of amazement echo off the cathedral chamber as a green mist appears and then vanishes with the water's surge.

The Tongans seem a gentle people, but they also carry an aura of oppression. It's taken for granted that the King cares little for elected politicians and appoints all ministers (some from his own family) but one's suspicion is drawn to the many foreign churches and missions in Tonga. After a collection in church, the amounts donated by each family are read out in descending order. A social status attached to the size of the gift is encouraged by these organisations and banks provide special loans to help people avoid the embarrassment of appearing low on the list. In effect, the congregation end up selling themselves to the church. All would be well if this wealth found its way back into the impoverished community but, after the King's cut, it disappears into the overseas bank account of the particular mission's headquarters. This has become big business with low overheads, considering that the villagers build each new church and then slaughter their animals to celebrate the opening.

Maybe things are not as straightforward as they seem, but these troubles in paradise provided food for thoughtful reflections as we sailed for Fiji.

Delhi Down Under

On this leg we really did cross the 180 degrees line. To celebrate the start of the second half of our world voyage, we worked out the longitude of friends and family in England and France and drank their health each time we crossed their respective patch on the other side of the globe. By the time we reached Ireland, it was difficult to tell who was where or what was the right way up.

'To be sure, a sort of tipsy-turfy don't you know.'

Fiji's main island was vast in comparison to anything we had seen for ages. With the exception of Panama, it felt like the first bit of mainland for over a year. We sailed straight for Lautoka on the drier western side – only the British could choose Suva for a capital, with its record breaking rainfall.

Native Fijians are not Polynesians but darker skinned Melanesians, who look very African with a tremendous seventies afro' hair style. They greet you with beaming smiles and an enthusiastic 'Bula Bula!' but Fiji is in a sad dilemma. To protect the Fijian tribal way of life, Indians were brought to Fiji by the British to work on the sugar cane plantations. After independence, the native Fijians retained ownership of the land (culturally their most valuable commodity) but the booming Indian population gained control of all the businesses. It's impossible for a Fijian to run a business, simply because, if a friend or family member walks into his shop and asks for an item, it must be given to him. There is no intermarriage and recently the Fijians have become a minority in their own country, resulting in the Indians winning the election. After two swift and bloodless *coups*, the place is now more akin to a dictatorship and the exodus of thousands of Indians has put the Fijians back in a majority – just.

This situation involving any other two differing races would be expected to lead to the most appalling confrontations, strife and even bloodshed. There is undoubtedly the faintest hint of tension and injustice, but the fact that this is about as far as it goes makes the gentle, warm and inquisitive players all the more remarkable. Away from the smells and noise of Delhi that comprise Lautoka, and into the outlying islands, not one Indian is to be found. Here the Fijian chiefs rule their villages and receive the visitors who bear gifts of *kava* – the root of the pepper plant and the basis of many cherished ceremonies.

After a month in Fiji, we hauled out *Upshot* and spent a few days scraping, sanding and antifouling the hull. I have touched earlier on the beauty of singing south sea islanders, but nothing quite prepared us for hearing these magical harmonies at midnight as we lay in the boatyard.

Ducking and Diving to New Zealand

Having witnessed the devastation of a Caribbean hurricane six months after the event, we were certainly not going to flirt with them throughout a tropical summer. A country with a population of only three million people and sixty million sheep, that can win the America's Cup, certainly deserved "a fair go". The thousand miles south to New Zealand takes you out of the tropical storm danger zone, but you need a certain amount of luck to avoid being walloped by a southern ocean gale on the final approach.

Unfortunately, weather predictions for more than three days ahead have to be treated with a lorryload of salt, so the only thing to do is hold your breath and set off. For the first five days we were lucky to have the most comfortable and idyllic ocean sailing to date. Sandrine even caught a glimpse of the elusive green flash as the sun set behind a cloudless horizon. Up ahead though, the weather pictures showed intense low pressure systems swiping the tip of New Zealand every three days. We felt rather as a hedgehog must, hoping to cross a motorway just behind a blind corner. In the end, our luck held out and on 19th November 1996 we slipped into the Bay of Islands between two active systems, after experiencing little more than a couple of weather fronts.

And what is it like here? Well, apart from a warm reception by the ex 15th/19th Hussars Customs Officer, it feels pretty cold after a year in the tropics, but the scenery is that of a subtropical Cornwall or Scotland. We look forward to seeing much more over the next few months.

Upshot is a 38' aluminuim cutter, designed by Groupe Finot, Paris and built by Metalaire Marine in the UK. She has a manual anchor winch, foot pumped cold water and an ice box. At anchor she has a large solar panel and a wind generator which is towed when underway and is almost too efficient. The navigation is comprehensively electronic with traditional backup provided by sextant and tables.

ARDFERN TO TIREE AND BACK

by Hugh Quick

Because of moving house I didn't expect to get much sailing in 1997, but an opportunity for a six day cruise appeared suddenly. About midday on 15th June I arrived in Ardfern on Loch Craignish on the West Coast of Scotland, and retrieved *Isis Tres* from her mooring. While enjoying a beer on board *Venture* with Ian and Eileen Taggart, Ian put the idea of visiting Tiree into my mind. As I had never been there, I returned to *Isis Tres* with an objective for my cruise. I was on my own because there'd been no time to find any crew.

After stocking up at the excellent Ardfern shop (open on Sunday) I set off at about 1600 and beat down Loch Craignish in sunshine against a gentle SSW breeze. I rounded the islets and rocks below East Makaskin (no signs of Conrad Jenkin who owns the island) and ran back up to East nan Gabhar and had supper in the cockpit. The breeze dropped away to nothing and the stillness was complete.

Next morning was gloriously sunny, but still a bit short of wind. I motored slowly through Dorus Mor, neap tide with me, and inspected Corryvreckan through the glasses. Even in these almost calm conditions at neaps I could see substantial waves. I decided this was not to be my first passage of the Gulf but, on my way up the Sound of Luing, I had a close look at The Grey Dogs (or Little Corryvreckan) between Scarba and Lunga. The flood had not developed fully so I decided to go through. There were some fierce eddies just west of the last islet, but no real difficulties. One advantage of The Grey Dogs over Corryvreckan is that the dangerous part is much shorter.

A light air started from the south-west, gradually increasing and veering so that I was able to beat slowly westwards all afternoon. It was lovely easy sailing with the sunlight and shadow passing over the headlands and hills at the eastern end of the Ross of Mull. At 1845 I dropped anchor in Tinkers Hole. It was quite crowded with four other boats there already and two more arriving after me. Seven boats in Tinkers Hole confirmed my impression that the west coast is rapidly increasing in popularity as a

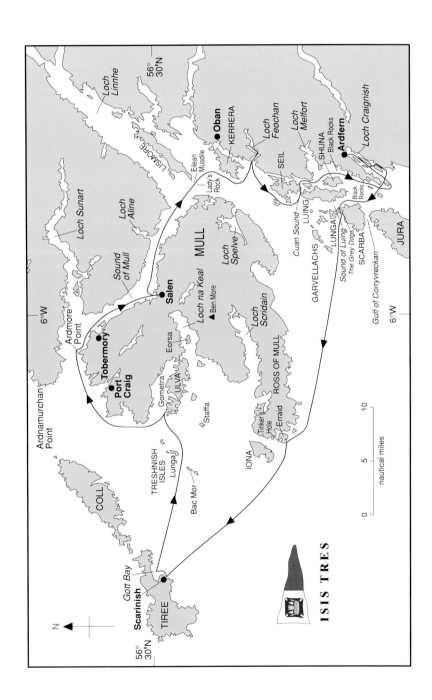

cruising ground. Judging by the English accents on the VHF, there is no doubt about the origin of many of the boats.

After supper the sun was still bright and I walked over to look at Balfour Bay, or Traigh Gheal as it is called on the chart, which is the other anchorage on Erraid. The small track is a bonus, as walking on west coast islands is often difficult with bracken, gorse and winbush covering boulder strewn ground. There were many small wild orchids I think (although botany is not my strong point). It was a perfect evening, the sun low in the west and the temperature in the 60s. Balfour Bay looked almost Caribbean with twin beaches of white sand and crystal clear blue water. It's a bit open to the south-west, but has plenty of water – I measured seven metres at half tide well into the bay where it starts to open out to the beaches.

The weather forecasts next morning suggested that Wednesday (it was now Tuesday) would bring heavy rain and winds up to F6 from the SSE. An overnight stay in Tiree therefore looked inadvisable because there is little shelter from the south-east in Gott Bay, which is the most practical anchorage for yachts. So it seemed that my visit to Tiree would have to be very brief and I should return to Mull for the night.

I had to motor to Gott Bay where I anchored at 1230. Martin Lawrence's book (Crinan to Canna) is right that Tiree has an edge-of-the-world feeling. There are banks covered with short, sheep cropped turf with huge clumps of yellow iris. Tiree has a lonely atmosphere, although the village of Scarinish fields quite a cluster of houses. Some of these houses are the old croft type known I think as 'black houses' although these were painted white. They have double dry stone walls and thatch held down by ropes weighted with stone. The thatch covers only the inner wall so that rain soaks into the earth filling between the walls, the idea being that the damp earth will exclude the fierce winter gales. The construction gives a strange effect, rather as though the dwelling is fortified.

I had forgotten to bring my camera and I wanted photographs in case I decided to write an account of the cruise (*quite so – Ed.*). While I was buying a piece of steak at Scarinish, I asked the butcher if he knew anywhere where I could buy a disposable camera. He might have given me an answer as silly as my question, but in fact his immediate response was to offer to lend me his camera, saying 'you can send it back later'. I declined his offer, but felt cheered that he had made it. On the walk back to Gott Bay I noticed plovers, oyster catchers and dunlin as well as the usual assortment of gulls.

At 1515 I got the anchor and set the main and genoa to a gentle breeze from south-by-east, heading for Gometra. I was sorry to have seen so little of the island, but there was a halo round the sun and high cloud was moving in from the west. Progress was slow and soon I set the cruising chute, which increased my speed to about 4 knots. I sighted a very large dolphin in the calm sea.

The Treshnish Islands were ahead with Bac Mor lying like a huge sombrero on the water. I don't know how this island got the name of Dutchman's Cap. In ten years in Holland I never saw a Dutchman wearing a cap that looked remotely like the shape of Bac Mor. The Scurr of Eigg and the hills of Rhum were visible to the north over Coll and the needle of Ardnamurchan light managed to look sinister even in this benign weather. I love the soft light of the west coast. Nearby grassland is a vivid green and the distant hills look hazy although one may be able to see forty miles or more. I was in the snug anchorage in north Gometra by 1930.

The wind and rain started early next morning, although not very fiercely. As I expected to have to beat down the Sound of Mull I replaced the roller jib with a smaller sail hanked to a spare forestay. I have found a partially rolled jib useless for beating. The wind was south-by-east force 5 and I was under-canvassed, but was running at 4½ knots with enough sea to make me concentrate on not gybing. Visibility was patchy with low cloud blowing across at sea level and sometimes I could barely see half a mile. I had intended to visit Port Croig, but when I got to the point where I should turn south for Croig, *Isis Tres* was reaching at 6 knots, the visibility was particularly bad and the course for Croig was straight into the rather increased wind. I decided to carry on round the north of Mull. What a contrast to yesterday's sunny ambling. The midday beer, which felt cold yesterday, felt warm today although it came from the same locker.

The lochs of the west coast of Scotland offer numerous peaceful anchorages.

When I rounded Ardmore Point, on the north of Mull, the weather began to clear and the wind to veer. I found I could just lay a course down the Sound of Mull and I carried on to Salen, which I had never visited in my many passes up and down the Sound. Salen is rather a wide open bay but there are pleasant wooded hills and the visitors mooring buoys are definitely a convenience. Ashore there was a shop (closed as it was Wednesday afternoon), a police station, ambulance, hotel, garage and telephone. My ordinance survey map suggested there might be some good walks, but I didn't try them, although it was now a sunny evening.

I was away early next morning as I wanted to catch the last of the ebb at the southern end of Lismore Island, where the stream runs strongly around Lady Rock. About 0800 a breeze came up on the nose, I stopped the motor and started beating. At 1030 I sailed slowly between East Musdile light and Lady Rock, dodging a Caledonian MacBrayne ferry on its way from Oban to Craignure. The tide was still with me.

Lack of wind made for slow progress and the entrance to Loch Feochan was not far off at the recommended time for entry (1½ to 2 hours after low water Oban) so I went in to have a look. The tide is strong in the entrance and the passage is tortuous but well buoyed, so it was all quite straightforward, apart from momentary jitters as the echo sounder went from 20 metres to 2 in a few boat lengths as we approached the bar. I had not been in to Loch Feochan before. It is a lovely soft loch with grass, trees and gentle hills, but is slightly marred by the main Oban to Lochgilphead road which runs along its south-eastern shore. Ardoran Marine maintain a good floating pontoon for loading and unloading; water and diesel are available.

At 1700 I left to catch the ebb through Cuan Sound and into Ardinamar before the tide dropped too low for *Isis Tres* to clear the rocks in the entrance. The stream was running fast out of Loch Feochan and care was required to see that *Isis Tres* was not swept out of the buoyed channel which, in places, leads across the tide. I anchored in Ardinamar at about 2000 hrs. This is one of my favourite anchorages – secure, peaceful, with good views out to Loch Melfort and Shuna and pleasant walks ashore on the island of Luing. It was one of those special west coast evenings with sun and cloud and the glorious, golden, hazy light on the hills.

As I passed close to the Black Rocks next morning, on my way back to Ardfern, there were more than a dozen seals lying out on them, basking in the sun. I drifted up Loch Craignish under the cruising chute, reluctant to reach the end of the cruise, and moored alongside at Ardfern at 1230.

It was the end of a most enjoyable little cruise and it was a pity I'd been unable to share it.

Isis Tres is a Nicholson 32 (Mark X) first launched in 1976. The main additions for short-handed cruising are a power driven windlass and an Autohelm 4000 tiller unit.

KNOCK-DOWN OFF USHANT

by Harry Franks

We were coming to the end of our summer cruise in Matawa (celebrating her 50th birthday this year). Having taken over from brother Tom in Brest, we had gone south to our old haunts in Iles de Glénan and Belle Ile, and had a delightful sail up the Vilaine river under full main and number 1. The weather had been light but we'd been able to carry our spinnaker for extended periods and managed to move well in spite of our weight. Much use had been made of Peter Cumberlidge's "Secret Anchorages of Brittany" and our total mooring fee for the two week period was 50 francs for one night in Port Tudy. Finally we had deposited Philippa in Brest in exchange for two Michael Blandys – father and son. After a quiet night a little way up the Elorn River attached to a convenient buoy, we had taken the ebb out of the Rade and were heading for Ushant.

The wind was light on our beam and we were intermittently sailing and motoring, wanting to make Ushant in good time for a run ashore that evening before an early start to head back across the Channel to Dartmouth. A few showers were threatened and there was some thunder about, but it looked like an uneventful sail as we passed Pierres Noires south-cardinal buoy and headed for Pierres Vertes west-cardinal. I was on the helm and the rest of the crew were variously loitering below, navigating, sleeping or reading. We had the engine on to hold us up to windward as the land breeze that had helped us out of the Rade had given way to the forecast northerly. The rather jagged rocks of Les Pierres Noirs were coming and going in the poor visibility to starboard, but we were well clear of them and to leeward.

As the thunder rolled round us I was idly pondering the likelihood of a lightening strike on our metal mast, when suddenly *BANG*, over we went as a massive gust hit us. For a moment I had that frightening feeling, remembered from dinghy sailing in times past, that we were going to go right over as I hung on desperately to avoid being pitched

over the lee rail. Thankfully Matawa did the right thing and slowly came into the wind, giving me the chance to check sheets. Down below, Henry on the windward bunk had been thrown across onto Michael junior on the leeward one and Tim, in the forepeak, was sure we were going to capsize. With the wind came torrential rain and much reduced visibility, and we were now, it seemed to me, being driven towards the rocks.

Fortunately Mike senior had recovered from the initial shock quickly, thrown oilskins on and was soon on deck. "Foresail down" was the order and this we soon managed, though as I checked away the foresheet, I had a glimpse of the comprehensive shredding of a sail – fortunately not a new one but a much appreciated inheritance from Christopher Thornhill's *Sai See*. We were still out of control and the wind seemed to be turning us around like a top, the sea flat but stirred by driven wavelets.

By this time Tim was also on deck and we had hands to lower the main; those rocks were looming closer in the mind by the second as we were driven on. Down came the main and I finally began to feel that I had some control, thankful that the engine was still on. I steered due south as gradually the wind subsided and the rain eased off from its frantic pelting. Soon, and with much relief, the rocks appeared still to the north of us – I'd half expected to have been driven past them! Fifteen minutes later we had the main up again and soon after that the number 2 jib, and were able to get back on our old course to Lampaul.

An hour later we were at anchor in Lampaul and entertaining three cheerful customs officers from a customs patrol boat as if we had not a care in the world. We did however notice that one or two other boats had their oilskins out to dry, which reassured us that we had not been hallucinating. The whole episode had only lasted half an hour at the most.

In retrospect, I suspect that we had experienced a mini cyclone or waterspout. This is surely why I had the impression of being driven at will through all points of the compass while we reduced sail. What warning had we had of such an event? The navigator says that he'd noticed the sky going dark; but obviously not dramatically enough to mention it to me. I suspect that I had not noticed it because I was wearing dark glasses. More important was our mind set – we'd enjoyed two weeks of calms and light airs and, perhaps out of ignorance, I associated thunderstorms with drenching rain and calm wind. I shall know better in the future. Fortunately the only damage was the sail, because that sort of experience really tests the seaworthiness of a yacht – not only the rigging but how well things have been secured above and below decks after weeks when the most extreme motion we'd experienced was the wash of passing trawlers. Full marks to the crew!

Bill Giles, Senior Met Office Forecaster at the BBC Weather Centre, comments on this incident as follows:

"It seems unlikely that a true waterspout was the cause of these locally strong winds. Waterspouts are infrequent visitors to UK waters and, when they do occur, are usually of a more savage but short-lived nature, such as the waterspout that caused such intense local damage on Selsey Bill in January 1998. However, it's interesting to note that in tropical and sub-tropical areas, waterspouts – which are essentially maritime tornadoes – can measure several hundred feet in diameter and persist for up to half-an-hour.

"The locally strong winds which *Motawa* encountered are more likely to have been caused by a kind of 'super-cell' thunderstorm phenomenon, in which cold dense air, falling very rapidly from the top of a thunderhead cloud, 'spills out' to give strong temporary surface winds that, over a small local area, seem to change direction very rapidly."

FIRST CIRCUMNAVIGATION OF BAFFIN ISLAND

by E Newbold Smith

Last August, at the instigation of the Explorers' Club, I joined 95 other creatures from many states and countries for what was billed as the 'first ever' circumnavigation of Baffin Island. The vessel on this voyage was the Russian icebreaker *Kapitan Klebnikov*, which in 1993 attempted a 'first ever' circumnavigation of Greenland. That proved a bit ambitious, as we were stuck for four days in multi-year ice north of Cape Morris Jesup, the most northern land in the world. But this 'first ever' I thought might work – and it did.

We flew 2,000 miles north from Toronto to Resolute Bay, Northwest Territory, and met the ship in a snowstorm. While waiting to board the vessel, we were bussed out to see some Thule Eskimo sites, which our resident archeologist explained in detail, bringing voices out of stones and bones.

Our first port of call was a little way east of Resolute: Dundas Harbour on Devon Island, which I had visited in *Reindeer* in 1991. The whole landscape was soft tundra, with colourful low-lying flowers – purple saxifrage and yellow arctic poppies. It was quite rocky, not easy footing for me.

In the afternoon we crossed Lancaster Sound to Cape Hay on Bylot Island, a perfectly magnificent mountainous scene, the cliffs teeming with kittiwakes and thick-billed murres. We jumped into our zodiacs to watch the profusion of nesting birds and luckily found a mama polar bear with her cub following her. Next day we visited Pond Inlet, a village of 700 Inuits, where I had spent three days in 1991. We then proceeded south, watching bowhead whales along the East Baffin coast, then stopping at Clyde Inlet, Pangmirtung in Cumberland Sound, and then down to Akpatok Island in Ungava Bay, a distance of 1,000 miles. At Akpatok there were bears on the narrow beach.

Suddenly, with no warning, a rock slide erupted and two women in

Working through the ice in Fury and Hecla Strait.

our party were struck and one seriously injured with multiple fractures of
the skull. She was flown by helicopter to Frobisher Bay and thence by
Medivac to Montreal, where she underwent surgery for four hours. We
were lucky more weren't hurt, or even killed. The Russian captain had
seen the slide and put out an emergency alert from the bridge. One
lesson of this: never explore a narrow beach with a steep cliff. The same
applies to a tall iceberg. Don't sail too close – they can tumble too.

Our next stop was Cape Dorset, the most famous source of Inuit stone
carvings. I had tried to reach Cape Dorset in 1994 in *Reindeer* but had to
bypass it, owing to an engine problem. The village dates far back in the
Inuit culture, and its location is neatly ensconced in igneous hills with a
polynia-type harbour that doesn't freeze over. Thus seals abound as well
as their predator (or other predator), the bears.

By 13th of August we were ploughing north-west in Foxe Basin
toward Fury and Hecla Strait, the very name of which sends a chill down
my back. *Fury* and *Hecla* were vessels of the Royal Navy under command
of Capt. Parry in 1822-1823. This was the second of Parry's expeditions
to find the Northwest Passage. After spending the winter amongst the
Eskimos of Repulse Bay and learning all he could about the pattern of ice
floes in the region, he managed to get his two square-riggers up into this
famous cauldron or choke point of ice flowing out of the Arctic. But he
could get no further west. With steam power he might well have made it,

because he was spot-on the most direct route to the Northwest Passage. As it was, it took another 83 years and countless lives for their dubious objective to be achieved.

Now, in August of 1997, a bunch of the boys were whooping it up on a Russian icebreaker as she cut through 9/10th ice with impunity. At Labrador Narrows, the narrowest point, we zoomed through with no resistance at all. But all of a sudden, as we turned north, we ran into 10/10ths ice with some multi-year ice three metres thick. The way the Russians steered around the hard, blue ice was like a star rugby back running wild down field without having to pass the ball. We were beginning to smell victory.

The ice in the southern part of the Gulf of Boothia began to thin and suddenly bowhead whales appeared and we watched for about an hour. Few of us, even the staff, knew that this whale even existed west of Baffin. They must have come down from Lancaster Sound, where there's apt to be less ice. Bird life also picked up – we saw Thayer gulls and arctic terns. Northern fulmars reappeared.

Once the ice pack receded we cranked up to 15 knots and headed for Fort Ross and also Bellot Strait. The latter borders the northern-most mainland of North America. Current runs up to twelve knots in the strait, so the Captain decided to tarry a bit off Fort Ross until the tide was right. Fort Ross is an odd name for just a Hudson Bay trading post. We went ashore and spooked around the two buildings that sit there,

Polar bears at play.

eroded by weather. There was plenty of evidence of animal life on the rough terrain. Indeed, a twin otter plane landed nearby with men who were going to fix up the houses for scientists to spend the winter conducting polar bear studies. One of our guides, George Hobson, pointed out where David Cowper left his lifeboat in the ice for the winter, during his successful solo transit of the Northwest Passage.

We traversed first westward into Peel Sound and then waited for the right current to return to Prince Regent Inlet. Peel Sound was chock-a-block with ice. At that point we were 120 miles north of King William Island, where Sir John Franklin is believed to have spent his last days. His vessels, H.M.S. *Erebus* and *Terror* are believed to have sunk near King William, and Canadian teams are still searching for them in an attempt to solve the final mystery in this greatest disaster of Arctic discovery.

Leaving Bellot Strait at 72° N latitude, we headed overnight for Prince Leopold Island and then Beechey Island, which at low tide is attached to Devon Island. Prince Leopold is high and steep-to, rising 1,300 feet straight up, pushed by plate tectonics that go back to the formation and reformation of Greenland and Baffin Land in pre-Cambrian times.

Prince Leopold, named by Parry after H.R.H. Prince Leopold Saxe-Coburg, is home to 86,000 pairs of murres and 62,000 pairs of northern fulmars. We made a short, non-anchoring pit stop for the bird watchers and those interested in magnificent sedimentary rock formation. We then stood on to Beechey, a talismanic piece of land that all Arctic explorers regard with hushed awe, because it's the resting place of six of Franklin's men, all young when they died during Franklin's first winter.

Entering the harbour, we passed some walruses and a few bears. After going ashore to look at the graves and the historical markers, I finally sat down on a rock and pondered. We had completed the first circumnavigation of Baffin Land. Interesting, but it wasn't that which occupied my mind. Albert Einstein once said, 'He who can no longer pause to wonder and stand rapt in awe, is as good as dead; his eyes are closed.'

My first emotion was reverence for the suffering of Sir John Franklin's men. My next was that whatever skills and culture I had accumulated over the years did not include the means of coping with an Arctic winter. Knowing Manet from Monet wouldn't be much use. My last emotion was that I did not belong there. This spit of land where I was sitting belongs to the indigenous people of the north and I was their uninvited visitor. After 3,260 miles, it was time for me to go home.

SOME MAGICAL HARBOURS
IN DALMATIA

by Rozelle Raynes

Rava Island   44°02′N, 15°04′E

This pretty green island of four square kilometres lies between Dugi Otok and Iž. It has a population of about 300, the men mostly fishing while the women tend the olive groves, vineyards and orchards. Vela Rava, the main village, stands on an inland summit and there are two small harbours, Uvala Marinica and Uvala Lokvina, on the west coast.

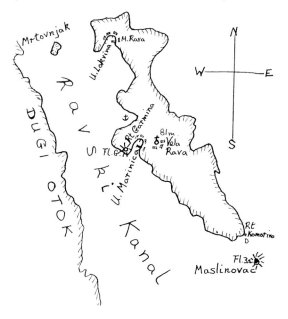

The lighthouse and monument on Maslinovac island.

Uvala Marinica, open to the south-west, has a post office, limited provisions and room for medium sized yachts.

Four cables north, after passing Rt Garmina lighthouse, is an unnamed cove, with deep water in the middle but 6–8 metres round the shore. It is open westward, but the fetch to Dugi Otok is no more than 6 cables. The cove was visited by an RCC member in 1996, who found ". . . one other boat, no houses, utterly peaceful."

Mala Rava, a hamlet around Uvala Lokvina, lies at the northern end of Ravski Kanal. It has a ferry quay and 10 visitors' mooring buoys.

Off the southern tip of Rava there is a white lighthouse and a stone monument on the islet of Maslinovac.

Uvala Statival – Kornat Island   43°51.7′N, 15° 15.5′E

Uvala Statival lies on the north-east coast of Kornat Island and is open to the south-east, but in a southerly blow there is an alternative anchorage nearby, at the north-west end of Svršata Islet.

Uvala Statival is divided into two coves. The western one is a pretty anchorage with a house on the north side and a fisherman's cottage and small vineyard at the head of the cove. There is a gently shelving sandy beach. Anchor in 4–10 metres, in sand and weed – good holding if anchor is well dug in.

You may pass either side of Svršata Vela when

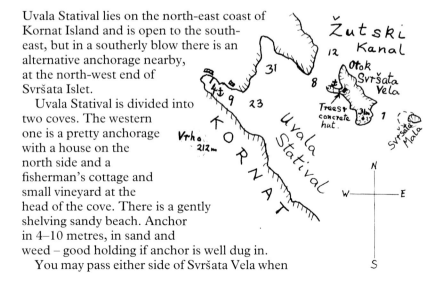

The anchorage at Uvala Statival

approaching Uvala Statival, but beware of the shallow spit jutting out from the west side of Svršata Mala if passing between the two islets.

There are no facilities at Uvala Statival, but the view from the top of Vrh, 212 metres above the bay, is magnificent. Holm oaks and strawberry trees can be found here.

Uvala Soline – Pašman Island   43°55.5′N, 15° 22′E

This bay on the south-west coast of Pašman Island is set among limestone hills covered with pine woods, olive groves, maquis and vineyards. It is the best anchorage around the island, with shelter from all directions (depending on where you anchor) and is quite unspoilt. There are no dangers in the approach, and V. Zaglav (127 metres), above the south end of the bay, can easily be identified. The central part of Soline, near the entrance, has a rocky bottom and is not recommended for anchoring, but the south end has all-round shelter, with depths from 5–16 metres and good holding in sand and weed. There is a fisherman's

The donkey shelter, my favourite house in Uvala Soline

hut and wall enclosing a shallow boat harbour there. Beware of snakes ashore!

During a strong north-westerly day breeze – the 'bura' – it's best to anchor in 4–8 metres sand at the north-west end of the bay, taking lines ashore. Pines, olives, holm oaks and pheasants abound, and you will find a charming pre-Romanesque chapel in the next bay, Uvala Sv. Ante.

Viška Luka – Island of Vis
43°04′N, 16°11′E

Vis, one of the outermost islands, is rich in traces of the Greek and Roman civilizations. In 1811 a British squadron defeated a Napoleonic one in the Vis Channel, and there are still four ruined fortresses – George,

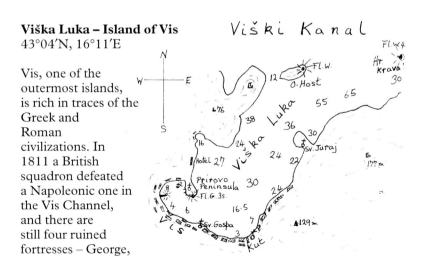

The old monastery on the Prirovo Peninsula

Wellington, Bentinck and Robertson – on the heights above the harbour.

The town and harbour lie at the head of a long inlet, open to the north-east. The 'bura' can blow with violence here and raise a big sea. The approach is straightforward with forts on either hand and beacons on off-lying rocks, all easy to identify and well lit at night.

The best anchorage is just west of the Prirovo Peninsula in 3–4 metres, keeping well clear of the ferry turning space and berth on the south side of the town quay. This is a beautiful anchorage.

Visitors may secure to the town quay, close to water, electricity, fuel and good shops. The town itself is fascinating.

Uvala Stiniva – Hvar Island
43°12.2′N, 16° 28.4′E

A small inlet on the north-west coast of Hvar, near the entrance to the Starigradski Zaliv. The surrounding hillsides are covered with lavender fields and vineyards, and a beautiful wild ravine leads

Our boat alongside the breakwater at Stiniva

up to Brusje (4 kilometres above) where there is a post office and bus-stop.

A breakwater from the west shore extends eastwards, nearly halfway across the inlet. This gives shelter from the 'bura', but a swell may cause discomfort. There are no dangers in the approach. A cross stands on the east side of the entrance, but there are no navigational lights on the breakwater. There is room for four medium-sized yachts behind the breakwater, or space to anchor in 6–8 metres in the south-west corner of the inlet.

Stivina hamlet consists of six houses near the head of the inlet. Čarne, a retired sea captain, sells fresh fish, honey and home-made wine and raki. A rough road now leads up to Brusje from above the beach. This is certainly a magical harbour.

Uvala Nečujam – Šolta Island   43°23.1′N, 16° 19.0′E

Uvala Nečujam is a wide wooded bay on the north coast of Šolta Island, where many new holiday homes are now appearing on the surrounding hills. But there are two unspoilt coves at the head of the bay, one to the north-west and the other to the south-east.

The north-west cove has all-round shelter in 3–6 metres over a sandy bottom, with good swimming. There are plenty of pheasants in the woods. We shared the north-west anchorage with two other boats in May 1997 and found it very peaceful.

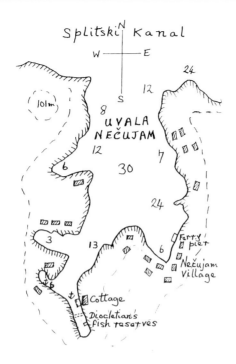

The cottage and landing-stage in the SE cove

In the south-east cove there is a primrose-yellow cottage with a small landing-stage (where you can bring a line ashore) and a path leading to Nečujam village, which has two shops and a ferry pier. A short distance south-east of the cottage, the cove is divided by an underwater stone wall, less than a metre below the surface. It was used, nearly 2,000 years ago, to enclose Diocletian's fish reserves.

Uvala Stipanska – Island of Brač   43°22.6′N, 16° 26.8′E

A delightful small cove on the north-west corner of Brač, only 10 miles from Split. No dangers in the approach, but the south-facing entrance can be difficult to find until the ruined mansion on the east side of the inlet can be seen.

Anchor in 3–4 metres, sand and weed, good holding. Sheltered from all directions except south. Take lines ashore to limit swinging space in midsummer, when Stipanska is very popular. Beware of various rocks near the west shore. We shared the anchorage with one other boat in May 1997.

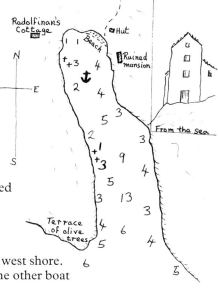

The anchorage and ruined mansion from Radolfinan'. cottage.

The Splitska Vrata – The Doorway to Split – between the Islands of Brač and Šolta, seen from the terrace of olive trees above Stiplanska Cove.

There is a hut and a small beach at the head of the inlet, with Radolfinan's old cottage above. A message painted on the front wall says; "Do not come here with evil in your heart." Olive and fig trees, climbing roses and millions of wild flowers abound, and there is a terrace of olives from which you can watch the ships steaming through the Splitska Vrata. The place is quite idyllic in springtime.

Uvala Luka near Povja – Island of Brač   43°20.4′N, 16° 48.0′E

This is the most westerly cove in a large bay on the north-east coast of Brač. One of the safest and most sheltered anchorages in this part of Dalmatia, the bay is entered from the Brački Kanal between Crni Rat and Rt Povja (with a lighthouse flashing 3s, 7M).

Do not hug this point too closely. There are no other dangers in the approach – the town of Povja lies ahead and Uvala Luka (no lights) due west. There are three coves to choose from, all with sandy bottoms and good holding. You can ride out a 'bura' with impunity

On the beach in Uvala Luka with the mountains of Bosnia on the farside of the Brački Kanal.

here. You'll find a farm house and small vineyard at the head of the middle cove, and a footpath leading across the hills. No other facilities, but Povja is less than two miles away. When the north-westerly day breeze is blowing down the valley further west, it sounds like a beautiful symphony in Uvala Luka. This is my favourite anchorage in Croatia.

GEE, SOLO, WOW

by Michael Richey

Jester had been standing on her keel outside the Museum of Yachting in Newport, Rhode Island, since the end of the last single-handed transatlantic race. After a brief refit we set sail on 25th June 1997 to arrive in Plymouth on 31st July. My preferred route lay along 40°N to about 40°W and thence, once sufficient northing had been made to allow for the Azores Current and the Iberian northerlies, more or less direct. This route has the advantage of getting off the continental shelf (where fishing vessels abound) fairly quickly and gaining a lift from the Gulf Stream into the general easterly drift across the North Atlantic. It is also the warm weather route. The weather was broadly favourable with few calms, virtually no headwinds and only the occasional blow. It was early in the year and I was in no particular hurry. All in all, 36 days seemed a satisfactory passage for a 25 ft boat. There were no incidents, although clearly some moments appeared more dramatic than others.

I had two memorable VHF encounters during the voyage, the first merely amusing. I did my best to answer a series of inconsequential questions from a pleasant sounding young American, perhaps a fourth mate bored with his watch. As he dipped over the horizon, still chatting, he asked how many were on board. One, I told him.

'Gee, Solo, Wow!' he responded splendidly.

The second encounter was more serious. In mid-July, 300 miles north-west of the Azores, a small American tanker, bound for Greenland, called me to ask whether I was able to receive weather forecasts. I was not (and cannot imagine circumstances in the ocean when I should want to be). We were, he courteously told me, in the track of sub-tropical cyclone Bill, possibly to be followed by yet another, now off the coast of Virginia, named Claudette. I thanked him for this disconcerting news and suggested he might like to report my position to Lloyd's. He seemed somewhat relieved, perhaps not quite clear where his duty lay. By then I was a bit anxious myself and wondered whether I should establish in which semicircle the boat lay, but the storm was plainly extra-tropical and there seemed little point.

That evening, however, the sky looked ominous and after running for a while at five knots under a single panel of sail I decided to heave to. The boat lay in comparative comfort that night, the wind whistling overhead. I slept fitfully, monitoring the situation from time to time. Just before daybreak the wind dropped suddenly and the seas became ungovernable. Inevitably I thought of the eye of the storm and the scene on deck was scarcely encouraging. The sky was streaked with lurid purple clouds and a great grey cumulo-nimbus cloud seemed to rise from the sea to thousands of feet.

I took all sail off and prepared to fit the hurricane hatch, a wooden plug that seals off the central control hatch. But confused as they were, the seas had little force in them and the glass stood comparatively high. In the event the seas died down fairly quickly and things started to improve. Within hours the old wind returned and we were on our way. However, next day the glass dipped suddenly and by noon it was blowing a full gale. The boat was hove-to again, heading the wrong way but being set in the general direction of our destination. An ocean gale with its vast fetch can be an awesome affair, and of course there are conditions where the sea becomes master. But the ability to ride out a storm hove-to or to lie a-hull in moderate comfort, imparts some sense of security. The

Setting off across the Atlantic towards England.   *Photo: Billy Black*

weather charts, incidentally, provide little information as to the source of this strange sequence of weather. Bill seems to have passed north-west of us, but I have no doubt we were within its orbit. Claudette, wise girl, seems to have headed for Nova Scotia.

One way and another, I seem to have spent most of my birthdays at sea since the war. The best chronicled was undoubtedly 1963, navigating the American yacht *Figaro* in the transatlantic race to Plymouth. The ebullient skipper, Bill Snaith, gives a hilarious account of the festivities in his book *Across the Western Ocean*. The most alarming was 1981, sailing *Jester* from Bermuda to Plymouth. I went north and we were off the Tail of the Grand Banks. That evening there was a sudden crash and the boat was thrown on her beam ends to port. We had been attacked by killer whales which followed us for a while, porpoising slowly, and then made off. Later in the voyage the boat suffered a knockdown which sheared the latch-gear on the wind-vane steering, so that I had to steer the last 250 miles by hand.

By contrast the conditions of my birthday this year, the eightieth as it happens, seemed idyllic. It was a day sent by the Gods, cloudless with a gentle following breeze, so that at noon I drew the cork of a bottle of champagne I had determined to keep for the arrival. I toasted my friends (not forgetting the contemplative ladies of my sister's convent who would be praying for my safety). The fact that champagne corks cannot be replaced I counted as a further blessing. *Jester*'s protective architecture meanwhile ensured that I remained inboard.

As the voyage drew to its close, with time to spare before catching the flood up Plymouth Sound, I hove-to for a sleep off the Eddystone. Later, as we approached the breakwater, boat after boat passed, their crews sitting out. I wondered what the hurry could be and why people at sea did not pace themselves better, as pedestrians and cyclists, and even motorists do. Perhaps I was still lightheaded.

Position fixing throughout was by hand-held GPS. With no call for transferred position lines, a daily fix – conveniently timed at noon – is all that is required, and four AA batteries will normally last the passage. The sextant was not used, but during the passage I tried to assess the practicability of using Sven Lundin's experimental 'Bris sextant' as a back-up to satellite navigation. My general impression was that, in spite of its limitations, such a device could well point the way towards a simpler and inexpensive form of back-up astro-navigation.

INCONSEQUENTIAL RAMBLINGS IN HOME WATERS *MORVEN* TO MORVERN

by Robin Bryer

Roger Pinkney told me that he never read or wrote another log after he finished editing the Journal. The latter has certainly proved to be the same with me – until now. Three blissful weeks on the west coast of Scotland bring me back into print again.

Morven is well described in the 1934 *Yachting World*, so I need say no more about her here. In any event, the blue book records that she was designed by Watson and built by Robertson. She was an impulse buy upon which I resolved during a ten minute chance visit to Ardrishaig. Her previous owner, Gordon McNair, agreed to my continuing to base her in those waters, so long as I kept her in perfect condition which (with his help) I resolved to do.

In the summer of 1996, Jinks and I split our time between *Frisk* at Dinan and *Morven* at Crinan – we strongly recommend basing boats at places with an 'inan' ending. Rediscovering the waters of Kintyre and the Clyde, I found that I had acquired a sweet vessel combining the qualities of a Folkboat and a Vertue, pre-dating them both and having the added attraction of being unique rather than oft repeated and adapted. This summer saw *Frisk* undergoing a major refit ashore with *Morven* the centre of my attention afloat.

Immersed herself in things equestrian, Jinks sent me north with Vicky. As dusk fell we sped along the shores of Upper Loch Fyne, round Lochgilphead to the still waters by the quay at Ardrishaig – to find *Morven* high and dry with (mysteriously) water up to her floorboards and her rigging incomplete. It was not a propitious start.

Jack Kaye, the proprietor of the boatyard, appeared at my side and explained that, when they put her in the water, they had decided it was prudent to remove her quickly and attend rapidly to her seams. A month longer on the hard than usual had probably resulted in the sun getting to them. The next morning, 30th May, it was a relief to find *Morven* floating and the water, once pumped out, returning in no more than the tiniest trickle.

I moved her to the pierhead where Jack swung from the jib of his crane to complete her rigging, following instructions from Gordon McNair who was understandably preoccupied with the imminent nuptials of his daughter.

"I'm just off to Oban to hire one of those," he said, pointing at my kilt. I offered to lend him one of my spares instead, but he declined.

By 1400 all appeared to be fairly ship-shape so we set sail, so we said, for Otter Ferry on the eastern shore of Upper Loch Fyne. However, the light south-westerly breeze found us instead laying a course southward towards the mountains of Arran, having first tea and then supper as we went until, in the gloaming, we picked up a mooring, as the log reports, "two coves short of Portavadie."

The next morning I slipped at 0600, sailed and drifted for two hours and finally motored to Ardlamont Point. This we rounded at 0900 and found ourselves beating against a fresh easterly up the Western Kyle, the water sometimes bright and glistening and other times calm and glassy as the wind played with us down the glens of Bute on the eastern shore. Tignabruaich somehow looked more French, Swiss or Italian than Scottish, with villas surely more reminiscent of a lakeside than a lochside.

We slipped through the southern entrance of the little harbour behind Eilean Dubh, waving to the yachts anchored there for lunch and out again into the entrance to Loch Riddon. Then we bore away to the Burnt Islands, just laying our course down the East Kyle. All the time, there was a procession of yachts motoring, fair wind or foul, in the opposite direction. They reminded us of a nature film of ants moving between one dung heap and another. In this case, however, we surmised that they were heading from Kip Marina to the marina at Tarbert. All, it seemed, had heeded the pilot notes that the winds are fickle in the Kyles, but it is just that fickleness which makes these some of the most attractive waters in which to sail. An honourable exception to these yachts with their sails tightly furled was the America's Cup Challenger *Sceptre* (like *Morven* in the waters of her birth) and a Gauntlet from my own native waters of Lymington.

In the less sheltered waters of Rothesay Bay we charged along, powered by a stiff breeze northward from Ardyne Point where I had been involved with the planning of the oil platform construction site but where all is quiet now. Then we were into the Firth of Clyde, sailing with a leisurely breeze abaft the beam down Bute's prosperous and wooded eastern shore, glimpsing the steep roofs of Mountstuart which reminded me of the hospitality of the much lamented John Bute, the late marquess.

In the mid afternoon we picked up a buoy off Millport on Great Cumbrae, happy not to have resorted to the engine from Ardlamont onwards. The previous year, Jinks and I had sat in the cockpit on a memorable Sunday evening listening to the carillon ringing out from 'the cathedral of the Isles' but never landed. This Saturday afternoon, however, provisioning beckoned. Vicky and I found ourselves sucked up by a mass of humanity come 'doon the water' from Glasgow. It was a relief to be back on board again.

Next morning I went ashore again to take the rubbish and find water. Our rubbish was nothing compared with what was blowing along the deserted promenade and the water, in the revolting public conveniences, did not inspire confidence. With relief we slipped away at 0730 with a brisk easterly behind us which, with *Morven's* large main and running backstays, tends to set the adrenaline a-bubbling, for it would be sad indeed to lose the upper reaches of her slender spruce mast. We past north of Little Cumbrae and south of Garroch Head, the southern tip of Bute.

Now this sparkling, spanking sail gave way to a gentler reach through Inchmarnock Water, across the entrance of the West Kyle and back whence we had come up Loch Fyne. It was amusing to see the procession of boats which had passed us in the Kyles the day before, solemnly motoring back towards the Clyde. Such is the attraction of Saturday night in Tarbert. How kind of marina operators to channel yachtsmen's activities in such a fashion, leaving us hundreds of square miles of water and deserted anchorages to explore, drifting at 0 knots or creaming along at 6 knots, according to the wind.

At 1300 we entered Upper Loch Fyne and there, on our starboard beam, was our original objective, Otter Ferry. However, it was far too early to lower sails for the day. Instead, we pressed on to Castle Lachlan, using Eilean Aoghainn as our turning point at the Minard Narrows before running back to Otter Ferry, picking up a visitor's buoy provided by the hospitable Oyster Catcher Inn there at 1800.

Otter Ferry is close to ideal. The white painted inn presides over the quay. Hills shelter the mooring from the east and the spit (or otter) curves westward, protecting Upper Loch Fyne as Hurst Spit protects the Solent, far down to the south. To get an appetite for supper, we walked uphill until we could see across the intervening Kintyre Peninsula to the Paps of Jura.

Supper was good but the night, though secure, was disrupted by tidal eddies bringing us up against the buoy. Though it would seem churlish to complain, it was a relief to slip the mooring at 0700 to head back to Ardrishaig and thence back south toward the in-tray on my desk. However, one last anchorage beckoned. At 0730 we dropped the hook in the little bay at Port Ann behind Glas Eilean, where we had the sort of breakfast that perfect cruises are made of. We were under way again at 0830 and into the sea loch at Ardrishaig at 0930, mooring alongside *Morven's* accustomed pontoon berth at 1000. It had been a roundabout way of moving her from the yard into the canal, but all the better for that.

Morven in the Garvellachs.

*A good supply of
Largavulin
whisky – perhaps
a little more than
Morven could
hold.*

One cannot read the sign as you leave Ardrishaig which bids "haste ye back" without a lump in the throat. Bowling along in an open car is a grand enough experience. Nonetheless, we looked with longing at Port Ann and the Minard Narrows as we motored by. Fortunately, however, no-one else was out there upon the water – our water – to make us feel envious.

I returned alone on 11th July on my way to Aberdeen to sign copies of the second edition of *Jolie Brise – A Tall Ship's Tale*. I had hoped to bring a bunch of hearty young men and women to help me get *Morven* through the canal from Ardrishaig to Crinan. Today, however, while students find time to go to really far flung places, they are far too busy serving behind bars and otherwise making money to find time to go to near-wilderness areas closer to home. So feeling very extravagant, I engaged the services of a professional canal man, Mr Ian Macondoer. Another yacht going through engaged a younger colleague of his. Together, they ensured us a smooth passage with locks opening as we arrived. I reflected that it was in fact no extravagance to give Mr Macondoer his fee of £35, compared with what I would have spent in keeping a bunch of youngsters in food and drink and being grateful for their 'free' assistance.

Mr Macondoer and I parted company at Bellanock, the wide bay which lies a lock and a bridge short of Crinan itself. Here I picked up a buoy, centre stage so to speak, below the little white chapel which presides over this semi-natural amphitheatre. This I resolved would be *Morven*'s new base, ideal for my son William, happier on a horse than in a boat, to use her as a floating croft which indeed he and his girlfriend happily did a week or two later.

3rd August saw me embarking upon my prime summer's objective – a voyage to the distilleries of Islay and Jura. Step-son-in-law Terence was my crew, his wife as immersed in things equestrian as my own. The next day, after fitting a new running backstay, we got underway at noon. Three minutes later the engine cut out. William, in his zeal to make sure that all cocks were turned off before departure, had cut off the fuel line. Drifting down a canal, however, you could not hope for a safer spot in which to learn how to bleed your new boat's engine.

Used to slipping in and out of the sea lock at Ardrishaig almost on demand, it was a revelation to find Crinan so busy. It was not until 1500 that we were out into the sparkling sea again. Most yachts make a bee-line northward towards the Dorus Mor. Perhaps one in a hundred go, instead, as we did south-west down the Sound of Jura. We had a light north-easterly which bore us gently down towards the Paps of Jura, which formed a marvellous backdrop beneath our boom – behind which, in due course, the sun set. We came at dusk inside the Small Isles to pick up a mooring off Craighouse on Jura, dominated by the none-too-smart distillery buildings.

Ashore the next morning I found Craighouse to be a 'take-us-or-leave-us' sort of place, more or less deserted. I found peaty water at a tap behind the hotel where there was a notice in the bar window which did not encourage either women or children. We slipped the mooring at 0900 on 5th August. *Morven* had a brisk reach along the Jura shore and then across the southern entrance to the Sound of Islay. I wondered for some minutes whether we had too much press of canvas, as I looked to windward towards the hazy outline of Kintyre and the serried ranks of breaking waves marching towards us. One, indeed, chose to arch over my head and drench me, but the inside of my kilt remained dry, so I resolved to press on without reefing. Soon we closed Ardmore Point, ticking off the islets as we sailed past until, first, we saw the distillery at Ardbeg and, just beyond it, that of Largavulin.

Navigating this way, it has to be said, is relatively simple because the distilleries are painted a brilliant white and have their names emblazoned, feet high, across them. Indeed, in the case of Largavulin, the admirable Martin Lawrence tells you in his yachtsman's pilot just which part of the name should be obscured as you approach it by the intervening Dunyveg Castle. We rounded up under the remains of the castle ramparts and lowered the main before negotiating the dog-leg entrance to the rock-sheltered bay and the visitors moorings, hospitably laid by the distillery. It was 1215 and we lunched, well pleased with our morning's sail. On the one hand we were looking at the fine stately buildings of the distillery where they make my favourite whisky; on the other, at the much smaller castle, a pile of stones whose diminutive size today belies its great significance in Scottish history. Stronghold of the Lords of the Isles, it served as a pivotal link between Scotland and the Irish coast, low down on the horizon to the south-west of us. Kintyre, with its tide rips off the Mull was – and is – far inferior as a 'stepping stone' despite being part of the mainland.

That afternoon we went on a guided tour of the distillery as impressive inside as out. As we returned to the boat down the alleyway which leads to the pier between the bonded warehouses, we almost swooned with the heady smell of the 'angel's share', the fumes that escape through the ventilators to the outside world. We then walked to Laphroaig and saw the house where lived an ancestor of Terry's, who had the agreeable job of being the Excise man attached to the distillery there.

That evening, we climbed Dunyveg Castle and then walked along the springy turf to the next bay. Never, surely, did industrial buildings have a finer setting; nor, indeed, such a noble calling. Back on board, our minds turned to more prosaic matters – the Calor gas only just lasted long enough to cook our supper. So we sailed at 0700 next morning down to Port Ellen, where we lay for half an hour alongside another yacht on the pier and acquired our gas and, for comparative purposes, a bottle of Jura to add to that of Lagavulin which we'd acquired at source.

We set sail again, tacking into a light north-easterly until, deserted by

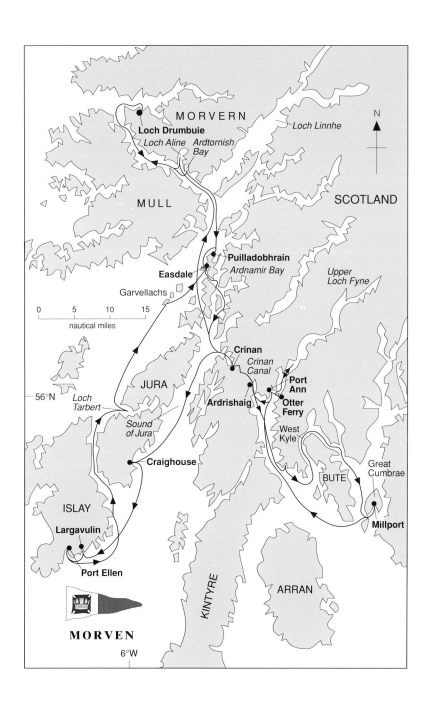

MORVERN

the wind, we motored up the coast back to Ardmore. Since we had to motor, a little close navigation seemed an appropriate distraction. I decided to pass inside the islets off Ardmore Point, posting Terry at the bow to look out for submerged rocks. Reading from the pilot, I told him that Michael Gilkes was credited with rediscovering this passage. At that moment, out from the shore, came a small motor boat with an un-mistakable figure at her helm. As she hove alongside I said "Hello Michael, we were just talking about you." He signalled to us to follow him through what has become known as Gilkes' Back Passage (inappropriately because, as an opthalmic surgeon, his concern is with an entirely different part of the body).

We waved farewell in good Dr Livingstone fashion, without any expressions of surprise at our encounter. Terry came aft, shaking his head, observing that, if I were to take him through the Magellan Straits, doubtless Magellan himself would come out to show us the way. I doubted he would, however, because (so far as I can recall) Magellan was not an RCC member. Terry mused a little more on the coincidence and said that, doubtless, Michael Gilkes lived nearby. "No," I replied, "he lives in Sussex." Terry shook his head at this further example of the mysterious ways of the Royal Cruising Club.

Clear of Ardmore Point, the tide carried us rapidly through the Sound, whisking us up past Port Askaig in blissful sunshine. As we came out along the western coast of Jura, the slackening current and increasing wind made sailing feasible once more. The four Paps of Jura, west of us at sunset on the first evening of our distillery cruise, were now to the east of us as we rounded into Loch Tarbert, that great loch which almost cuts Jura in two. We coveted the house at the foot of Glen Battrick as we sailed by, and some miles on came to the only other house on the loch, the so-called Bothy on the north shore. We anchored in the bay by this deserted building and, appropriately, drank long and well from our bottle of Jura whisky after a good supper.

Next morning we went ashore at 0800 and climbed the hills immediately above the anchorage, photographed deer and then returned to the boat again for a good breakfast. Then we set out on a lively sail down the loch and up the Jura coast, standing westward to avoid the Corryvreckan, laying a course for the Garvellachs for good measure. As the wind died completely away, the opportunity to land on the southernmost of these seemed too good to miss. We anchored between the island and the off-lying sheltering rocks and explored the remains of the monastery where St Columba's mother lived and died.

Calm though it was, this was no place for the night, so we pressed on over still-glassy waters to the old slate harbour of Easedale where we anchored off the pier and, after a good pint of beer ashore, watched the sun setting over Mull.

Next morning (8th August) we weighed at 0700, sailed out of the northern entrance and thence close hauled to Fladda. We tacked north of Grey Dogs, cleared Ardluing and laid a course to the south side of Loch Shuna. Then inside Reisa Mhic Phaidean and through the Dorus Mor, arriving at Crinan at 1330 having had an extremely light head wind but a fair tide all the way. Others, apparently with no concern for fuel consumption and no particular regard for sailing, motored past us in a steady stream. They need not have hurried because we joined quite a traffic jam at Crinan. The fishing boats took priority, since the weekend was upon us, passing through the sea lock ahead of us yachts. It was not until 1500 that we picked up our mooring again at Bellanock. We left the next morning at 0600 hours in pouring rain and a gale lashed at us as we drove over the Rest and Be Thankful Pass, well pleased at choosing our sailing weather so well.

It had seemed hardly worthwhile bringing the bottle of Jura whisky with us, so little remained in it. Back home in Dorset that evening, I found among my post a box from the *Daily Telegraph*. I had recently won a *Telegraph* competition and been promised a bottle of champagne. I assumed this was it, but I found instead they had sent me . . . a bottle of Jura.

I sipped it thoughtfully, looking out over the soft Dorset landscape, remembering the Inner Hebridean loch where I had last tasted it. Why had they sent me whisky rather than champagne? Perhaps it was because I'd been clad in a kilt when they came to visit me. Even so, why did they send me Jura? Ours not to reason why, but simply to be thankful for good sailing and good drinking.

Fashion Note: I strongly recommend the kilt when sailing. The pleated backside cushions the buttocks when sitting on hard cockpit coamings. There are no trousers to get wet when leaping out of a dinghy onto a seashore. It is infinitely easier to get into in a small cabin or to find ones way out of in the heads. Spread from chin to toe, a kilt also makes an adequate substitute for a sleeping bag. When raining, an oilskin coat covers all. The navy blue and dark green of the Universal tartan is particularly appropriate when sailing along a wooded shore. When falling in, initially it billows out around you, giving support. When sodden, however, it can easily be discarded.

A LOOK AT THE LOFOTEN
TROUBADOUR'S MAIDEN CRUISE

by Stuart Ingram

This is the cruise for which the Claymore Cup was awarded.

Now there could be no excuses. A new boat, purpose built to our requirements, a strong crew and a clear month away. *Troubadour*, designed by Mike Pocock, is a solid 13½ metres of wood and epoxy, bringing together all the yacht building expertise of Lymington. She had been launched at the beginning of April. Over the years, Annabelle and I have invested to ensure that our two sons took to sailing; now was the chance to look for the return. Peter, a cadet member of the RCC, has already appeared more frequently in the Journal than his father twenty years a member. Alistair at 22 has also had much sailing experience. But although we had all been cruising in various parts of the world, it was seven years since we last sailed together as a family.

Just before 0200 on Sunday 15th June, the boys staggered on board. Alistair was finishing at University and he and Peter had been engaged in the final round of parties. As we motored out of Lymington I felt like the captain of a New England whaler with a crew recruited from the grog shops, but by the time the sea breeze picked up in the late morning, after a night of motoring through the calm, they were fully recovered. The smaller spinnaker was set at Beachy Head and there followed a great run down to Dungeness before the wind died. At 1900 we passed Dover, catching the turn of the favourable tide and gaining the extra push into the North Sea.

A night of light south-easterly wind carried us across the Thames Estuary and along the East Anglian coast, but high pressure was building over Dogger. Peter and Alistair worked hard to keep *Troubadour* moving over the smooth sea in the dying breeze until finally, at 2330 on Monday night, the engine was needed to maintain progress through gas and oil platforms. Over the next two days progress continued with long periods of motoring interspersed by short periods of sailing. On the smooth sea, nine knots of true wind from anywhere on the beam would give us six knots of boat speed through the water, but if the wind dropped below this our progress, even with the feathering Maxprop, slowed.

The calm conditions did allow time to come to terms with some of the new equipment on board. At the chart table Peter had set up the ICS Navtex, but surrounded by computer and printer he was having less success with the Weatherfax. Meanwhile the PUR water-maker got quietly on with turning 15 amps of 12 volt electricity into 2½ gallons of freshwater each hour. Four hours a day gave enough for comfortable usage including showers when wanted. The refrigerator was closely monitored. A generous four inches of insulation had been built in and we expected to have little trouble keeping meat frozen in cool northern waters. The full range of Autohelm's new ST-80 instruments and autopilot were a daunting prospect and the manual was constantly being consulted. When I complained about alarms going off all over the place and never knowing which new toy was the source, Alistair sought to reassure me.

"Don't worry Dad, they're young, its just attention seeking. When they get older they'll stop communicating with you altogether." A wry sense of humour.

Just before midnight on Wednesday the wind began to pick up from the south. At 0200 Annabelle came to take over the watch. She found both the boys up and reluctant to go below. It was a beautiful night and as the sky began to lighten the grey outlines of mountains appeared on the Norwegian coast. We ran on steadily with the full main and the genoa boomed out. By mid-morning, as the wind eased slightly, we set the big pale blue spinnaker with its decoration of musical motifs, covering 40 miles in the next five hours before the wind began to die. Eventually we motored through the outer islands into the skærgård, the inshore lead, crossed the entrance to the Sognefjord and anchored at Hosvåg (Ytre Sula) (61°02′N, 4° 43′E), having covered 710 miles from Lymington in five hours short of five days at an average speed of just over six knots.

When planning the cruise we had known that with the Lofoten over one thousand miles as the crow flies from Lymington, we had set ourselves a tough target to get there and back in one month. Having reached Norway, we'd have to use the long hours of daylight to keep moving through the skærgård. It was fortunate that Peter and Alistair, with university training, were almost entirely nocturnal creatures, whereas Annabelle and I had our body clocks set to more conventional hours. A pattern was soon established whereby we made the early morning start and the boys surfaced mid-afternoon to take over; having all had supper together, it was parents turn to flake out. *Troubadour* then continued to follow the intricate route piloted by the boys, who would

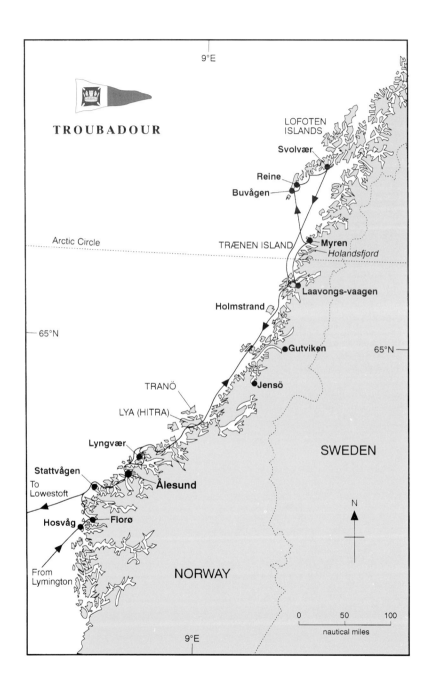

TROUBADOUR

LOFOTEN ISLANDS

Svolvær

Reine

Buvågen

Arctic Circle

TRÆNEN ISLAND

Myren
Holandsfjord

Laavongs-vaagen

Holmstrand

65°N

Gutviken

TRANÖ

Jensö

LYA (HITRA)

Lyngvær

SWEDEN

65°N

Stattvågen

To
Lowestoft

Ålesund

N

Hosvåg

Florø

From
Lymington

NORWAY

0   50   100

nautical miles

9°E

usually find an anchorage in the early hours, enjoy a final cigarette and night cap before turning in themselves.

We did linger a night in Florö (61° 36′N, 5° 02′E) for when we went in for fuel and to clear customs, the town was decked out for the annual midsummer herring festival. It was a lively evening, eating herring from tables set up along the main street as the town resounded with music. Peter and Alistair disappeared and Annabelle and I eventually got some fitful sleep despite the noise. Just after 0400 we woke to bright sunlight and splashes as the drunken giants of the local basketball team threw themselves into the harbour, our two sons giving full encouragement but declining to join them.

Having a full, if not entirely sober crew, I took the opportunity of extricating *Troubadour* from the mass of moored boats and getting underway. As bacon sandwiches were prepared to counterbalance the alcohol, there was a minor panic as the echosounder gradually descended, finally registering under two metres. According to the chart we were in very deep water, but later we theorised that freshwater from the melting snow coming down the fjord was forming a layer on top of the heavier salt water and the echosounder was fooled by the barrier between the two. Soon we became used to the phenomenon and learnt to ignore it.

This was the longest day. The sun shone and snow glistened on peaks further inland. There was little to no wind as we motored on north. There is a gap in the inner lead at the notorious headland of Statt and the FPI warns that it can be a difficult headland to round in bad weather, but we only experienced a flat oily swell.

Aware of the high cost and limited range of food available in Norway, Annabelle had stocked the boat to ensure that we would be essentially self sufficient. As all the guide books describe the ease of catching fish, I was optimistic of supplementing our diet. In Florö I had invested in a devilish looking device called a Svenske Pilk which I was assured would not fail to yield results. North of Statt is a rocky bank with a depth of 10-15 metres – I set a GPS waypoint to find it. Once there we set about drifting slowly across. Annabelle was sceptical as I lowered the apparatus into the water and began to jig it up and down. Almost immediately there was a tug and up came a mackerel, followed a few minutes later by a large pollack, big enough to satisfy the whole family at supper. My reputation as a fisherman soared as we continued on our way.

Three days later it was 24th June, midsummer's day and our silver wedding anniversary. At 1915, as we slipped into the deserted anchorage at Jensö (64° 35.2′N, 10° 50.0′E) formed by a group of islands and populated by sea eagles, the telephone rang. Friends and family called with their congratulations as the champagne corks popped. It seemed quite incongruous that with the high mountains VHF reception was poor along the coast and even the Navtex signal disappeared for days despite our expensive masthead aerial, yet the GSM mobile phone never lost its signal. They may be the curse of modern society, but that evening it was wonderful to be right away yet still in touch. After a celebration supper we sat in the cockpit at 2300 enjoying a brandy in the daylight.

Light northerlies and clear blue skies persisted and continuing north we enjoyed wonderful scenery. Torghatten, the mountain with a hole right through, was inspected in the evening light, and next day passing Alsten we were able to admire its seven snow dusted peaks, the Seven Sisters. Just over a week after reaching Norway, and 500 miles through the skærgård, we crossed the Arctic Circle. The line was marked by a metal sculpture of a terrestrial globe set on the islet of Vikingen – five sea eagles wheeled around it in the clear blue sky. It was just after midday and, with the breeze picking up, we bore away to sail the 15 miles up the Holandsfjord and tied to a pontoon at its head.

Walking ashore around the lake to the foot of the magnificent Svartisen Glacier, we split apart. It was as if after almost two weeks together on board with only the briefest of breaks ashore, each needed to find their own space. As we returned to *Troubadour* to sit in the cockpit and admire the magnificence of the glacier, the Norwegian royal yacht *Norge* came to do the same. We sailed and then motored back down the fjord in the evening to reach Myren (66° 47′N, 13° 20′E) a quiet anchorage close by.

Next day, as we passed the headland of Kunna, a wonderful vista opened up. The snow covered peaks of the outer Lofotens could clearly be seen 60 miles away to the north-west. It was too tempting. We set a course for the southern end of Moskenesöya, gliding across the smooth sea of the Vestfjord in a light force 3. The whole semicircle of the Lofotens, Vesterålens and snow-capped mountains of the mainland opened around us.

We sailed on through the gap between Moskenesöya and Værøy. This is the Mælstrom of Viking legend, but it was showing barely a popple. Out in the ocean west of the Lofoten, with an unencumbered northern horizon, we watched the midnight sun before anchoring close-by in the remote bay of Buvågen (67° 50′N, 12° 49′E) at 0130, the sun climbing steadily in the sky.

The following day in Reine we enjoyed an excellent fish supper at 'Gammelbua' restaurant, but moored up by a warehouse full of dried cod one's nose ensures that you never forget the primary local industry. Sund, close-by, is much visited by summer visitors either in coaches from cruise ships or touring in campervans.

In a cold northerly wind blowing off the mountain tops we had a glorious reach across to Svolvær. As the BBC World Service described Britain as enjoying the wettest June this century, there was a certain vicarious pleasure to find oneself north of the Arctic Circle in the Lofoten with clear blue skies and snow capped mountains. In Svolvær

A typical village in Lofoten.

Troubadour creaming along.
Photo: Patrick Roach

we did a little shopping and, having reached 68°14′N, prepared to start south.

At 0540 next morning, 1st July, Annabelle and I got *Troubadour* underway. Clearing the harbour we found a force 3 from the north and set full sail. For sometime the boys had made clear their view that Dad was not sailing his new boat as hard as he should. So at 0730 Peter came up and we set the smaller spinnaker as the breeze increased, and then increased. Soon the windspeed was over 20 knots true and we really began to move. Peter and Alistair took turns to helm, the seas built up and *Troubadour*'s speed reached 12 and then 13 knots as she surfed. A further increase in the wind and suddenly the boat speed hit 16.1 knots! It was a long way home and enough was enough. Despite having a snuffer, recovering the spinnaker proved far from easy, mainly as there were four different opinions on how it should be done.

We woke early in the Trænen Islands next morning. The weather was overcast with drizzle and the wind had switched round to the south. Our anchorage was unsatisfactory in these conditions and we got underway to reach back into the inner lead. Over the next few days as we headed south, the weather became more mixed including a morning of fog. Inevitably, the northerly winds that had dogged our progress north disappeared. Revisiting some anchorages and exploring new ones, we reached Ålesund six days later. The morning was spent topping up the tanks and preparing for the return across the North Sea. Here, as we had often found in other harbours, there was a fishing boat selling excellent shrimps.

Having gone outside between Statt and Ålesund on the way north, this time we followed the Sulefjord, Vartdalsfjord and Rovdefjord route. This gave us an impression of the fjords, but how much we wished as we passed its entrance that we had time to turn into the Geirangerfjord and travel the 50 miles to its spectacular head. At 2330 Peter and Alistair anchored *Troubadour* in Stattvågen (62° 11′N, 5° 12′E), a dramatic inlet with a dredged entrance, well protected by breakwaters.

Annabelle and I were up early to start the return passage. At first we motored over a long smooth swell with clear skies, but in the afternoon a light wind came up from the SSE and for eight hours we sailed, covering 40 miles before the calm returned. With 400 litres of fuel, we had sufficient to cover around 400 miles, and looking at the chart and lack of wind it seemed sensible to motor towards Peterhead, 300 miles away. However at 0945 next morning there was 7 knots of wind from the NNW and we hoisted the large spinnaker which allowed us to creep forward at just under 4 knots in perfect peace. Our spirits dropped with the spinnaker when the wind disappeared again at midday, but three hours later it was back up once more and now the wind picked up to just over 10 knots and *Troubadour*'s speed increased to 7.5 knots in the absolutely smooth sea. Peter's log entry at 1800 just said 'Good, Good, Good.'.

It was something of a surprise that night when it became quite dark for a while. We ran on in the light winds, switching to main and boomed genoa as there were now dense fog patches and a close radar watch was needed. At one point a large course alteration was required to avoid two dots on the radar which appeared to be fishing boats pair trawling. The forecasts told of thick fog in Shetland and on the Scottish coast and we were grateful for the light breeze that had alleviated our concerns about fuel. During the day the fog cleared and it became warm enough for shorts. The spinnaker was up once more and we were entertained by white nosed dolphins, a group coming and going throughout the day. In the evening the light spinnaker caught on a mast step making a small tear, so the small spinnaker was substituted until 0230 when the wind began to go round to the east and drop. We had covered a further 200 miles under sail when the engine was restarted and were now on the latitude of the border between England and Scotland.

Throughout Friday the Yanmar thumped away except for a couple of hours in the afternoon. It was only as we approached the Norfolk coast that the wind returned and we beat down to Lowestoft, where we tied up at 1230 on Saturday, 613 miles from Norway. It seemed extraordinary that given the ease of refuelling in Norway, in Lowestoft we were reduced to filling cans at the local garage. We made two trips to collect 100 litres. Meanwhile Annabelle dashed to Marks & Spencer – we had run out of wine and the crew wanted steak for supper. In less than two hours we were at sea again, beating in foggy conditions across the Thames Estuary. Next day the sun shone but the wind went round so that we were still beating on the south coast.

We hove-to off Bognor in a SW F3 to enjoy Sunday night supper seated around the saloon table. The cruise was nearly over. Our intention had been to test the new boat and *Troubadour* had come through magnificently, but in the process we had certainly tested ourselves. Older but wiser we returned to the Solent. On Monday morning I was put ashore at 0530 in Portsmouth to catch the train to London in time for work. The rest of the family took *Troubadour* on to Lymington. The log showed that we had covered 2,766 miles in our 28 days away. "Next year" said Annabelle "we'll go to Brittany and potter." Perhaps.

Troubadour was designed for the Ingrams by Mike Pocock and built by Stephen Etherington using the Speed-strip method, in which cedar strip planking is sandwiched between epoxy glass layers. She is rigged as a cutter, although the two headsails are intended to be used either/or, not set together. Troubadour is 43ft 8in LOA, 36ft 3in LWL, 13ft 4in Beam with a draught of 6ft 6in.

IN SEARCH OF THE SALT WATER HIPPO

by David Mitchell

Steve Jones' description of the Bijagos islands in his West Africa Pilot, published by the RCC Pilotage Foundation, intrigued me – deserted islands, girls in grass skirts, outstanding fauna (the world's only salt water hippos), challenging navigation and rarely visited. I found the grass skirts and the hippos, but came away chastened by the sandbanks which recently claimed seven lives.

Dakar to Bissau

Guinea-Bissau is about 200 miles south of Dakar, past the Saloum and Cassemanche rivers (much loved by the French) and The Gambia. Bissau, the capital, is on the north side of a large estuary – the Canal do Geba – 50 miles from the coast. Members at the yacht club in Dakar

171

advised me to keep a good 30 miles off the coast to avoid the local fishing boats, most of which carry no lights. One yacht spotted a piroque just in time from the spark of a cigarette lighter. Another smelt charcoal from a stove on board a fishing boat. So every 20 minutes I turned on all the deck lights, illuminating the sails, on the basis that if I could not see them it was just as well they could see me.

It was a gentle southerly run, blown by a wind that was always in the north, until I turned in towards the coast about midnight on day two. There was a bright moon but little to see as the headland was low and the lighthouse not working. I was surprised to see that there was only 26 feet of water 12 miles off the coast and pathetically relieved when it increased to 30 feet. The ebb started just before I reached Bissau, so I had to motor against the four knot tide. In the early afternoon, I anchored in 35 feet opposite the piroque landing place, and slept.

Bissau

Immigration came alongside the next morning, asking why I had not checked in the day before and demanding $100US. I roared with laughter and we settled for $10, which was still probably too much. Ashore I found that the Harbour Master's office was shut until Monday, so I explored the town, found the British Consul, Jan van Maagen, but no mail. Nothing can have been spent on the town since Guinea-Bissau gained independence from the Portuguese in 1974 after a protracted war. The old colonial bungalows with their verandahs, shutters, painted walls, pantile roofs and attractive gardens lay neglected. Streets were heavily pot holed and unlit. From a distance, the waterfront looked charming with painted buildings of varying heights set back behind palm trees. Close up you could see the vultures on the rooftops whilst others picked amongst rubbish dumped in plastic bags. The tarmac on the port roads had long since disappeared and the buildings were splattered by mud up to fifteen feet, giving some idea what conditions must be like in the rainy season (July – August).

In the port lay the rusting hulks of barges (relics of Russian aid) and a fishing trawler. There were a few smart four-wheel drive vehicles, but most cars and lorries were battered, bent and rusting. I helped push-start a taxi with no silencer. People squatted in the roadside dust behind piles of charcoal, rice from Taiwan, peanuts, a few bananas and tomatoes. Most people are very poor, which explains why the gentleman at the Harbour Master's office demanded $116 for entering his port. I laughed, resisting the temptation to say that I was not Father Christmas, and said that I did not have the money (*never say you will not pay*). I picked up my completed papers and, forcing a chuckle, left. No one stopped me.

Bissau offers no shelter and the tide sweeps through the anchorage at 3–4 knots, so I moved three miles upstream to the Canal do Impernal,

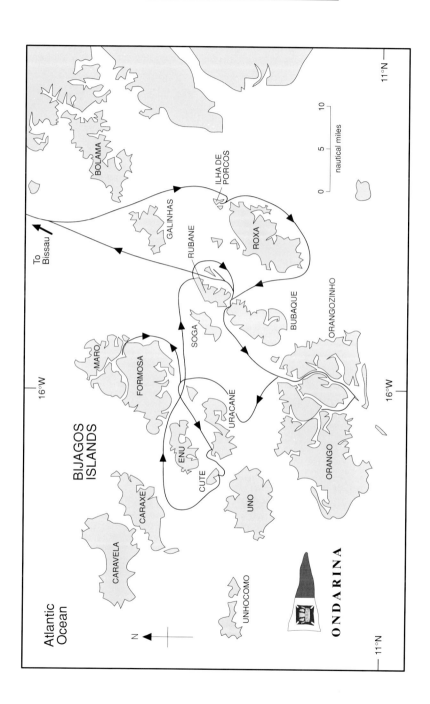

which divides Bissau island from the mainland. This mangrove lined
creek offered good holding, protection, peace and quiet. Two former
naval gun boats lay rusting in mud berths, one alongside a dilapidated
pier by an abandoned repair yard. Two dugouts ferried people to and
from the village on the mainland side across to the Bissau side. Bee eaters
darted across the water, waders worked the water-line, spoonbills, ibis
and pelicans flew up and down the creek. At night, lying in the cockpit
gazing up at the stars, I could see large fruit bats flitting around the mast.
This is the only place I used mosquito nets.

Getting ashore through the mud at low water was a novel experience.
The mainland side was not too bad, since you could land on the marine
railway and walk up the sleepers. I used this route to explore the village
hidden by palm trees at the top of a hill. Here were clusters of four to
eight huts, most built with mud walls and a palm frond roof. Each cluster
was surrounded by an insubstantial fence, while pigs, chickens and goats
wandered freely in the undergrowth. The people were friendly and there
was a boy of fourteen who spoke some English.

Going ashore on the Bissau side was more tricky, and the three mile
walk to Bissau started over dried mangrove flats, then between paddy
fields and water courses filled with blue and white water lilies. Egrets
were everywhere and I saw sandpipers, spurwing plover, three different
kinds of bee eaters, brown hooded shrike, a common pratincole and two
lovely, purple Abyssinian rollers. On the edge of town, by a rubbish
dump, I paused at a stagnant ditch for a final wash and to change out of
my sarong and bare feet into my 'meet the officials' kit of long trousers,
short-sleeved shirt and sandals.

Bijagos

Once I had cleared with the Harbour Master, I was free to leave for the
Bijagos islands, an archipelago of approximately 14 islands or, in some
cases, groups of islands covering about 180 square miles. South-west of
the islands, and protecting them from the full force of the Atlantic, is a
largely unsurveyed area of about 160 square miles described on the
Portuguese chart as *'zona periggosa com haixos e rochas'*. The Admiralty
chart says much the same but not so lyrically. The charts were a little
vague about depths in the channels separating the islands – some
channels appeared to be accessible at all times, others dried out.

My search for hippos took me to Orango. I anchored off a tiny
unnamed island where a group of straw huts, sheltered by palm trees,
overlooked a white sandy beach where two dugouts were pulled up. I
rowed ashore to explore. The huts, made of palm fronds with an earth
floor, were clustered in a haphazard way just above the high water mark.
Some people were sitting in the shade of a tree and I asked if I could walk
around. Pigs were scuffling on the beach and in the bushes. A narrow

path led through the palms and shrubs, and in the distance I could hear waves crashing on the exposed sandbanks.

I came across five men laying gutted and split fish on wire netting stretched about three feet off the ground. They were about to light a fire to smoke the fish. One spoke a little English and told me that the hippos walked along the shallows in the mornings. Sure enough, next morning, with a watery sun coming up over a vast expanse of exposed sand, I saw three hippopotamuses, two on the south side of Orangosinho and one walking between *Ondarina* and the little island. An extraordinary sight. Given more time, I would explore the island to the south which is where the hippos must come ashore at night.

The mud and sandbanks support a myriad of shore birds from the exotic – flamingos, spoonbills, pelicans, sacred and glossy ibis – to the more mundane, such as whimbrels, redshanks, oyster catchers, sandpipers, godwits, stints, plovers and terns. Anchored between the islands of Formosa and Maro, I saw wave after wave of waders flying up the channel as the flooding tide flushed them off the banks. Before dawn, I would be woken by the swish of their returning flight.

I felt safe on all the islands and left the boat unlocked when going ashore. People either ignored me completely (very African) or were extremely friendly. In Guinea-Bissau, Portuguese is the second language. The Bijagos people have their own language which other Africans find impossible to understand and learn. Anyone with a knowledge of French or English was always keen to try it out. Most had learnt their language in Senegal or Nigeria. At Urcane, I was approached by a young man who had seen *Ondarina* come in whilst out fishing the night before. He told me he was learning English from an American volunteer in Bissau. I gave him some books and received a woven basket in return.

When *Ondarina* left Guinea-Bissau it was from the anchorage off Bissau itself. It was here that I made the final preparations for our Atlantic crossing and the 2,500 mile passage to Tobago. As *Ondarina* starting to swing on the first of the ebb, it was time to leave. I motored for about ten hours until we picked up a northerly wind and cleared the coast, but we were still ducking and weaving round sandbanks made visible by the heavily breaking seas. Seventy miles from Bissau and twenty from the coast we still had only 46 feet under the keel. I dozed for a while, then woke to find the depth was over 200 feet and I could relax. West Africa had let us go, at last.

Ondarina is an Ohlson 35, launched in 1973 and refitted for a single handed, five year world cruise. She has twin 800sq.ft jibs on Profurl, Stowaway Hood furling main, two Autohelms (an old 4000 and a new 800 – both broke on the crossing) one rigged so that I can steer from the cross trees, Aries, Furuno radar to help with the watch keeping (new but broke on the crossing the scanner flooded with condensation in spite of being fitted by a qualified marine electrician).

CRUISING FOR THE MORE MATURE

by Tom Straton

A couple of years ago I began to find that sailing was getting more difficult – don't we all some time after reaching the allotted three score years and ten. I wondered if I should take to a motor boat, as many do at that time of life, but I was reluctant. Most people I've met have regretted it, and at least one went back to sail for a few more years. *Styria* is a NAB 35, ketch rigged with rolling headsail and furling main, so both these sails can be controlled from the cockpit, which is reasonably well protected. The mizzen is quite small and can be managed easily. The mizzen staysail is a fair-weather sail that is not difficult to control. I have a spinnaker which goes up in a tube, but it's only used nowadays if there is a keen youngster aboard.

In order to make life a bit easier and avoid the change to a motor cruiser for as long as possible, I had a more powerful engine. This makes it possible to travel against a strong wind and short chop, so I am able to get to shelter in adverse conditions without having to tack too much. I know there are club members who take a dim view of using the motor, but I felt it was better to have a motor boat that can be sailed, rather than just a motor boat or even no boat at all. I have also fitted davits which are a great saver of effort. An improved auto pilot took away a lot of the strain of constant compass watching on long passages.

Pat Stafford is a friend from the late 1920s, when our respective mothers bought cottages on the Devon coast to which we went in the summers, fishing and catching lobsters from rowing boats. She has become a regular crew for me since my wife Rae had an unfortunate accident with a rotary mower which deprived her of her right thumb and parts of her fingers. In mid June we worked our way west in easy stages via Portland and Salcombe, where we anchored in the lower reaches of Frogmore creek. Then on to the Yealm where we joined some friends who have a mooring right at the head of the river. The weather was not kind, so we returned home, leaving the boat in Plymouth at Clovelly Bay marina.

Bill Evans is a retired chief superintendent of police whom I first met in St Peter Port on another boat in 1966. He has sailed with me extensively since and joined *Styria* again in early July, when we set off in fine weather for France. The tide was strongly against us at the southern end of the Four Channel and we were glad of the poke provided by the new engine. In L'Iroise a pleasant breeze came in from the north-east, so we put up the spinnaker and had a grand, increasingly fast sail through the Raz de Sein to Audierne where we anchored outside at Ste Evette. Early next morning we set off in a flat calm heading south. We were between the Plateau des Birvideaux and Belle Ile motoring in bright sunshine with the autopilot in charge, when I saw a yacht on a reciprocal course coming towards us. I changed course to avoid a collision and looked expectantly over the side to give a friendly wave, but the only occupant of the cockpit had his back to me and his eyes fixed on his book. We were no more than the length of my boat apart. He was flying the burgee of a very well known Solent yacht club. I'm sure that if I'd been doing the same as he was, we would have been in collision out of sight of land and any other boat.

We spent a night in Port Haliguen, which is quite handy for stores and fuel. Then into the Gulf of Morbihan and up the Auray river. A lot of mooring buoys have now been laid where we used to anchor opposite the Bono river, so it was necessary to tie up to one (for 46 francs) as there was no room for anchoring. Next day we sailed with a brisk head wind to Lorient, picking up a mooring off the north side of Port Louis. There is a small marina here and a much larger one on the other side of the harbour at Kernevel. We then went up the river Blavet to Hennebont, which was a first for me. Moored alongside a pontoon in the town, *Styria* was the only visiting boat. The distance from Port Louis was about seven miles and the depth at the pontoon was 15 feet at HW and 7 feet at LW – the tides were neaps. It was a worthwhile diversion, attractive wooded banks, many laid up old fishing boats in varying stages of disintegration, some with masts still standing.

We sailed, and at times motored to Bénodet, where we picked up a mooring buoy above the bridge for the night. Then up the river to 'The Secret Anchorage' where the minimum depth was 13 feet. Next day we went down to the marina in Bénodet to get stores. It was slack water when we moored alongside the visitor's pontoon, but by the time we came back from shopping the ebb was very strong. *Styria* was pressed violently against the pontoon, boats were passing continuously, it was quite windy, so there was much unpleasant movement and grinding against the pontoon. As soon as the tide slackened a bit, we managed to get away with the help of four strong men and went to a mooring under the bridge. Here, next day, a charming young lady called Navette came to collect our fee and offered to run us ashore to Saint Marine marina as part of the service. She spoke very good English and was waiting for her A level results from a school that she had attended in Cheshire.

The days were fine and very windy, but the nights were quiet so we slipped at 0120 in moonlight. Although it was still dark when we passed Menhir tower off Penmarc'h point, there was no light on it. Sailing and motoring as necessary we worked our way into the Rade de Brest, and up the Aulne river to Port Styvel, where there were about eight warships laid up. This is a handy sheltered place to spend a night if you plan to go up to Châteaulin.

We slipped at about three hours before local HW and went upriver, reaching the lock an hour before HW. *Styria* spent a quiet night tied up to the bank at Port Launay and next day we went up to Châteaulin, which has a good supermarket for stocking up.

On the way back down we anchored in Porz Coz, which is about a quarter of a mile upstream from Port Styvel. This is a pleasant quiet spot with room for three or four boats just out of the main tide. We left early in the morning to head for home, reaching Fowey 25 hours later with the log reading 153 miles. Next morning, as Bill was feeling unwell and wanted to get to his home, we slipped the mooring in Wiseman's Pool and had a breezy sail to Plymouth, ending with very poor visibility off Rame Head. I was glad to have a radar as there were quite a lot of boats about.

A little 'mature' cruising in south Brittany.

In the first week of September Pat and I went to Plymouth by train and brought the boat back to her home base in Lymington, stopping for nights in Salcombe and Dartmouth. We had a pleasant trip across Lyme Bay, sailing over the Shambles four hours before HW and fetching up at anchor in Lulworth Cove. Conditions were calm, but as usual before the night was out I wished I'd put out a kedge to hold my bow towards the entrance as we did quite a lot of rolling later. Next morning we landed at Lulworth and did some shopping – there is a shop about half a mile from the landing place with very limited supplies, and a slightly better one a further half mile inland.

We were a bit put out by being requested by the firing range safety launch to sail three miles towards Portland Bill, then a further three miles south before turning east for St Alban's Head. The tide was east-going. Previously I have only been asked to go two miles off the coast. But it was a lovely day and we had a pleasant sail catching four mackerel, then anchored for the night in Poole harbour, between Goat Horn and Green Island.

The next day we had a sail tight on the wind to Buckler's Hard, where we tied to a mooring for a couple of nights and I was able to get a coat of varnish on all my bright work, before returning to Lymington for a month. I hoped to have another two weeks pottering about between Chichester and Portland before laying up.

Although I have used the motor quite a lot this season, I have also had some good sails and several short cruises, I am sure I enjoyed them more than I would have done if I had changed to a motor cruiser.

THREE HOLIDAYS IN ONE

by Katharine Thornhill

This year *Sai See* took us to the west coast of Ireland. My parents had sailed her as far as Westport, County Mayo, so I had five weeks to return her to England. Some of my friends now actually have jobs, so they were unable to sail for the whole five weeks. This worked brilliantly and instead of having one holiday, I had three twelve day cruises, dropping one entire crew and replacing it with another. Each was totally different, the only recurring theme being the huge numbers of dolphins we saw.

The first cruise was made up of university friends. Peter Ingram joined once again with a friend of ours, Nik Devlin, who sailed with us for ten days on old *Troubadour* in Greece two years ago. For a long weekend we were also joined by Clara Dolan, whose two days on *Sai See* last Autumn were her total sailing experience. This cruise was notable for its perfect weather. We started heading north as planned and had a very exciting beat up the coast of Achill Mor. The north-east wind increased and increased until we were fully reefed and we anchored in a lovely 'Irish green' bay on the north-west corner of the island, fascinated by squalls coming off the steep hills.

Conference decided that the prevailing south-westerly was bound eventually to set in again and the chances were that if we went further north we'd end up beating both there and back in order to meet the next crew in Galway ten days later. So the next day we put up the spinnaker and set off southwards aiming to reach and climb Skellig Michael – The Great Skellig. From this point on we couldn't have had more ideal weather.

We had the most dramatic night sail to Blasket Sound, with dolphins in the phosphorescence as we surfed down a rough sea with a strong following wind. For climbing the Great Skellig we had a totally calm, windless day. We motored up in low mist and the boys got into the dinghy, rowed ashore and, defying the guides, climbed the lonely rock to look at the monastery on the top. While they found a friendly

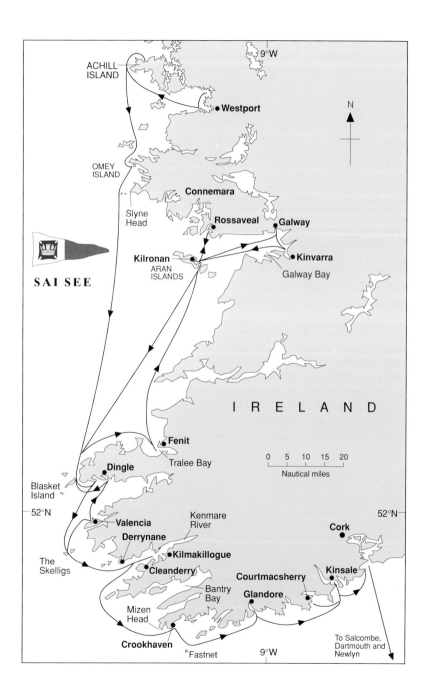

ACHILL ISLAND

9°W

Westport

N

OMEY ISLAND

Connemara

Slyne Head

Rossaveal

Galway

SAI SEE

Kilronan
ARAN ISLANDS

Kinvarra

Galway Bay

IRELAND

Fenit

Tralee Bay

Dingle

0 5 10 15 20
Nautical miles

Blasket Island

52°N

Valencia

Kenmare River

Cork

52°N

Derrynane

Kilmakillogue

The Skelligs

Cleanderry

Courtmacsherry

Kinsale

Bantry Bay

Glandore

Mizen Head

Crookhaven

Fastnet

9°W

To Salcombe, Dartmouth and Newlyn

archaeologist to tell them all about the mad monks who lived on this exposed rock, I drifted off the island in the evening light, chasing puffins and basking sharks on the water.

This was one of only two calm days in the whole fortnight and next day we had to head north again - sure enough the wind blew strongly from the SE, sailing at its best! The weather was so perfect that Nik complained he had come sailing for 'action and adventure' and we had not heeled enough for his liking. We put in a detour in order to get a windward sail.

In twelve days we'd been from Westport down to The Blaskets and Valencia, on to the Skelligs and then back to Dingle – where we had to go because Nik had read in the pilot it had 50 pubs! We then had a fantastic sail to Fenit where we picked up Clara. Another brilliant sail to the Aran Islands and a perfectly timed calm day to explore them, swim and pick up water. This was done with jerry cans. Clara and I decided to get our own back for doing more than our fair share of cooking and watched from a nearby pub while Peter and Nik lugged the heavy supplies over three fishing boats.

Galway was where we changed crew. We left Nik and Peter on the pier and motored out of Galway docks with an entirely new crew. Alistair Ingram, Digby Morrison and Cate Worsley had all been with me last year in Scotland. The only newcomer was Fiona Clark, pretty much new to sailing, and terrified she was going to be sea sick! We had eleven days to get the boat to Kinsale.

Our first stop was Kinvarra, south across Galway Bay. We were told in Galway that there was a festival of Galway Hookers, the old boats that took turf from the west coast out to the Aran Islands. Kinvara was alive in the evening with incredibly nice people, many of whom were experts on the Hookers, the far west of Ireland and the Aran Islands. The

Sai See on the west coast of Ireland.

following day we came right into the village on the tide and happened to anchor on the start line of the day's races. We couldn't have had a better view. Then we weighed anchor and followed the fleet, having a private race with one of the bigger Hookers, the *MacDough*.

Back to Kilronan on Aran Mor and again we walked along its amazing south-west coast. The plan was to sail overnight for the Blaskets. This very nearly had to change because at 1800 on a Sunday night we discovered there was not enough diesel in the tanks. We really expected to have to wait until Monday but, to our amazement, a fisherman, whose skipper was not on board, drained some diesel from his tanks and filled ours. He would not take any money but was pleased with some Guinness.

The crossing from Aran to the Blasket Sound was mostly motoring; it was very rolly and poor Fiona was quite unwell! The morning made up for the night and we had the most incredible sunrise, with a mass of diving gannets and dolphins, some with their babies. It was the most beautiful morning in the whole world, ever.

The second trip to The Great Skellig was less successful than the first. There was much more wind which made for a great day's sailing, but it was not so easy to land. Yet we braved it and Al stayed on board while the rest of us put on life jackets and clambered into our rubber dinghy with our ancient Seagull outboard, only to be met by a guide. She absolutely would not let us climb, telling us it was a spring tide. We said we knew and had decided to risk it anyway, but she stood there and refused to let us go any further. So we just had to turn around and get back into the dinghy. Our opinion of her really does not bear repeating!

Light winds followed, giving us the opportunity to fish and stroll around the beautiful gardens at Kilmakilloge, in the Kenmare River. The wind filled in just for the last three days and the final sail of this cruise was really exciting as the wind got up and up and we ran into Kinsale with a double reefed main. We didn't realise that the wind was going to keep on increasing and we were going to be gale-bound for the next few days.

On our last night, which was Fiona's birthday, we were very lucky to find a fishing boat willing to sell us enough lobster to feed us all. Whether we got a good deal or not did not really matter because we had the most amazing meal of lobster, salad and birthday cake, topped off by a midnight swim (for some of us) in the phosphorescence. A perfect end to a second perfect cruise.

The next crew joined in Kinsale and was met by a dreadful evening's weather. We saw 58 knots of wind on our anemometer in Kinsale Marina and the next morning another boat was reporting 72 knots. Once we had made sure the boat was safe, we lit the fire and had a snug evening listening to the rain pounding the deck.

The third complete crew was my sister Mary (RCC) who came almost

A bit of traditional boating, to be sure.

straight from her year off in Africa, Australia, New Zealand and North America to join us. There was also my Irish cousin Luky Barrow, who comes for a week or so every year, and two very old friends, Peter Lewin-Harris and Calum Lindsay from Oban.

Our first forecast warned of a force 10 so we decided to spend the day in Kinsale. We had met a friend of Peter's, Tinny, who had sailed with us for a few days in Scotland, and her boyfriend, Sasha. They had a car so we all piled in and went to look at the weather on the Old Head of Kinsale. We were quite glad to have stayed in! The next day they were still forecasting force 8-9. This waiting was getting boring so after a telephone consultation with my Father we decided to dash downwind to Cork. Dash we did. Peter got the boat surfing down the waves at 11 knots with just half the jib flying. It was the quickest 15 miles I have ever done in *Sai See* and probably the most exciting. Everyone really enjoyed it and we were able to take Tinny and Sasha for the sail of their lives.

Next day the forecast was for NE 3-4. There was another depression on its way but it was moving fairly slowly so we hoped to make a dash for it and cross St George's Channel between depressions. The passage began with plenty of wind, a reefed main and semi-rolled jib, and then the wind completely died and we rolled uncomfortably in a big sea. This was short-lived and we were, in the space of about half an hour, thrown into a force 8 or more. We shortened sail repeatedly until left with a tiny corner of jib. Once under control it was very exciting, but I must admit that the speed with which the wind got up was alarming.

The wind died almost entirely off Lands End and we motored most of the day, but finally got a head wind causing us to miss the tide. Eventually, we arrived in Salcombe at 3 o'clock the next morning. In Salcombe we said goodbye to Peter Lewin-Harris and picked up another friend of mine, Lizzie Wearn. She has been on every one of *Sai See*'s cadet cruises, but this year she too has a job so only had time for a week on board. Unfortunately we spent the day weather-bound in Salcombe, but eventually we left and continued our journey eastward. Dartmouth was the next stop and we all really enjoyed wandering around the town and having tea with Robert Franks. It was here we discovered that our efforts to get the boat east were futile as the Beaulieu Meet had been postponed. We therefore had to turn into the wind and try to return to Milford Haven. We were held up again in Newton Ferrers by bad weather. We did attempt to go sailing, but decided that thick visibility, driving rain and gusty winds were not going to be much fun, so we all dressed in full oilskins and went for a walk instead!

Unfortunately we only got *Sai See* as far as Newlyn before we had to leave her. My parents drove along the quay just as we sailed in and took our lines. Excellent timing.

Three perfect holidays rolled into one, and although the last was slightly taken over by the weather, they were all completely brilliant. Long live endless summer holidays and no permanent job!

Sai See is a 40ft centreboard yawl, designed by Sparkman and Stephens and built in teak, with varnished spars and bright work, by the Wing on Shing Shipyard, Hong Kong. She prefers remoter waters and is now more often than not under the command of an RCC cadet.

FEANOR'S CRUISE TO SCANDINAVIA

by Jeremy Parkinson

It was calm when *Feanor* left Kristiansand, so we motored gently through the Randösund and then the Ulvösund to enter the Blindleia. Tony and Jill Vasey had told me this would be good practice for the Swedish skjaergärd, and so it proved, although we found few leads in Sweden that were as narrow. It all looked very beautiful in the windless sunshine and, this still being early June, there were very few other craft. We anchored for lunch in a small bay on the north coast of Skaggerö, opposite Lillesand, and later had a walk through the woods on the island.

After negotiating Dybesund, a light southerly sprang up and we were able to hoist the spinnaker and have a lovely evening sail at about three knots. There was a note on Oliver Roome's chart strongly recommending the anchorage at Koalö, but the sailing was so glorious that we didn't want to stop and eventually anchored in a small pool, 2½ metres deep, amongst some rocks named Brathölne in the middle of a bay called Somskillen. Most of the anchorages in south-east Norway seem to be overlooked by summer retreats, but this one was quite isolated and sheltered from all directions except the north-west. The next day we continued through the skjaergärd anchoring for lunch in the beautiful anchorage of Dal which, according to the FPI, is 'where peace is' – and so it was. Then we had another lovely spinnaker run in bright sunshine as we sailed north through the Havefjord to Lyngör, mooring to a vacant mooring buoy for a couple of hours while we looked round the small town which is built on three islands with the attractive harbour in the middle.

The Coastal Radio station of Tjøme gave us a forecast of south-west, 10 metres per second (about force 5) so we set off eastward for a night passage across the Skaggerak. Twelve and a half hours later we berthed at Fjällbacka, where the marina was practically empty and where we were told they would not be collecting charges as it was too early in the season. Another couple of months though, and it would be a different

The outer skerries of the Stockholm archipelago, even here you'll find a sauna.

story. The next day we meandered southward through the leads and sounds of Sweden's west coast archipelago, whose granite rocks were smoother and more rugged than those of Norway's east coast, until we reached the large pine-clad island of Orust where we'd been told Hallberg-Rassys, Najads and Mälos are built. Derek and Chris left and Peter and Mike joined at Uddevalla, which had good connections for crew changing but other facilities were poor.

We reached Gothenburg via Marstrand (the Cowes of the west coast) where a retired Lloyds agent from Gothenburg, Johann Collin, introduced himself. He said he had known Peter Pye. Later we entered the Göta river and moored in the Lilla Bomen marina in Gothenburg, right next to the new Opera House.

The Göta river took us up to Lake Vänern, one of the biggest lakes in Europe. Lake Vänern is 160 feet above sea level and to get there we ascended the six big Trollhättan locks, a major engineering feat by-passing a hydro-electric scheme. In the first lock I sent Peter scrambling up the thirty foot vertical ladder with the mooring ropes, much to the amusement of the onlookers. He was politely ticked off at the top by the lock-keeper, who explained that because these modern locks filled from underneath there was no turbulence and one only had to hold on to the hooks recessed into the lock walls. On Lake Vänern we visited Spiken, a charming fishing village hidden in the reeds, and the fairy-tale castle of Lackö, each with its own small gästhamn. At Spiken we bought smoked

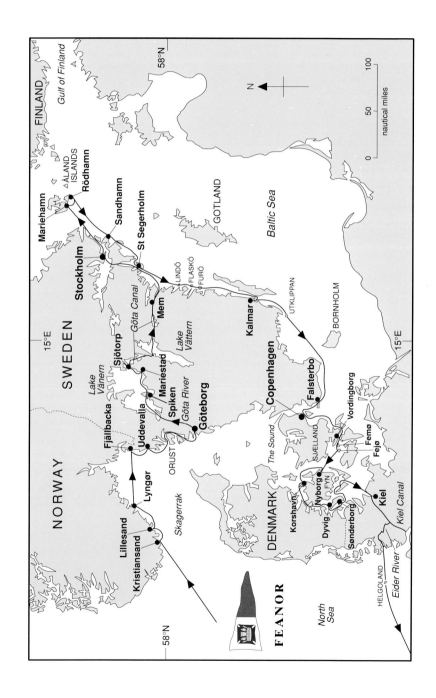

trout direct from the smokery and picnicked on the uninhabited island of Onsö, whence we fled at 4am to escape the voracious mosquitoes. At Mariestad, where David joined us, I was able to buy mosquito netting to go over the main hatch at night; it was worth its weight in gold, far more useful than the anti-midge application we had with us.

We entered the Göta Canal at Sjötorp. While we waited for a lock, a young Englishman appeared and seeing *Feanor*'s transom, exclaimed 'I bet they don't see many yachts from Weymouth up here!' He told us he had a brother living in Weymouth. Then it was up another 154ft to Lake Viken, where our channel passed close to an osprey's nest on a post in the middle of the lake. There was a large single chick in it, but unfortunately no sign of its parents. Thence it was downhill, 56 locks altogether, but the locks were made far less tedious by the beautiful girl lock-keepers doing summer holiday jobs. These girls were very efficient and were constantly talking into their mobile phones, so you had the impression that progress was being constantly monitored at a central control. This feeling was strengthened by many of the bridges being controlled by closed-circuit television.

The camaraderie of the locks does prompt one to talk to other vessels and amongst people we met this way was a Swede taking his 33ft cutter from Gothenburg through the canal for a cruise on the Gulf of Bothnia, two Norwegian brothers taking their 40ft vermillion-painted ocean racer '*Hotlips*' through for the 'round Gotland race' and a Northern Irish member of the Irish Cruising Club who had bought a Nicholson 31 in Finland and was taking her back to Ulster via St Petersburg. The owner of the Swedish yacht was most helpful, providing us with all the information needed to get the Stockholm Radio shipping forecasts in English at 0733 and 1933 GMT on various VHF channels round the coast.

At Mem, when we emerged from the last lock into the Baltic Sea, the crew of the yacht astern of us let out a tremendous "Alleluia!" so they were as pleased to get out to sea again as we were. We'd taken eleven days for the 250 miles and done a little sight-seeing without dawdling.

After leaving the Göta Canal we sailed north to Stockholm. It was midsummer day when we arrived and the exodus of boats of all sizes making their way out to the islands was amazing. Many were decorated with birch branches in leaf, as is the Swedish custom at midsummer. Here David and Mike left and Douglas and Clem joined. Stockholm is a marvellously clean city, not a scrap of litter anywhere. I found the Swedes as helpful as the Norwegians, and they can nearly all speak English. It is amazing how many Swedes have spent time in the UK doing courses or on holiday, and many seem to have relatives living here. English is Sweden's second language at school and they even learn about our history, yet we know almost nothing about theirs; all the battles they fought with Russia, for instance.

The highlight of our time in Stockholm was a visit to the Wasa Museum, where a sixteenth century warship has been raised from the seabed and preserved, in the same way as the *Mary Rose* at Portsmouth except that the *Wasa* is much more complete. Apparently teredo worms and other wood borers do not like the semi-fresh waters of the Baltic.

After Stockholm, where everyone seems to have a boat of some sort, we had some wonderful sailing northward through the thousands of picturesque islands which form the Stockholm archipelago. Although most of the larger islands have wooden summer houses on them, each complete with its own sauna, there is no law of trespass in Sweden. So long as you don't tramp through someone's garden, the yacht can be moored to a tree almost anywhere the water is deep enough. Because there is no tidal rise and fall in the Baltic, the Swedes like to drop an anchor over the stern and nose their yachts right up to a rock where they can jump ashore and make the bow fast without using the dinghy; a custom we very quickly adopted.

It's only 50 miles from this wonderful cruising ground across the Åland Sea to Mariehamn in the Finnish Åland Islands. This was the furthest goal of the voyage at 60 degrees North, the same latitude as the Shetland Isles. Mariehamn was an important port in sailing ship days and in the 1920s a dozen or so windjammers still sailed out of Mariehamn. To commemorate that era, a four-masted barque, the *Pommern,* is preserved afloat in the harbour. She is maintained as if she

Feanor in Scandinavia.

were still working and it was fascinating to see the complexity of the rigging and appreciate the enormous skill and strength the crew needed to sail a ship of that size.

We spent another lovely day cruising amongst the Åland islands, where we grounded on a rock for the first time when navigating at slow speed into a beautiful anchorage out of the main channel near Rödhamn. Before we had time to lay out a kedge, a summer resident, who had witnessed our plight, came over in his motor boat, took our jib halyard and pulled us off. He had obviously done it before.

Then it was time to turn for home. We worked south through the outer leads of the Stockholm Archipelago, visiting some of the slightly more barren outer islands as well as Sandhamn – Sweden's premier yachting centre – which was in full preparation for the 'Round Gotland Race', the principal offshore race in the Baltic.

It was now almost July and, as we voyaged south, there were many more yachts going our way, starting their summer cruises through the well marked channels inside the outer islands. We only had a week before we were due in Copenhagan for the next crew change, but it would have been a shame to rush this idyllic area so we dawdled, mooring up to bathe in the surprisingly warm water and exploring some of the many charming anchorages such as Lindö, Flaskö and Furö. At St Segelholm a couple hailed us from their summer house at 11 o'clock in the evening, when it was still light, and asked us if we would like a sauna as theirs was all stoked up. Of course we jumped at the chance, but it seemed very strange to be entertained 'au nature!'. Our host's wife, I might add, had already had hers and took her plunge while we were inside. Mixed saunas, we were informed, do not happen in Scandinavia, except in families. Afterwards we shared a bottle of wine sitting in the garden in our towels and dressing gowns until well after midnight. It was certainly very relaxing and we all slept like tops afterwards.

Douglas had to leave at Kalmar, in order to attend his daughter's graduation ceremony. Clem and I pressed on for Copenhagen via Utklippan, a fascinating harbour built in the early part of the last century by Russian POWs to serve the lighthouse on the island at the south-eastern corner of Sweden. We fetched up in the comfortable Langelinie Marina, just a stone's throw from the Little Mermaid statue.

After an idyllic cruise of the Danish Islands, Feanor returned to England by way of the Kiel Canal, the Eider River, Helgoland, Norderney, Vlieland, Schleveningham, Zeebrugge and Dunkirk. She arrived back in Weymouth on August 9th after 2,868 miles.

Feanor is a Contessa 28 designed by Pelle Peterson and built by Jeremy Rogers in 1981. She is a comfortable cruising boat for three people and performs particularly well to windward in light to moderate conditions.

THROUGH THE BIG APPLE

by Jill and Tony Vasey

We had laid up little *Clara*, our Cornish Crabber, at Wellfleet on Cape Cod, snugged down in the woods behind our friend's workshop. It only took a couple of days to ready her for the summer so when we launched on 23rd May, we still had three weeks for our intended 500 mile passage to Chesapeake. Our partner, Harvey (CCA) had volunteered to take *Clara* as far as Rhode Island and we were pleased to find him there on schedule just as the weather cleared and the wind turned to the north-east.

We have cruised this area several times but had never visited Block Island so fashioned a course for a sparkling sail with the wind well round on the quarter. We just missed the tide so had to skirt the considerable race off the north-west corner of the island, eventually resorting to our trusty Yanmar to push us through the man-made cut into the fine natural harbour known as The Great Salt Pond. It is more than a mile long with several good anchorages, but we chose to go to the southern end as near town as possible to allow a run ashore before dark. This early in the season the place was virtually empty, tempting us to explore further, but we were loath to squander a fair breeze this early in our cruise, so left at dawn to catch the tide into Long Island Sound.

The eastern end of the Sound has a shallow bar running north-east from the tip of Long Island, through Plum Island and Fishers Island and on to Mystic on the mainland. Although the tidal range at the eastern end of the Sound is only about three feet, the bar creates currents of up to five knots, so it's essential to get your timing right. We carried a fresh north-easter all day and just caught the last of the fair tide through The Race and on to the Connecticut River, where we anchored in a shallow creek north of Essex town with barely enough depth even for *Clara*.

In the morning we drifted down river on the ebb in hot sun, a change from the day before when it had been bitterly cold, and wandered west along the shore in light airs. There are many good harbours along the mainland shore, but the pilot book's description of several as 'yachting meccas' frightened us off so we made for Guilford as more our style. It has a rock encumbered approach into a tortuous shallow river with hardly room to swing, ideal Crabber stuff, and the walk into town was well rewarded with good shops and a most attractive tree lined park in the centre. The night was utter peace.

Another lovely morning with sandpipers all around on the tidal mud. We were in an Audubon Society reserve of coastal marsh which was a haven for shore birds. This is the joy of a small shallow boat. The last time we cruised this area we had six foot draft and worked up the coast in greater style, but little knowing what joys awaited behind the shallow bars. The small breeze took us along to unaccustomed opulence at the smart Norwalk Yacht Club where we had arranged to meet Forbes and Ernmy Morse (CCA). They secured us to a generously stout mooring (the dinghy dock was full) before carrying us off to their retreat in the forest for a splendid 24 hours R.& R.

We had read that it was still possible to ask that the bridges on the Harlem River be opened for a passing boat, but could find no record of this having been done in years. To our amazement the Director of Bridge Operations quickly agreed to our request, so we made a rendezvous at Broadway Bridge with the proviso that their engineers would help to get the mast down if a recalcitrant bridge refused to open. So, with three days to kill, we drifted on to City Island where the yacht club was most welcoming.

Next day dawned foggy and drizzly and we were tempted to go back to bed, but the current through Hell Gate waits for no man and we were already late so oozed off into the murk. We were swept under Throgs Neck Bridge barely visible in the fog and driving rain, and carried on past La Guardia with unseen jets passing low overhead. At best this back door entrance to New York is uninspiring, but in good visibility at least the lure of Manhattan's skyline promises better things to come. In thick weather we groped across Flushing Bay out of sight of land but within smellshot of the Sanitation Department's refuse barge depot, past the forbidding Rikers Island prison to Hell Gate, the junction with the Harlem River. Here the current flows hard and changes abruptly at high water; hence the need for correct timing. We were a bit late, measuring 10 knots over the ground as we went through the overfalls in the narrows, and were rewarded with a breathtaking passage south down the East River. The tall buildings reluctantly emerged from cloud as the rain eased so that abeam the UN building we actually glimpsed the top of the shining Chrysler Tower. Under the magnificent Brooklyn Bridge we dived into the South Street Seaport Museum, hoping that our quaint little gaff cutter would elicit enough sympathy to allow a stopover. They were polite but firm, pointing to the empty pier where yachts were once berthed but which was now condemned, and it wasn't difficult to see why. Even *Clara* would have been in danger of carrying it away.

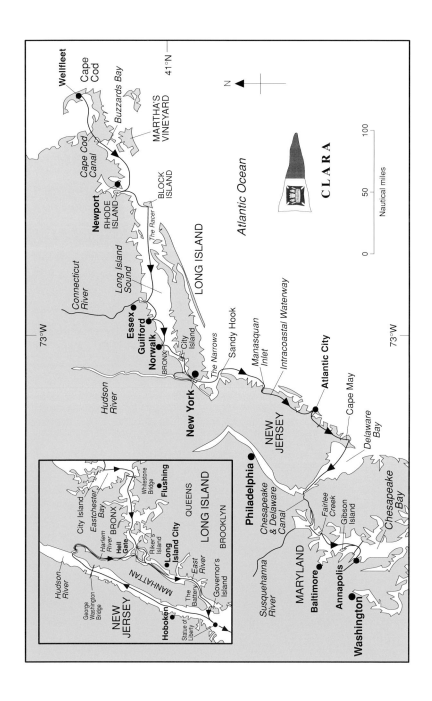

We next tried Governors Island but again were politely shown the door, so crabbed across the strong ebb and tucked in behind Ellis Island where the old railroad piers have been removed to leave an attractive shallow pool well suited to our three foot draft. After a lazy lunch, during which the sky cleared completely, Jill put to sea in the dinghy whilst I sailed *Clara* round the Statue of Liberty for photos before taking the flood north up the Hudson. The wind filled in, allowing us to beat through this magnificent city all the way to the 79th Street Boat Basin which caters for the impecunious by offering $10 moorings only five minutes walk from Central Park.

The day of our assault on the Harlem River dawned as foul as could be, but the rain stopped and the sky cleared right on cue for our approach to the first bridge, the Spuyten Duyvil Railroad Swing Bridge. Our greatest difficulty was not persuading the bridge to open but pronouncing its name on the RT. Once round the first corner we realised the enormity of our demand. The mass of Broadway bridge stood before us carrying two lane rail and four lane highway traffic, and the crossing subway trains seemed almost continuous. Its massive bulk was swarming with men in yellow jackets and hard-hats with flashing vehicles at both ends.

Our photographer Brooke Davies hailed us from the river bank and told of her arrangement to join the convoy of engineers hopping from bridge to bridge so as to record our historic passage. We were kept waiting for half an hour but were encouraged by RT messages from the bridge saying that they only had a slight problem when from our vantage point it looked as though they were trying to rebuild it. Eventually, with blaring sirens, the 1,000 ton truss rose majestically between its lofty towers, going all the way to the top despite our gesticulations that we only needed a few feet to clear our diminutive mast. Perhaps they were taking the opportunity to test its full travel but the bridge was open for fully five minutes and must have backed up the subway all the way to Wall Street.

With two miles before the next low bridge, we stopped the engine to enjoy a wild sail as the wind funnelled through the canyon beneath three high-level bridges. Mercifully it eased before Malcombs Dam Bridge, which appeared to be resisting the efforts of yet another armada of engineers. Our consciences were salved by the lack of traffic, and such is the bridge's remoteness in this industrial Bronx that it did not appear to have barriers. Eventually sirens sounded and the men obstructed road traffic with cones and vehicles as latecomers tried to run the gauntlet. Pedestrians would sneak through only to be shooed back by the engineers, but a large lady pushing a pram outwitted them and was chivvied across in a most unseemly manner as spectators gathered to witness the spectacle of this ancient piece of machinery cranking itself into action. Our shouted thanks were reciprocated by the workmen, who seemed to be enjoying their day out as much as we were.

Next came 145th Street bridge which from a mile away looked rusty and decrepit. Certainly the long delay in opening confirmed that it was not giving in easily. Years of accumulated rubbish had filled the joint between bridge and road and crowbars were much in evidence. Eventually, with loud groans from its corroded cog wheels, the span slowly edged round sufficiently for us to squeeze through, but at the next bridge, Madison Avenue, there was an even longer struggle, making us doubt if we should make it all the way.

We were not surprised to hear the Metro-North Railroad on the RT, urging Madison to get a move on as they had main line trains out of Grand Central waiting. The railroad was another lift bridge, like Broadway, but this time each carriageway rose independently. An up-train sped by and was hardly off the span before up it went with such alacrity it was clear they were trying to shame their Madison brethren. A down-train steamed through and up went that truss with such urgency that we were spurred to match their speed. No full travel here! With barely a foot clearance it stopped and we were under to receive a cheer and triumphant gesture from the well practised workmen.

3rd Avenue bridge was a mere bagatelle but we hadn't reckoned on

Clara meets the Statue of Liberty.

our last obstacle, Willis Avenue. This bridge takes the north bound traffic from the double-decker Theodore Roosevelt Drive, the main artery of East Manhattan, and an unbroken line of cars crossed which the bridgemen seemed reluctant to interrupt. Eventually, after a quarter of an hour, we saw the traffic lights turn red but the Gaderine herd pressed forward with little heed. The barriers began to lower but still the traffic surged on so that a workman with a red flag was forced to intervene. Slowly it opened, again to full travel, and we hid our heads in shame as the frustrated motorists backed up for miles.

We were through and felt like early explorers who had forced a passage into the unknown.

We had missed the tide down the East River, so that at Hell Gate we were already stemming two knots. We had the alternatives of turning east to find an anchorage in Flushing Bay for the night or plugging the flood tide down the East River. The wind was still fresh from the north so we chose the latter course and slowly struggled south with full sail and engine. Whereas two days earlier the river had been dead under low cloud and rain, now it was alive with rush hour traffic. High speed ferries sped past, helicopters clattered overhead picking up commuters from the several Manhattan sky ports, the funicular to Roosevelt Island slid across above us and a small float plane landed perilously close whilst the steady hum of executive aircraft signified the return of the more opulent to their nightly retreats. And little *Clara* slowly carried us to our favourite retreat behind The Statue of Liberty for a quiet night after her adventures of the day.

Cruising a 24ft boat is a 'back to the womb' syndrome. You don't sail in her, you sail with her; you don't get aboard, you put her on. But she reaches places that other boats can't and takes you to quiet backwaters where there isn't another boat in sight and the only noise is the chuckle of the bows, the sucking of the tide and the cry of the water birds. In my youth I craved adventure but in maturity I find peace a fair substitute for waning energy.

'YOU SHOULD HAVE BEEN HERE A FORTNIGHT AGO . . .'

by Peter Bruce

Loch Roag, at the extreme north-west of the Outer Hebides, was chosen as the target for *Owl's* 1997 biennial cruise to the Scottish Western Islands. Loch Roag is a large bay bestrewn with islands which looked interesting on the chart. And so it was. The cruise was to follow the usual routine for my Contessa 33, namely a cruise up to the Clyde in May, participation in the Clyde Cruising Club's Rover Series, a ten day break for some office work and then the expedition to the islands. Two weeks were allowed for the cruise north from the Clyde and a week for the passage back to Lymington.

For the first week I had Tim Jefferys, Vicki Watson and Maggie Widdop, and for the second week Lucy James was to change places with Maggie. Lucy, Tim and Vicki had done the cruise north from Lymington, Tim and Lucy had also done the Rover Series, and Maggie had been on board for the bruising all-upwind sail to Ireland in 1996. They made a bold, resolute and experienced crew, familiar with the boat and with Scottish waters.

On 8th June we arrived back at Troon, where the boat had been left after the racing, to be met by a southerly gale which prompted a well meaning local lady to say that we 'should have been here a fortnight ago'. Of course, *Owl* had been racing then and we had experienced glorious sunny weather, but frustration owing to very light airs – rather unsuitable for our heavy displacement boat.

The ancient caravanners of central Asia used to make their first encampment just outside the city walls and with this in mind we spent our first night on a buoy at Lamlash, Arran. Next day we took the direct route to the Outer Hebrides passing the Mull of Kintyre, Islay and Skerrivore to starboard and, after an uneventful passage, dropped our anchor in Village Bay, Mingulay, 25 hours later. We found ourselves in company with the Royal Navy Contessa 38 *Gawaine*, which had been built alongside *Owl* in 1984.

During the exchange of pleasantries as *Gawaine* got under way we heard that someone was apparently living on Mingulay, but this hardly prepared us for the sight, a little later as we ate our porridge in the cockpit, of a young and lovely lady walking down to the beach, taking all her clothes off and swimming unattired in our bay. This turned out to be Julie Brook, an artist who, having lived in a cave at the north end of Jura for a previous summer, was now spending the summer alone painting on Mingulay. We presented Julie, who was living in the shepherd's cottage, with our three day old newspapers, and she entrusted us with her mail.

Strong northerly winds were forecast, so from Mingulay we hurried north while we could do so in comfort, past Mingulay's puffin colony and on to Loch Skiport. From here *Owl* passed through the Stanton Channel of the Sound of Harris. Our arrival into the Atlantic Ocean coincided with the expected rain and strong northerlies so we made for Loch Amhuinnsuidhe – pronounced *almond-suey* – for the night. The first landing party of the morning met Kenny who was painting the main door of Amhuinnsuidhe Castle which was just about sheltered from the rain. He was very friendly but complained of the December-like weather. 'You should have been here a fortnight ago,' said he.

In view of the rain and the grim forecast it was tempting to stay another night, but by lunchtime we had seen all there was to see and time was pressing so we climbed into all three layers of Musto and thrashed our way northward. Happily, *Owl* is at her best on a beat to windward in a strong breeze and seaway. We tacked off the Flannan Islands and by dusk we were off Loch Roag. The big swell sent white water high up the bluff cliffs and the Kyles Pabay entrance was hardly visible in the murky conditions, but with the assistance of our GPS before too long we were safely at anchor in the sheltered inlet at Meavig.

Next day we met John and Fay Hay, their daughter and son-in-law Murray and Janet Macleod, and also Iain Buchanan, the gentle manager of the fish farm. All were immensely kind and hospitable, and after most welcome showers and being entertained from one house to another we didn't get to bed until after 1am.

We set off south in sunlight to visit the enchanting lagoon at Pabay More and the delicious anchorage between Scarp and Kearsay Island, where the bright green machair under the gneiss cliff makes such a contrast with the ultramarine water and the pale beige sand. Whilst taking the passage inshore of Mealasta Island we must have passed over a shoal of small fry as we had gannets plopping in on all sides. The clear weather allowed an easy passage eastwards through the Sound of Harris.

Owl entered Finsbay in semi-darkness and spent the night off the promontory with the ruined cottage. We dined off Iain Buchanan's excellent salmon. The planned crew exchange required a return to land easily accessible by motor car so, next morning, we took a route close under the cliffs on the south-west side of Skye. Visibility was over 50

Owl in Loch Slapin, Skye.

miles, and off the Cuillins we could see much of the Outer Hebrides and the high hills of Mull. Lucy had arrived and next morning we took our kind hosts to Scavaig, where the seals outnumber the humans about 5:1. A lone golden eagle soared high above as the shore party explored the valley at Loch Coruisk.

Another depression with southerly winds was now forecast, so we decided to round Ardnamurchan and tuck into the Sound of Mull. After a quiet night in Loch Aline, the rain and forecast southerlies were only too apparent in the morning. Spring tides were approaching and, with a strong contrary stream, we had to use the eddies under the Mull shore to make satisfactory progress.

One of the aims of the cruise had been to visit Bagh Gleann, the bay at the north of Jura, facing the Gulf of Corryvreckan. We decided to try to motor through the Grey Dogs and approach Bagh Gleann from up-tide. *Owl*, flat out, motors at 6.6 knots and at first that didn't seem enough to break through the narrows between Eilean A'Bhealach and Lunga. However, by going closer to the shore we made progress inch by inch. Scarba has an interesting westward side, but as we approached the famous Gulf we were more concerned with keeping a good margin up-tide for the crossing. At first we hardly noticed The Great Race but this abruptly changed as we neared the Jura shore. Our plan had been to leave Eilean Mor to starboard, but as we got closer this approach looked horrifying – a tumbling wall of white water was evident on its north side.

We altered course firmly to leave Eilean Mor Island to port, and soon found ourselves in more white water and dramatic streams running so fast that the adjoining surface appeared to be running at about 8 knots in the opposite direction. It was quite exciting stuff but no green water came aboard, and we were soon in the calm waters and unspoilt scenery of Bagh Gleann Nam Muc – the Bay of the Boar's Glen.

We left at slack next morning and passed close to the pretty, wooded eastern shore of Jura where red deer abound. The next stop was on the visitor's moorings off Gigha. We found the Archamore gardens very attractive in the afternoon sun and also much enjoyed meeting Jennifer Guinness and her amusing crew Alex and Jack, at the hotel bar. Dinner on board was the final portion of salmon, converted into Zanzibar soup, one of Tim's specialities of which everyone had become increasingly fond. Meanwhile we could hear Jennifer, at the next buoy, goading her crew into making preparations for an extremely early start.

We left at 0720, no doubt some hours after Jennifer's *Alakush*, with a view to arriving at the Mull of Kintyre at slack water. Though we arrived nearly an hour earlier than planned, even by then the tide had fully changed and we were obliged to take note of the Clyde Cruising Club's recommendation to pass the Mull of Kintyre some hours before the Hydrographer suggests. Clearly Jennifer knew about this, and now so did we. It was rough, and the tide was running at over four knots against us, so we worked our way close along the shore, taking advantage of any eddies and slacker water that we could find, whilst hoping that the offshore rocks were as charted.

Back at Troon Tim, Vicki and Lucy left in the car after sharing lunch with the crew who had arrived for the passage south. For this I had happy and excellent sailors Terry Wilkinson and Mike Currie, both old *Owl* hands, and welcome newcomer, Alex Hemsley, a friend of Mike. After a fast and enjoyable sail, *Owl* was back in Lymington a week later, having completed 2,036 miles since her departure on 13th May. The second half of June 1997 had been unusually cold and overcast for cruising, but the good days were so wonderful that the attraction of the Scottish Islands remains as strong as ever.

Owl is a Contessa 33 designed by Rob Humphreys and built by Jeremy Rogers in 1984 as a successor to the Contessa 32. Owl is roomier and more comfortable than a Contessa 32 and, though of equally heavy displacement, has won her class many times at Cork, at Tarbert and at Cowes Week. This was her third cruise to the Scottish Islands.

FLIGHT OF TIME TAKES OFF

by Graham and Margaret Morfey

This was the cruise for which the Irish Cruising Club Decanter was awarded.

This was the voyage Graham had dreamed about for years. With retirement and a new boat I overcame my earlier misgivings, and we spent a year preparing for a cruise which would take us to new lands and people, new seas and harbours.

On 22 August 1996 we set off from Southampton and headed west for Falmouth. Peter Ingram and Dominic Oldridge were our young crew, both sailors from an early age. The exhausted skipper and mate were glad to hand over the sailing of the boat after a hectic countdown to departure. The weather was foul, the stores were all over the place, but the boys got us safely to Dartmouth for food and sleep. By Saturday 24th we had arrived at Falmouth for the OCC meet – an opportunity to ask the advice of those blue water sailors for the months to come. We were richly rewarded with information, even to the extent of a disk full of wisdom given by Gavin McLaren which we loaded onto our computer. On Sunday night we had a farewell meal with old RCC friends and said *au revoir* to Peter.

Dominic stayed with us for the Biscay crossing and we were blessed with fair winds and fine weather, reaching La Coruña on 30 August. At the approach to the marina we stopped dead with a fouled propeller, but Dominic went over the side with the bread knife and cleared yards of fishing net and rope. We were glad to have reached Spanish sunshine before September and enjoyed four happy days in this beautiful old town, which has improved its waterfront tremendously since our last visit in 1980. Dominic flew home, Alistair Ingram joined us and we sailed on via the fishing ports of northern Spain. In Muros we met several Scandinavian boats which formed the nucleus of a small fleet heading south – we met them again in Portugal, Madeira, the Canaries, and one re-appeared from time to time in the Caribbean. This was a new kind of sailing for us, always moving on and not having to count the days and turn for home.

We reached Leixões on 23 September and found three of the Scandinavian yachts there. Arriving in Porto by bus, we saw the ferocious waters of the Douro and a few yachts firmly tied up at the bank. Porto was a fascinating mix of grandeur and squalor, humming with life and activity. We visited all the sights, walked miles and admired the traditional port barges on the river.

For the passage to Lisbon we had light winds, some fog, a dramatic eclipse of the moon and a sea full of phosphorescence. At dawn we were doing seven knots with the yankee boomed out, then the fog cleared and we entered the river Tagus in sunshine. This was an experience I shall never forget – the fortifications at the river mouth, then the white medieval tower of Belém on the port hand and the long, majestic monastery of San Jeronimo behind the towering modern monument to the Portuguese discoverers – *Los Discobrantes*. Ahead lay the high road bridge and on the right an immense statue of Jesus. Further along the north shore lie the classical piazzas and monuments which rival those of Paris and Rome – as they were intended to do. Portugal was once a powerful nation and Lisbon is still a magnificent expression of national pride. We found a berth in the *Doca de Alcântara* and spent a few days sightseeing; high spots were the maritime museum and the old city with its castle.

English Harbour, Antigua, from Shirley Heights.

On 1 October we set off towards Madeira. Coming out of the Tagus we found strong winds and high seas, and by afternoon the sails were well reefed down. Later we lowered the main but the Aries coped well with the conditions. For the next three days we roared along in northerly winds, varying the amount of sail but usually under yankee and reefed main. We set up the Aquair towed generator which produces seven amps at seven knots and enables us to run a small freezer. On 3 October Alistair sighted a forty foot whale with a small dorsal fin (probably a Sei whale). He seemed to be interested in our towed generator and came alarmingly close, but left us after about half an hour.

We were very glad to have Alistair's help in the strongest winds we'd met so far, and on 4 October arrived at Porto Santo. We had a wonderful meal ashore of *espetada* – skewered steak in the local fashion, and a chance to relax in comfort. Colin and Marylyn Ford in *Nandisa* were anchored outside the harbour, but we had to move on to Madeira for Alistair's flight home.

Everyone had said it was impossible to get into Funchal harbour, but on a quiet Sunday evening after the harbour master had gone home we had no trouble. It was crowded but friendly on a trot of seven boats, and here we met Alistair and Margot Pratt and our Danish friends, and an American crew with whom we later spent Christmas in Grenada. Funchal was excellent for laundry, shopping, fuel etc. and full of good restaurants. The old town is interesting, but like the rest of Madeira very overcrowded with a crazy road system and no signposts. We hired a car and got lost repeatedly, but did find some wonderful walks at higher altitudes, above the heavily cultivated slopes of bananas, vines, fruit and flowers of all kinds. One day we walked the famous *levadas* – man made irrigation channels around the mountain contours with paths alongside. The dizzying height and steepness of the mountains was a revelation. Another day we walked above the pines and chestnuts on the bare mountain peaks, with wonderful views down to the sea.

On 15 October we left Funchal and headed for the Salvagem Islands. We had our permit to visit the Salvagems, but when we arrived a heavy swell was running and it wasn't safe to anchor. We took a few photos, saw the Cory's shearwaters and Madeiran petrels which are a speciality here, and headed on towards the Canaries. That evening we were doing over seven knots under full sail in a perfect force 3 from the NNE. Next day at dawn we sighted the island of Graciosa and came to the lovely anchorage of Playa Francesca at 0900.

This was the first true anchorage we had found, and the terrain around us was utterly different from green Madeira – sandy and barren, with two strange peaks of volcanic rock ringed with black and brown. Across the water the long dark cliff of Lanzarote stretched away into the distance. About a dozen sailing boats lay at anchor, from a big Baltic trader down to a 29 foot cruiser. Among these were circumnavigators from Australia,

New Zealand and Canada, and of course some Scandinavians. After a few days' rest we moved on to the smart marina of Puerto Calero at the southern end of Lanzarote and made this our base for exploring the island. We loved Lanzarote, a strange volcanic place with almost lunar landscapes and fascinating houses, art galleries and viewpoints designed by the local artist Cesar Manrique.

From Lanzarote we crossed to Las Palmas on Gran Canaria, where Pete Ingram joined us again. He was a great asset, having already made one crossing of the Atlantic. We also met Niels from Denmark and Margaret from Austria, Bowman owners who became our firm friends over the next few months. Las Palmas was hot and noisy and dirty, but in a peaceful quarter of town we found Christopher Columbus' house, built around a courtyard and housing an excellent museum about the great man's travels. By car we toured the island with its craggy mountains, tree sized cacti and extinct volcanoes – and enjoyed the hot sun and exotic flowers.

Next we sailed down to San Sebastian on La Gomera, a quite different island off the main tourist track. Exploring inland we found the ancient laurel forest which traps mist and moisture for the island, saving it from drought and erosion. Driving towards Vueltas we passed through the Valle Gran Rey with beautifully terraced sides, green with vines and vegetables and studded with pretty red roofed cottages.

On 1 November we sailed from La Gomera towards the Cape Verde Islands; here is a log extract dated 4 November:

"Sea area Sahara. This is the first time we have had an unbroken spell at sea, so that we are a self-contained world, a space capsule. The outside world doesn't seem to matter much, although we can hear other sailors talking on the SSB. What does matter is the state of wind and sea and sky around us. Although we are on the same latitude as north Africa, it isn't really hot; the sky is absolutely clear but not an intense blue. The colour at the horizon is a flat, neutral grey. This is because of dust from the Sahara, which has settled on the boat to some degree. We have not had the dust-laden Harmattan wind from the east which can seriously reduce visibility and coat everything with red dust.

". . . We have had a moderate north-easterly wind most of the time, sailing goose winged with yankee and reefed main. The sea is smooth and friendly with only an occasional dollop of spray to wake us up. Few signs of wildlife, though we have seen storm petrels, shearwaters and the occasional migrating butterfly. No dolphins since our first day out of La Gomera, but flying fish on the deck in the morning."

We reached the Cape Verdes in exactly 5 days. Merryl Huxtable was due to fly into Sal on 6 November, a good friend who has helped us with delivery trips before. We arrived at the port of Palmeira right on time. At anchor was David Mitchell in *Ondarina*, with plans to sail down the coast of Africa.

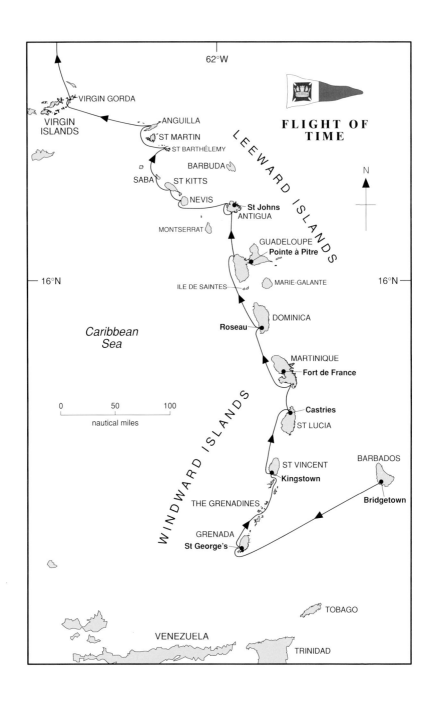

Soon there was Merryl being rowed out by three black boys in a wooden fishing boat. One put out a hand, I grasped it to pull them alongside and then he passed me a short, frayed piece of rope which only just reached our guardrail. These are poor people. Their boat was painted in bright colours but faded and scarred with age. A broken oar blade was bound together with rusty wire.

Palmeira village was simple and bare. A queue of women with containers stood waiting for the water to be turned on – the islands have little rainfall and the water supply is limited. The houses were painted in pastel colours, with spiny acacia trees for shade. There was a church and a small bar, but no shops in Palmeira. We set off along the dirt road to Espargos. On the outskirts of town, at a butcher's block under a tree, they were selling the parts of a recently slaughtered cow. We saw a man walking away with a couple of legs under his arm, complete with fur and hooves.

We headed for the *supermercado* and the vegetable market. The major buildings in town – post office, hotel, bank, church and school, were quite smart. The airport nearby brings in some much needed income. The houses and shops were spartan, but the people were cheerful and welcoming. A young Spanish yachtsman we'd met in the harbour was suffering from hepatitis, but the locals had taken him in and cared for him.

With our supplies replenished we moved on to the island of Boa Vista, mostly sand dunes, with one commercial harbour, an anchorage and some wonderful beaches. If there were an infrastructure of water, power and drainage the Cape Verdeans could build hotels and bring in some tourists, but it's hard to see how they can get started. We enjoyed the wild beauty of the beach, the wind patterns in the dunes, the brilliant blues of sea over sand and the sandpipers running along the water's edge.

We set off south to Santiago, one of the larger islands, reaching the Tarrafal harbour at night via an unlit headland. Radar and GPS helped, and when we reached the anchorage the other yachts turned on their lights to help us in. Tarrafal is a small town with a few primitive fishing boats in a good natural harbour – a beautiful place with protecting cliffs and a palm fringed beach. The town has a bank, telephones, a health centre, a big church, a market and a few shops including a good bakery. There are swarms of children of all ages, many barefoot and ragged. In the market we could buy onions, yams, sweet potato, lemons and oranges, cassava root and fresh fish.

One day Merryl and I set off into the interior to find a botanical garden and a giant silk-cotton tree. We travelled in an *aluguer* – a minibus rather like a Turkish *dolmus*. The southern part of the island is bleak and mountainous with little cultivated land. Further on we came to fields and orchards, with many villages and stopping places. We eventually found the garden after many wrong turnings, and later (much later) we came across the enormous tree in a long, deep valley, meeting children just out of school who were fetching water for their mothers. We squeezed into another *aluguer* and got back to the boat by sunset, to Graham's evident relief. At no time did we feel threatened or unsafe in the Cape Verdes, and most people were friendly and helpful.

The weather turned grey and rainy, but by common consent the fleet in the harbour felt ready to move westwards. *Flight of Time* set off across the Atlantic on 17 November, at the same time as *Katinka*, *Patton* and *Cortana*. We passed Fogo wreathed in cloud, then Brava, and that was the last land we saw. With a steady ENE wind we were averaging 7 knots.

From now on our world was the boat and her crew, and we'd been together long enough to have great confidence in both. *Flight of Time* was one year old, chosen by us with this voyage in mind. We had a good suit of sails to meet all weather conditions, a sturdy hull and a comfortable cabin. The windmill, towed generator and solar panels helped keep the batteries charged, and our water-maker enabled us to have showers whenever the water was warm enough. We'd had time to get to know the electronics and radio systems, and with a laptop computer could even receive weather maps. So we set off cheerfully into the rainy seascape, with storm petrels and flying fish for company, and the sky cleared auspiciously for a dramatic sunset.

Next morning was grey with a heavy swell, but the third day dawned fair. The sprayhood came down, the bimini went up and we dried out the damp cushions. A white egret flew round several times before settling on the rail. He looked keenly at me, and I at him; only on a boat at sea could we get that close.

We were now settling down to the rhythm of life at sea – sextant sights three times a day, breadmaking, regular radio calls to *Katinka* and *Patton* to exchange positions and weather news. We were all awake for a drink in the cockpit at noon and at six, and with four good cooks on board, mealtimes were the highlight of the day. Even being woken for a night watch was rewarded by that magical climb up the companionway into the soft night air, a flood of moonlight and the water whispering by. We hardly ever saw another vessel at night, but checked the radar from time to time. By the fourth day we were tasting flying fish for breakfast and Merryl was learning to use the sextant.

Day six, and a big swell running. A sheave at the top of the kicker had sheared, but Graham managed to replace it by adapting an old one. It was so rolly that I fixed up the pilot berth in the saloon – a lovely breezy position under an open hatch. Next morning an enormous wave came right over the deck and through the hatches, swamping the pilot berth, table, cabin seats and galley – but luckily missing the chart table and instruments. I had just hung everything out to dry when a big black

Coral Beach, Barbados.

Pete and friends in Palmeira, Cape Verdes.

Safe arrival at Newport, R.I.

cloud came up astern with a heavy rain squall. I gave up and dumped everything in the shower, turning my attention to more important matters – champagne and silly games to celebrate reaching halfway across the Atlantic. We caroused in the cockpit until dark and then went below for a feast: smoked salmon, a leg of lamb with apricots and all the trimmings cooked by Merryl, and treacle pudding with cream served by Pete. We had a merry time serving it up with the boat rolling more than ever, and while eating we had to grip our wineglasses between our knees.

Eighth day – a bright sunny morning and the wind and sea had calmed down. We got everything pretty well dried out and back to normal. Two pilot whales appeared briefly. Next day there was even less wind, so the spinnaker went up and pulled steadily for twelve hours – a splendid smooth run. We watched brown boobies skimming the water and diving for fish, and saw a big silver tuna leaping.

Over the next three days the wind was light but the spinnaker and the Aries kept us on course. It became hot and sultry with a sprinkle of rain and distant flickers of lightning. On our twelfth day out we had to motor for the first time, the wind dropping to seven knots. Next day was uncomfortable – a tiresome swell but not enough wind; the slatting of the sails kept me awake. The kicker sheave broke again and Graham replaced it with a rope. Then a school of dolphins lifted our spirits, playing and diving, and crossing our bow in sparkling spray, squeaking to one another. Only 300 miles to go.

November 30 and getting closer to land. It was hot and steamy, with tall pillars of cloud and light winds. More dolphins appeared, and our first tropic bird with its long streaming tail. We were still speaking every day to *Patton*, now far astern, and to *Katinka* who would reach Barbados first. In anticipation of our arrival, Pete started mixing rum punch, and we had stirring music and hilarity in the cockpit while watching a stupendous technicolour sunset. Next morning I was woken with a cry of "land ho!" and scrambled up to see Merryl looking through the binoculars. Soon I could see a long, low island, and we all swung into action with a major clean up of the boat, inside and out, with high spirits, elbow grease and Beatle music. We arrived off Needham Point under sail and turned into Carlisle Bay to see palm trees and casuarinas growing along a gleaming white beach, an anchorage of clear blue water and our friends in *Katinka*.

Niels and Margaret came over to share our champagne, and then took Graham with them to see the harbourmaster. Later we landed through the surf and walked through soft white coral sand to the Boatyard bar, right on the beach beneath palm trees. Long rum punches while we watched the beautiful sunset over the sea, and as darkness fell a chorus of tree frogs started chirruping, a lovely sound which will always remind me of Barbados.

We spent two weeks in Carlisle Bay, getting to know Bridgetown and then hiring a car to explore the island. Barbados is a friendly place, where we were often greeted by passers by who wanted to talk and make us feel welcome. The women and girls were elegantly dressed, particularly in Bridgetown, and their hairstyles were works of art.

We visited old plantation houses, wonderful gardens of exotic trees and flowers, and a windy beach on the east coast where the Atlantic comes crashing in. This was our first visit to the Caribbean, so everything was new. We'd seen the posters – and it was all for real! The week passed all too quickly and then Pete and Merryl had to fly home. They had been a wonderful and supportive crew and we were sad to see them go.

We sailed on to Grenada and anchored in Prickly Bay on 15 December. Barbados was beautiful, but the sight of those Grenadan mountains covered in rich green forest was even more dramatic and enticing. By car we saw St George's and its wonderful central market full of spices, paw-paws, mangoes and bananas, and then we headed for the hills. Grenada is nearly all forest. Apart from St George's, some small towns around the edges and a few fields, the rest is filled with big, juicy, dripping, vigorous trees and ferns and creepers – real rain forest, with the occasional heavy downpour. Under the trees, along the roadside and tucked away in the forest, are little wooden houses on stilts, painted in pink, turquoise, blue, green and lilac, with washing drying underneath.

The waterfalls on Grenada are wonderful and we asked a guide to take us through the forest to the Concord falls. He showed us all the spices growing and opened our eyes to so much we might have missed. The waterfall was about fifty feet high, in a green clearing like the Garden of Eden, the most beautiful place I have ever seen.

Back in Prickly Bay, we began to think about Christmas. With more boats arriving all the time, we got together with *Segera* and our American friends on *Night Watch* and planned a joint Christmas dinner. Then the sail training ship *Astrid* came in and invited us to their Christmas Eve drinks party, quite a grand occasion to dress up for. Christmas morning was blazing hot and we went ashore for a stroll and a cold beer at the beautiful Moorings hotel. We thought fondly of our family at home, but I was glad not to be cooking the usual gargantuan meal. We had a wonderful Christmas dinner together aboard *Flight of Time*, with christo-phene and tropical fruit in place of brussels sprouts and Christmas pudding.

Soon after Christmas, Annabelle and Stuart Ingram joined us for a cruise through the Grenadines. Stuart had sailed these waters 25 years ago and could show us the best anchorages among the Tobago Cays and beyond. It was very hot in Prickly Bay and we were all glad to put to sea again, heading north past Isle de Ronde and its girdle of rocky islets in a lively breeze. We anchored in Tyrrel Bay on Carriacou on New Year's Eve, dined in the cockpit and saw the New Year in among the other anchored yachts with fireworks, flares and bagpipe music.

On 3 January we sailed to an idyllic anchorage between the two small coral islands of Petit St Vincent and Petit Martinique. This is millionaire country, with an exclusive hotel complex hidden among the trees on Petit Martinique and some very grand yachts at anchor. By now we were constantly looking out for coral reefs and it was nerve racking at first, but we learned to read the colour of the water and approach the reefs with the sun behind us whenever possible. We were approaching the archipelago of the Tobago Cays, perfect little desert islands surrounded by brilliant blue water and crests of surf over the reefs.

We anchored first at Saltwhistle Bay, a palm-fringed cove sheltered from the strong east wind. Next day was calmer and we found a lovely anchorage at the heart of the Tobago Cays for two days of swimming, snorkelling and basking in the sun, before moving on to the delightful island of Bequia, one of our favourite spots in the whole Caribbean. Bequia is a small island, but its serpentine shape forms the wide, deep anchorage of Admiralty Bay in the lee of a green mountain. The bay is always busy with inter-island cargo boats and ferries, sailing vessels of all sizes and a resident fleet at anchor. This was a nostalgic visit for Stuart and Annabelle, and they showed us the path over to Friendship Bay where there are still whaling boats.

Port Elizabeth is really just a village, with one road and a few taxis, but much of the waterfront is served by a footpath under palm trees between the gardens and the sea. The village is full of flowers and birdsong, happy people strolling and shopping in the market, with a few hotels, restaurants and bars where you can sit outside under the trees. At 'Sergeant's' they make exquisite scale models of local whaling boats, and of yachts too. You can watch the craftsmen carving every part in wood, right down to tiny oars and harpoons. Another local craft is screen printing sea island cotton, which is made into beach clothes and sold in the boutique. In the evenings you can go to a waterside restaurant with a steel band playing and dance on the sand. Little wonder we returned to Bequia three times before the month was out.

Flight of Time is a Bowman 45, designed by Chuck Paine and built in GRP in 1995. She is cutter rigged, with a scheel type keel, displacing 13 tons. The mainsail is fully battened, with lazy jacks, and the yankee has roller reefing. Large capacity fuel and water tanks and a water-maker provide for comfortable long distance cruising.

HAVE WE GOT THE RIGHT YACHT HERE?
MUSKETEER IN ESTONIA 1997

by Michael Lewin-Harris

The new crew had joined at Mariehamn and the destination was Estonia. We had charts (not all in Cyrillic writing) and the Estonian 'Mini-Loots', a slightly sketchy yachting pilot in five languages, including English. A cruise in bright sunshine down the rocky channels and islands to the Finnish clearance station at Kökar became a fast spinnaker run through the night (although it never gets properly dark in June at 60°N). 0100 found the wind backing to the north (chilly too), the spinnaker down and the shore lights of Hiiumaa island in the distance to starboard. These disappeared as the light strengthened, leaving us in 10 metre soundings with nothing in sight at all. The GPS confirmed our position and course was shaped for the Hari Kurk channel, 10 miles distant.

Gradually the leading light structures on Vormsi island appeared above the horizon, followed by pine trees and finally the low sandy shore. As we drew level with Vormsi's southernmost point, soundings dropped into single figures, where they remained for the next five days. Now a turn to port, and for a nerve-racking 14 miles we followed buoyed channels and leading lines in ever-decreasing depths to Haapsalu. The 2.5 metre soundings given for the quay were a trifle optimistic, but with a heave-ho through the soft mud we were bow to the staging, in company with two Finnish and three Estonian yachts.

Not much seemed to be happening, but thanks to Peter's left-over 'Kroons' from two years before we were able to buy some garfish from a small fishing boat for the equivalent of 60p. Estonian is a language akin to Finnish or Hungarian. At the yacht club / hotel on the quay, the lady in charge, whose English was at least better than our Estonian, insisted we sign the visitors book and assured us the officials were coming. They were courteous and the only requirements were passports (no visas) and copious crew lists. At last we could walk to the town centre half a mile away.

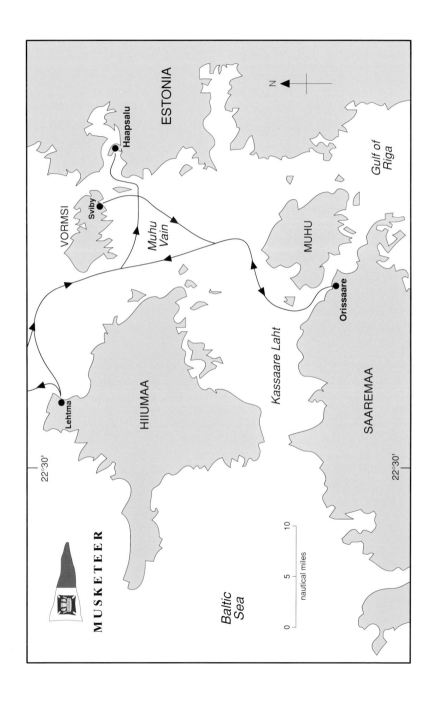

Picturesque wooden houses, which had not changed in centuries, led to a bustling centre dominated by the castle on its hill. An enormous amount of restoration work and modernisation is taking place. With enormous energy, the country is recovering from decades of communist apathy. Shops and the supermarket were well stocked. Currency exchange is easy (the Kroon is linked to the Deutschmark) and you can eat out quite cheaply.

Next day, eager to see more of Estonia, we sailed for Saaremaa Island, pausing at Svibi on Vormsi. This small ferry port has a tiny yacht pontoon, sufficient for four or five small boats, again needing a heave-ho through the mud. The island has a gentle rural aspect with wild cowslips and loud birdsong.

A Finnish yacht had recommended Orissaare, whose approach is four miles up a bay marked by well lit leading marks. The channel is marked as 2.7 metres, but with 2½ miles to go in the dusk, the 'ogginometer' read 2.5 metres. We need 2.3! There was no sign of the three small buoys marked on the chart. Mad to go on, but it was flat calm and we could see the harbour lights ahead. Hearts froze as the depth fell to 2 metres for an instant.

"Have we got the right yacht for this?" someone asked.

At last, conflicting instructions from the quayside, stern line to a buoy, more heave-ho and a hard shove with the engine, and there we were. There on the quay too were the missing buoys, freshly painted! The local people were wonderfully helpful and friendly. At the small timber yacht club we were assured we were the first British yacht ever to visit. Slightly to my alarm, we were also told the water level had been half a metre lower the previous week, but the panic dropped with the level in the bottle of Vana Tallinn (the local liqueur) as we concentrated on the serious business of cards, laughter and conversing in our respective languages.

Next morning we walked past a derelict factory (which had once made GRP sailing dinghies) whose sole occupant was now an abandoned Volga car of 1930's vintage. A short stretch of marshland and woods brought us to a pleasant small town sporting barracks, a classical Town Hall, shops old and new, again well stocked, and a main street of largely timber houses. Virtually nobody spoke English but all were friendly and even in this backwater repair work was going ahead, all co-ordinated by the ubiquitous mobile phone.

To our relief the water had risen slightly and our departure was uneventful. A delightful sail to windward in a pleasant breeze brought us to deep water again and our departure port of Lehtma on Hiiumaa, a commercial fishing harbour with good shore facilities and easy clearance. From there it was a gentle day's sail to Hangö, Finland's Lands End.

THE THREE GRANNIES GO BACK TO OLD HAUNTS

by Gill Lloyd

This year's RCC meet at Carteret, a new port of call for all three Grannies, inspired us to venture across the Channel again, to visit old haunts and old friends in the Channel Islands and St Malo aboard trusty *La Snook*.

On Monday 30th June we had an easy day's sail across to Cherbourg, checking our 50-year-old trailing Walker log against 'Maggie', a newly acquired hand-held Magellan GPS, connected to the service battery by a splendid Heath Robinson DIY job.

After a day in Cherbourg, we had a bumpy, wet and chilly passage to Alderney, which we could just lay. Ashore for an excellent supper at the 'First and Last', we sat next to a boatload of four friendly and chatty men, including two Ancient Mariners whose Yachting Yarns Helen could easily cap. The evening ended with the youngest of the crew taking us three old women off for a drink at the Divers pub. Waiting for the last water taxi in the wind and rain down beside the tiny harbour, I was reminded of the spooky night we spent dried out there in 1952 in *Chal*, our pre-war gaff cutter, sheltering from a nor'-easterly blast with three small children aboard. Then we were haunted by the ghosts of the unfortunate foreign workers, forced by the Germans to build the fortifications still towering above us, who were said to have been just tipped in with the concrete if they happened to die on the job.

Next day, cold and wet again through the Swinge and a very bumpy passage to St Peter Port, creeping in early over the sill to a convenient pontoon berth. Helen remembers pre- and very early post-war RCC Easter gatherings there, drying out for scrubbing and antifouling in company with the Commodore, Roger Pinckney, and *Dyarchy I* or *II*.

Saturday 5 July. Summer at last, and a balmy downwind sail to Jersey, bumbling along under the 'Snooksl' (cruising chute), all the islands sparkling in the sunshine. We anchored for tea in St Aubin's Bay, off the castle where Helen and her father in *Emmanuel*, a 24-ft gaff cutter with no engine, had found peaceful haven in 1930. Alas, buzzing motor scooters and wash from passing ferries spoilt today's peace, so we drifted on round the bay to the modern convenience of St Helier marina. In the old days, to stay afloat, we moored to a rickety pontoon just inside the harbour entrance, and a succession of convivial French boats would attach themselves outside, with a few bits of string one to the other, see-sawing back and forth with the slop of the tide.

A gentle potter over to St Malo next day, although the vis. wasn't good enough to thread the 'Minkies', as we'd hoped. We took the west-about route, ending up in St Servan marina at whisky time. Not so romantic as locking into Bassin Vauban, but more convenient tidal access for local pottering. In 1946, Helen and John Tew sailed over in *Mary Helen*, a 24ft gaff cutter without an engine. Extracts from her log in that year's RCC Journal make intriguing reading:

'August 22nd. Entered basin and tied up alongside quay by the old town walls. The gaunt ruins of the old town made the approach to St Malo deserted and desolate . . . The centre of St Malo was destroyed by the Germans out of sheer vandalism, after most of France had been liberated. The ruins and destruction have to be seen to be believed, but fortunately the old walls and a few buildings at the edge of the old town still stand.'

When Liz and Jim Bate arrived in 1950 on a cruise from the Bristol Channel in their 23ft Beer fishing boat, they found the town still in ruins but rebuilding proceeding noisily from dawn to dusk.

Two days of morning fog and no wind were enlivened by convivial evenings, first with French friends at Minihic-sur-Rance. On a perfect evening we sipped champagne on their terrace, looking across the river to St Suliac. In 1966, when the Rance barrage was still being built and we anchored there in *Pleiades*, Jean-Pierre and Florine rowed out to warn us that the water might suddenly disappear (luckily it didn't), stayed on for a protracted lunch party and have been firm friends ever since.

Gently sailing up the Rance, we were making for Plouër when the wind died and the engine failed. *La Snook* drifted up to a mooring off the Restaurant de la Cale, just before the marina entrance, as by the time I'd coaxed the engine back to life it was too late to get in. A dinghy trip ashore revealed a peaceful and very sheltered little marina, an old mill pond tucked away in a corner with six feet depth, a boatyard, but no nearby shop.

On Saturday 12th July we came back through the barrage and set sail eastwards along the coastal Chenal de la Bigne, but the breeze came round north-easterly and gave us a rock-dodging beat. Progress became minimal and the engine again failed to start, so we eventually turned tail and drifted back at the turn of the tide to St Servan marina. I rushed ashore and just managed to catch the *chantier* before the long weekend –

Ann alongside in St Malo, 1950.

Emmanuel

Old Dyarchy in St Peter Port, Easter 1930.

La Snook

le Quatorze Juillet. A charming young *mecanicien* got the engine going within 20 minutes. Air in the fuel system. Hurrah! Not stuck here for the weekend.

Next morning we enjoyed a fascinating coastal crawl, finally cutting close round Pointe de Grouin behind the islands. On a rising tide, *La Snook* threaded through the oyster beds into Cancale harbour, a new port for all of us. With massive holiday crowds ashore, we sat on a mooring enjoying the view with drinks in hand, before setting sail across Baie de Mont St Michel. Misty visibility and tricky tides made Maggie's readings reassuring, and eventually we hastened into Granville marina with half a metre to spare over the sill on a falling tide.

Next day, we waited until the last of the tide before setting out for Chausey, to be rewarded by a splendid view of Mont St Michel, like a distant battleship, as we crossed the bay. Reaching Chausey Sound near low water, we moored between two vacant buoys and settled to a lovely calm moonlit evening.

Aiming to carry the tide up to St Catherine's Bay at the north-east corner of Jersey, we left at midday to pick our way through the north passage, just touching the sand on the hump (reckon on about 1½ metres depth at half tide). With a bare force 2 westerly, engine running and an ancient large-scale chart (rocks and towers stay the same) we took a daring short cut through the dreaded rocks off the south-east corner of Jersey to the Violet Channel buoy, and thence up past Gorey to moor inside St Catherine's breakwater.

Wednesday 16 July: Drizzle again and confusing leading marks dissuaded us from attempting Les Ecrehous *en route* for the new Diélette marina. Early on the tide we crept in on 125° to the pierhead as directed, then over a sill into a large, near empty marina full of smart pontoons. We had an excellent meal at the hotel up the steps, just above the corner of the old inner harbour.

Next day, *La Snook* joined the RCC Carteret Meet, a happy, action-packed event, expertly organised by John and Sue Sharp. The Grannies, in the smallest boat by well over six feet, were much cosseted with expert help when the service electrics failed, and transport ashore magically materialised before we started to flag, including a car to Portbail to view the 'unmodernized' harbour, reminding us what it was like visiting these small ports in the old days. By breakfast time on Sunday the next generation had arrived by car to take over La Snook and we drove home via the afternoon ferry.

SEA ANCHORS AND DROGUES

by Richard Clifford

Those of you that read my last account in the 1976 Journal may recall that we were severely knocked down during the OSTAR and again on the return passage. In the 1980 CCA Journal I recorded a similar experience whilst alone off the Irish coast during the 1979 Fastnet gale. It was after the Fastnet incident that I made my own drogue using a discarded parachute, with a diameter of just under a metre. However it was not until last year that I performed trials on this and other drogues and sea anchors.

To avoid confusion, my definition of a sea anchor is a device which when streamed ahead of the boat holds its head into or nearly into the seas, while a drogue is a device streamed astern to slow the boat and give it directional stability. Streaming warps over the stern, like many of us have done, does seem to give some directional stability but, as I found during my recent trials, not as much as I had previously thought.

Claude Worth expounded on the virtues of sea anchors while the Hiscocks, like many British yachtsmen, dismissed them. This, I believe, was largely because the size of sea anchor used was too small. In 1964, Tilman (in the yacht *Patanela*) used a military parachute as an effective sea anchor on a Heard Island venture, although on its second deployment a bronze fitting parted and the parachute was lost. Since then, development of these devices has been slow, although the RORC has commissioned the Wolfson Unit at Southampton University to do trials on both sea anchors and drogues.

The aim of my own trials on board *Warrior Shamaal* was to compare, in as quick succession as I could physically manage, various heavy weather techniques from lying ahull, streaming warps, streaming a number of different drogues to lying to a sea anchor. I carried out these tests in Biscay and twice in the Channel, in force 6 maximum. During the last trial Peter Bruce accompanied me. The results were not conclusive and all are subjective. I used a GPS to record speed over the ground.

Sea Anchors

I had the use of a 15ft diameter parachute sea anchor said to be suitable for yachts up to 35ft (*Shamaal* is a Warrior 35). The literature stated that an 18ft sea anchor would be suitable for up to a 40ft monohull. The bigger the boat the larger diameter required. One also needs a minimum of 100m of rope rode. Three lay nylon is preferable to braided line, of about the diameter you'd use to anchor your boat – I used 18 mm nylon, plus about 10m of anchor chain (possibly too light) to help sink the sea anchor below the disturbed surface water. Finally I used 30m of 10mm polypropylene with a fender on the end as a tripping line to aid recovery.

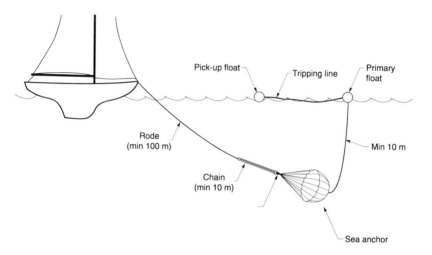

All this was dumped over the windward side in reverse order – i.e. pick up float (fender), tripping line, primary float (fender), parachute (in its bag), chain and then the main rode which was paid out slowly. As soon as the parachute developed I could feel its immense power – not a device to be trifled with. Once the rode was fully out, I used a plastic pipe in the stemhead fitting to reduce chafe. The rode was led via a snatch block on the toerail to the sheet winch.

With the wheel lashed amidships *Warrior Shamaal*'s bows swung into the seas and wind. We did yaw, but only to about 15° either side of the wind. Also the motion is rather lively. Some recommend a steadying sail, either a reefed mizzen or a storm jib hanked onto the back stay, although in the storms I have experienced, including the October 87 storm, a sail would not have survived for long. Also it's vital that the fittings on board are sufficiently strong to take the loading. Recovery of the device took 20 minutes and is hard work. The tripping line only

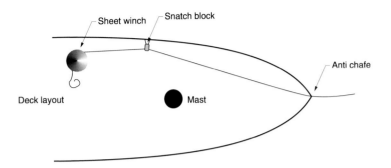

came within reach of the boat with the use of the engine as it was blown off to one side. Do not underestimate the weight of a wet parachute.

Drogues

I took several different types to sea. Three were cone drogues and one a Delta drogue as illustrated. The recommended minimum diameter for a cone drogue is 10% of your LWL. Again I used 100m of 18mm rode and a 10m length of chain to keep the device as far below the surface as possible. I'd fitted a substantial swivel ahead of the Delta drogue.

My home made parachute nylon drogue, one metre diameter, was no more effective than streaming warps. A similar sized cone drogue made of vinyl-coated fabric gave better performance. I then tried two vinyl cone drogues in tandem, the second about half a wave length behind the other and this was even better at reducing speed and giving directional stability.

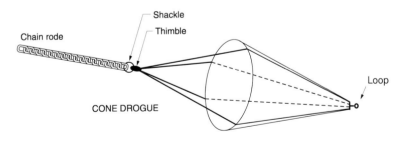

The Delta drogue, also of vinyl-coated nylon fabric, was very effective at keeping the boat running downwind and slowing the speed, thus reducing the risk of a broach or pitchpole.

The distance the drogue is astern can be controlled on the sheet winches. If possible the drogue should be drawing on the back of the second wave astern. Although some recommend lashing the wheel, I do not, as I believe one should have immediate access to the rudder to counter any likely broach. With drag devices one must be prepared for wave impact from astern. Recovery is much easier than the sea anchor.

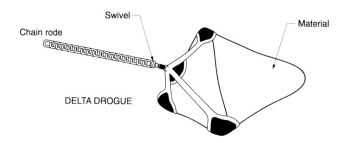

I did try locking the wheel and steering with the Delta drogue. By tying a 20m mooring line onto the rode, thus making a bridle lead to the sheet winch on the other side, I was able to steer to bring the wind from just abaft the beam through to just abaft the beam on the other tack. A useful emergency steering system.

When the late Colin McMullen wrote about this subject, he mentioned the Jordan drogue which consists of a series of small drogues fitted to a 100m line. I have not tried this and would not be prepared to give stowage space to a line which has only one use. He also mentioned the Attenborough sea drogue, a metal frame which again I have not tried, although Charles Watson has some experience with this device. There are other drag devices on the market, but beware of salesmen's claims.

Conclusion

As to which of these devices you should carry; ideally both. If you don't want to loose ground or are off a lee shore in a storm, I would recommend using a sea anchor providing you have the muscle power on board to set and recover it. If, however, you have sea room and wish to use the strong wind to make some progress safely, a drogue seems to be effective and also provides a useful emergency steering device. Whichever you use, the device must be large enough for your boat and kept well below the orbital water.

GETTING THE WIND UP

by Hugh Marriott

Three hundred overseas yachts visit New Zealand each year, said the Customs Officer at Opua, North Island, as he cleared us in. Of those, ten go down to South Island, but only one goes as far as the fabled Fiordland cruising ground at the south western tip. In a surge of over-confidence, I immediately decided we had better be that one.

First we had to do something about the hull blisters and fix a few hundred other defects ranging from crucial to desperate. After that, I thought, how about a circumnavigation of New Zealand before sailing north to Fiji? A four-thousand mile cruise extending down to the Roaring Forties and up to the Tropics. A taste of the Tasman Sea, Southern Ocean, and South Pacific. Albatrosses to flying fish.

It took a year to cosset the boat into reasonable shape, working on her ourselves. During that time we became part of the local community. The problem with this was that our friends at Te Uenga in the Bay of Islands turned out to see us off. It was 14th December, blowing quite fresh with rain so dense that it was hard to make out the figures waving to us from the shore. We wanted to wimp out, but didn't dare. Even with fine weather we would have been scared. Everyone in New Zealand is a sailor in one way or another, and all of them had warned us about the horrors of sailing down the west coast:

'The Tasman is the worst sea in the world, a lee shore, no harbours, it's too early in the year . . .'

In fact, there *are* harbours, including the port of New Plymouth, but they either have bars or nowhere for yachts inside them. We had decided to go non-stop down the west coast of North Island, pause in the Marlborough Sounds, then carry on non-stop down most of the west coast of South Island. It would get the worst over quickly.

I set the staysail and single-reefed main, and sailed off our anchor. Within five minutes our well-meaning friends, and everything else, had disappeared in the greyness. Luckily, the Bay of Islands is not called that for nothing, so we stole round the corner and hid in a cove, feeling guilty. Next day the weather cleared and we sailed 30 miles north to Whangaroa, a harbour as safe and scenic as Falmouth. There I removed the dorade ventilators and screwed in stainless steel plates; triple-lashed Jemima the Duckling dinghy; took the spinnaker pole off the mast and secured it on deck; sealed the hatches and dogged them down, finished off the preparations for our new parachute sea anchor. Then I stowed away the oil lamp glass chimneys and anxiously studied weather faxes. Really horrible lows down south, one going through Fiordland. But the glass was rising.

By 0600 next morning we were under way. Still, clear, quite cold. Little blue penguins dived in front of us. Fluttering shearwaters fluttered. In the afternoon, bashing into a force 5 headwind, we saw Mount Camel abeam. Twin humps. Did that wit Cook name it? At 1700 we tacked round North Cape and then plunged along the top of New Zealand through the early part of the night. Lots of shipping, bound for Auckland. At 0415 started our run south, standing well offshore. Wind force 4 from the north-west. Breathe out. Relax.

It was then that the glass began to fall, and continued falling until the very hour when we arrived in Nelson, four days later. But now that we were on our way, we felt ready for anything. Not that it was ever all that bad. The worst parts were the forecasts. They gave winds of 45 knots (force 9), but either from the beam or abaft the beam, and the sea was never wicked. Respectful of the Tasman's reputation, I watched it suspiciously. It looked much the same as any other bit of sea.

Three days out, I took the mainsail down and hoisted the trysail. I had long ago furled the big headsail and changed down to the storm staysail. The trysail and little staysail together don't amount to much, but during the night – must have been at about 0300 – I woke to the sound of serious wind. Poked my head out and looked around. Nothing evil about the seas and the boat sauntering along, all under control. I thought 'she's okay,' and went back to bed. Next morning I put the trysail away and re-set the main.

That evening Cape Farewell, at the top of South Island, lay unseen to starboard. We were in the relatively sheltered waters of Tasman Bay, with forty miles to run to Nelson. Having supper below, I saw a rain squall coming up on the radar. Thinking there'd probably be wind in it, I went on deck to tuck in a pre-emptive reef. Doing so, I could see the rain coming up fast. So while I was at it, I tucked the second reef in as well. Before I had quite finished, the wind struck. It came off the Tasman mountain range, and suddenly we were in woolly hat and gloves conditions. It put Nelson on a lee shore, so I knew I ought to heave to rather than try to enter in the dark. But, obligingly, it took off and then disappeared altogether, allowing us to motor in, wallowing on the swell, grope past the port hand lights and anchor just outside the fairway. We had sailed 515 miles from Whangaroa. Up with the riding light, off with the hat, gloves, coats, jerseys and gumboots –out with the whisky bottle, on with the woolly pyjamas, into the bunk.

Next morning we woke to shouts of 'Taceet, Taceet', and tumbled out on deck to see a French boat we had met in the Bay of Islands. They circled us and giggled. It was my pyjamas. 'You are so English, even on the other side of the world.'

They were heading out. It was 21st December and we didn't know a soul in Nelson. Panic. The only other Christmas with no family around us had been in Bequia in the Caribbean, but then we had rafted up to friends, shared a barbecue on the beach and had dinner ashore to the plinking of a steel band. This time things looked bleak. But nobody is friendless for long in New Zealand. A stranger turned up with hot mince pies for us, and delivered a letter from someone else inviting us to go into the hills to fish for trout. At a carol concert we spied a yachty family with whom we had explored the jungle in Guatemala. A pile of packages was waiting for us in the Post Office. Relax, breathe again.

On the day that our Christmas decorations came down, so did brother-in-law Billy and his new wife Heather (ex-Watson, ex-McMullen, RCC). Set off with them for the Marlborough Sounds. No pilot book aboard: we can't afford to buy pilots for everywhere we go, but we have the charts. Have to go through French Pass, the Kiwi equivalent of the Raz de Sein, with currents of 7 knots. I work out that slack water is at 1900, although Billy thinks it's 1600. We agree to split the difference and go through at drinks time. So having passed the Beef Barrels we head towards a little bay on Durville Island, inside Audibert Point, one-and-a-half miles before the pass, for a tea-stop. On our way in, we spot a lone bottlenose dolphin. It swims under the boat, comes up on the other side and slaps the water with its tail, splashing water into the cockpit. We take cover. He dives under, comes up and splashes us again. Grunting, he accompanies us for ten minutes, slapping and splashing, criss-crossing and grunting.

Later, we read about Pelorus Jack. Thirty five years ago there was a lone dolphin that accompanied ships through French Pass. He did it for so long that a legend grew up round him. So who was our dolphin? Pelorus Jack had been harpooned. Was this his ghost or his son, carrying on the family business?

For the next fortnight we investigated the channels and climbed the hills of the Sounds, peering in vain for the hordes of yachts who, we had been warned, would infest this rich cruising ground at the height of summer. But the word 'crowded' means different things to Kiwis and to those accustomed to the Solent or the Caribbean. In Pelorus Sound we had Deep Bay, Homestead Bay and Waterfall Bay virtually to ourselves. But talk on the radio of cyclone Drena, which was heading straight for New Zealand, sent us scurrying for Queen Charlotte Sound.

Hugh Marriott at the James Cook memorial in Ship Cove, Queen Charlotte Sound.

With a light northerly breeze we passed Duffers Reef and Goat Point, left Titi Island and Alligator Head to port, and swirled between Cape Jackson and its lighthouse with two knots of tide under us. Got it right this time. North Island was clearly visible on the other side of Cook Strait. Drena, about 275 miles to the north, was closing. We anchored on the east side of Papatoia just under Cooper Point, but it offered less shelter than we hoped. Never mind, purple mussels clustered on the rocks everywhere, and at low tide we filled a bucket. Time enough next day to find a real hurricane hole in Tawa Bay – Endeavour Inlet. There we anchored in 20 metres, setting a single anchor with concentration. But dreary Drena drably dragged her draughtless drizzle, and the centre of the storm passed almost directly overhead with plenty of rain, but no wind.

It got up after Drena's passing, though. As we sailed up Queen Charlotte Sound to Kumutoto, fierce blasts came from all directions, but mainly downwards, off the surrounding hills. Hoping to go into the town of Picton next day, we called the marina on VHF. But New Zealand is a land of mobile phones and the almanac lists telephone numbers, not channels. In any case, when we arrived at Picton immediately after breakfast, we found that the marina is for mastless motor boats (the footbridge doesn't lift or swing). However, we found a space alongside the town wharf.

Back down Queen Charlotte Sound, we anchored at Ship Cove, Cook's home from home. In 1774 he planted a vegetable garden there and turned out pigs and goats, returning four times in later years to draw on these supplies. The place is just as it was then, except for a stone cairn, at which we paid our respects.

The south-eastern, or Queen Charlotte, part of the Marlborough Sounds seemed luxuriant to us by comparison with the cropped bare look of Pelorus Sound. It was here, in Ketu, that Heather kindly cut my hair – or rather cut it off, perhaps in sympathy with our surroundings.

Crewless again in Nelson, we found someone staring at the boat.

'Is she yours?'

'Yes.'

'I was looking at the size of her sheets and lines. Have you come from England in her?'

'Well, yes, but only slowly.'

'I'm about to set off round the world. Do you mind if I pick up a few tips?'

He was the proud new owner of a 38-footer on the hard close by. He told us his background:

'I was a fisherman, out of Fiordland.'

'Well, good grief, I should be asking you questions, because that's where we're going.'

'Only one thing to tell you about that, mate. Don't go.'

So once again we set off heart in mouth on a passage down the inhospitable west coast. We'd decided on an anticlockwise circum-navigation because it seemed the best way to get round the bottom of Stewart Island at the southern tip of New Zealand. If there was a long spell of hard westerly weather, we thought we could always blow round with the wind behind us. We'd heard tales of boats waiting for two months to beat round from the other direction before giving up. On the west coast, the wind blows out of the north-west as the fronts go through, and if we have to have gales we prefer them to blow from aft. As for going up the east coast, well, we would deal with that when we came to it.

First we had to retrace our steps northwards from Nelson up Tasman Bay, before turning west past Cape Farewell (Cook said goodbye to New Zealand from there). The fresh westerly was in our teeth as we plugged round Cape Farewell, getting nowhere. Then it died, and we motored for three days solidly, the longest continuous period under engine we have ever had. Not a breath. We came across an albatross sitting on the water, unable to get airborne. We sat in the cockpit in warm sunshine staring goggle-eyed at Mount Cook and Mount Tasman sliding by seventy five miles away. The twenty-year-old Perkins purred on and on. From time to time I patted it and dipped it and took its temperature. Then the signpost of Mount Tutoka, 2745m, appeared on our port bow, snow glowing in the dawn light. We sidled surreptitiously into Milford Sound, the northernmost of the fjords, in 44°S, well into the Roaring Forties, everything holding its breath. Seals sunbathed. The famous waterfalls dribbled. We massaged our necks, stiff with craning back. We tapped the echo sounder, which gave no reading at all as we altered course to avoid another sheer rock face. We puttered into the fishing boat harbour where, gently, we ran aground, 380 miles, and many litres of fuel, out of Nelson.

Before we left England, Billy's son Robin, our nephew, had asked if he could come with us if ever we decided to sail round Cape Horn. I sent him a message to say that southern New Zealand was the next bit of land to the north, and would that do instead? He replied, in three lines on a postcard: yes, and he'd be on the quayside, if there was one, at Milford on 1 February, and if Tacit wasn't there he'd happily occupy himself by fishing. That's the kind of crew I like.

Robin arrived a day early, in a Cessna. I just happened to be in the pub at the time with Ray, who runs the fishing boat harbour where we were moored and is also the manager of the Fiordland Lobster Company. Ray drove me back to the harbour in his truck, and had just offered to let us have a couple of spare lobsters when I saw Robin on our deck. 'Can you make that three lobsters?' He gave us six.

There are too many fiords to investigate them all. North to South, they are: Milford, Poison Bay, Sutherland, Bligh, George, Caswell, Charles, Nancy, Thompson, Secretary Island, Doubtful, Dagg, Bradshaw, Deep Cove, Breaksea, Dusky, and Preservation. We became confused till Robin said: 'Easy: Milford was Poisonous, Sutherland was Blythe, but George Caswell's and Charles and Nancy Thompson's Secretary was Doubtful about Dagg, so she looked him up in Bradshaw; he was a Deep Cove.' He's still working on the last three.

Our Holy Grail was Dusky Sound, where Cook had spent four months in HMS *Resolution* in 1773. He charted it meticulously and when it was next surveyed by HMS *Acheron*, John Lort Stokes, in 1851, Stokes couldn't improve on Cook's work. It was not re-surveyed till 1996, when the Royal New Zealand Navy tackled the job. But the new chart had not yet been issued and we wanted to explore the area before it was. We soon discovered that although Cook was a genius, Stokes was just an ordinary mortal. When we arrived off what our GPS said was George Sound, it turned out to be a shallow bay. We were in Catseye Cove, two miles to the north of George.

Our 1970 large scale chart, based on Acheron's survey, was two miles out, and not just in longitude. Inside George, we picked up a standing line in the all-weather harbour behind a little island. I had worried needlessly about anchoring in these deep, ice-gouged fiords. Cray fishermen have strung webs of lines in most of the best anchorages; yachts can make use of them so long as they don't object to the sudden arrival of a fishing boat alongside. Not that anyone could object, since these visitations are always accompanied by gifts of live crays and fresh cod. Less hospitable are the other denizens of Fiordland: sandflies. These midge-like creatures launch intensive airborne sorties throughout the day, and their bites, if scratched, turn septic. Our answer was copious mosquito netting in the companionway and dorade vents, and a full-time burning coil. Ashore, the trick is to keep moving. But pause to listen to a bellbird or investigate deer tracks and you're done for.

The fishermen of Fiordland are friendly partly because they're New Zealanders, and partly because there aren't many people for them to talk to, so that they welcome company. This seems also to apply to the dolphins. Each sound has its resident family, and they are always pleased to see you. Dolphins have prodigious appetites. We had been warned that the deep fiords only support life around their fringes so have a fragile ecosystem, yet there is no shortage of the delicious blue cod in them. We always caught two or three when we tried, and one even came up on an unbaited hook. The average time to catch dinner for two days was eight minutes. We duly went through this laborious procedure before leaving for Charles Sound. We also changed down to the storm jib, in view of the williwaws which had been buffeting us all night. Willies, as we came to know them, are catabatic winds that come whooshing down from the mountain tops rather like avalanches, slam into you with appalling violence, then suddenly stop.

Tacit going well.　　　*Photo: Roberta Etter*

With one reef in the mainsail and our small jib (which was to stay on the forestay for the next thousand miles) we set off down the sound, gaining speed as we neared the mouth. The wind was off the land, and I knowledgeably explained that this meant the sea would not be rough. But when it opened up before us, patches of it were smoking as wind gusts tore across. Before I could comment, a willie descended and laid us flat on our side. Three water containers lashed on to the starboard sidedeck instantly disappeared. The helm was useless, and the poor old boat lay there like a dog that's been run over by a lorry. Then she heaved herself up and belted off, straight out to sea. I was steering for all I was worth, trying neither to gybe nor come up a single point. We had to get the main off her, and as I didn't want to leave the wheel, it would have to be Robin. He looked a bit shaken, but bravely struggled into a harness. When he was ready, I tried to round up to free the main, but we were instantly laid over on our side again.

Then the wind paused to draw breath, and we were able to take in the second reef, and roll up the storm jib altogether. After that we crabbed inshore under deep-reefed main only, making about two knots, until we closed the land. We found ourselves off the entrance to Charles Sound, which was not where we had been hoping to go, but seemed good enough in the circumstances. For three hours we tacked painfully slowly up the sound till we could find somewhere - Gold Arm - sheltered and shallow enough to let go the anchor. We had sailed from 0800 till 1800 to make good about twenty miles. Strangely, though, this was one of the few passages we made under sail in Fiordland. For most of the time we skulked while the winds went through, then motored for all we were worth through the in-between calms.

What was good, though, about being out there when it was blowing true Southern Ocean style, was to see the albatrosses. I never saw one flap its wings. These are so long they appear to be articulated at two points along their length, instead of following a single curve. There must be uplift from the waves, and they use this instead of flapping. The sheer power of the weather was, I have to admit, daunting to us. But then you stole a glance at one of these enormous birds as it swept by, leaning negligently on the wind, at home and at ease, and suddenly you felt, though I can't explain why, better about being there.

As for the strength of the wind, I can't tell you. We have no anemometer. But I spent the following morning re-whipping the ends of the jib sheets, which had been shredded into old-fashioned shaving brushes.

Next day we had a fine two-tack beat to Thompson Sound in search of the Blanket Bay Hotel. Where Thompson meets up with Doubtful, on the shores of Secretary Island, is the charmingly but inexplicably named Blanket Bay. There, on a rock, is a shack built by the local cray fishermen. They have run a pipe to it from a nearby stream so that they

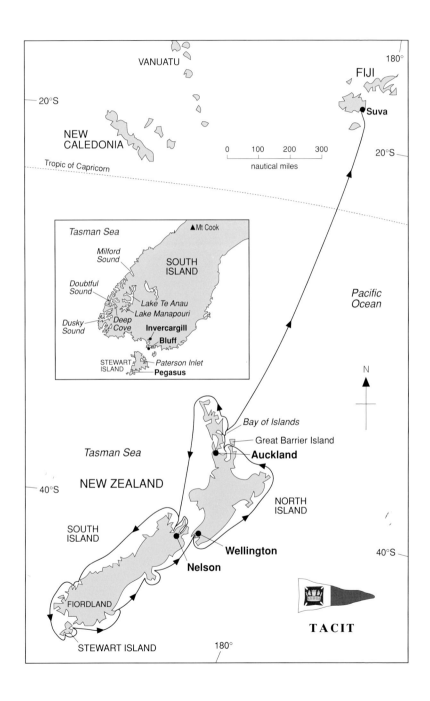

can take on fresh water, and made an incinerator for burning their rubbish.

Two other boats were there already. One was a single-handed fisherman, who lobbed a few crayfish into our cockpit. The other was a dive charter boat full of tough Invercargill wives taking a week off from their families to dive for crays. We made fast alongside her. After our lobster supper, the party began. Robin went to represent the Poms. One of his new friends said to him: 'Hope your auntie and uncle didn't come here for a bit of peace and quiet.' Another showed him one of her tattoos, the one on her thigh. A third told him he sounded like Prince Charles. 'You should hear his uncle,' chipped in a fourth; 'he talks as if he's got a hot plum stuck in his throat.'

Our social life continued next day. It was raining, the sandflies were out in force, and the forecast was NW 40kts, sea very rough. So we went twelve miles upstream to Deep Cove at the head of Doubtful Sound, protected all the way by massed mountains. A hostel there provides educational holidays for young people. They are bussed to the village of Manapouri, boated across a lake, and then driven in the hostel jeep along a dirt road to Deep Cove. For some reason, they invited us to dinner. During it, we suggested that one or two might like to come out and visit the boat next day. They came, and one at least we sent away with a wistful faraway look in his eyes.

This, we thought, would be the last we would see of people for two weeks. Not that we would be out of contact, because we talked every day to Bluff Fishermen's Radio, run by the apparently unsleeping Mary.

Only once did Mary fail us, when we asked her to get a message to Andrew and Bette O'Grady on *Balaena*, who we knew were also in Fiordland, a few days ahead of us. But *Balaena* does not carry a radio, and we never met.

Hugh and Cathie Marriott are cruising full-time in their cutter-rigged Valiant 40, built in 1976. They left Lymington in 1992 and after completing their circumnavigation of NZ Tacit set off for Fiji and to investigate the Pacific further before returning.

BENSERSIEL – 29TH NOVEMBER 1897

by Richard Coleman

' "Sou-west to north-east – only the worst sort do that," said Davies.' Chapter XV of Erskine Childers' *Riddle of the Sands* then continues with a description of *Dulcibella*'s run into Bensersiel in the storm.

In the Club Journal for 1897, there is a brief account by Erskine Childers of his cruise that year in his 7 ton yacht *Vixen*. In that account he wrote ". . . on the German mainland there are half-a-dozen little miniature cottage-rimmed basins which can be reached in broad daylight by tidal channels at high water. It was into one of these that we ran under exciting circumstances during the great gale of November 29th, the first half of which we rode out safely in the open." Childers' manuscript diary of the cruise is now in the National Maritime Museum.

The cruise began at Dover in the middle of August. By the beginning of November *Vixen* was at Flensburg. Here, the diary tells us: "Henry arrived . . . brought loads of guns, cartridges etc and a big new double oil stove and our fine old 'Shulah' compass."

On 11th November they were at Schleimunde: "Wind S. Thick fog all day. About mid-day heard step on deck and next moment who should tumble down hatchway but our old friend Bartels of the *Joannes*. He was on his way to Hamburg from Kappeln without cargo . . ."

By 17th November, *Vixen* had passed through the Kiel Canal and was at Cuxhaven, where they were delayed by bad weather until 21st November.

"It was thick unsettled weather, so we decided to cut in across the sands behind Neuwerk Island following the boomed channels . . . explored for Stickers Gat, our first boomed channel . . . found it, but also a strong ebb running out of it."

In 1897, the distance between Cuxhaven and the deep water of the Weser by way of the boomed channels across the sands was about 28 miles. There were (and still are) three drying, or almost drying watersheds to cross. The channels were unlit and *Vixen* had to anchor between tides and overnight in great discomfort. It was not until 24th November that they reached the Weser. From the Weser they sailed across the Mellum Plate into the Jade and then westwards into the channels south of Wangerooge and Spiekeroog.

On 27th November they reached Neuharlingersiel, a small tidal harbour on the mainland shore opposite the western end of Spiekeroog. Although they didn't know it, a depression with a central pressure of around 980mb was moving south-east from Iceland and deepening. Strong gales were sweeping eastwards over Ireland.

Vixen spent the night of 27th-28th November at Neuharlingersiel. On the morning of the 28th "Wind SW fresh to strong (Glass 30.0)." As soon as *Vixen* was afloat they set sail and "stood away WNW over the sands in 5 or 6 feet towards Langeoog Island. . . . Anchored under a bank in the Rute Channel."

The centre of the depression was now just north of Scotland and had deepened to 975mb.

"Glass began falling with frightful rapidity almost visibly as you watched it. Two anchors out. Blew a heavy gale in night. Heavy sea at high water. At midnight glass was 28.50 having fallen 1½ inches in 24 hours."

The centre of the depression was now moving south-east across the North Sea and had deepened to around 960mb.

"November 29th. Wind SW. Gale abated but strong still. Very thick. Rain.

"Under way at light – determined to seek shelter at Bensersiel, a little place exactly on the lines of Neuharlingersiel, about 4 miles away on the mainland shore approached by a boomed high water channel. Fearful job to get anchor – found it bent! Groped three-reefed to the Bensersiel channel and anchored outside for water. Wind grew to an even worse gale with heavy rain and a hurricane look in the sky. A water spout passed us at a distance of about 400 yards.

"We were in the centre of cyclone, we supposed, about 1100, for the wind suddenly veered to the NE and blew a hurricane, making our anchorage and Bensersiel a lee shore.

"It was half flood and we decided to start, but how to get up anchor. Could not get in an inch as it was. In view of slipping we buoyed it ready: then got up sail three-reefed and tried to sail it out of the ground. Just giving up when it came away and we got it up. Then bore away for Bensersiel. Got into the channel but found booms almost covered by abnormally high tide and very hard to see . . . Soon got into breakers and found it a devil of a situation. Fearful work with the tiller under so much sail. One or two heavy gybes at turns of channel. When close inshore sea less bad – missed booms altogether and grounded but blew off again. Whole population on the beach yelling . . . Tide so high that all clues obscured . . . We were soon tearing into mouth of the 'harbour' about

15 ft wide, at about 7 knots. It was tiny harbour with not even room to round up. Tried to get sail down but peak jammed: let go anchor with a run, luffed and just brought up in time with the bowsprit over the quayside and received the bewildered congratulations of the people who seemed to think we had fallen from the sky. Boat and everything wet through inside and out. But she had done well, for she might well have broached to in the breakers."

After the storm *Vixen* left Bensersiel (under tow through the approach channel) and sailed westwards through the islands, laying up for the winter at Terschelling on December 14th.

ARDENT SPIRIT TO THE SERENISSIMA

by Arthur Beiser

To go to Venice in one's own yacht is such a wonderful experience that we dare not do it too often lest we perish from a surfeit of joy. So, although Germaine and I first sailed in the Adriatic 31 years ago, our cruise to the Serenissima this year in our 58-ft sloop *Ardent Spirit* would only be our fifth. We were last in the Adriatic in 1991 just as Croatia was seceding from Yugoslavia and open warfare was about to begin. Now the Dalmatian coast of Croatia, with its 1185 lightly-populated islands, was again safe and we looked forward to another marvellous summer there, with a visit to Venice as the cherry on top.

We left our base at Ile des Embiez, which is just west of Cap Sicié off the Mediterranean coast of France, on Sunday, 18 May. With us for the outbound passage were Alicia and Peter Moore, whom we have known forever and who have their own yacht in New England waters, and Dargar Bjorksten, a younger friend whose family's summer place in Finland we regularly visited when we owned the ketch *Minots Light*. We headed southeast toward the Strait of Bonifacio between Corsica and Sardinia, an overnight passage Germaine and I have made often yet always enjoy in anticipation of the landfall on the dramatic Corsican coast. Our destination was Porto Cervo in northeastern Sardinia, playground of the super rich in July and August but usually deserted at this time of year. We enjoyed a day ashore there even though the billionaires' yachts were not yet in evidence and we had to make do with gawking at those of mere millionaires.

A front passed by the next day, bringing rain and gusty winds, but the weather moderated by evening. A deep low was due next and it seemed a good idea to get going at once in the hope of covering the 300 miles to Vulcano, an island just north of the Strait of Messina, before it arrived. The plan worked, and we even had a fair wind all the way. At Vulcano, which sports an active volcano as one would expect, we showed our crew the various sights, notably a natural hot mud pool filled with bathers out

237

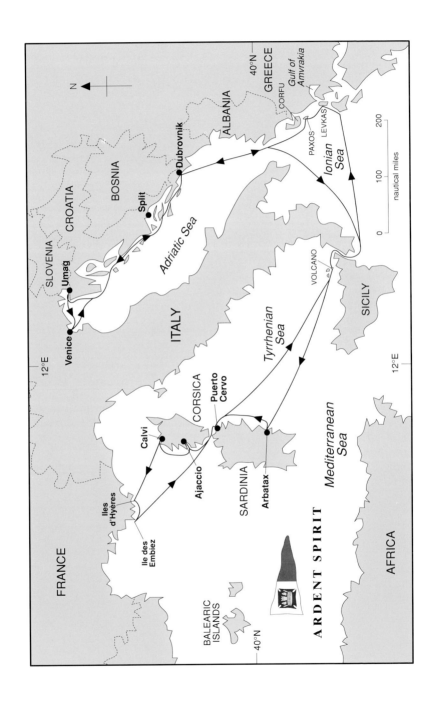

of a Fellini movie, and then repaired to Maurizio's fine restaurant for a splendid lunch.

On the Calabrian side of the Strait of Messina near Capo dell' Armi is a well-protected harbour built for an adjacent petrochemical plant that had been abandoned unused. On previous cruises we had found this harbour, called Saline Joniche, in just the right place for an overnight stop, and we went there from Vulcano. We took off early the next morning for Greece, chugging along most of the day over an unruffled sea. In the evening a wind picked up from the north and we gratefully set the main and yankee. Soon we were creaming along at 8-9 knots in the dark with a phosphorescent wake gleaming astern. By daybreak the wind had increased rather more than necessary, so we rolled up some of the yankee and eased the main; with full-length battens, one can spill wind from the main without any flutter. At noon Cephalonia was in sight, and by mid afternoon we were anchored in Port Vathy on Ithaca, a pleasant town in a handsome setting with Gregory, of the eponymous taverna to port as you enter the harbour, always ready to dispense good cheer and good food.

From Port Vathy we went north to Levkas, where we were glad to find our friends Mervyn Hall and Paula Massey on the ketch *Baily of Howth* in Tranquil Bay opposite Nidri. We anchored a mile away in Vlikho Bay, which we prefer because, though a longer dinghy ride to Nidri, it has better holding and is less crowded. We stayed there for two days during which we swam in the warm water, explored Levkas in various vehicles, saw a lot of Mervyn and Paula and caught up with one another's adventures, and ate surprisingly well at the Trata taverna in Nidri.

The almost landlocked Gulf of Amvrakia is an hour's run north of the Levkas Canal. We spent a few days exploring this peaceful inland sea and then anchored off Vonitsa, a Potemkin village rather attractive seen from the water but dismal inside with shabby buildings and dusty streets full of idlers and the occasional scurrying chicken. Alicia, Peter and Dargar left for Athens from here and then flew on to New York, leaving us with memories of three harmonious weeks on *Ardent Spirit*.

Our daughter Nadia, her son George (now a useful 15), and her partner David Richards were due to join us in Corfu in ten days. In the interval, while Germaine and I were lazily cruising around the central Ionian, the grapevine brought disturbing news of a crime spree in Corfu by Albanian gangsters. Greek officials and the press confirmed that over 200 night-time robberies of and from yachts in Corfu harbours had recently taken place, plus assorted piracies of yachts under way in Greek waters opposite Albania. A Greek coastguardsman had been killed and a Greek customs launch stolen. All this was not quite our scene, so we asked Nadia and company to meet us in Nidri instead of Corfu.

Nadia and George have sailed with us almost every summer of their lives, and David has learned fast on previous cruises, so life on board slipped into a comfortable pattern at once. Our first stop was Lakka on Paxos where we picked up 26 litres of the superb local olive oil. The forecast was for SE winds the following day, just right for the 240-mile passage north to Croatia. We left at 0500 in light airs that hardened later to F6, staying west of Corfu and well away from Albania. *Ardent Spirit* roared along at 10-12 knots under a bright gibbous moon, glorious going although steering was strenuous at times. In the morning we tied alongside the quay in Gruz, the commercial harbour of Dubrovnik, where we got our cruising permit for £184. As its name suggests, Gruz is not a particularly lovely place, and when the formalities were over we went up the river to the marina at Komolac, a decided improvement.

The war damage to the marina and to the old city of Dubrovnik had been largely repaired and both were back in business, although noticeably less crowded than on our earlier visits. A stroll around Dubrovnik is always rewarding to the eye, and several good restaurants are there for the time when the stone pavement becomes too much for one's feet.

On 26 June we shifted back into cruising mode and sailed in light winds to Polace harbour on Mljet, one of the loveliest spots in this lovely region. The next day brought more wind and we flew to the outer island of Vis, in the past forbidden to foreigners. We found a beautiful bay with the town of Vis at its head, but unfortunately the wind, now quite vigorous, was blowing parallel to the main quay where a gaggle of smallish yachts were moored stern-to and jumping wildly about. It seemed imprudent to try to join them, so we went to the windward corner of the bay to anchor in calm water off the hamlet of Kut. We dragged three times and finally, at the suggestion of a restaurateur on the quay, picked up a mooring.

The SE wind that had caused us such grief in Vis was just what we wanted to give us a swift broad reach to U. Soline on Pašman island. Most of U. Soline, a pretty place we had visited on earlier cruises, is too deep for comfortable anchoring, but now we found a number of government-laid moorings there and picked up the last vacant one. Then on to U. Maracol on Unije island, like Vis previously forbidden, and finally up the Istrian peninsula to Umag where we tied up in the marina to get ready for Venice. Going north from Dubrovnik we found more and more yachts enjoying the coast and islands, mainly under German, Austrian, and Italian flags. But there was always room in the anchorages, especially at night when most of the powerboats had fled to the many (and excellent) marinas that were never far away. And, best of all these days, no jet skis – not, I hope, a temporary absence.

The surface of the Adriatic was a sheet of glass when we left Umag. In an effort to raise a wind we covered the furled mainsail, always effective in the past but to no avail today. At 1400 we entered the lagoon of Venice, the bell towers of the city in the distance piercing the sky merrily atilt. Soon the splendour of the Doge's Palace was to starboard, the white dome of the Salute ahead, and to port the island of San Giorgio Maggiore, next to whose imposing church lay our destination, the narrow basin of the Compagnia della Vela. We tied alongside the brown-hulled ketch *Mattutina*, whose owner is our old friend (and the local RCC representative) Gianpietro Zucchetta. (I belong to this club, but non-members are welcome if there is space, as there often is in the summer.) As usual – I never seem to get the timing just right – the tide was not quite high enough and *Ardent Spirit* dragged her keel through soft mud the last few metres.

Venice needs no gloss from me, and all I will say is that we found being there as enchanting as ever. It is hard to imagine a better base in Venice than San Giorgio, which stands majestically apart from the bustle of the city itself yet is only one vaporetto stop from San Marco. Unending streams of scurrying vaporettos, gleaming varnished water taxis, humble freight barges, multideck Lido ferries, and the occasional ocean-going freighter or cruise liner pass in front of San Giogio where our cockpit provided front-row seats for the spectacle.

Nadia, George and David left for home on 9 July. Venice is not an easy place to leave – even its mud had a grip on us – but Germaine and I managed to get away a week later. Not much wind, so we motorsailed in bright sunshine the 75 miles to U. Kanalic, an anchorage just south of Pula on the Croatian mainland. There, to our pleasure, we found *Mattutina*, which rafted alongside *Ardent Spirit* the next day.

Ardent Spirit in Port Vathy, Itaca.

A brisk SW wind the day after was just what *Mattutina* wanted to start her return passage and she took off, but it was on the nose for us and raining besides, so we stayed put. That night a violent squall struck with gusts over 40 knots and a deluge of icy rain that blotted out nearby yachts as we all swung wildly about. Several yachts dragged and had a struggle to re-anchor in the darkness and confusion. By midnight it was all over with only jangled nerves and a sharp spike on the barograph trace to show for a hellish hour and a half.

We now had four weeks by ourselves to cover the 130 miles to Trogir where Joan and Peter Noble were to join us. Hardly an epic voyage, but an opportunity to immerse ourselves in, not just sample, the delights of the good life afloat in an incomparable setting. This year's exceptionally mild temperatures meant that we were never too hot during the day and slept well during the cool nights; we even needed a light blanket now and then, as never before in a Dalmatian summer.

From U. Kanalic we sailed south to one of our favourite spots in this region, the angle formed by the uninhabited islets of Veli ("large") Orjul and Mali ("small") Orjul. A few yachts come there during the day for their crews to enjoy the crystalline water and remote atmosphere, but usually leave in the evening for nearby Lošinj or Ilovik and we are then utterly alone overnight.

Not much of note occurred in the days that followed as we made our gradual way to Trogir. After Orjul came cute little Luka Sv. Ante on Silba, Zapuntel on Molat, where we found moorings and a good

Ardent Spirit leaving Venice, Germaine Beiser at the helm

restaurant; and Zaliv Pantera, a large sheltered bay on the north end of Dugi Otok ("Long Island") that has 50 moorings scattered about and a launch that comes every evening to collect garbage.

The southern end of Dugi Otok is a two-tined fork four miles long that encloses a cruising Eden called Luka Telascica. It boasts perhaps ten distinct anchorages (several with moorings) in a variety of handsome settings, garbage is collected daily from yachts, and a bum boat provides fresh bread, fruit, vegetables, eggs, cheese, and wine. The FPI is luke-warm about L. Telascica in a commendable effort to minimize visitors to its clean waters and wooded shores, but this did not seem to be working when we were there. Fortunately the bay is large enough not to be overwhelmed by the dozens of yachts that came and went every day.

South of Dugi Otok is Kornat, another long, narrow island, which has a string of islets along its western shore, a treeless world of carved limestone. After a few days there we found the lush surroundings of U. Potkucina on O. Kokar welcome until a young man on an Italian sloop anchored nearby turned on a loud boombox. Irate, I went over in the dinghy to ask him to moderate the racket. Before I could say anything, he presented me with a fine watercolour of *Ardent Spirit* sailing in that he had just completed; he turned out to be a professional artist, and the watercolour is before me as I write. After I thanked him, he wondered why I had come over just then. "To invite you and your friends over for a drink," I said with a straight face. They were a jolly bunch and we had a pleasant hour together during which I managed to hint that we liked peace and quiet. Later the immaculate Freedom sloop *Mermerus* came in and we went over for a chat with Gail and Christopher Lawrence-Jones who were on their way to Venice. Had we not just come from there their good fortune would have been hard to bear.

We got to Trogir a few days later and tied up in the marina in the only berth available for a vessel our size, unfortunately amid a herd of large motorboats. We like Trogir, an ancient town of great presence with an excellent market nearby, but we did not care much for the incessant and usually dramatic comings and goings of our neighbours. On 14 August Joan and Peter Noble arrived three hours late from London via Zagreb. ("Is normal," the woman in the marina office told me when she dismissed my request to call Split airport to inquire about their nonappearance.) Peter is a psychiatrist who has written and lectured on psychological factors in sailing and is the author of a compatibility questionnaire for *Yachting Monthly* to determine if prospective crews would make good shipmates. It seemed extraordinarily brave of Peter to come with us under these circumstances, so in return I was tactful enough not to apply the questionnaire to them. Joan and Peter in fact fit in very well with our ways of doing things, and their competence, experience, and good cheer were tremendous assets during the three weeks and nearly a thousand miles we were together.

Our Honorary Representative in Venice, Dott. Gianpietro Zuchetta, in his new private gondola. Built to an 18th century design, it is propelled by two young ladies in period costume.

To give Joan and Peter a taste of Dalmatia, and to give Germaine and me a sort of going-away present, we sailed first to three of our favourite anchorages south of Trogir: Tarsice on Sv. Ante, Loviste at the end of the Pelješac peninsula, and Polace on Mljet. Then on to the Dubrovnik marina for the Nobles to see the old city and to get *Ardent Spirit* ready for the long passage home.

We are not especially fond of southern Italy, so our plan was to go from Dubrovnik to Sardinia with a stop only at Vulcano to enjoy Maurizio's cuisine once again. The 415-mile hop to Vulcano was uneventful, two nights underway in mild northerlies, and all our meals were at the cockpit table. At Vulcano we introduced the Nobles to the mud pool and the marvels of Maurizio's kitchen. (As the reader may already have divined, we consider gastronavigation a vital element of our cruising lives.)

An oily calm greeted us when we left Vulcano for Arbatax on Sardinia, but that evening a robust southeasterly came up that gave us a mighty shove. Toward morning we were assailed by a series of squalls with heavy rain and gusts up to 35 knots. To cope we rolled up the yankee and feathered the main; the radar showed that the squalls were only a few miles across, so no point in reefing the main when depowering it sufficed for the short span of each squall. Soon after sunrise the squalls were gone and we unrolled the yankee for a fine fast sail the rest of the way.

Arbatax, though a handy stop, has nothing else to recommend it, and after a day there we headed north to wait out a forecast westerly gale in the more attractive Costa Smeralda. In Porto della Taverna we dug the anchor in solidly with 45m of chain in 6m of water. The gale considerately waited until we had finished dinner in the cockpit before climbing to F7 with intervals of F8 during the night and the next day. The day after that the wind subsided to F6 and we ran under staysail alone to Cala di Volpe where we anchored off the beach. We tend to think of *Ardent Spirit* as a largish yacht but now she was one of the babies of the anchored fleet, which ranged up to a gorgeous Perini ketch 155 ft overall.

When the gale was finally over we went up to Porto Cervo, which was getting ready for a meet of classic yachts. Already there were a number of giant schooners, including *Te Vega* and *Mariette*, all polished to inhuman perfection. Just as interesting were two famous Olin Stephens designs, both now under loving Italian ownership and looking just out of the box: the 52-ft yawl *Dorade*, whose racing invincibility made Stephens' name six decades ago, and the magnificent 73-ft ketch *Capricia*, whose photo graces the endpapers of my book *The Proper Yacht*.

On 1 September we tore ourselves away from Porto Cervo and motorsailed in light airs to Ajaccio on Corsica's west coast. After two days there the Nobles left for London and the real world. From Ajaccio we went up to Girolata and then to Calvi, where we found Warren Brown (RCC) in *War Baby* leaving for Venice. He had just come down from northern waters, Venice was a long haul away, and it was now September, but Warren was game to press on.

From Calvi we sailed to the Iles d'Hyères off the French coast west of St. Tropez, where we like to spend a few days at the end of each summer to unwind. We had hoped to stay in these beautiful islands still longer, but after three days a severe mistral was forecast, so we returned to Ile des Embiez on 12 September and secured *Ardent Spirit* in her winter berth. The mistral never materialized, but we couldn't really complain after nearly 4 months (half the time by ourselves) in which we covered about 3000 miles, visited 51 different harbours, and enjoyed the company of some wonderful crews.

Ardent Spirit is a 58-ft glassfibre sloop designed by Bill Dixon and built by Moodys at their Hamble yard. With full-length battens, lazyjacks, roller jib, a forestaysail, and electric winches, Germaine and I can handle her by ourselves in all conditions. Large tanks, a watermaker and ample refrigeration provide autonomy, and her size confers speed and comfort. There is almost nothing we would change about her.

SIX CANADIAN ANCHORAGES

by Eve Bonham Cozens

Gemervescence, our 50ft wooden cutter, spent five weeks in Nova Scotia in late June and July, and the sailing varied from slogging upwind in fog or dashing downwind in sun, usually some distance offshore. The coast, mainly low-lying, either wooded and deserted or rocky and deserted, is one of solitary splendour, where we saw seals and whales, eagles and ospreys. Outside Mahone Bay, Lunenberg and Halifax, other sailing vessels and even houses are few and far between. We set off from Camden, Maine, and returned to Newport, Rhode Island, and went all the way to Cape Breton Island in between. We sailed nearly 1,400 miles in just over a month, and, yes, it was too fleeting and too fast.

So I've decided to write about a few of the places where we made a stop – at some memorable and superb anchorages – which now seem to me like clear moments of idyllic calm in a swirl of foggy speedy passage-making. These places are without doubt some of the finest anchorages we have ever found. Occasionally we had to share them with another yacht or two – but in Canada three is a crowd and we were mostly on our own. Cruising on the Nova Scotia Atlantic coast is a solitary affair and you need to like your own company – which we do. There is little scope for socialising and a lot for communing with nature. Despite the chilly air, cold sea and mosquitoes at dusk, this is a wonderful remote region of great beauty.

After a sparkling downwind sail from Penobscot Bay some 75 miles 'down east' along the Maine coast, Michael and I and *Gem* slipped into a narrow inlet at dusk leaving Moose Peak lighthouse to port, and found a peaceful small anchorage out of the ocean swell in Mistake Harbour. There was absolutely no sign of habitation anywhere. An apricot sunset glistened on the sleek backs of the black seals as they lay motionless on the granite rocks around us. It was cool and peaceful.

We made the passage across the Bay of Fundy to Nova Scotia next day, anchored for a few hours just outside Yarmouth, and set off again in the early hours to catch the tide and light round Cape Sable. This fearsome headland was kind to us and we sailed past in light airs and calm seas with clear visibility – a rarity here. And so to the first of our seven chosen anchorages.

The Town Anchorage

I recommend anyone cruising Nova Scotia to come to Shelburne – there is a marvellous deep bay and the entrance through Eastern Way is easy and safe at any state of tide and in any weather. On the starboard side, past Sandy Point, you can anchor or moor off the Shelburne Harbour Yacht Club, and it was here we made our official entry into Canada, with a simple phone call to Customs, who cleared us in and issued a Cruising Permit number there and then. The club is charming and friendly and one of the flag officers, Harry O'Connor, tries to greet every visiting boat personally.

However, it's worth venturing further up the bay and anchoring off the town dock, keeping clear of the rock and shallows between the dock and Government Wharf which you pass to starboard approaching the town. You are some miles from the open sea and therefore in flat water, though it can be quite breezy. This is an attractive, open but safe anchorage, opposite a charming and picturesque waterfront. Most of the houses and buildings still have their original wooden façades, and this small town has starred in several historical films. There are several restaurants but the best is the superb Coopers Inn – an old family house where we had an excellent meal in a delightful ambiance.

The Beach Anchorage

En route from Shelburne to Lunenburg, we stopped overnight at Port Mouton, pronounced 'Muttoon' by the locals. We were recommended to this place by friends, who said that Wombakek or Carters Beach just a mile south of the Harbour was one of the most stunning beaches in the whole province. We passed north of Spectacle Island when approaching, but the locals creep in between the southern tip of this island and the high sand dunes at the south end of the beach. *Gem* anchored in crystal clear water in sand off a small wooded islet towards the north end of this two-mile white beach, where a small stream flows out. We needed an anchor light at night because there were a few fishing boats around. The dunes and sand in the moonlight were eerily beautiful.

After a couple of nights anchored off the wharves in Lunenburg (no moorings left and ground very foul and muddy), we entered Mahone Bay with its many islands and anchorages, where, together with Halifax, most of the sailing takes place in the province. We moored at South Shore Marine in Chester (probably the best boatyard in this area), having sailed 350 miles since Camden. We met up with Ted and Liz Brainard, who invited us to dine at their house on Big Gooseberry

Island. They also very kindly lent us their car so that we could drive to
Halifax Airport to meet our two children Julie (11) and Jack (9) who flew
in direct from school in England.

The Hurricane Hole

The afternoon after our children joined *Gem*, we all set sail across
Mahone Bay to Deep Cove on the eastern shore – probably the most
secure anchorage for hundreds of miles. This narrow inlet extends nearly
a mile into the 500ft high hill surrounding it. The entrance was difficult
to spot until we were almost north of it, and then we kept close to the
port side going in (where the deepest water was) and we could see ledges
on the other side. We wafted down the creek with its high pine-forested
banks, past a small but attractive hotel development with a few docks, to
anchor in a secluded small basin at the far end, near a small fish weir and
minor road. The children happily and safely pottered about in the dinghy
and went ashore to a small grassy area to explore. Wonderful place.

The Ultimate Hideaway

Near Prospect Bay, on the granite coast between St Margarets Bay and
Halifax, there is a famous and unique anchorage known as Rogues
Roost. This is not easy to find or get into, but once you are there it's
superb, with marvellous views from the surrounding hillocks. I will not
attempt to describe the way into this small and enclosed place. What you
need for cruising these waters are Canadian charts and Peter Loveridge's
'Cruising Guide to Nova Scotia' (published 1997 by International
Marine). This new book is a really serious yachtsman's guide with good
sketch charts, and we found our way into Rogues Roost with his help,
passing a few feet from the rocky side all the twisty way in.

We anchored *Gem* in Swan's Cove, tiny and enclosed, and walked to
the top of the hill to see an unexpectedly wide panorama across the inlets
and islands to the open sea. On our way to the Roost, we had stopped for
a few hours to have a good walk round Hearn Island, where we anchored
off a small white beach. Jack actually had a swim here – but only for a few
seconds! On our way out of the Roost, the fog began to roll in and we
luckily made it to reasonably clear water before losing all visibility.

We sailed and motored the 28 miles round to Halifax, seeing nothing,
but often hearing the surf on the rocky shore close to port. We couldn't
have done it without GPS. Indeed, most of those we met were amazed
that we should be cruising in Maine and Nova Scotia without radar! At
Chedabuckto Head the fog cleared and we sailed up to Queen's Wharf,
downtown Halifax, where Mary Barton joined us. After a day in the city,
we headed off north-eastwards along the coast, finding our way into
Jeddore Harbour for a night. Next day was a rollicking 66 mile run in
bright sunshine, with Mary helming much of the time while Michael and

I put the spinnaker up, adjusted it, and later dropped it and boomed out the yankee.

The River Reach

We were making for the Liscombe River, which is easy to find and extends some miles inland. Whilst there are some pleasant hills with a few farms and fields near the estuary, further up the river becomes narrow with virgin pine forest down to the water's edge. In the upper reaches, the wind dropped and we continued under power, round many bends and often just yards from the bank. We were careful to keep in the main channel which was narrow and only just deep enough for *Gem*'s 8ft draft. Arriving in the final navigable reach, we anchored off Liscombe Lodge, a surprising anomaly in this remote area. It is an attractive resort lodge/hotel with excellent facilities – swimming pool, jacuzzi, any number of sporting activities and a tiny 'marina' with four moorings (though we anchored as we always do). Here one can get fuel, water, ice, laundromat and showers, and eat in a restaurant – a relaxing and sophisticated stopover in the wilds on the way north.

Gemervescence in Swan's Cove, Rogues Roost, Nova Scotia.

From Liscombe, we had another day's fast sunny spinnaker run all the way up to Canso, on the north-east tip of Nova Scotia, and from there we sailed across in thunder and rain to St Peter's Lock from which a canal runs into the extensive Bras d'Or Lakes. Passing through, we anchored for the night near the small town of St Peter's and ran ashore for some provisions next morning (shops being few and far between in this area). It was 15th July and when we set off to explore the lakes the wind increased to 25 or 30 knots, so we stopped for a few hours for a boozy extended lunch in lonely Damien's Cove. Full of good cheer, and rather too late in the afternoon, we decided to press on to a spectacular anchorage 20 miles further on. With two reefs in the main and only a staysail, we bounced and beat across Little Bras d'Or to arrive at our destination just as night fell.

The Lake Anchorage

Leaving Cameron Island to port in the gathering dusk, we crept forward until we were close to the northern shore, which is very steep-to, with Marble Mountain soaring above to about 1,000 feet. We then turned into a small cove to starboard and anchored off the end of a white pebble spit, as we dared go no further in the failing light. Next morning we woke to find that we were in a very special, tranquil and beautiful place, with a few houses and a wharf about a mile to the west. We all went for a walk along the pebble shore, skimming stones across the calm surface of the dark water.

Passing through the Grand Narrows and the swing rail and lifting road bridges at Iona, we entered Great Bras d'Or and anchored for the night in Maskell's Harbour, sheltered, pretty and popular (there were five other yachts here!) After a walk ashore to the lighthouse, we sailed across to Baddeck, where Mary had to leave. After a brief stay in this lovely town, we set off, just the family, to sail back again, beating the whole way to Halifax in thick fog, lumpy seas and lots of wind. There my Canadian cousin, Gary, joined us, whilst we moored off the hospitable Royal Nova Scotia Yacht Squadron.

Leaving at dawn from Halifax we saw a large number of minke whales to the delight of us all. We spent a night at Liverpool and then Shelburne again, where Christina, a young Canadian student, joined *Gem* for the 330 mile passage to Newport, RI. We tacked across the Gulf of Maine in fog, rain and some 25 knots. Having passed through the Cape Cod Canal and Buzzards Bay, we entered Newport on 31st July in brilliant sunshine to see both 'J' class yachts *Shamrock* and *Endeavour* sailing majestically out into Narragansett Bay. We were dazzled by the multitude of yachts and motor boats and the famous waterfront with the noisy summer crowds – all rather bewildering after our solitary sojourn in Canadian waters and our quiet anchorages.

A SPANISH CIRCUMNAVIGATION

by D Scott-Bayfield

Many years ago we set out in *Bow Bells* to circumnavigate Spain, when the ex-captain of cadets was less experienced (at 5 months) than she is now; but we rounded Sardinia instead (Journal 1973). This year, the family not agreeing on where I wanted to go, we compromised on a three and half thousand mile round trip in *Physalian*, the 40 foot Jeanneau Sunfizz we bought in 1995.

There are two obvious problems with such a trip; the Portuguese northerlies and the French canals. Most of us have tasted the summer strength of these northerlies – after Porto the die is cast. The Canal du Midi, with its five foot draft limit, means the main alternatives are the Rhône and canals of central France, back up the Portuguese coast at other times of the year, or a lorry across France. Less obvious alternatives are the Azores, the Danube-Rhine Canal, via the Don and Moscow, or via the West Indies. This is why we have a hydraulic lifting keel, reducing our 7½ foot draft to 4½.

We left a delightful anchorage off Brownsea Island in thick fog to pick up Sandy and Winkie Watson in Portland. Leaving there, again in thick fog, opinions varied on the length of a 'biscuit toss' off the Bill. I commend the Watsons as crew; organised, disciplined and tactful, a contrast to my dog and family. We were headed off Ushant and eventually departed from Audierne, always well placed for Galicia.

An easy run gave the Watsons a taste of the delightful Galician Rias until they and Julie had to return to the UK. Off Cape Villano we spotted a yacht heading north. Rapid closing and deduction proved her to be Tom Fenwick in *Fair Joanda*. We have the happiest memories of *FJ* in three long Aegean cruises (Journals 89 and 90); equally memorably a day earlier a 50 foot whale dived close under our stern.

I was on my own for 10 days for some relaxed riding and cruising. Totally unplanned were two dreadful days anchored off Combarro, an ancient fishing village at the head of Ria de Pontevedra. I'd returned from a long bike ride after arranging a day out with a stables in the mountains. The wind had freshened sharply into a south-westerly 6 up the Ria, though Isla Tambo and a new low breakwater gave shelter to the anchorage. Fifty yards under my lee was the crowded fishing boat wall with a shoaling bay beyond that. *Physalian* has a 45 pound Bruce anchor and a 35 pound Danforth anchor, with 3/8 inch chain and multi-plait. I put down a 28 pound Chum-type weight to reinforce the Bruce and served the rope round the roller. Single-handed, with a manual anchor-winch, moving was not an option and there were no satisfactory alternative harbours nearby. Clearly we were in for a dirty night.

The first night was not cheerful but not too uncomfortable. The glass only dropped slightly, the wind speed was not much more than Force 8 and next morning the glass rose slightly. It was still too strong to get ashore to recover the bike or buy fresh food. Fishermen and others on the shore watched with interest and anticipation as we veered around, though the rope and Chum had improved the jerking substantially. Steering into gusts with the engine ticking over helped in the worst snatching.

I cannot claim to have slept well the second night either, for early next morning the wind increased beyond anything I had been through on board. Like me, the anemometer goes to pieces in a crisis, and it expired over 40 knots. For about five hours the whole sea was SMOKING with the water droplets being sucked into the air by wind sheer alone, since the waves themselves were small. With no yardstick, I estimated the wind strength at about Force 11, consistent in direction and strength and not gusty.

Rather sheepishly I considered a PAN PAN call or flares but gave up the idea. If the anchor had parted or dragged we'd be on the breakwater or shore instantly with no chance of motoring off with the few seconds or yards available. The bower Danforth, though ready, would be no more than a futile gesture. The rubber dinghy, inflated, had to be lashed on deck and would serve as a wind surfer, or more likely a hang-glider, to get me ashore. The engine was useless in the violent pitching and yawing although I left it ticking over. Lifejacket and flares were ready. I had to ring Julie on the mobile to explain my absence (long intended) at a wedding. It did not seem helpful to go into detail so I just regretted the lost riding due to it being 'a bit gusty'.

Eventually the wind dropped. I had assumed these were purely local conditions, since the barograph movements were minimal and nothing appeared on local radio, but over the next weeks we met damaged yachts and shaken yachties.

Julie rejoined via Santiago and we were three days stuck in Bayona waiting for the strong south-westerlies to ease. We had to BEAT to Porto. The old city is fascinating and a dramatic sight, since most of coastal Portugal is dull holiday developments. Portuguese officialdom is tedious, pointless, usually civil, and has to be repeated at each harbour. With the winds still southerly, we took the train inland up the Douro valley with its dramatic shots of the river and the vine terraces, but at last the normal weather patterns took over.

The original plan was to try a twin headsail system (our roller foil has two bolt rope grooves) but the strength of the northerlies discouraged experiments. By afternoon each day, wind strengths were Force 7 or more with steepening, although never vicious, seas. Looking aft from the cabin encouraged thoughts of gardening. With just the two of us, each hour's trick was hard work.

Our best stops along the Portuguese coast were at Sesimbra, with its castle, Sines with Vasco de Gama's statue, and Sagres. We much appreciated the contrast between the winds and seas off Cape St Vincent and the smooth water and isolation under Henry the Navigator's monastery.

The Algarve coast is an easy contrast to the northern coast, with several harbours or anchorages. We were underwhelmed by modern Vilamoura, but liked the Guadiana River, going 20 miles up it. Storks nest in the village church at Alcoutim. The gear lever cable parted on this stretch and fitting a replacement was an irritating nightmare not achieved before Gibraltar. Cadiz we enjoyed, but only because we carry folding bikes; the yacht harbour is a long way from the city.

We put into Tarifa, a pleasant town, as the African mountains came into view. Tempted by what I thought was a dying afternoon wind, we flew the spinnaker for a brief but exciting run towards Gibraltar, a wonderful sight. The wind freshened and we had a horrendous wrap to confirm Julie's view on spinnakers, and we were fairly shaken by the time things were back under control. Gibraltar is a fascinating place and the bikes served us well; there is even a dramatic new mosque under construction at Europa Point under the old 9.2 inch guns. Alexandra joined us here.

The original plan included Morocco and Tangier, but we only had time for a day in Ceuta, which is totally Spanish, though Moroccans pour daily across the frontier three miles away. The Spanish seem unable to relate the politics of Ceuta and Melilla, the enclaves they seized from Morocco in 1890, to Gibraltar.

We handed the boat over to Alexandra at Benalmádena, next to Torremolinos. Alex skippered *Physalian* to Barcelona with her friends, where she handed the boat back to us (intact). Interestingly, she had no hassle from either macho marina staff or officialdom.

The most attractive part of Mediterranean Spain is the short coastline between the French border and Blanes, where the Pyrenees generate anchorages instead of the usual marinas. Just into France, Collioure with its Templar castle is as lovely as ever. We have always enjoyed this stretch and did not come alongside again until the southern entry to the Canal du Midi at Port la Nouvelle.

Julie left, Gilly Watson and two less marinized friends joined here. Dismasting was easy and our new yacht legs, still unused, became a trestle. Unfortunately, 10 foot of mast and clutter still stuck out at each end and we had to use the first railway bridge to reduce the mast height further. This bridge was used by the TGV trains, which made life exciting for me and interesting for my crew.

At Narbonne, the Roman bridge builders had not borne us in mind and further lowering was necessary. Crossing the Aude was no problem; I have never seen it so high. However, there were endless delays in the locks up to and beyond Carcassonne, due mostly to the volume of hire boats. At one stage we brought the system to a halt by my refusing to have a large fourth cruiser in the lock with us. The lock keepers in summer are very green and young students. We were travelling in convoy with a friendly French yacht and an English cruiser I knew from Dover, so my mutiny was pre-arranged and supported. After two hours of hubbub (we had the English Sunday papers), the section chief arrived in high dudgeon. He rightly said (officially) I was totally in the wrong and subject to penalties ranging from 'infractions' to guillotining for treason. He then came aboard unofficially, had a whisky, told me he was surrounded by idiots and amateurs and arranged a solo passage for us for the next 30 miles.

It's interesting watching peoples' psychology change as the hire boats learn the ropes. They come off the motorways having juggled for position as individual motorists, and only slowly learn the need to co-

Physalian alongside a fishing boat in Muros.

operate as teams in the locks. In the Midi, the uphill locks can be violent. Yachts, with keels and masts, need continuous control on warps, while the hire boats, with all round fendering and nothing under water, float like ducks above the turbulence. In general, once we had explained our problems and limitations, everyone co-operated, though I have a happy memory of a startled squeak as the mast butt went through somebody's French windows and goosed Madame in her galley.

Further difficulties occurred when low arched bridges crossed the lower end of a lock, accompanied by a strong cross current in the lock bypass overflow; our mast clearance meant we always had to go for the highest point of the arch. However I found *Physalian* much easier to handle than *Bow Bells*, even though two feet wider and 13 feet longer. An alert crew of 4 helped; Julie and I had always done it on our own on the previous six trips.

Medieval Carcassonne was as wonderful as ever. At the 700 year old tavern, we had the same table and menu as last time, and later watched skilful horsemanship and jousting in the lists at a local pageant between the double walls.

After Castelnaudary, the hire boats thinned and we made faster progress to Bordeaux. Here we planned to remast by the old U-boat pens, out of the river, but the crane there had just fallen on top of the yacht being remasted. We therefore had to continue to Royan at the Gironde entrance, another 70 miles with the mast down; this cannot be recommended in any wind, but the Pauillac crane is still unacceptable. The whole passage took 12 days compared with the seven it used to.

Although I had scraped the hull as far as I could reach in the Med, and the fresh water should have killed most of the weed, *Physalian* was still dirty and slow in the long tedious light air beats of the French west coast. At one point the engine started racing and it took two days to clean up and tighten all the fuel lines to clear this. I also learnt the expensive way (£50) that the ignition bulb is an essential part of the alternator charging circuit.

Older members may remember my old friend Nigel Ringrose (ex-RCC) who, after a tour in Khazakstan, is retiring to Auray. He joined us up to Loctudy, finding enormous changes in boat equipment in the 30 year gap since his last transatlantic passage.

And so back to the Solent, after 3½ months and 3,500 miles. Too much ground, too little time, the cruising man's lament. So much exploration frustratingly left undone. I was blessed with a first class crew, the essence of any cruising.

Physalian is a 40ft Jeanneau Sunfizz sloop, built in 1983. The Sunfizz is a comfortable cruising yacht and her French design incorporates many practical features. Her hydraulic lifting keel allows access, not only to the French canals, but also to a wide range of secluded anchorages.

KEEP IT SIMPLE

by Michael Manzoni

In theory, plans for our winter sunshine were faultless. A leisurely four week shakedown cruise from Trinidad to St Lucia with the easterly trade winds, followed after a few weeks merry-making back home at Christmas by three months idyllic downwind sailing through the Windwards to the offshore islands of Venezuela. To get things ready, my brother Bill and I flew out to Peake's Yard in Trinidad where *Blue Sonata* had spent the summer of 1996. We were soon stimulated by the gaiety of the Trinidadians personified by Crosby the mechanic and all those willing hands anxious to help prepare the yacht for sea. Fitting out was a cheerful affair, even though the seeds of future problems were sown at that time.

Julie and Cicely arrived a fortnight later and as new RCC members we were conscious of our first duty to find a stout piece of bamboo 8 or 9 ft long to fly the burgee from the masthead. We ventured into the jungle, if that is not too dramatic a word for the dense growth on the side of the country roads, to find two or three straight shoots standing majestically tall, waving gently in the breeze. 'This is it' said Cicely 'this is what the pandas were eating when I saw them'. A crew of worldwide travellers is a boon on these occasions and we returned to the boat delighted with our prize. But while the mechanical expertise of the resident population may occasionally be more enthusiastic than skilful, there can be no criticism of their local knowledge and the hilarity of our many helpers knew no bounds when they told us that this was not bamboo but elephant grass! Those of us who faced the embarrassment of disposing of it determined to go alone on the next search, justified we thought by cross examination of our traveller, which revealed that the pandas had been seen not in China but in the London Zoo.

A few days later, with new cutless bearing in place, alternator re-aligned and the boat looking trim, *Blue Sonata* was launched and we motored gently to a nearby marina berth for provisioning before departure. On the way the new fan belt broke.

Blue Sonata in Chimana Grande.

It's surprising how much one learns about the simplest things when well-known products are not readily available. Who would imagine that one manufacturer's 43 inch belt is the same size as another's 42 inch, or that the best quality belts would be considered too expensive for a place like Trinidad?

'What you need,' everyone said 'is a Gates belt, . . . but we don't stock them.'

'Perhaps you could try . . . . ' Thus began the great fan belt hunt which was to play some part in our adventures as we progressed north.

The more experienced sailors' wives grow sceptical about promises of sunshine sailing off the wind, and it was not easy for me to admit to Julie and Cicely that the first leg would take us dead into the wind against a foul current for the 65 mile passage to Tobago. With resignation clearly showing on their faces, we cast off at midnight in full moonlight, prepared to motor-sail most of the way. Adjacent to the coast the wind is usually less strong at night and so it proved to be, but dozens of fishermen in small boats with outboard engines and no lights create a considerable hazard. Often they will flash a torch as you approach, but it's difficult to identify their presence and their movements. Recently reading Hugo du Plessis' account of his trip to the Rio Grande, I now wonder whether the locals were lighting rags in bottles of petrol which they could throw at us if we came near! By dawn we'd arrived at the north-east corner of Trinidad and edged out into the passage between it and Tobago. Both wind and current increased during the morning, forcing us to batten down against a lumpy sea as we hammered our way close-hauled to the harbour in Scarborough, arriving about lunchtime. The sun shone and the Caribbean began to come into its own, but there was a hint that all was not perfect with *Blue Sonata* as we reflected on the Autohelm which had failed to work throughout our journey. How we come to rely upon these labour saving devices. We found immigration and customs procedures in Scarborough straightforward and the officers very friendly and we were able to take a brief look at this busy little town, which is not a tourist centre and none the worse for that.

After a lazy day round the corner at Pigeon Point, the crew instructed the skipper to set sail for the north-east of the island. It is possible that they meant motor to the north-east corner, bearing in mind that the Trades were then blowing ENE, but even so they would soon have been disappointed when the best of Trinidad's fan belts failed again, providing the skipper (now chief engineer) with the perfect justification for sailing once more directly into the strong wind. We had a glorious beat up the coast to arrive in Man of War Bay just as the sun was setting. If the name conjures up images of square-riggers and sea battles, pirates and derring-do, nothing could be further from today's reality of this magical deep water harbour against the backdrop of lush vegetation on steeply rising hills, with the charming town of Charlotteville spread along the shoreline.

There is a moment in every cruise when a sense of belonging to a new world takes over and the life left behind fades from memory. This moment came to us in the north of the beautiful island of Tobago. Cicely started painting, Julie walked in the hills to see the myriad birds and

A traditional schooner close-hauled into Admiralty Bay at sunset.

butterflies, we all swam and snorkelled and watched the seine netting of the fishermen who in this area are the core of the fishing industry of Trinidad and Tobago. The Engineer, now comfortably into his stride and ably assisted by brother Bill, tried and tested two or three of the assorted fan belts on board without success.

It's ironic that our purchase of *Blue Sonata* in Marblehead six years ago was accompanied by strong advice from the broker that it was better to buy a simple boat like this, albeit 10 years old, than one of the many more complex boats on the market. I was reminded of this as we contemplated the failure of cheap motor vehicle belts to drive our heavy alternator, and I began to wonder whether maintaining an old boat 3,000 miles from home for only three or four months sailing each year was a bit optimistic.

Fortunately, the capricious mechanical and electrical systems of the yacht cannot endanger the freedom to sail in regions of the world where the wind blows constantly day and night. Our cruise could happily continue, although we decided not to by-pass Grenada as originally intended but to make for one of the harbours on its south coast where spares might be available and repairs more easily effected. We weighed anchor at 1900 on 29th November and sailed into the night on a course of 315°. We covered the 83 miles to Prickly Bay in just under 13 hours and by 0900 next day were tied up at the small jetty which passes for a marina, where we were able to recharge the ship's batteries.

Perhaps surprisingly for late on Saturday afternoon, we were also able to track down the highly recommended Basil St. John, who looked at the refrigeration system and pronounced that we appeared to have an electrical fault, for which he would need to fetch his meter. He would do that 'one time', which we'd learnt in Patois means straightaway. I have since consulted the Oxford English Dictionary to find that straightaway means continuous in direction and time, and in fairness to Basil that is probably what he did, except that his continuity must have taken him past many usual drinking haunts where he made good use of his own definition of time. He finally arrived back on board late on Monday, when he replaced the fuse and left happy at being so successful. It wasn't until we were heading north on the next leg of our journey, with the refrigeration under load, that Basil's fuse and one or two others failed and we decided that a more thorough investigation 'one time' would be a good idea.

This was our first visit to Grenada and we were to learn more about the island on the second half of our winter cruise, but a few days were sufficient to convince us of its delights. We were driven by one of the many friendly taxi drivers to the capital St. Georges, while he proudly told us something of the island's history, talked about the trees, plants and wildlife and showed us the sights. He also steered us to every supplier in town until finally we found a fan belt of reasonable quality,

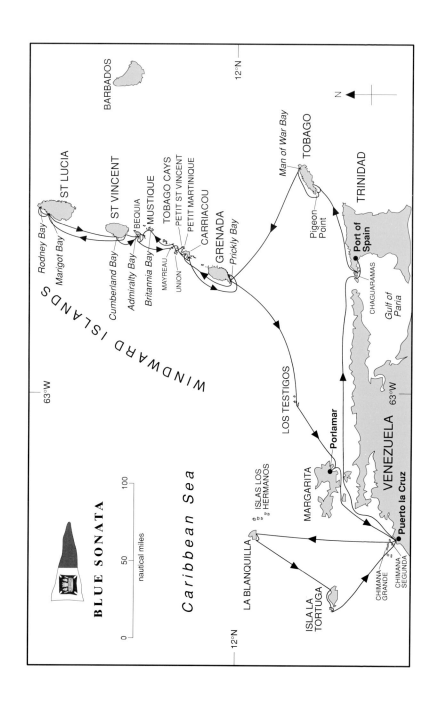

not quite up to Gates' standard, but certainly better than anything found so far. Spirits rose accordingly and it was later fitted with due ceremony and saw us safely through the remainder of our cruise.

We found navigation up the island chain relatively straightforward, so long as due allowance is made for the north-westerly current which runs at one or two knots – occasionally more in the short passages between some of the islands. You also need to avoid the numerous reefs projecting from many of the islands, most of which are unmarked. In these days, armed with GPS, a good chart and the latest guide books, it's good fun weaving one's way between the hazards to the many glorious anchorages available, and the Grenadines are certainly among our favourite places for enjoying this challenge. We worked our way north, calling first at Sandy Island and then Hillsborough in Carriacou to sign out from the jurisdiction of Grenada. We obtained some ice, in the book store believe it or not, and gin for £4 a bottle, before moving on to spend a few nights at Petit Martinique (in the Petit St Vincent Islands) and Union Island, *en route* to anchor behind the Horseshoe Reef at Tobago Cays.

Despite the number of yachts attracted here, the kaleidoscope of colours and the clarity of the water in the lagoon, which lies protected by the reef from the ceaseless roar of the Atlantic, never fail to thrill us. Our day was made when we picked our way between the reefs guarding the narrow southern entrance to anchor securely in about 18 ft of water. A few days here, where the snorkelling is superb, are likely to be among the highlights of any cruise in the Eastern Caribbean and so it proved again. Yet although protected from large waves, the anchorage can feel exposed if the trade winds increase much above 20 knots. We were unfortunate on this occasion to have winds in the 25-30 knot range, so we didn't stay as long as usual and continued our island hopping, making an early start for yet another beat north-east to Mustique.

As we cleared the reef, meeting wind and sea head-on, the skipper's credibility was again in danger of looking thin. But with a few rolls in genoa and main, *Blue Sonata* started to show her paces, performing well against wind and current. In the sparkling Caribbean sun the promise of gentle off-wind sailing appeared to have been forgotten and we all enjoyed the brisk sail to an anchorage in Britannia Bay, some 17 miles north-east of Tobago Cays.

The following day was 9th December, six whole days since we'd put mechanical problems out of our mind. We reached (at last) for a few miles to a lunchtime stop in Petit Nevis before rounding the south-east corner of Bequia for a beat into Admiralty Bay as the sun was setting. Crossing tacks with a traditional sailing schooner, we edged our way into the anchorage with Bill skilfully plumbing the depth with the lead line – I forgot to mention that the depth sounder had succumbed to a mild attack of corrosion somewhere along the way. There is an unmarked reef down the middle of the anchorage area, towards the south side of Admiralty Bay. The holding near the reef is not too good, so you need to look carefully for a suitable spot. As we manoeuvred under power, *Blue Sonata* didn't seem to be responding as she should and it was a few moments before we discovered to our horror that the propeller shaft had slipped backwards out of the gearbox – fortunately prevented by the skeg from disappearing altogether. As we drifted helplessly seawards, a rapid change of plan involved dropping the anchor in 50 ft of water before we found ourselves beyond the safe depth for our chain. My mind flashed back to Crosby's cheerful smile when he assured me that the shaft was perfectly reassembled with its new cutless bearing – good for at least another five years.

It was not long before one of Bequia's ubiquitous water taxis pulled alongside, seeking to give us a lift ashore or at least sell us a few bananas, take the garbage or do anything else which might earn a few dollars. Who better to ask if there was an engineering repair shop on the island?

'Yeah boss,' he replied, 'you need de Fix man'.

Waving his arms in explanation with his glistening eyes and black face in the fading light, it looked like some incantation to secure a visit from the local witch-doctor who would cure all ills with his magical spells. We felt rather foolish following his explicit instructions to call up 'Fixman, Fixman' on channel 68. In the silence which followed we could imagine

Trading vessels in Carriacou.

the laughter of those who might have their radios turned on, listening to yet another sucker who had fallen for the old gag. We didn't repeat the call more than once or twice.

Our informant had promised to return early next morning, in case we'd been unable to summon help. After a partly wakeful night I was up, breakfasted and ready to be ferried ashore when he arrived precisely on time. Within a few minutes he was nudging his boat into the shore where, just across the road, there was a narrow alleyway between two houses.

'See dat man up dere,' he said. 'He know where Fix man is.' With that, he was away for his next assignment. As I emerged into a clearing at the end of the alley, I didn't need to ask any further. There in front of me was a small tin shed bearing a large notice:

'FIXMAN ENGINEERING'.

Peter is a Norwegian who sailed and lived abroad for many years before finally settling in Bequia. His workshop was clean and tidy, giving me confidence in him and in his promise to come to the boat after lunch. He duly arrived and soon saw that the studs holding the shaft had worked loose and the key had disappeared into the bilge as the shaft slid backwards. 'I'll make another key' he said 'and I'll drill the studs so that when they are replaced they can be wired to prevent them coming loose again.' That seems such an obvious precaution, one wonders why it isn't done that way in the first place. True to his word, Peter Fixman was back before long. With Bill acting as fitter's mate, the shaft was soon reassembled in perfect order. By four o'clock we were having a drink in the cockpit with the repair done and paid for, with Peter offering Bill a permanent job. Magic or Voodoo it may have been, but I doubt if any yard in England or America would give service like that – it would take that long to prepare the invoice.

A peaceful evening, a good night's sleep and rising with the dawn, presented us with one of those rare occasions in a sailing life which will remain in our memory for a long time. In the stillness of the morning, with only a gentle breeze rippling the water, a small junk-rigged schooner tacked gracefully into the bay, the only movement in a still-sleeping harbour. We watched as she worked her way quietly into a space between the dormant yachts, and as the couple on board effortlessly dropped the anchor, lowered and stowed the sails and sat back to enjoy the rising sun and the slow awakening of all around them. Some time later we saw them lower a small wooden dinghy and row ashore, and while they were away we felt free to take out the binoculars and look more closely at their yacht. To our delight we saw the name *Badger* and the RCC burgee and realised this must be Pete and Annie Hill, whom we had not met before. We were due to leave after lunch, but seeing them return about noon we went across to introduce ourselves. We were welcomed aboard a yacht which was looking immaculate by two charming people who, we presumed, had been sailing for some if not all of the night, but who nevertheless looked as relaxed and fresh as could be. Imagine our surprise when we discovered that, far from crossing from one of the adjacent islands, they had just arrived from the Canaries. They have clearly mastered the art of living and sleeping on board rather better than many of us can manage on land.

The last leg of our journey took us briefly into St.Vincent and Marigot Bay, before we came to rest in Rodney Bay, St Lucia. We left *Blue Sonata* after approximately 400 miles which, though sometimes more of a shake-up than a shake-down, had been great fun and gave us much to think about, not least the difference between *Badger* and the American version of 'simple'.

Epilogue

When I called her from home in Birmingham during the Christmas break, Cicely's greeting 'Have you found any good fan-belts recently?' prompted me to ring Perkins for advice. They give me the number of Gates Power Transmission in the UK, who said I should try the Gates Rubber Company.

'Where are they?' I asked. 'Oh', they said, 'Gates Rubber are in Birmingham'.

For the price of a local call I received as a gift the best, strongest looking fan belt I have ever seen – I think I'll frame it.

Blue Sonata is a 46ft centreboard sloop, designed by Dieter Empacher and built by Bristol Yachts at Rhode Island in 1981. She draws 5 feet with the centreboard up, but 11 feet with it down. She now carries an extensive range of spare fan belts.

ALL GOOD FINNS COME TO AN END

By Pete Lewin-Harris and Sam Edenborough

While writing this log, we found that we sometimes had differing viewpoints about how events panned out. Accordingly, where Sam's (the Mate's) memory differed from the official one, his thoughts appear in italics.

It is quite a shock to find yourself in charge of your father's pride and joy for the first time, especially in some of the rockiest waters in the world. That said, we arrived bright-tailed and bushy-eyed on *Musketeer*, berthed peacefully in Helsinki. We had high hopes, a spring in our step and lashings of ginger beer.

We'd decided while planning the cruise that the best way to see the Finnish archipelago was at a leisurely pace. This enables a cruising yacht to explore the myriad leads of the area and spend a while nosing around for the perfect anchorage. So what follows is a more intimate view of the archipelago's appeal.

The voyage to Tallinn

Helsinki. The name on every sun-worshipping pleasure-seeker's lips. Well, perhaps not, but as we cruised into town from the airport in a plush air-conditioned Mercedes (a taxi, naturally), we wondered what the Finnish Tourist Board had been up to all its life. Sweeping down the wide boulevards towards the harbour, we caught sight of *Musketeer* tied up at NJK Blekholmen marina, and just as quickly lost sight of her again behind one of the largest ferries we had ever seen. There would be times later on when we feared the foredeck might suffer the same fate.

With a due sense of priority my father began his briefing. Naturally concerned for the welfare of his beloved, (that's the boat) he left nothing to the imagination. A day later the crew cheered his parting shot, which concerned the vast quantities of beer neatly packed into a locker that we came to know and love.

Having done all the necessary victualling, we took one look at what we had bought to keep us alive for the next week and decided that eating out was probably the way to go. That evening we enjoyed a superb meal, entertained by the Mate's enterprising if fruitless banter with the waitress, including the classic: 'That tasted as good as you look.'

Well, that's what it says in the ship's log. I definitely remember saying 'That tasted as good as IT looked' although I did wonder why the bill arrived so fast.

The next morning(ish) we set sail for Porkkala – our first berth in an NJK harbour. The NJK or Nylandska Jakt Klubben is a Finnish Yacht club which owns about ten secluded and beautiful private anchorages with mooring facilities around the archipelago. The RCC is privileged to have a reciprocal arrangement with the NJK which allows us to take out a temporary membership for the season and use these anchorages.

When we awoke there was not a breath of wind and it was obvious that sailing our intended route to Tallinn was out of the question – no-one seemed to want to spend Christmas on board. This freed us to try the engaging sport of windless sailing down some beautiful leads and watching Finns motor past us, with baffled expressions on their faces

At this point I would like to discourse on the finer points of navigating in Finland. It is said that on the Seventh Day the Lord, just before popping off for a rest, had a handful of leftover stones. So he threw them out of his celestial window and lo! they became the Finnish Archipelago. Fortunately the Lord had the excellent sense to imbue the Finns with consummate chart-making abilities, for which we gave thanks repeatedly.

A few leads later, we enjoyed an unexpectedly invigorating beat into a wind that blew up from the south-west, no doubt to spite us for deciding against the Tallinn option. Undeterred by this meteorological perversity, we made Hangö at sunset. Picturesque as this may sound, our westerly course made the recognition of navigation marks a tricky task. In the end some unusual rock formations gave a satisfactory alternative to the black and white sticks, since the rocks at least stood out in the blinding sunlight. We soon found ourselves at rest in Hangö's voluminous marina, which the visitors' brochure proudly assured us was the largest in all Finland.

Keen to convince my crew that my planning was spot-on, I made a vigorous case for eating the lurid-green minced beef lurking in the fridge that evening before it went off. With the utmost consideration they gently argued me away from this position and laid out before me visions of the culinary delights of Hangö, so I conceded.

As I recall, we threw it in the bin first and argued the toss later. So we trooped ashore and ate pizza, that well-known Finnish speciality.

Uusikaupunki or bust

With the barometer sky-high and the crew dipping themselves in the water by means of increasingly tortuous contraptions made from the bosun's chair and several halyards, we motored north into the archipelago proper.

As if the mind-boggling number of rocks was not enough for any aspiring invader to contend with, the Finnish military has dotted the coastline with strategic bases. These emplacements gave us an eerie reminder of the reality of the Cold War for this nation, located as it is in Russia's backyard. The surrounding areas are marked on the charts as restricted: one can sail through them but stopping would be ill-advised. During the rest of the cruise a sense of Finland's territorial anxiety was increased by sightings of customs launches that looked as if they might be more at home fighting off a couple of destroyers.

We arrived at NJK Langholmen ready to perform the now-familiar bows-to mooring drill. In this case it was tested to its limits . . . and beyond.

In other words, the stern line ran out while I balanced precariously on the pulpit ready to spring, catlike, ashore. It was too damn nearly fishlike for my liking.

After the ritual evening fridge inspection, it was decided that a spot of charcoal could not harm the food any more than the passage of time

Musketeer moored to a rock, Baltic style, in Lill Kalvholm.

already had. A barbecue was faultlessly planned, although the execution
proved somewhat haphazard. Later, a pink sky softened the rocky
landscape, and we sat, watching our sobriety disappear under the
horizon, singing shanties. A hefty dent was made in the beer locker's
supplies that night.

*That's for sure. I believe it was me who, to cheers of approval, attempted to
annexe a small rock inconveniently far from the shore in the name of Australia.
Well, I figured that the Finns would never notice one small island bearing the
Aussie flag. Unfortunately, as in World War II, the channel proved
insurmountable.*

Setting out the following day, I was pleased to be able to fly the
spinnaker for the first time in the cruise. The bright sunshine held, so the
shipping navigating the main southerly approach channel to Turku from
the Åland Sea was treated to the sight of *Musketeer* under full sail, darting
northwards.

The log begs to differ:

*1000: Some bright spark thought it would be a good idea to fly the kite (the
Skipper, of course). Two gybes later, after much rope-untangling, the Mate is
exhausting the thesaurus of violent swearwords and threatening to make
incisions in the beloved balloon at the dead of night.*

1130: Headed again, and dropped the spinnaker.

*1200: Wind veered. Veiled threats and the dull glint of sharpened steel have
subdued the Skipper's ambitions in the kite department – for the moment.*

The chart offered many tempting anchorages around the island of
Inio. As we approached, still with the kite up and with Gemma and
Caroline navigating us towards our destination, we averaged an
extravagant seven knots. As evening began to fall, so did the wind, and
after some trial and error we anchored in a secluded, idyllic bay. By this
time we were becoming expert at the art of visual sounding. Nosing in
toward a promising anchorage often involved Caroline and Trevor
peering over the bows for the tell-tale tips of weed that grows in
profusion off the shelving shores in these waters.

The six o'clock whisky materialised as usual, thanks to Gemma's
weirdly accurate bodyclock. Soon the galley became our focus of
attention, and after a huge meal, I found myself unable to sleep. The
boat was lying uneasily to the wind and I couldn't help wondering if the
anchor was about to become nomadic. Eventually I fell into a shallow
sleep having checked our holding several times – all seemed to be well.
Until, in the small hours of the morning, Sam sat bolt upright in what
appeared to be a fit of Mately concern and shouted, 'drat! drat! drat!' (or
something of that ilk, perhaps a little more industrial) at the top of his
voice. Within seconds I was shivering on the foredeck anxiously grasping
the anchor chain, listening for ominous grumblings. Nothing. I returned

to bed not a little confused. In the morning, I quizzed Sam, who was as mystified as I was by his fit of sleep-talking.

To Uusikaupunki or not to Uusikaupunki? That was the question. In need of stores, we planned to visit a nearby marina – until someone thoughtfully pointed out it was Sunday. So a visit to the scenic town of Uusikaupunki was mooted; my objections revolved around the sheer inventive madness of the Finnish language. I couldn't see how anywhere with a name like that could be a desirable holiday location. But I was overruled and to Uusikaupunki we went. Humph.

Owing to excellent planning, we were able to provision again in the interesting town of Uusikaupunki on Monday morning. During our passage there, I persuaded the crew to fly the kite: by now, we had ironed out the kinks in our drill and of course in light airs the sail worked wonders. That is, until we saw the oil rig, which appeared to be blocking the narrow lead. Even more puzzling was that despite the spinnaker we seemed not to be closing on it.

The glasses again, please . . . Ah yes. It's under tow . .

Let's try that again: leaving the lead and starting the approach to Uusikaupunki, we passed an interesting dredging platform under tow.

Finally the weather changed. Our dramatic approach to the town was marred by the first rain for a week, and a drop in temperature. Trevor took a manful stint on the helm, volubly enjoying the eight knot peaks on the clock, and taking the holiday's speed record by storm.

An interesting problem was posed when we finally reached the visitor's wharf (complete with 4-language 'Welcome' fenders). I was not quite sure how to moor the 46 ft yacht when the stern buoys were placed about 40′ from the shore. So we broke the Scandinavian custom and moored alongside. No-one seemed to mind: the (closed) harbour office doubled as a small café staffed by charming Finns who, nevertheless, didn't know a bosun from a baggywrinkle.

Things that go bump in broad daylight

In the event, the metropolis of Uusikaupunki afforded us no more than some excellent fish, a decent supermarket and the bizarre appearance in the gents' showers of a matronly cleaning lady.

We began the second leg of the cruise, making our way south towards Mariehamn, our final destination. By now we had become used to the peculiar double-think required of the navigator in these waters. A helmsman, too, must have nerves of steel as he is invariably directed through the narrower of two channels as it is 'the clean one'. Conversely, what may look like open water regularly contains nasty surprises lurking deep enough to be invisible but shallow enough to remodel your keel.

Once this point had been rammed home in no uncertain terms, I decided that we should gingerly put into Lappo for the night. This little harbour boasts newly-built facilities and was an ideal place for us on what was promising to be a windy night. As if our close encounter with the local geology was not enough to fray all our nerves for one day, the sky went berserk toward nightfall. Huge, sickly brown thunderheads filled the air and I dragged the Mate to the shrouds where we rigged up the most contrived lightning conductor imaginable. With good reason – we had the tallest mast in the marina by a clear 20 ft.

The storm had gone by morning leaving a stiff force 7 in its wake. Our unshakeable confidence somewhat shaken, we gathered our wits and prepared to change the headsail down. This process was aided by Trevor's prop-forward build which allowed him to tackle the 700 square feet of genoa as it flogged merrily in the breeze. Leaving Lappo put us through our paces once again. We exhausted ourselves with a three-hour beat through the narrowest leads yet.

That afternoon brought us into the busy ferry routes between Turku and Mariehamn. These channels make for lively sailing, as they are only just wide enough for two ferries to pass. In one of the many bottlenecks, we were confronted with the office-block architecture of a passenger ferry which threatened to leave us carrying *Musketeer* over an island to keep clear. The ferry smartly turned on the mark and we breathed a sigh of relief. I prepared to wave to the kindly soul who gave the order to turn – only to discover that the bridge appeared to be utterly deserted.

We anchored not much later in a pretty bay on the island of Gripo. The next day was spent without moving *Musketeer*, giving us time to explore an islet at the mouth of our anchorage. During the inevitable watersports a strange thing happened. To quote from the log: 'We were rowing along in the dinghy when suddenly the oar fell in half.' Oh well, stranger things happen at sea.

I should interject with the remainder of the log entries for the day:
1300: Up rather late.
0100: Didn't go anywhere.

A day later we motored into Mariehamn marina, with its wonderful facilities – including the largest ablution block known to humanity – and its affable, laid-back harbourmaster. Having taken advantage of the extremely reasonable price of beer in the waterfront café, we felt ready for the cleaning, packing and marathon voyage home.

But that, as they say, is another story...

Musketeer is a wooden yawl – forty-six feet overall – built by Camper and Nicholson in 1963. She was designed for ocean racing and has (because of handicap rules) been a sloop for a good portion of her life. She has a long keel, giving her a draught of just over 7 feet, which is a consideration when cruising in the Åland islands.

CLIPPER 96

by Colin de Mowbray

She hesitated briefly before looking across the room:

'I only have one question. Would it please be possible for me to sit at the Captain's table for dinner?'

So ended the interview and this particular candidate's chance of signing on for the Clipper Round the World Race. 250 crew *were*, however, selected for the paying berths in the eight new boats for this 11 month race. About a third were female and a good half of the total had no previous sailing experience.

The Clipper is not a formula one race like the Whitbread and it's not a head-banging event like the BT. By using the Panama Canal, the route included Japan, Shanghai and Hong Kong as well as Singapore, the Seychelles and South Africa. The return took the fleet to Brazil before the third Atlantic crossing on the way home. At 34,000 miles it is the longest of all the races and despite excellent Trade Wind sailing the route has plenty of cold and wet weather to satisfy the masochists. Close and exciting racing was ensured by having a strict one-design fleet which also provided a reassuring feeling of mutual support.

The initial concept surfaced in June 1995. A company was formed and the eight boats were commissioned and built at Colvic. The crews were recruited and trained, the skippers appointed and the fleet was on the starting line on 12 October 1996, a mere 14 months later. This remarkable feat would not have been possible without the determination and energy of Sir Robin Knox-Johnston, the race Chairman, and Spud Spedding, the inspirational project manager.

The hulls were based on the David Pedrick Nicholson 58. They have a shallow draft of 2.5 metres and their relatively large rig resulted in a surprisingly good performance especially in light winds. They were all named after famous clippers although, in truth, I had not heard of *Chrysolite* which was to be my command. Each boat had a professional skipper and up to 14 crew. The accommodation is best described as comfortable when compared with a racing boat, but Spartan compared with a cruising boat.

The crews were a delightful mixture in every sense. In age they ranged from students to retired people who were seeking adventure. The majority, however, were professional people, many taking a career break from life's escalator which they perceived was denying them any outside challenges or lasting memories. Nearly half signed up for the whole race and the rest did one or more of the six legs. They all paid for the privilege of crewing – the whole circumnavigation cost much the same as a Volvo estate, in other words a clear bargain.

During my introduction, when I was sailing as mate to Mervyn Wheatley in *Thermopylae*, he played the combined bands of the Royal Marines on the stereo. Immediately the crew, all perfectly normal and decent people and captains of industry in their own right, picked up cleaning gear and started to scrub with a vengeance. This master stoke of indoctrination later backfired when one crew member wrote complaining that whenever the Royal Marines were playing on her radio at home she found herself going off to get her bucket and scrubber.

Despite the rush, the crews all completed their training and *Chrysolite* and the other boats were ready for the start in Plymouth. As we beat out into a strong south-westerly there was a sudden feeling of reality. We had been extremely busy without time to think and dwell on our undertaking. Now we were on our own and wondering just how sensible we all were to be committing a year to the project. For me I had a wonderful flashback of my mother Louise, and her sister Lexie, waving from the forecastle of a supporter's boat, resolutely hanging on in the spray while everyone else had taken shelter.

The first leg to Madeira was a mere warm up, but as the first four boats finished within 40 minutes of each other it was apparent that the racing was going to be close. Although at the end of the whole race Ras Turner in *Ariel* was the clear winner, five of the eight boats recorded leg victories. The start at Madeira was unusual as the Captain of the local patrol boat admitted he had no ammunition for his main gun so would use a machine gun. One burst at the ten minute gun, two at the five minute and the remainder of the magazine at the start. By remarkable coincidence no one was over the line! The Princess Royal arrived just before we departed and was visiting her husband in H.M.S. *Monmouth*, so we did a fleet sail past with a cheer ship.

The Panama Canal

Going through the Panama Canal was a crucial planning factor for the Clipper route as it enabled new places to be visited. The procedure for yachts is that you report to various offices at Colon and then have to wait until they are ready for you – sometimes over a week later. We had a good agent and set off barely 24 hours after arriving. This was fortunate as Colon is no place to hang around. The agent's advice was on no account to walk the 200 yards to his office from the jetty.

We transited the canal in two groups and, unusually, at night. The great scenic experience was therefore slightly limited, especially as torrential rain lasted for most of the time. I can honestly say that I really did not see the transit at all. Our pilot was extremely good and entered into the spirit of the race. After some devious manoeuvring, we ended up on the outside of the raft in the last lock and then burst out in front of the others. We then sent our signal home:

'Pleased to inform you *Chrysolite* first Clipper to reach the Pacific.'

Our stop at Balboa on the Pacific side of the canal was dominated by our spinnaker repair. It had been decreed that there would be penalties for sail damage and if my repair bill was greater than $305 I would start losing places. As neither of the two local sail-makers seemed interested in work, I took a hotel room with the use of a vacant ladies hairdressing salon. By afternoon the team had the sewing machines going and material everywhere. It was a fine sight but a daunting task.

Galapagos

The Galapagos Islands lie on the Equator about 600 miles west of Ecuador. Charles Darwin did much of his fieldwork there and the Darwin Institute remains an important research establishment on the islands. The Galapagos are not colonised and the wildlife and fauna remains much in its natural state. They are typical volcanic islands with a fairly rugged landscape, but located at an interesting crossroads of several currents. Sea temperatures vary a great deal and we experienced a range of over 8°C. All these factors make the Galapagos a naturalist's paradise, but the population from the mainland has grown recently and, although strictly controlled, tourism continues to increase.

Passages

Most boats had a straight two-watch system (four on, four off) with some form of mother watch. We worked a three-watch system with an active standby watch, which I believed had the benefit of not having surplus hands around when they were not required. We also had a trickle change of personnel in each watch

We would get together at midday for a shareholders meeting to discuss professional and domestic matters, and then met at 1800 for Sundowners. This was normally yet another cup of tea except on Saturdays or birthdays, which we celebrated with a warm can of beer. Feeding fifteen was a big issue and, as we didn't have a fridge or freezer, food was mainly dried or tinned. Predictably there was a language problem in the USA. Digestives became thousands of small mints, pork beans are baked beans and the quantities ranged from hundredweight sacks of flour to individual jars of Hellmanns.

Despite all this I think we didn't do badly and I suspect *Chrysolite* had the best food in the fleet. The daily baking became very successful and took on a competitive turn. We developed a system to graduate the bakers into Day Bakers, Coastal Bakers and then all the normal stages up to Offshore Baker.

Walter the watermaker deserves special mention as he was of such importance. He worked on the principle of reverse osmosis (which I still am unable to understand) and produced about a litre of very pure water a minute. We topped up the tanks every time we charged the batteries, normally about 1½ hours per day.

Galapagos to Hawaii (4,200 miles direct)

This was one of the longest legs and is a good illustration of our passages. My personal scribbles read so:

One Third Down

We took the southern route which will be 300 miles further, but I believe the guaranteed winds and favourable current will give us this back. Mervyn and Spud went north, two others came south with us and three sat on the fence in the middle. The next event was an amazing dash by Spud at about 2°N. He put in several runs over 240 miles a day and seemed to have the monopoly on a very favourable current. Merv headed north through the Intertropical Convergence Zone as we continued further south, finally reaching 5°S. We have far out performed my calculations have had some great Trade Wind sailing, clocking up daily runs of up to 230 miles. Unfortunately the plan also relied on the others doing less well and this has not yet happened. There are still over 2,500 miles to run and all of us, bar Merv, have yet to cross the ITCZ and I feel there will be several twists to come. At one point we were 750 miles displaced from *Thermopylae*.

New Year's Eve

On 28th December, in the noble pursuit of PR, I sent a slightly early press release describing our Hogmanay. A Scot was playing his pipes in full dress, another crew member had baked cakes to a recipe given to her by the Queen Mum and we gorged ourselves on haggis made from wild Galapagos boar. Whales were calling in the background and coal was passed around for first-footing. It was our moment of glory and was given two columns in the Telegraph.

Two Thirds Down.

All boats have crossed the ITCZ and we are converging on Hawaii. We were forced up from our southerly position slightly early and crossed the zone before it started moving north with us. I think we were lucky and got through in 24 hours. We are currently fifth and will be hard put to catch Merv, but there is still time for changes. What an intriguing problem and when asked the question 'which route would I take next time' I'm really not sure I have an answer.

700 miles to go
Events continue to be exciting. This morning we gybed for the second time in nearly 4,000 miles. We had been reeling in Merv, cutting his lead from 240 miles to 67, but now our friendly NE winds are dying too.

600 miles to go
Crew performed the wind dance which had previously been very effective. Shortly afterwards, Spud radioed that he was in a force 9 off The Big Island (Hawaii), *Mermerus* has very little sail up and Merv has 3 reefs in and thinking of taking his main down. Meanwhile *Chrysolite* is charging along at 1 knot in 2.5 knots of wind. I have arranged for the crew responsible for the wind dance to be executed after Shareholders – this should encourage the others.

Hawaii

Well it was a thriller to the end. The wind died and the last 100 miles proved a real test of patience for all boats. Merv got within a mile of the line late at night and then spent 10 hours drifting with his host motor boat astern. Finally we finished and then experienced the most amazing reception at the Hawaii Yacht Club at 0100. Every member of the crew was announced over the PA system and drinks were waiting on the jetty. What a place and what a reception!

To Japan the Orient

When we left Hawaii for the start, the club tied lucky tea leaves on the bows of all the boats and threw rose petals onto the start line. This was all to help keep the evil spirits away. No one dared take the long leaves off their pulpits.

The passage to Japan was another long leg and we sailed nearly 4,300 miles in 22 days. We went well south again and then cut north with the pack. In the end, the first six boats finished within 12 hours. An amazingly close margin after all this distance.

One current South of Japan, which played an important part later on, was the Japan or Kuroshio Current. This is about 40 miles wide and runs like a snake along the coast. In some places it meanders like a river and circles of current up to 100 miles wide break off. Although difficult to follow exactly, the rough position is transmitted by fax along with the weather forecasts.

Shanghai

Our visit to China was a first for a yacht race and this was part of the attraction. All eight boats were required to take pilots as they could only equate us as fully crewed merchant ships. We embarked our pilot, Mr Wee, at about 0900 and he remained with us until we docked just after midnight. The river trip through Shanghai at night in the pouring rain was dramatic. The centre of the city still has the fine old colonial buildings including an exact copy of the Liver Building. There are absolutely no yachting facilities in the area and as the river was frantic with traffic, berthing was a serious problem. Robin had found a new basin where the authorities agreed we could berth on a barge. This was not ideal but, considering the options, we got away quite lightly.

The following Clipper press release sums up our stay . . .

On arrival Sir Robin was interviewed by Dow Si Hatch, China's best known yoting correspondent and editor of Classic Junk. He asked 'Do you mean people actually pay to sail in your boats? Surely only reason to go sailing is to fish or avoid oppressive political regimes.' Sir Rob replied that these were indeed good reasons and certainly helped the marketing at home, however many of the crew were businessmen and women who were simply taking a break.

'If they have money, why they not buy bigger Mercedes?' Dow interrupted.

Colin de Mowbray shows Daisey the route sailed by the Clipper fleet, Salvador, Brazil.

The British Consul, Mr Ric Shaw, intervened and explained the advantages of building high-tech junks in UK with laminated GRP hulls, carbon fibre spars and mylar sails. His remarks were greeted with total silence.

Sir Rob remarked about the magnificent yoting facilities in Shanghai and was most impressed with the 24 hour watch of 5 immigration officers, 16 soldiers, 14 Marine Police, two launches and a reserve of two battalions of the Red Army Guards, although he was sorry he was having to pay for all of them.

The visits to Hong Kong and Singapore went as planned and then we set off south to pass through the Selat Sunda and into the Indian Ocean. Here we were denied our return to trade wind sailing by Rhonda, a tropical storm that the pilot said only occurred every seven years, and then from the other direction. We found the position reporting of Rhonda on the Inmarsat-C excellent and it was a great comfort to know her exact position and track.

Everyone enjoyed the Seychelles, but sadly we did not have the opportunity to explore the numerous islands which make them a delightful cruising ground. We pressed on to Durban and then Cape Town. The passage round the Cape in early July was of special interest as there are vicious fronts charging up the coast. These work against the strong SW Agulhas current and create the infamous abnormal waves which have caused the destruction of several large ships. Assuming you cannot get 100 miles or more out to sea, one is left seeking the relatively calmer water inside the 200-metre line. The problem here is that this leaves a thin ribbon of sea room sometimes less than four miles wide, to beat down. Reaching Cape Town was a great milestone, but there was a dangerous feeling that the back of the challenge had been broken when actually there were 7,500 miles and two Atlantic crossings still to go.

Just before midnight on 14th September, eleven months and 34,000 miles after the start, we slipped past Plymouth breakwater with *Mermerus* tucked five feet to leeward and *Antiope* half a mile astern. When we had time to look around, there was *Fidget* with the reception committee.

Looking back, I believe we achieved our aim and proved the Clipper formula. The boats behaved magnificently and averaged eight knots on some legs and seven on most of the others. The crewing system worked well and they all took away lifelong friendships and memories. It was a shame to rush past so many wonderful places, but the racing was an essential part of the equation as without it I am sure the crews would not have found the satisfaction that was so evident. I would not have missed the opportunity for anything.

USHANT REVISITED

by Wallace Clark

The further south you go in Brittany the more crowded the anchorages, the more expensive the marinas and, for those who like it wild, the less interesting the islands. So there is much to be said for not venturing far south of Penmarc'h.

Wild Goose tucked her head under a canvas cover in October 1996 in L'Aberildut and spent the winter safely in the hands of Georges Rennes, owner manager of Lanildut Marine. We did some day sailing with grandchildren in the Rade de Brest in May, then spent pleasant weeks renewing acquaintance with Ushant and her southerly neighbours. Good companion on board was *Ianthe Cruises* by H. J. Hanson, doyen of the Cruising Association. His unvarnished words recreate pre-war days when engines were a novelty and yellow wellies and marinas hadn't been invented. His Brittany scenes were similar to those we pensioner sailors can recall from the early fifties, when tunnymen still fished under yawl rig with a line from the mizzen masthead, and single-handed *pêcheurs* could be met far out at sea in small chunky boats under nothing but a well patched lugsail.

A volume of James Naval History 1800/04 was also picked through for local references and entertainment. It describes under *'Light Squadrons and Single Ships'* how the inshore squadron acted as eyes for the admiral blockading Brest; incidents like the taking of the lugger *Affronteur* off Ushant, the cutting out of the twenty gun *Chevrette* off Camaret and risky reconnoitres in the Goulet to ascertain the state of readiness of the French Fleet. The events come easily alive as so many parts of the rocky coast can have changed little in appearance in 200 intervening years – tides and winds not at all.

Wild Goose had several crew changes but only one skipper and no insurrections. A hand said, 'There couldn't be a mutiny on this ship; the old man would join it.'

The most active period was three weeks voyaging in August/ September among the islands, with a crew change each weekend. My trusty mate June was sadly unable to join, but Mefo and Peter brought good cheer on board when they drove to Bénodet, their first ever sortie to Brittany. Mefo Harland, a talented marine poet, owns the nearest thing that exists to a sister ship of *Wild Goose. Jorrocks* (Maurice Griffiths 1936) was appropriately named for her owner, a foxhunting baronet who held on to her for years and never altered a thing. Mefo, since rescuing *Jorrocks* from a mudberth in Wivenhoe, has put in hundreds of hours restoring her to become a beautiful time capsule.

Jorrocks has her galley forward while a generous loo occupies what would now be counted valuable space just forward of the main hatch. In this and other ways she is almost the opposite to the *Goose*, which has been modernised year by year, cruised mainly in exposed waters and taken a fair number of knocks as a result.

Mefo had planned to sail out so that we could voyage in company, but the fitting of a new deck in Alan Chapel's yard at Faversham was not finished in time. So she and Peter raided us by car at midnight and took over the saloon bunks, galley and cocktail cabinet. A car on the quay can be the dearth of cruising. It's far too easy to say, 'Headwind today; let's go off and have lunch at Jack's at Bélon, or the *Hôtel du Port* at Guilvinec.' June and I had found ourselves weather-bound under this heading several times; car-bound might be a better word. The temptations of Brittany are manifold.

Iles de Glénan

After a couple of days, Mefo set the big drifter and we reached south for Glénan. The Breton sailing season comes to a fairly abrupt end by September. Where two weeks earlier 400 yachts had filled every niche, there were now less than 50. A westerly swell was running in the pool and we chose the bight east of the spit between Nicolas and Bananec for the night, as giving a lee and less stream; that meant picking up a white buoy as there was no room to anchor clear of visitor moorings. A French singlehander came in and we shouted over an invitation to cockpit drinks. An Aussie voice in the next berth yelled, 'Can we come too?'

The owner of the voice and his wife, on a weekend charter out of Loctudy, were soon alongside to join the Frenchman, a Professor of Engineering from Lorient who'd just finished building his smart steel 50 footer. So in a matter of minutes a party developed in our tiny cockpit; thereby we acquired much local lore. Hours later Mefo produced food for all.

The main fun in the Glénans is exploring the outliers by dinghy. *Wild Goose* has few luxuries, but I'd count as one having room on deck for a ten foot wooden dinghy. In this we had earlier made extended sorties in the gin-clear shallow water. Archipelago islands tend to suffer from similarity and thus be less interesting than those in isolation. But the Glénan remains varied. Each of the seven main islands has its own personality. Loch with its bird marsh and beds of salicorne, a plant which bears the components for making soda, once produced on the island. Ponies graze there and rodeos are not unknown.

Penfret with its almost two hundred year old light and mansion for the *Gardiens*; beaches where many waders feed and a rusty carronade abandoned in the grass. Drenec with its forest of dinghy masts and stone huts for sailing school staff. The vegetation appears to have been flattened by much lovemaking. Cignone with its arresting circular 1760 fort and hideous daymark tower. Bananas (sorry Bananec) with its wooden huts, a boardwalk to keep visitors from trampling campion and trefoil, and extensive batteries of solar cells.

There's a wee reef out west where lies in eight fathoms the wreck of the 14 gun sloop HMS *Arab*. Built as a corsair called *Jean Bart*, she was captured and renamed. In 1796, *Arab* was part of the task force under Sir John Borlase Warren preventing French landings in Ireland – she ran ashore in fog and heavy swell. Guns, musket and rigging parts are being recovered by *scaphandriers*. What splendid sea words the French have; I wonder if Mefo will find a rhyme for that one.

Ile Nicolas with its Café of the Four Winds and disused lobster vivier. There is more to take in than could be absorbed in several visits. In winter the population shrinks to one man; I wouldn't mind swapping places with him for a month or two. The Glénan group gets several stars in the *Wild Goose* catalogue of islands.

The Saints

Later, from Audierne, we made a dawn start to catch the end of a fair tide to the Ile de Sein. Cutting across west from La Vieille we found the tide had turned and we were not going to be able to fetch the east entrance The alternative was to 'bout ship for Portzen on the mainland or push on and get the pick down south of the island. This lead to the discovery of an anchorage I had not previously thought of. The chart shows a patch of sand south of the harbour, a bit over a mile east of Le Chat beacon (with Men Brial light bearing 350°). There for the south-going stream we found no tide (it was neaps) and the kedge warp lay slack under the bow in a light north breeze. So we spent a pleasant four hours swimming and lunching until the tide turned and enabled us to move again. The usual anchorage off the lifeboat pier by the harbour entrance is weedy, shallow and restricted. In summer it's not easy to find a berth clear of other yachts.

We made friends with the crew of the Canot de Sauvetage as they came in from assisting a coaster, were given stiff shots of *pastis* and invited to use the ferry buoy for the night. This was a relief because the tide runs briskly through the anchorage and brings in a swell. At low water great coils of maiden hair weed lolled in the blue water around us: the island dolphins gambolled.

Around midnight the thrifty islanders turn off the six street lamps. Darkness leaves a pleasant sense of being anchored in mid-ocean, yet guarded by stand-off skerries, illuminated now and then by the low power beam of the light on the pier end. All was still and the evening had a sense of magic.

If Glénan feels like Scilly, or even a mini Scapa Flow, Sein resembles Tory Island. Both are flat slabs of rock surrounded by reefs, four miles or more from the nearest mainland. Each has many legends of ghost ships, pirates, rescuers and wreckers. Sein is called the Isle of Blue Cormorants from the blue coats of its sailors. In 1940, after the 18th June speech by General de Gaulle, the entire male population got into their boats and sailed for England to join his Free French army. De Gaulle announced Ile de Sein as the First Province of France.

Beside an untidily abandoned shellfish processing plant at the west end of Sein is the tiny chapel of St.Corentin. By it is a grave or two; also an 'auge' or stone trough, which looked old enough to be one of the stone boats in which early saints commuted here from Ireland and Wales. Must have taken a lot of faith.

Today the island population is 500, jammed into an area of one square kilometre, of which the highest point is only six metres. There are so many fascinating things to be seen around Sein that it's worth visiting often; but usually briefly while good conditions last. The anchorage is not secure enough for a long stay and drying out in the harbour is a messy business.

If on departure you find the north entrance easy, cast back your mind to the cutting out activities of Lieutenant William Deane and the boats of HM frigate *Naiad*, as reported by Captain Wallis on 5th July 1805. Having heard of a French schooner in at Ile de Sein for repairs, they rowed in and '*notwithstanding the rapidity of the tide, the state she was in, being made fast to the shore, and the number of rocks and shoals they had to pass, brought her off without the smallest accident.*' She was the *Providence* of

Shipping off Ushant.

200 tons, carrying newly cast guns from Nantes for Brest. Good for William, a remote relation of my wife June's.

So we left for Ushant but did not quite have the luck of Thos. Usher commanding a hired armed cutter who reported to Admiral Cornwallis on 17th Feb 1804: '*Coming thro' the passage de Raz this morning I fell in with and captured the chasse marée Quatre Soeurs, laden with brandy and wine.*' I'm sure he handed every litre of it over to the Admiralty Prize Court!

On the way north we passed the jagged teeth and great light on Pierres Noires. It seems curious today that this was an anchorage in 30 fathoms regularly used by the blockaders. The 74 *Magnificent* struck an uncharted rock beside the Pierres in March 1804, while attempting to get east to capture a storeship at anchor off Le Conquet. She became a total loss; all the crew were saved, 84 as captives of the French.

Ushant

My first Brittany port ever was Lampaul in 1952. We'd come straight down from Ireland in *Caru*, a 27 foot McGruer sloop. Having missed the tide south, Ushant seemed a natural stopping place. There's no time like the first time and as very raw sailors basking in a feeling of achievement, we gorged Muscadet and *moules*. In '52 women still wore lace coiffes, ankle-length black dresses and wooden clogs. Visitors were few, a tiny fraction of the present when 1,500 a day can spew ashore at Stiff from the ferries.

Seeing Ushant again this year, we were not too proud to use a visitor mooring in the bay. It's usually calm in summer but could be mighty uncomfortable in a sou'wester. Lampaul has the great advantage that few *vedettes* come there and not many fishing boats nowadays, so peace is rarely broken.

Equally, time spent on licensed premises is rarely wasted and in L'Ocean Bar we found a tall Irishman with a lightsome eye, slaking the cement dust from his throat. Beside it he and his hirsute friend Garry were rebuilding a perilously perched stone wall behind his boutique. John Moran from Achill has been living in Lampaul for 15 years, married to a local beauty. He has become perhaps the *Grand Fromage* of Ushant and shows no inclination to leave.

We had a lazy starter on the engine. Peter had kept it going, but now he had jumped ship. John called up the garage man at the top of the town who identified the trouble. A new solenoid was flown out from Brest on the afternoon plane and fitted by our 'mousse' Lewis Purser the same night. It took him two hours of contortions to do so.

Why do engine manufacturers commonly mount the starter low down where bilge water is likely to get at it, and the studs are virtually inaccessible? We proposed and seconded, while downing champagne at midnight to celebrate the completion of a disagreeable job, that manufacturers should invent self-rotating nuts which screw on or off in response to coded taps.

Gourmet John Moran recommended L'Ocean for dinner and we duly enjoyed the *Rillettes de Rouget* of Corsican José. As a fisherman, John knows the rocks and introduced us to the Fourche Passage which from the south-east brings you inside La Jument. This not only saves a couple of miles distance but avoids the strong tide outside, which always seems to be foul and producing a *mer démontée*.

Fourche itself is a twin-tit rock with little iron spikes coming out of the top. You line it up with a conspicuous white mark with a red centre on the far shore and steer boldly in. But a big scale chart and a rising tide are advisable. There is a fine beach at the head of Lampaul Bay where we spent pleasant afternoons. On hired bikes we circled the island, using muscles I'd forgotten I possessed. Not having ridden for ten years, sudden meetings with other ancient mariners coming the opposite way on a narrow track three feet in from the cliff edge produced some exciting moments. But after an hour or so I was standing up on the pedals like a circus clown. Well, sort of!

The sandy track winds right round over headlands and down gullies along the south-east side of the island, up stiff little slopes too. Negotiating it slowly and enjoying the savagely beautiful cliffs on one hand and sweetly tame pairs of wheatears on the other is an abiding recollection.

The Eco Museum is an excellent example of what a display of past village life should be. Créach lighthouse, with the aspect of a palace, and the Phares et Balise Museum it contains, are worth a walk. But most memorable are the anfractuous rocks of the west with the background of the steady, almost mesmeric procession of ships plodding by in the north-going separation zone.

It's curious that tiny Sein, without any museum that I have seen, gets almost as many visitors as Ushant. The smaller and more isolated the island, the more the mystique; it is this and the desire to see what island life is like that draws visitors, according to a recent survey published in Nord Ouest, the Breton paper. We read it often, mainly for the excellent Météo maps.

Picnics on the smaller uninhabited islets – Bannec, Balanec and Quéménes – made good objects for day sails from Lampaul. Familiarity breeds content. This, my fifth visit to Ushant was enjoyed more than ever. Don't miss it next time you are passing! Now that 45 years have flashed by since my first arrival there, I wonder what Ushant will be like in 2037. If the present pace of change maintains, I guess Lampaul Bay will have a seawall right across the mouth and a jam-packed marina within.

Wild Goose, a 33ft Maurice Griffiths yawl built in 1935, has owned the Clark family for the last 40 years. She has taken them to the Mediterranean through the Midi Canal, often to Brittany and has nosed into most inlets on our western coastline. New hands soon become 'Wild Goosed' and learn to appreciate her sense of humour.

FINDING LONGITUDE BY DEVIOUS MEANS

by Mike Pocock

After an enjoyable cruise down to La Rochelle, a short hop across to Bilbao, an excursion as far as the French border and back and then port-hopping west to Cedeira, we found ourselves hard on the wind, on the starboard tack, 24 hours out on our way home. With a clear sun and a crisp horizon, I gathered all the gear together with a view to improving the DR, our position fixing systems having reverted to traditional methods since the death of our GPS three years ago.

I had adjusted the clocks to within a second, we had Macmillans Astro supplement, the sextant and so on, but imagine my dismay when I found that the one item I'd omitted to bring aboard was the AP 3270 Vol 2 Sight Reduction Tables. Not being a former naval person, I am not skilled with the sines and cosines needed to work without these tables, so I had to accept that our resources were somewhat reduced. We had access to noon sights, a Hercules 190 automatic DR facility, a first-class Homer 5 RDF and reliable soundings, generally in depths of up to 150-200 metres.

When our dilemma became apparent we were already out of soundings, with nearly three miles of water beneath us. The nearest RDF station on Ushant was 200 miles out of range. The north-easterly was steadily driving us out to the westward and in the evening we worked our way through the shipping and out beyond the Ushant to Finisterre rhumb line into the Atlantic. This suggested the solution to our lack of longitude input. The column of shipping is so concentrated and con-sistent that we only needed to tack inshore, preferably before dusk, and our position could be established with sufficient accuracy by crossing the shipping line with our noon sight.

As it happened the wind relented that night and we were able to set a more direct course towards home. We made good progress and our course varied between about 035° and 050° as we tried to keep the ships just over the horizon, particularly at night. During the afternoon watch, 2½ days out, I began to juggle the clues as we neared the time when a firm position became desirable. The noon sight had given a latitude of 47° 20′N and at around 1400hrs soundings of 198 metres began to appear. What one might call 'run-of-the-mill' ships seemed to be well below the east horizon, but we were seeing the odd supertanker which we presumed would be using the dangerous cargo lane on the outside of the Ushant system.

Our target was the SW Lanby, which marks the southern inshore limit of that zone, and to round Ushant outside the main shipping. The visibility reports in the Channel areas were not very promising and our choice, having got on the outside, was to stay there and sail the extra distance. By now we had the wind on the port quarter and if conditions held we would be able to gybe in mid-Channel and stay clear of the worst of the shipping all the way.

RDF began to come in increasingly sharply and at the 2300 change of watch I had great satisfaction in pointing out the loom of the buoy to Pat as she took over. She had a storming sail throughout her watch, pulling down a reef just after midnight and passing the buoy at 0110. The wind backed sharply at 0400 and on the other gybe we soon ran into rain and poor visibility. The wind did some silly things in the afternoon, trying to turn easterly and head us, and even failed completely for a couple of hours, when we motored. Strangely there was a clearance in the evening and Start light was bearing 030° at 2230hrs.

That sighting of Start was our last glimpse of anything as visibility closed in once more and any passing sailor with a GPS to sell would have found a willing buyer. With only one useable RDF beacon on Portland Bill, fetching the Needles is not easy with a roaring tide and no sight of St Alban's or Anvil. Bearings on Hurn Airport at least told us we were getting close to home and by picking up the 20 metre contour we eventually made an accurate landfall on the Needles Fairway buoy as several other yachts emerged out of the murk. In these circumstances nowadays there is a temptation to assume that 'they all have GPS' and we were the only ones groping our way around by guess and by God. For all we know, they may also have been planning to buy GPS or Radar for Christmas.

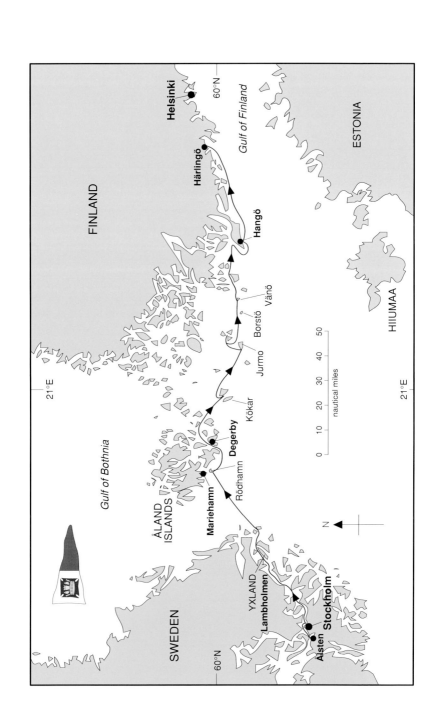

A SHORT SUMMER CRUISE TO HÄRLIGÖ

by Aran Williams

Våga II is a Maxi 77 and belongs to my girlfriend Hanna's parents. They keep her in Ålstens harbour, next to their house in Bromma, on lake Mälaren in Stockholm. *Våga* sounds like the Swedish word for 'wave', but actually means 'to dare'. *Våga I* was the family's first boat, the original 'dare' being to borrow the money to buy her. She crossed many times from Stockholm to the family summer island of Härligö, on the south coast of Finland. Now, after several years without a boat, *Våga II* has been bought; the dare perhaps this time being to allow Hanna and me to take her on her first trip across the Åland sea to Härligö.

We flew to Stockholm on a wet Saturday morning and left Ålstens harbour (59°18.0′N 17°57.0′E) after lunch. As we motored out to the lock that separates Mälaren from the salt water Stockholm archipelago, the weather cleared up. The shores of the lake were busy on Saturday afternoon, as we passed discreet yellow and red villas, classically elegant white passenger ferries and the towers and grand façades of old Stockholm. We sped underneath the bridges and headed out through the islands following the main channel running to the north-east. The wind stayed very light, so we motored on until nightfall, anchoring at 2200 in the perfectly sheltered anchorage of Lambholmarna, on Yxland island (59°36.00′N 18°48.00′E).

Next morning we stopped at Furusund, where the channel narrows, for diesel and basic provisions before setting out for Åland. Åland is almost entirely Swedish speaking, although it has been part of Finland since Sweden relinquished Finland in the 19th Century.

As the low islands were swallowed up in the haze, a good breeze filled in from the south-west and we could sail at last. We danced across the Åland sea, passing Nyhamn lighthouse and reaching on to Rödhamn with the wind freshening all the time. The headland at Nyhamn has always registered magnetic deviation, and 100 years ago this excited people to mine for iron ore there. They finally gave up after they had dug a kilometre long, entirely ferrous-free tunnel, under the sea.

Rödhamn is visible from afar – bright red rocks with a solitary white cottage standing proudly on top. The island is a popular first stop in Åland. The well protected anchorage (58°59.1′N 20°06.4′E) has recently been developed to include a wooden quay with off-lying buoys to offer easy bow-to mooring. Thanks to naval visits there are also plenty of well positioned iron rings in the rocks.

This was my first attempt at mooring bow-to and I must admit to severely underestimating the distance from the buoy to the shore. With Hanna standing on the bow poised to leap ashore, I passed a rope through the ring on the buoy and carried on towards the shore. My first rope soon ran out, so a quick bowline attached the reserve. However with this reserve also rapidly coming to an end, and with the distance from bow to shore still comfortably exceeding Hanna's long jumping range, the only rope to hand was the the main-sheet. This was speedily attached so as not to break my approach. The boat was slowed as the main sheet pulled tight and I reached frantically for the topping lift to give me the necessary extra few inches. This was judged 'to perfection' as Hanna leapt nimbly ashore.

The island has been a pilotage point for several hundred years. We scrambled around, checking out the new developments. There are now three saunas and a large barn in addition to the pilot's house. A fishing family used to live there, selling cod, perch and flounder to visiting

Phoning home.

yachtsmen, but they have left. A small café/shop opens in summer, run by people from the mainland. We bought fresh flounder from them.

It rained hard in the night but cleared by nine when we set off east again. The wind was fairly fresh and we had to harden up to beat through a narrow channel. Unfortunately I was a little sharp on the mainsheet and the mainsail ripped from the leech along its lowest seam for almost a metre. We continued under genoa to Degerby. There we found a new swimming pool and restaurant, showers and a new boat pontoon with buoys for about forty boats. There is also a supermarket where we were able to buy some strong nylon thread. I spent the rest of the day sewing, only drawing blood three times! Hanna navigated along the narrow passages that weave through the clusters of islands. At times the well buoyed channel is no more than thirty feet wide.

Later that day the wind faded and it began to rain. We motored south to Kökar ('Sherka'). This island too has changed over the last few years as it tries to attract more tourists. The inlet of Hellsö (59°57.1′N 20°55.6′E), where we stopped, now has buoys and a pontoon. The inlet is long and well sheltered by flat rocks and small shrubs and trees, and is relatively empty as most boats go to the main settlement on Kökar. At Hellsö we found three small saunas, pleasant showers and mini-golf. The least modern feature was the harbour master, who seemed reluctant even to acknowledge the existence of, let alone charge for, his newly built facilities. On a hill above the harbour is a little restaurant.

It was blowing hard on Tuesday morning, so we stayed in harbour and went running. Later I was encouraged by the arrival of a yacht carrying full sail, so I refitted the newly stitched mainsail and we ventured out. The yacht I'd seen was in fact a traditional Finnish boat, unable to reef its mainsail, but the wind moderated slightly and we were on a broad reach, heading for an outer island called Jurmo. The visibility remained good, although rain showers pursued us.

The harbour at Jurmo (59°49.6′N 21°35.3′E) is not so well protected from westerly winds. The new visitors pontoon proved too exposed, so we lay alongside two boats that were nestling snugly behind the old pontoon, sheltered by a fisherman's red hut. Jurmo is a rather special island. By the harbour on a smooth round pink rock, an unusual glass telephone booth is perched. There is a fish smoker and five small huts, one bearing three brass nameplates, which announce in Finnish, Swedish and English, that electricity came to Jurmo in Autumn 1996. Jurmo's rugged beauty is striking, particularly on a blustery overcast day. The long pebble beach is a bird sanctuary and the west end of the island is covered in heather and small wild flowers.

The archipelago is so huge that large parts of it are not accurately charted. The charts show the main passages through the islands and mark the positions of scattered rocks, but do not pretend to be a definitive guide. Straying from the channel is best done in fine weather

Moored by the ferry landing on a Finnish island.

and is well worth the effort as there are many interesting islands to explore. Next day we sailed north to the island of Björkö (59°54.5′N 21°41.0′E). There is a long inlet with an unusual entrance, that ends close to a freshwater lake some 200 metres across. We dropped a stern anchor and tied up to a tree ashore, then scrambled over to the lake to bathe. The lake is cut off from the sea by a thin rocky isthmus at the western end, which only allows spray in during storms.

With the wind light and from the west it was unfortunate that *Våga II* had not yet acquired a spinnaker, or even a pole. We took turns at holding the genoa out with the boat-hook as we ran past hundreds of small islands, past Borstö ('Brush island') and on to Vänö ('Fair island'). This island has a community of eighteen people who live there all year round. We knocked on the door of a beautiful yellow wooden house, and an elderly lady led us down to her boat-house to sell us fresh fish. She netted four flounder from a floating wooden keep and prepared them for us outside as she chatted away in Finnish-Swedish, the dialect of the Swedes living in Finland. She had lived all her life on the island.

On Thursday the weather was fine again and we had a moderate south-westerly to push us east. We left the outer islands behind and joined the 'inner channel' that leads all the way to Helsinki. The wind was light between some of the islands, but freshened as we reached across Hangöfjärden to the Hangö peninsular. This is the headland that all small boats dread, as it is the point where they must leave their sheltered channels and brave the open sea. In rough weather it can be nasty as there are hundreds of skerries. However the weather was kind to us, and we were able to sail around, beating nimbly up through one of the shallower inshore channels.

Hangö is the sailing centre of Finland and we arrived at the same time as a race back from Estonia. There is a large new marina with guest pontoons, but we were not staying long and tied up in a vacant private berth in the inner harbour. Hangö has the best ice cream in the world, and as soon as we were tied up Hanna was racing for the nearest ice-cream kiosk. The ice cream comes in enormous scoops and in many flavours, notably liquorice. In the town there are beautiful wooden villas and the whole place has the feel of a well-heeled Victorian seaside resort, with splendid gardens, gaily painted houses and shadowy boulevards.

We continued east in the evening and anchored behind the island of Sjöbjörkskär ('Sea birch island' – 59°51.0′N 23°11.8′E), leaving us a day's sail to Härligö next day. This we would have covered in no time with the winds we'd had to date, but our final day found us beating, again along narrow channels. In glorious sunshine we worked our way up the outer passage to Härligö.

Härligö has an interesting history. Last century it was owned by Bäck, a rich brewer, who treated the island as his personal fortress. He imported stone and foreign soil to grow superior plants, and built himself a tennis court, fine houses and sea defences. One winter a local man walked across the ice to ask Bäck for employment. Upset at being rejected he proceeded to cleave Bäck's skull with his axe, and run up to loot the house. Bäck fell immediately in cold snow so he did not die, and despite his split head was able to walk up to the house and surprise the robber, who was by then attacking a servant in the house. The robber ran away terrified, and the servant lived to tell the tale, although Bäck soon died. Bäck's wealth was never found, although villagers and indeed Hanna, have spent much time trying to find the buried treasure.

Bäck's most evident legacy springs from the soil he imported. Härligö has a beautiful lawn and some of the tallest trees in southern Finland. The largest fir tree had to be pulled down a few years ago as it was threatening the main house, but before then it was so tall that it was marked on charts of the area.

As we made our approach in the early evening, a welcoming tail of smoke was already rising from Härligö's gay yellow sauna.

SNOW AND SUN IN PATAGONIA

by Kit Power

Early October found Penny and me in a most luxurious hotel in Puyuhuapi, 180 miles south of Puerto Montt on the coast of Chile. There were hot springs to frolic in and an attentive waiter who addressed Penny as 'Miss' which, after some re-education, he amended to 'Missus' and eventually, with exaggerated emphasis, to 'Madaaam'. We had flown out with minimal baggage and a great quantity of ship's stores, trying to look as if the 100 metres of 12 mm rope in our hand luggage was as light as a feather and successfully informing the Chilean customs that this was 'equipment temporarily imported for a tourist activity'. Now we were awaiting the arrival of *Northanger*, the yacht (and home) of Greg Landreth and Keri Pashuk, 1996 Tilman Medalists, which was en route from Tierra del Fuego to Ellesmere Island in the Canadian Arctic. There they will take part in the Otto vedrup Centennial Expedition, re-enacting the overwintering of the *Fram* a century ago.

Northanger had not turned up and despite attempts to contact her on the hotel's SSB and VHF radios, we had no idea when she would. So on 8th October, we packed our bags and were waiting by the jetty for the launch that would take us to less splendid accommodation. Suddenly *Northanger*'s red hull was spotted two miles away across the channel. We raised her on VHF and soon we were celebrating our (and her) arrival in the saloon. On board were Greg and Keri, plus Keri's nephew Joey and his cousin Blake – two Canadians aged 18 and 20 neither of whom had sailed before.

Northanger will be known to members as the boat in which Rick Thomas made the first transit of the North-West Passage by a British yacht in 1988/9 and for which, after his tragic death climbing a few weeks later, he was also awarded the Tilman Medal. Greg Landreth was on board for that voyage, and bought the boat after Rick's death. She is very much an expedition boat, a Michel Joubert designed Damien ketch, 49 feet overall, immensely strongly built in steel and with a draft of 3 or

11 feet as you wish. She is designed around the huge keel-box containing her lifting keel, which not only incorporates four tons of ballast but a large fuel tank as well. The keel-box is open on deck and you can look eerily down, past the keel and into the blue depths below. Fenders, garbage bags and all sorts of other things can be hung there for stowage.

Below, there are two double cabins to port, two pairs of single bunks to starboard, and a massive forecastle with 8 ft workbench and large diesel stove. Right aft are the saloon and galley. There is massive stowage, under the sole and elsewhere, and the yacht swallows up such exotica as skis, snow shoes, a hang-glider, a petrol chain saw, mountain bikes, snow shovels, ice axes and two kayaks. Accommodation ladders, to port and starboard, lead through hatches in the after coach roof. There are no spray hoods and in heavy weather you have to time your entry and exit carefully through the lee hatch. In the best Tilman tradition, Greg regards the mountains as the real objective – the boat is only the means.

Next morning it was raining hard and we motored up to the village for stores. Puyuhuapi has about 600 inhabitants, living in a motley assortment of old shingle houses and newer tin ones. Everyone has a smile, and in the trees we could hear the loud, hysterical laugh of the chucao bird. Daffodils, yellow berberis and escallonia flowered everywhere. We shopped in one of the 'supermarkets', picking our way past bags of flour

Tic Toc Bay and Mount Yantelos.

and bags of cement stacked together under a 1995 calendar, and repaired back on board with 40 litres of diesel in cans.

"It's stopped raining," Greg announced. He was right – it was snowing, and next morning we awoke to a good four inches over everything. We shovelled it off, turned up the stove and were away by 0745, squeezing under the cloudbase at mast height. Snow was lying down to the shore, and on little ice floes around us, as we turned north-west into the Canal Jacaf.

A colony of 100 or more fur seals lay on rocks on the north side and we nosed in close, watching their increasing nervousness as one by one they slipped into the water until only one remained ashore, elderly, agitated and arthritic but defiant. Across the Canal Moraleda, we anchored for the night in Puerto Ballena, between Isla Mike and Isla Mulchy. The clouds were clearing and the boys took the RIB ashore to fill cans at a waterfall. Penny and I clambered about on the boulders on the shoreline lamenting that even in a remote and beautiful spot like this, plastic bottles, polystyrene foam and other detritus litter the shore.

Next day, 11th October, a high was establishing and in bright sunshine and a light NW wind we motor-sailed towards Tic Toc Bay, 45 miles to the north-east on the mainland. Suddenly the sparkling sea and blue sky were gone and *Northanger* was bracketed between dense curtains of streaky grey rain. As we entered the anchorage, cliffs enclosed us, two penguins dived away as they saw us and an albatross sailed past with incredible grace. We anchored at the head of the south arm of the bay, perfectly sheltered beneath a sheer, but wooded, cliff, with the Bruce anchor well dug into thick mud.

The following morning we could see what a perfect anchorage this is. The sky was cloudless, the snow sparkled on Mount Yanteles and we put on our shorts. Penny and I took the kayaks ashore, starting gingerly and gaining confidence until in the shallows I disturbed a shoal of large brown fish. Suddenly the sea was boiling around me with fish banging the canoe on all sides and seriously threatening my equilibrium. We walked along the volcanic sand, with wild strawberry plants above the tide line and banks of gorse flowering under notro trees covered in red flowers like honeysuckle. A white-necked heron stood motionless in the shallows. Back on board, we drank gin and tonic and watched the sun setting behind the snows.

October 13th dawned cloudless and the wind blew from the south. Progressively it boxed the compass through east, north and finally west, which was where we were going. As we left the anchorage, Greg and Joey went off in the RIB to take photographs. Leaving the coast, more mountains opened up. Yanteles, now looking exactly like Mont Blanc, was astern. Corcovado, giving a passable imitation of the Matterhorn, was to starboard and on the port quarter was Melimoyu, a vast rounded chunk of smooth icing sugar with two jagged peaks protruding from the

Clearing snow off the decks before getting underway.

top. Under all plain sail we close reached across the Golfo Corcovado towards the southern end of Isla Chiloé, encountering several sudden and quite severe tidal rips en route. Predictions for tidal streams in these waters are confined to the heavily used narrows – elsewhere there seems little guidance available.

We'd set up a SSB radio schedule with *Plainsong* and *Ardevora* with the object of arranging a meet. In the event, a three boat meet proved impossible but that night we anchored in the fishing port of Quellon on Chiloé with *Plainsong* close astern. After drinks aboard *Northanger*, we all went ashore for dinner.

Our arrival on board had to be recorded on the *zarpé*, the Armada Chileana's way of keeping tabs on yachts on this coast. Passports were presented and the *zarpé* duly notes that 'Mr & Mrs Christopher British' had joined the ship. We fuelled, hugger mugger in a melée of fishing boats, then headed north under engine inside Isla Chaullin, passing little farms backed by rolling wooded hillsides and punctuated by the occasional distinctive Chiloé church with a stepped tower. Yellow gorse blazed everywhere and three pelicans flew past in perfect formation. We anchored for the night in Puerto Queilen on Chiloé amongst painted trawlers anchored on incredibly long ropes. A fiery orange sunset was complemented by a complete double rainbow above the village.

Morning dawned sunny, clear and windless yet again. We were underway soon after nine, motoring north through the channels. GPS is of limited use in these waters as the Chilean charts can be two miles or more adrift from true positions. Radar seemed to solve the problem and was the main navigational aid used. We anchored for lunch off the west side of Isla Apiao, opposite a little wooden church, apparently prevented from falling over by two large wooden props wedged against it. Suddenly the church bell started a rhythmic toll and we watched in shirtsleeves as the congregation came straggling along in little groups. Penny painted the scene while Greg baked bagels for lunch. This is the area where fishermen still work under sail but we saw none of them under way.

That evening we anchored at Isla Mechuque in a small lagoon perfectly sheltered within a steep shingle beach where women in brightly coloured dresses were gathering clams at low water. The following morning we explored the village; rickety houses were balanced on stilts perched on the banks of a creek and there was a little church surrounded by a mass of enormous white lilies. There are no cars here – or even roads – and if you want to go anywhere you ride on horseback.

From Isla Mechuque we sailed, still with little wind, across the Golfo de Ancud. The sun still shone, the Andes sparkled above the horizon and I nearly jumped out of my skin when I caught a glimpse of what I took to be jagged rocks breaking surface close to starboard. Closer inspection revealed three pilot whales keeping station alongside. We passed into the Canal Calbuco inside Isla Puluqui south-west of Isla Calbuco. It was a fortunate choice – our chart showed an equally satisfactory channel to the north-west of Isla Calbuco but as we rounded its northern tip we saw that this channel has now been closed by a causeway.

We raised Tim and Sophie Trafford in *Ardevora* on VHF and headed up Est. Huito where we had arranged a rendezvous. This is a large inlet with many fish farm tanks and a number of big fishing boats being built in wood, precariously balanced high on the banks. Launching must be rapid, dramatic and hazardous. That night we secured alongside *Ardevora* for a memorable dinner and sing-song. In the whole cruise we had seen only four other yachts and two of them flew the RCC burgee.

Next morning we motored north between islands fringed with gorse, but soon reached Puerto Montt with banks, shops, markets, even a marina. After the spectacular wilderness we'd become used to, civilization was a major shock to the system and we had to steel ourselves to leave for our plane. It flew us to Bolivia and we went on to Lake Titicaca, but that's another story altogether.

SCOTTISH SUMMER

by Peter and Gill Price

Peter and Gill Price wintered Lectron at Ardfern and cruised up the west coast of Scotland before crossing to Shetland. After circumnavigating Mainland, they headed south towards Fair Isle, where we join them for just a small part of their 2,200 mile cruise.

A gentle north-westerly took us to Fair Isle in seven hours, where we moored alongside *Calico Martlet* in the North Haven. A new breakwater gives good shelter so that the *Good Shepherd* mail boat is no longer hauled out of the water every time she's in harbour.

We were soon ashore for an excellent, if rather dangerous walk over the hills. Both Sandy and Peter had direct hits on the head from the legs of angry Arctic Skuas, luckily with no damage. We wrapped our heads in jerseys and held up sticks which seemed to spoil their aim. The weather was calm and we were not surprised to hear that Kirkwall was the coldest place in the UK that night while our Eberspacher kept us pleasantly warm.

On the last day of June we left under a cloudless sky and drifted for a while as Peter had his Monday morning Ham session talking to members in Badcall Bay, the Azores and Sheffield. Then, with a light north-easterly, we were off southwards again. Lumpy seas off North Ronaldsay, but things were quiet again as we entered the North Sound in Orkney. Gales were forecast by evening so it was good to be close to Westray, as we'd heard on the Ham network that Pierowall is now one of the few secure harbours in Orkney. *Calico Martlet* was already there and we moored alongside again. The harbour has been built of large metal caissons and gave good shelter from the NE gale. The acting Harbour Master asked for dues of £9.21 for four nights and then we were free to collect stores from the two shops, about three quarters of a mile from the harbour.

At 2200 a fishing boat came in and moored stern to the wall to try and repair a stern trawl. They failed and left again at 0100 into the teeth of a 40 knot gale to go to Aberdeen to get the trawl mended. Just like that! It blew hard in the night, so next morning was boat maintenance and reading time. In the afternoon we braved wind and rain to visit the ruined Notland castle, still several floors high but almost all unroofed. The wind blew but the barometer hardly moved at all.

On 2nd July we left quietly at 0615 and had a good sail, well reefed, in sheltered waters between the islands. Suddenly we heard our name being called by the coastguard. We responded to be told they just wanted to know where we were. Apparently *Islay* were aware of the gale, knew that we'd left Fair Isle and had not heard from us at the morning net. They had asked Stornoway coastguard if we had reported in at all and they in turn had passed the message to Orkney who found us at the first call. No panic, just a simple question which in those waters seemed quite sensible. How different from the Solent.

By 1030 we were moored in Kirkwall ready to sample the public showers opposite the Cathedral. A towel, soap and unlimited hot water for 50p didn't seem bad! The two supermarkets, butcher and baker supplied our needs and then we visited the magnificent St Magnus Cathedral and the Tankerness House museum, which had a special exhibition of the Viking 'Skaill Hoard' of silver treasures unearthed in 1858. Leaving *Lectron* safely in Kirkwall, we hired a car for another day trip. We saw the Churchill Barriers which enclose Scapa Flow to the east and quite by chance noticed *Grey Gannet* at anchor and met Pat and Ann Thomas as they rowed ashore. We learned about their engine failure off Cape Wrath which had delayed *Grey Gannet*'s departure to Orkney.

Our next stop was enthralling when we saw the Italian Chapel, where the interiors of two Nissen huts are beautifully decorated with painted plasterboard and concrete to look like brick and stone. The chapel was built by Italian prisoners of war and in 1960 the original designer, Domenico Chiocchetti, was traced and persuaded to return and help with restorations.

No tour would have been complete without a visit to the ancient sites at Maeshowe. The large chambered burial cairn dates from about 3,000BC. We saw the stones of Stenness and some even bigger stones at the Ring of Brodgar, followed by the prehistoric village at Scara Brae which dates from 3,100 BC. The village was buried by sand in 2,400 BC, uncovered by a storm in 1824 and excavated in 1928. You can look down into the stone houses with stone beds, shelves and hearth all connected by passageways. By now it was raining again and we made our way back via Stromness and its interesting museum.

In the evening we sailed to Deer Sound to spend the night, ready for our departure to mainland Scotland next day. *Lectron* was underway by 0715 on a grey, misty morning. As we rounded the bird cliffs of Mull Head, the wind came gently ahead, very disappointing after all the days of north winds. The rough and breaking seas calmed down once we had crossed the Pentland Firth, but we still needed hot soup for lunch to ward off the cold. We moored alongside the wall in the almost deserted inner harbour at Wick and in the evening we all went for a walk and saw the imposing memorial to J. Brenner, who had built 18 harbour break-waters and salvaged 260 ships including the SS *Great Britain*.

We spent a rolly night in Cromarty, followed by a choppy sail up Inverness Firth to enter the Caledonian Canal and climb the first flight of locks to Caley Marina with its excellent facilities and chandler. Here the Watsons left us and we were sorry to see them go. Needless to say, the sun came out and we dried ship!

Lectron is a Moody 376 modified for light crews, with winches near the helmsman, Starcruiser roller jib, slab reefing, separate trysail track and removable inner forestay. The Aries vane gear is offset to allow stern boarding. The electronics are comprehensive. There is an Eberspacher heater and a WC holding tank.

Anti skua tactics.

CLUB MATTERS

THE 1996 AWARDS

Judge's Commentary by Loftus Peyton Jones

This year we saw some remarkable achievements by Cadet Members, which reflects great credit on their parents for many years of training, trust and encouragement. The logs reveal two venturesome passages through the Finnish archipelago by Peter Lewin-Harris in *Musketeer* and Aran Williams in *Vaga II*; and two most competent cruises by Katharine Thornhill in *Sai See* on the west coast of Ireland, and Hamish Southby-Tailyour in *Black Velvet* on a homeward passage from Iceland.

Further cruises to Scandinavia were recorded by the family Ingram taking *Troubadour* on her maiden cruise to the Lofotens, and John Marsh in *Harrier* who cruised the Finnish archipelago, the Saimaa Lakes and St Petersburg. The only other recorded venture to the Arctic Circle was by *Black Velvet*. Ewen Southby-Tailyour's outward passage and remarkable surveying cruise of Iceland's unsounded fjords deserves admiring recognition.

Apart from the circumnavigation voyages, we have three accounts of transatlantic passages. The first was a nonchalant note by Michael Richey, describing a solo west to east crossing. On this 36 day passage in his 25 foot *Jester*, Michael once again celebrated his birthday afloat – his 80th this time! The second was a complete North Atlantic circuit by Alistair and Margot Pratt in their 35 foot *Border Raider*.

The third was a splendid log of Margaret and Graham Morfey's new Bowman 45 – *Flight of Time*. This was a long planned passage to celebrate retirement and took them 7,000 miles down to the Cape Verdes, across to Barbados, then island hopping up to the Virgins, before finishing at Newport. All mishaps and misfortunes were most cheerfully surmounted, during a voyage that was evidently very much enjoyed.

On that same eastern seaboard of North America, Ian Tew completed a three-day shakedown cruise from Sandy Hook to Chesapeake in his newly acquired *Independent Freedom*, while Gill and Tony Vasey spent three weeks sailing the 500 miles from Cape Cod to Annapolis in their 24 foot Crabber, *Clara*. This coastal passage was remarkable for its transit of the Harlem River, bordering New York, which required an armada of engineers to lift road and rail bridges that had remained in their customary down position for many years.

Most notable of the ventures on that side of the Atlantic was Pete and Annie Hill's account of their passage from Newfoundland northwards along the little known coast of Labrador, across the Hudson Strait to Baffin Island, and thence to the Azores – a journey of some 3,000 miles in their 34 foot junk rigged schooner, *Badger*.

To return to warmer climes, we have only to read the log of *Blue Sonata*, the 45 foot centreboard sloop belonging to Michael and Julie Manzoni. From Trinidad they made a thorough exploration of the eastern Caribbean as far as St Lucia, returning after a Christmas break for an interesting detour to Venezuela. Much nearer the equator, and often in much shallower waters, was David Mitchell in *Ondarina*, seeking grass-skirted girls and salt water hippos in the archipelago off Guinea-Bissau. A fascinating account of a most original solo venture.

Now I come to the yet more seriously addicted deep water sailors, to whom the first few weeks of non-stop sailing are but the prelude to the adventures that lie ahead. Leading this group must be Noël Marshall, who last year completed a three year circumnavigation in his 38ft Hallberg-Rassy, *Sadko*. After crossing to St Lucia, *Sadko* cruised up the Atlantic seaboard to Nova Scotia, before returning to Panama, by way of Bermuda and Belize. Then across the Pacific to Hawaii and another diversion to Russia and Japan, before homeward passage through the Med. A wonderful voyage with solo legs when crews were lacking.

Another long distance passage was undertaken by Jeremy and Sandrine Swetenham in their 38ft aluminium cutter, *Upshot*, from Poole to the Bay of Islands. Crossing the Atlantic in company with others on the ARC circuit, they cruised the Caribbean before voyaging across the Pacific. Their account makes it all seem deceptively easy and was quite delightful. Already in the Pacific was *Plainsong*, Francis and Marilyn Hawking's 35ft Tradewind, which sailed from California to Chile via French Polynesia and Easter Island, a jaunt of some 9,000 miles spread over five months.

Still on that side of the world were two accounts of rounding Stewart Island off the southern tip of New Zealand – the next most southerly point to Cape Horn. Andrew and Bette O'Grady took their 42ft gaff cutter, *Balaena*, from the Bay of Islands westabout to fiordland and return. Surrounded by 4,000 foot mountains and many miles in from the sea, they found wonderful anchorages in virtually every fiord and enjoyed some splendid explorations ashore. Following a similar route, but completing a circumnavigation of New Zealand and then onward to Fiji, were Hugh and Cathie Marriott in their 40ft cutter, *Tacit*. To have completed this voyage in the prevailing stormy conditions was an example of enterprise and endurance of the highest order.

Closer to home, Arthur and Germaine Beiser made the round trip to Venice from their base in the South of France in their 58 foot *Ardent Spirit*. Their log gave a wonderful feeling of the enjoyment of leisurely cruising in familiar waters, with many friends to meet along the way. For Christopher and Gail Lawrence-Jones in *Mermerus*, a Freedom 38, it was a first visit to the Adriatic, having completed a coastal voyage around the toe of Italy from north of Rome. Their cruise among the 700 islands of the Dalmatian Coast ended in Venice, where our Club representative, Dr Zuchetta, is evidently extending the warmest of welcomes to all visitors.

Also in the eastern Mediterranean were Simon and Catherine Butler in their 35 foot Rival, *Haigri*, voyaging with their two young children as crew. They sailed clockwise around the Aegean with an interesting detour up the Sea of Marmaris to Istanbul, before returning westwards to lay up in Tunisia.

One of the most enchanting logs was Gill Lloyd's account of *La Snook*'s cruise to the French haunts of yesteryear. Among her crew of grannies, in what must be the smallest boat in our fleet, was the same young lady whom I had seen receive the Challenge Cup at the first Club dinner I ever attended – at Grosvenor House in 1939. Her name of course was Helen Tew. Equally evocative and historically compelling is Wallace Clark's account of Ushant Revisited – a wonderful lesson in how to identify oneself with one's surroundings.

Jonathan Virden found friends and sunshine on the Ile de Ré, but had to spend five times as long motoring as sailing to get there and back. Tom Fenwick also had a fair amount of motor sailing to get *Fair Joanda* back to the Solent from Seville, but he does record a few unexpected days of fair winds on passage northwards up the Portuguese coast – and much else besides. His very readable log was matched by Scott Bayfield's account of circumnavigating the Iberian peninsula by way of the Canal du Midi, which includes a terrifying description of riding out a gale in harbour that forced him to regard his rubber dinghy, moored astern, more as a hang-glider than as a liferaft.

Dawdling in Donegal aptly describes Mike and Hilde Gill's passage from the Shannon to the Clyde in *Quicksilver* – a well planned cruise which allowed time to stop and stare and for the young crew to enjoy harbour pursuits. By contrast our gallant Honorary Secretary and his stalwart Mate covered over 2,000 miles, visiting many little known anchorages in the Shetlands, Orkneys and Hebrides in a voyage full of interest and not a little excitement.

No summary would be complete without mention of Bob Shepton's engaging account of his participation with Willy Ker in the Three Peaks Race. He excuses this rash, and almost unmentionable, adventure by revealing that they came in last, and saying 'I knew it was only a cruise really.'

To nominate awards from among so many memorable and well documented ventures was a taxing task. If winners have to be named they win, in most cases, by the narrowest of margins over their fellow voyagers.

RCC Challenge Cup	Noël Marshall
Romola Cup	Francis Hawkings
Founder's Cup	Andrew O'Grady
Claymore Cup	Stuart and Annabelle Ingram
Juno's Cup	Pete Hill
Cruising Club Bowl	Ewen Southby-Tailyour
Royal Cork Vase	Simon Butler
Goldsmith Award	Ewen Southby-Tailyour
Irish Decanter	Graham and Margaret Morfey
Sea Laughter Trophy	Hamish Southby-Tailyour

Ladies' Cup

The Commodore had no hesitation in awarding the Ladies' Cup to Gill Price, for her contribution to *Lectron*'s 2,000 mile cruise and also her continued stalwart work in supporting our roving Honorary Secretary.

The Seamanship Medal

Christmas 1996 had barely passed into Boxing Day for competitors in the Vendée Globe round-the-world non-stop single-handed race when Peter Goss, aboard *Aqua Quorum*, received a satellite message that his fellow competitor Raphael Dinelli (*Algimouss*), 150 miles behind and upwind of him, had activated his emergency distress beacons. *Aqua Quorum* was the nearest vessel that could be contacted.

With no second thought, Goss turned round and started back into the teeth of a Southern Ocean storm and vicious sea. With 55–60 knots of wind and unable to lay the course, *Aqua Quorum* was knocked down three times in the first two hours. Nevertheless Goss continued into the unabated storm for the next 30 hours, during which time the Royal Australian Air Force had found and dropped a liferaft to Dinelli shortly before the capsized *Algimouss* sank. It was not until 27th December that, despite still atrocious conditions, *Aqua Quorum* came alongside the liferaft and was able to signal:

"I've had the best Christmas present ever. Raphael is aboard, very cold but happy, with no injuries. I've just given him a cup of tea." This was an outstanding feat of courage and seamanship in the very highest traditions of seafaring.

The Medal for Services to Cruising

Anybody who has cruised the West Coast of Scotland will be aware of, and has probably used, the Clyde Cruising Club series of pilot books covering that lovely area. Those who race there will also know of the series of inshore and passage races that the club runs up and down the coast (often with prizes for those who race less seriously – like first family crew, or best fish caught during the race). What is less widely known outside Scotland is that Sandy Taggart has been the driving force behind all this. Indeed his firm's staff might be forgiven for wondering whether the firm was engaged in accountancy or yachting. As well as everything else, Sandy has somehow found the time to be Scottish Area Governer of the Ocean Youth Club and, later, a Trustee of the Jubilee Sailing Trust. His contribution to sailing in general and cruising in particular over the past 20 years has been prodigious. The medal is awarded for this service.

The Tilman Medal

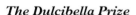

South Georgia is a remote South Atlantic island which became better known in 1916, when Shackleton and his crew arrived there having sailed over 1,000 miles in an open boat following the loss of *Endurance* in the ice. In 1992 the Carrs arrived in South Georgia aboard *Curlew*, their 28ft gaff cutter Falmouth Quay Punt, a boat already 18 years old when Shackleton made his journey. Like Shackleton's boat, *Curlew* has no engine. The Carrs remained at Grytviken for the next five years, looking after the whaling museum and exploring the island. During that time they have not only explored every cove and inlet under sail alone, an extraordinary feat by any standards, but have also climbed and skied extensively, summer and winter, traversing the island in both directions. All this has been achieved with a boat built a year before *Sea Breeze*, the oldest of Tilman's Bristol Channel Pilot Cutters. Tim and Pauline Carr are true followers in the Tilman tradition.

The Dulcibella Prize

This year's Dulcibella Prize is awarded to Wallace Clark and *Wild Goose of Moyle*. Wallace Clark has been a regular contributor to the Journal over many years, and his pieces are well known for their warmth and style of story-telling. This year he takes us gently back to some favourite Biscay haunts in his inimitable way.

FLEET MOVEMENTS

Name of Boat	Name of Skipper	Area Cruised
Adrigole	Jeffrey and Sally O'Riordan	Mediterranean Spain and Balearics
Ardevora of Roseland	Tim Trafford	Cape Verde Islands, Tobago, Venezuela, Cuba, Belize, Guatemala, Honduras, Panama, Easter Island, Chile
Artemis of Lleyn	John Hodges	Norway, Bergen / Stavanger
Ayesha of Yealm	John Lawson	Kusadasi to Kemer in Turkey, across to Malta
Barada	Ted Hawkins	Channel Islands, North Brittany, Normandy
Cardhu	Sir Tom Lees	Isles of Scilly, SW Ireland
Caressa	Christopher Perkins	Falmouth, L'Abervrac'h, Galicia, Spanish Rias, Bayona, Camariñas, Falmouth
Countess of Elloughton	Paul Roach	Southern Turkey, Greek Islands
Felicia	Robin Faulkner	South coast England, Normandy, Channel Islands
Foggy Dew	Michael Gilkes	Argyll and the islands
Foxtrot of Rhu	Bill Ludlow	Falmouth, SW Ireland, Dingle Bay, Isles of Scilly, West Country, Weymouth
Grey Gannet	Pat Thomas	West coast of Scotland and the Orkneys
Island Moon	Peter Craig-Wood	Eastern Caribbean
Juno II	Geoffrey and Sue Nockolds	Guatemala, Belize, Cuba, Florida
Kwai Muli	Kit and Penny Power	Channel Islands and North Brittany
Lectron	Peter and Gill Price	West coast of Scotland, Shetlands, Orkney, St. Kilda, Hebrides, Ireland, Chichester

Marlin	John Lancaster-Smith	South Brittany
Merilintu	Jamie Heron	Göteborg, Anholt, Copenhagen, S. Denmark, Keil Canal, Helgoland, Nordeney, Holland, France, Lymington
Moongazer II	David Pirie	Azores
Morning Shot	John Broomfield	Normandy, Channel Islands, Brittany
Morning Sky	Oliver Roome	Brittany, SW Ireland
Morning Star	Dick Trafford	Aegean, Turkish coast, Greek Islands
Nandisa	Colin and Marylyn Ford	Trinidad, Venezuela, ABC Islands, Honduras, Guatemala, Belize, Mexico, east coast USA to Maine
One and All	Robert Burdett	North Brittany
Oriole	John Lytle	West Country, west coast of Scotland, the Channel Islands
Oyster Belle	Robin and Tricia Stevens	Jersey to La Rochelle and back
Penelope's Ark	Jill and Tony Vasey	Canals of Holland
Quiver	Anthony Browne	Channel Islands, North Brittany, South Brittany, Morbihan, West Country
Rapscallion of the Russel	John and Ruth Button	Inner and Outer Hebrides
Response	Rory Macnamara	Burnham-on-Crouch to North Brittany, Camaret and back
Roving Topsy	Conrad Jenkin	West coast of Turkey
Squail	Elizabeth Bourne	West coast of Brittany
Taichi	Henry Hugh Smith	Trinidad, Venezuela, Dutch Antilles, Honduras, Guatemala, Belize, Mexico, Florida Keys, Chesapeake Bay
Tatsu	Lester Smith	North Brittany, Isles of Scilly
Te'Aria	Colin Barry	Canaries, St Lucia, Martinique, Saints, Dominica, Guadeloupe, St Vincent, Grenadines
Triculette	Terry Gerald	Ionian Sea, Croatia, Venice, Slovenia
Valkyrie of Guernsey	Loftus Peyton Jones	West Scotland and East Ireland
Wandering Moon III	Christopher Buckley	Scotland, West coast of Ireland, Normandy, Belgium, Holland

MEETS

East Coast Meet

The Meet saw far fewer than of recent years gathered at Suffolk Yacht Harbour in the River Orwell on a warm sultry afternoon with a light south-east wind. For once, boats from the south coast outnumbered by two to one the only local able to attend.

The presence of *Kwai Muli* with the Commodore and Penny was particularly appreciated, not only for their effort to be with us but also for having a boat large enough to accommodate all who stepped aboard to receive a warm welcome. This gave the evening a happy start in grand style which continued throughout dinner aboard the light-vessel of the Haven Ports Yacht Club, where we were fed superbly in splendid fashion. It was a happily convivial evening – some rated it the best East Coast meet yet.

Oliver Roome brought *Morning Sky* for the eleventh consecutive time, regardless of wind or weather. They arrived on Saturday morning, sailing again early on Sunday bound towards the Isle of Wight. We were privileged to have the Vice-Commodore too, his first visit for many a year. As a past Commodore Geoffrey Nockolds came, though sadly without Susanna on this occasion.

It was of particular interest to hear, from so many unable to come, comments such as 'Sailing in Croatia' to 'Going south this year' as well as 'Cruising the East coast of the United States' or 'In the West Indies' to quote just a few. Others had their boats in Scotland, Ireland, Norway and elsewhere too no doubt.

Boats attending were: *Kwai Muli*, *Morning Sky*, *Rollicker*.

Scottish Meet

An RCC blockade of Puilladobhrain didn't prevent the entry or departure of any other overnight cruising yachts on Friday 15th August. However the inner end of the arm leading into the anchorage, a handy Firth of Lorne 'lay-by' at the north end of Seil Island, was admirably suited for the gathering of our yachts for the Scots Meet.

The overnight forgatherers were *Thomasina*, *Islay*, *Lectron*, *Venture* and visiting yacht *Ceres* owned by Jim Pitts and crewed by two Club worthies, Bill Spiers and Michael Gilkes. Later in the morning we were treated to a fine sight – *Revel* beating in the light airs, short tacking dinghy fashion as she wove her way through the pool to the weather end to anchor under sail. *Nordlys* arrived to fill the first gap in deeper water. *Temptress* was followed closely by *Valkyrie* (a loaned yacht with Colin Maitland Dougal and friends). *Megget* and *Soilta* came in with *Quaila* bringing Katie Christie, CCC Commodore and her husband, Frank. This completed the jolly rendezvous. Despite the damp drizzle, everyone across the raft started to get to know each other, sharing lunch and good things amongst the fleet.

On the early flood, anchors were lifted and the whole lot of us proceeded in line ahead into Loch Feochan's narrow entrance channel. *Ceres* led the way, ensuring that all her HR 48 draught and hefty keel would clear the way for the rest of us. Our tidal predictions and calculations were perfect and soon all were comfortably anchored again and lying off the Scottish Salmon Centre where we enjoyed a delightful supper in the warm evening as the sun set in a glorious scale behind the mountains of Mull.

Next morning, with a fresh south-easterly whistling out through the loch, eight of the muster left at first light for breakfast anchorages near Oban and thence to continued fellowship in Loch Spelve, joining up with the Clyde Cruising Club at their August West Coast Muster.

Carteret

This splendid gathering took place on the weekend of 18th-20th July in glorious weather, and was attended by 24 yachts. It was the second meet organised by John and Sue Sharp and we hardly believed there could possibly be an improvement on their first event in Jersey and Chausey in 1996. However, they excelled themselves and provided a truly memorable weekend. This included a fiercely competitive *boules* match, an excellent dinner for 82 people, and a ride on a rather eccentric train to Portbail. For the second year running, John and Sue organised a superb barbecue, this time on a headland outside Carteret. The Meet culminated in a visit to Les Ecrehous which, thanks to excellent pilotage from Martin Richardson and Nick Bailhache, went without incident. The whole weekend ran like clockwork thanks to the enormous amount of work put in by Sue and John.

CCA Maine Rally

Maine is a wild and beautiful cruising ground at the north-eastern limit of the States. Granite shores are deeply indented by bays and rivers, and thousands of islands offer an endless variety of anchorages.

The four Commodores at the Maine Rally

Our first meeting with the CCA was a welcoming party hosted by CCA commodore Bob Drew and his wife Mindy on their yacht *Knight Hawk*. We met in Seal Cove, a lovely backwater just south of Fox Island Thorofare, surrounded by pinewoods. There was ample space for all the yachts, which carried visitors from Scotland, England, Ireland and New Zealand – and we converged in our dinghies to meet our hosts and new friends, and of course old friends from the RCC.

Next morning we sailed round the corner and anchored off Hopkins Point where Bill and Janie Saltonstall welcomed us to a wonderful brunch in their garden high above the Thorofare in blazing sunshine. A jazz band played on the verandah, while under the pine trees and in airy marquees we began to get to know the CCA members – some from local waters, some from Boston and New York and many from Chesapeake Bay.

In the next couple of days we had a spell of the infamous Maine fog, but we found a snug anchorage with two other CCA boats at Buckle Island. When the sunshine came back we made our way north to Mount Desert Island and the famous Somes Sound. It was indeed beautiful with hills on either side and a bay at the end where we all anchored for the dinner at Abel's Boatyard. We had a wonderful meal at long tables in two immaculate boat sheds.

Next morning John and Nancy McKelvy welcomed us with drinks on their spacious verandah and a sumptuous lunch in the comfort of their home – again in honour of the very fortunate foreign visitors. After this the fleet divided into two groups, some to explore the mid-coast area and some to go 'down east' beyond Schoodick Point to more wild and remote shores. Down East means further north in our terms and we went up with the northern fleet, including *Kataree*, to Roque Island. Passing through a narrow winding channel, we emerged into a wide, beautiful bay with a mile long crescent of golden sand. In the evening there was a Raft Party given by Shell Brown on his cat ketch *Long Reach*, which was a very jolly affair.

Turning south again, we called at Winter Harbour with its venerable yacht club, Back Cove and Bar Harbor. The next big party was in Frenchman's Bay, a spectacular area surrounded by hills and islands. In these superb surroundings there were two large schooners rafted up for the Commodore's Cocktail Party. After the excellent company and superb food we returned to our boats by moonlight in high spirits. The next morning we all skimmed gently along in the sunshine, gliding past Bass Harbor Head towards Pretty Marsh Harbor, which lived up to its name. Here *Flight of Time* rafted up with *Strathspey* and other chosen boats for the Scottish Classic Malts party hosted by Commodore Katie Christie of the Clyde.

August 7th was our final day. We set off in calm sunshine towards Naskeag Harbor, but as we were threading our way through the many small islands the fog began to descend. We quickly selected a good local boat to follow and didn't let her out of our sight! By the time we were approaching the anchorage at Brooklin, the fog lifted. By midday we were enjoying hot sunshine on shore and lining up for an excellent barbecue with all the trimmings. We sat in comfort under shady awnings while the farewell speeches and presentations were made in great good humour. We had all had a wonderful cruise, thanks to the good planning and warm hospitality of our American hosts.

The RCC members at the rally were: Kit and Penny Power, John and Caroline Power on *Kataree*, Colin and Marylyn Ford on *Nandisa*, Graham and Margaret Morfey with Merryl Huxtable on *Flight of Time* and John and Sue Sharp, with Tristan and Philip on *Canard*.

RCC members who were being entertained on American boats were: John Gore Grimes on *Knight Hawk*, Oz Robinson on *Hope*, Dick and Sheila Trafford on *Manukai* with Stanley Livingston (RCC) and Jonathan Trafford on *Fair Tide*. Other RCC members present were Warren Brown, Ed Kendrick and Jennifer Guinness.

Beaulieu Meet

The Meet had to be postponed by one week, but fortunately everybody got the message and it took place successfully a week later, with 32 boats attending. *Jolie Brise* could not be present, but *Hosanna* filled the breach and her enormous 86ft length was anchored fore and aft alongside the buoys. This gave an excellent base for the raft and her huge sitting room provided the ideal venue for an evening sing-song ably led by our Cadet

Captain, Emma. The world-girdling courtesy flags from *Sadko* were kindly lent to us by Noël Marshall and included many difficult colours for the younger members to identify. Unfortunately they were few in number, as most had returned to school because of the postponement. Boats attending were: *Albatross, Astros, Autarchy, Bluejacket, Brilleau, Chinita, Cyn III, Enki III, Felicia Fisher, First Lady, Hookey of Hamble, Hosanna, Kwai Muli, Lectron, Marlin, Merilintu, Mikonda, Morning Sky, Oboe V, Ocean Grace, Owl, Oyster Belle, Physalian, Saga of Sakrow, Sarie Marais, Squander, Starwalker, Tehari II, Tidecatcher II, Troubadour, Wandering Moon III, Warrior Shamaal.*

Christmas Meet

A spring low water at lunchtime dictated Yarmouth for the Christmas Meet on December 28th. Eleven yachts and two open boats arrived in weather more like spring than mid-winter. Assuming that, like ordinary clubs, we would have need of the services of local hostelries, the Harbour Master had berthed the fleet alongside, with the advantage that rafts could be visited without recourse to dinghies. The Sandy Watsons and Peter Bruce and his crew arrived in open boats, and David Ellis called in while waiting for the Lymington ferry. Great was the telling of stories of last summer, the laying of plans for next and the mulling and subsequent consumption of wine.

Boats attending were: *Kwai Muli, Enki III, Sarie Marais, Warrior Shamaal, Troubadour, Wandering Moon III, Cloud Walker, Merilintu, Hekla, Squander, The Otter.*

OBITUARIES

Major General C.W. (Bill) Woods, CB, MBE, MC and Angela Woods.

Bill and Angela Woods, who both died in 1996, made a dedicated husband and wife sailing team, racing and cruising in their own boats for 43 years. When they first met, Bill was an oarsman at Cambridge, and it was Angela who introduced him to sailing which became his prime pastime, although he was a competent and life-long skier as well.

Bill Woods also fitted in a full military career. Commissioned from Cambridge in 1938 into the Royal Engineers, he was badly wounded at El Alamein, won a Military Cross for gallantry on D-day in Normandy and took part in the bitter winter fighting on the Imjin river in the Korean campaign. He retired from the Army in 1970 and then worked for Service charities for 12 years.

From 1952 to 1994 he and Angela owned successively six boats, in two of which, *Tula* and *Tula II,* they took part in RORC races for 20 years, interspersed with annual cruising. Bill was Commodore of the Royal Engineer Yacht Club from 1968 to 1970 and of the Royal Lymington Yacht Club at a difficult period from 1981 to 1983. He was a friendly, calm and quietly spoken person, even in moments of crisis, and an expert and meticulous navigator, given to finding buoys in fog and cross-tides with quite uncanny accuracy before the days of Decca and GPS. Angela, equally charming and friendly, was no less competent a seaman and navigator, but also took care of the creature comforts aboard.

Bill and Angela came to the Royal Cruising Club in 1985, rather late in life, when they were both 68. But they already had many friends in the Club, and made others, by all of whom they are greatly missed.

OMR

Martin Tomlins

Martin Tomlins was born in 1909 and joined the training ship HMS *Worcester* in 1923 from University College School, London. His first seagoing appointment was six months as a Midshipman RNR – mainly on the battleship *Revenge* – before joining the P&O shipping company as an apprentice; he subsequently served with them as a Third Officer and held a Mate's Certificate . . . his service included a time in ice-bound Vladivostock where armed Bolsheviks confined the officers to their cabins!

His career changed direction when he joined de Havilland Aircraft,

313

training as both a pilot and a Field Service Engineer. Later, in the 1930s, he ran a family-owned laundry business which steadily grew from 50 to 450 employees and became known as the *White Knight* group.

Martin Tomlins joined the Cruising Association in 1937 and later became Editor of their Handbook, a natural extension of his meticulous planning for the many small yacht voyages he made. He visited most parts of north-west Europe under sail and owned a series of yachts culminating in his favourite *Xanthe*, built to his specification by Tucker Brown at Burnham.

Elected to the Royal Cruising Club in 1957, Martin won several trophies for his cruise accounts. His final home was Chichester Harbour, overlooking his mooring in the Bosham Channel, where he died peacefully last September.

GD

Robert Ballantine DSC

Robert Ballantine was a past President and Trustee of the Cruising Association and served on almost all its committees. Born in 1922 and educated at Highgate School, he joined the RNVR in 1941, serving first in HMS *Gambia* on Atlantic convoys and in the Indian Ocean. After gaining his commission he volunteered for Special Service and was posted to the Combined Operations Pilotage Party in Egypt.

Robert was then posted to the Levant Schooner Squadron, a clandestine unit formed in 1942 and operating first from Beirut and then from bays in south-west Turkey. He commanded what was claimed to be the smallest warship in the Royal Navy – a 30 foot Greek caique with a crew of three – undertaking many secret night missions into the Aegean Islands.

After the war, Robert became a chartered accountant and later senior partner with the City firm of Bagshaw & Co. He and Wendy moved with their three children to Landelmere Hall, an 18th Century manor house on the Walton Backwaters. Here they kept *Rollicker*, their Stella One-Design 25 foot sloop. Robert was elected to the RCC in 1988. On retirement, he bought *Rollicker II*, a 36 foot Westerly Conway ketch, in which he and Wendy sailed out to Turkey. Based on Kusadasi, they cruised widely in the Eastern Mediterranean.

CAH

Geoff Pack

Geoff Pack, Editor of Yachting Monthly since 1992, died aged 39 on 28 May 1997 after an eight month fight against cancer. Geoff was a big man in every respect. This Falstaffian figure had a big personality, a big sense of humour, a huge enthusiasm for boats and the sea, and a vast eclectic retinue of friends scattered around the globe.

When he joined Yachting Monthly at the age of 19, I realised that

Geoff was someone with a natural ability as a seaman. He could move around a boat with the agility of someone half his size and tackle seemingly impossible tasks with alacrity. As he developed into his job, so he honed his skills as a writer and tireless researcher. But no sooner had he started to carve a real niche for himself as a yachting journalist than he started to make plans to leave, buying the first *Foreigner*, a Wharram catamaran, and spending a year rebuilding her for a cruise 'wherever and with no determinate end'.

After an incident-packed crossing of the Atlantic, he and Lou Lou worked as charter skipper and hostess in St Lucia. Few couples survive a single season, but Geoff and Lou Lou managed two before returning to the UK after selling *Foreigner*, not to settle down but to start again, buying the Rival 34 *Euge* with which they successfully completed a two year Atlantic and Caribbean cruise.

Once again Geoff fell on his feet as there was a vacancy on Yachting Monthly and he returned as senior staff writer, later Assistant Editor. Here he made his indelible mark on the magazine with his enthusiastic and active writing programme. Geoff was also notorious for his mischievous sense of humour and many of his friends were the butt of his practical jokes, myself included.

Once again wanderlust struck and he left Yachting Monthly on the start of what was planned as a round the world, leisurely cruise on the second *Foreigner*, an Apache catamaran. Their cruise was cut short when Geoff was appointed Editor of Yachting Monthly after I joined Yachting World. I know he found this a difficult decision and one he confided he

regretted each time he sat on the early commuter train to London on dark winter mornings.

As well as being a colleague, Geoff was a close personal friend and Godfather to my son, Adam. He leaves his wife Lou Lou and four young children, Oliver, Claudia, Theo and Tilley.

AB

Robert Forbes Perkins

Forbes died last winter, aged 80, following a brief illness. After graduating from Harvard in 1940 and attending the U.S. Naval Reserve officers training program, he saw his first action as a Lieutenant at the attack on Pearl Harbor aboard USS *Pennsylvania*, flagship of the Pacific fleet. Rushing back from leave, he manned his battle station wearing a seersucker suit, an officer's cap and sidearms. He later became a Naval Aviator and piloted dive bombers from the USS *Ticonderoga*, receiving the Distinguished Flying Cross for participating in a successful attack on a Japanese cruiser in the Philippines. He was wounded in 1945 during a kamikaze attack and subsequently retired as a Lieutenant Commander.

After the war, Forbes pursued his careers of banking and investment management in Boston until retirement in 1989. He lived in Manchester-by-the-Sea, only minutes from his Concordia 39 yawl *Goldeneye*, which he owned for 29 years. In 1979, while Commodore of Manchester Yacht Club, he sailed *Goldeneye* to Plymouth with his two sons, Rob and Tom, as part of the MYC, CCA and Royal Western cruise in company. Later, while Commmodore of the CCA Boston Station, he organised the CCA Sexedecimal (a Forbsian word!) 'Down East' Cruise in which many RCC, ICC, RCYC and CCC yachts participated. He became an RCC member in 1984.

Forbes combined his love of the sea with love for family and friends. With his devoted wife Flo, he was a genial host of many happy gatherings. He leaves Flo, five children, four grandchildren and a sailing legacy being carried on by his two sons who are CCA members.

EK

Commander F. M. Crichton RN

Michael Crichton was born in Hampshire in 1909, the second son of Captain Reginald Crichton RN. Throughout his childhood, Michael spent much time at Netley Castle, the home of his grandfather, where he and his brother were allocated two sailing dinghies, the Chip and the Chop, becoming expert sailors younger than most at that time. In 1922, Michael went to the RN College Dartmouth, adding greatly to sailing experience there. His time as a Midshipman, and much of it as a Junior Officer in the 1920s and early 1930s, was spent in the Mediterranean Fleet, during which he was a member of the Royal Malta Yacht Club. He joined the RCC as a Naval Member in 1934. Michael's later naval experience included service as first lieutenant of a gunboat on the Yangtse just before World War II, first lieutenant of an Aircraft Carrier during that War, and command of a destroyer immediately after it.

In peacetime, wherever he was with the Navy, he sailed whenever he could in a variety of boats. He crewed in a Plymouth to Santander race in 1930 and sailed a lot in the Mediterranean and on the China Station. At one stage, during the 1930s, he was asked to coach young Prince Philip of Greece in sailing. As a consequence, in the late 1940s, Michael was invited by the Duke of Edinburgh to become the first Royal Sailing Master, combining the job with a staff appointment ashore. In that capacity he raced *Bluebottle* in her early days.

Michael Crichton skippered some very large yachts in the Mediterranean in the 1960s and then retired to the Crichton family territory on the banks of Lough Erne. In the 1970s and 80s he continued enthusiastic membership of the Lough Erne Yacht Club. From the late 1980s he spent every winter in Gibraltar, ending his days there in December 1996.

DPS

John Young

John died suddenly in February 1997. After leaving Stowe, his career as a chartered accountant was interrupted by his wartime RAF service and he spent the rest of his National Service with the RAF in Germany. Following demobilisation and completing his articles in Norwich, he built a 12 ft Firefly racing dinghy. In a regatta at Wroxham Broads, Gill was asked to crew for him. This was the start of their highly successful marriage.

John joined the firm of Pauls of Ipswich as company secretary and later became Financial Director. He took on many local public commitments and was also Commodore of Waldringfield Sailing Club. He took his 25ft Shenandoah to Holland with his young children and then owned a 28ft Twister before building *Quetzal*, a 34ft Legend hull which he completed at his home and sailed for 12 years with Gill. After retirement, John bought *Quern*, a Moody 34, taking her to Cornwall, the Channel Islands and Brittany. Later, he and Gill went through the French canals to the Mediterranean and cruised Spain, Italy and Corsica.

John was elected to the RCC in 1985. He was a great supporter of the Club and always flew the burgee. As a skipper he was meticulous in his instructions and everything went happily. All who knew him will remember him with great affection.

CL

Dr Peter Burnett

My father, Peter Burnett, qualified as MB, BS, LRCP from the Middlesex Hospital. The Second World War interrupted his medical career, but he joined the RAF and served with the medical units of Fighter Command as a Squadron Leader, attending some harrowing incidents. He married my mother, Yvonne, in 1940.

At the end of the War, he took over his father's practice and the sailing bug was able to germinate and grow. His first real vessel was a small converted fishing boat, soon replaced by *Mazurka*, an X boat with a cuddy forward and a non-functioning engine; her fate was probably sealed by my arrival. My mother tells the story of a Solent trip with me as a babe in a carry-cot floating in bilge water during a patch of nasty weather.

His next boat, *Airlie*, was a delightful gaff cutter built in 1898 of about 28ft with 6ft beam and negligible freeboard. Being narrow and graceful she was as fast as a witch. *Airlie* provided many happy family holidays and it was a sad day when she was replaced by *Nausikaa*.

Nausikaa provided wonderful sailing and cruising for the next 42 years. An 8 ton Gauntlet, teak on oak, she was as tough as a church but sailed well and was a terrific seaboat, cruising as far and wide as a busy practice would allow. In the late 1950s, a lasting friendship was forged with Roy and Helen Bailhache of Jersey. All through the 1960s and into the 1970s there was an annual family cruise in company with *Monica*. Perhaps as a legacy to these wonderful times, not only did I become an RCC member after being a Cadet, but all the Bailhache "young" did as well.

Pa retired from practice in 1976, which gave the opportunity for cruises to Scotland, Ireland and France. Advancing years reduced sailing ambitions to the south coast and the Solent, often single-handed, but none the less happy for that. It was a sad day when *Nausikaa* had to find a new home after 42 years.

A warm, kindly man with a lively sense of humour (often naughty but always witty), he was for ever the Doctor ready with help and advice. He was intensely loyal and a devoted husband, father and grandfather.

RB

Christopher St J Ellis

Chris, as he was universally known, died on 18th December 1997. He was a man of enormous talent and an inspirational teacher. Perhaps his greatest gift was his ability to encourage young people to develop their talents, whether they were academic, artistic or sporting, by a com-bination of persuasion, encouragement and sometimes even a little mild bullying. Many will recall his somewhat provocative style, which encouraged debate and brought ideas out into the open.

Chris was born on June 20th 1920, son of Major L F Ellis CVO, CBE, DSO, MC. He entered Eton on a scholarship and subsequently went up to Magdelen College Oxford where he read maths. Joining the Navy at the outbreak of war, he was unable to serve at sea because of lung problems which had plagued him all his life, but he served his country

with great distinction in the field of bomb disposal both in England and Malta. Chris was awarded the George Medal for exceptional bravery in defusing a bomb in Plymouth.

After the war Chris was appointed a master at Radley. In those drab post-war years he brought an unconventional approach which did not balk at challenging anything he considered pompous or stuffy. During his time at Radley he bought his beloved pilot cutter *Theodora* in which he took part in the first Tall Ships Race in 1956, winning his class in the second race. Chris won the RCC Challenge Cup in 1959 for a voyage across the Atlantic crewed by school leavers.

Countless young Radleians had their first experience of sailing on *Theodora* and Chris was able to see the obvious benefit which arose from the development of teamwork. With Christopher Courtauld he founded the Ocean Youth Club as a means of using boats and the sea to teach young people from all walks of life the qualities of teamwork, self confidence and consideration for others.

The Club started in 1960 with the two co-founders both lending their boats: *Theodora* built in 1911 and *Duet* in 1912. From that very modest beginning has sprung the largest sail training organisation in Europe. Fortunate indeed are those who worked and sailed with him and privileged are we who were taught by this exceptional man.

IE

John Wells OBE DSC

John's love of life and enthusiasm for everything he did inspired all those with whom he came into contact. He had a distinguished naval career and an interesting business life. His close association with the preservation of HMS *Warrior* will long be remembered. Parallel with his career was his enduring happy family life, his love of sailing, and his pride and enjoyment of RCC membership. He was elected in 1958 and was Honorary Steward from 1983 to 1988.

John was born in 1915 into a family with a strong naval tradition; he could count three admirals in his immediate ancestry. His own career followed an almost classic pattern for his generation: Dartmouth, destroyers, the Royal Yacht *Victoria and Albert*, gunnery expert at Whale Island (HMS *Excellent* of which he became Captain in 1961) and then six years of action-packed war service.

He was at Dunkirk in 1940 and in May 1940, aged 24, was given his first command – a small Dutch ship *Pascholl* in Poole harbour. John was ordered to St Valéry and Boulogne where his ship rescued 330 troops under intense shelling and dive bomb attack. He was awarded the DSC. Thence to the Mediterranean as gunnery officer of *Phoebe*, where he took part in many furious actions of the campaign including the August 1942 Malta convoy and the 1943 action to capture Kos and Leros. In 1945 John was aboard *Swiftsure*, our first major warship to enter Hong Kong, and it was a proud moment for him to be chosen to lead the 50th Anniversary Remembrance Services there in 1995.

There followed a series of interesting and varied peace time appointments in Athens, Canada and Malta, aboard the carrier *Warrior* as second in command and, after Whale Island, as captain of the guided missile destroyer *Kent*. After retiring he moved on to develop the Aviemore Skiing Centre, then four years with Clarkson Holidays and managing Gulf-Stream, a barge and container company.

He was then asked to write the history of HMS *Excellent* and there quickly followed his leading role in the preservation of *Warrior*. Many will recall his lectures and tours of *Warrior* and it was a fitting tribute that the dinner to celebrate his 80th birthday took place there.

In the early post war years, John brought back a 100 sq m windfall yacht from Kiel, did some ocean racing and became part of the *Fidget* crew. He owned a Contest 27 and then spent time sailing with Diana on *Josanta*, as well as crewing with other RCC members.

His last book, 'The Royal Navy – An Illustrated Social History', shows his sensitive insight and natural ability to comment on dramatic changes in Naval life. This book, with the immortal *Warrior*, will be our lasting legacy and his memorial service attested to his tremendous capacity for making and keeping friends.

RHT

Rattcliff Rowson MA CEng MI Mech E

Those who met Rattcliff Rowson (Ratty) will not forget him. He was outgoing, friendly, modest, often noisy. He was funny, the best of company. He was a courteous man, always more interested in hearing the activities of others than relating his own. He was kind, and an incomparable host, at home and afloat.

Ratty was one of five brothers, brought up on the Sussex coast where dinghies attracted him to the water. Oundle was chosen as the foundation for an engineering career, and the river appealed, so it was no surprise when subsequently he stroked the first boat at Clare, Cambridge, which went head of the river and earned him the Captaincy of the College Boat Club.

In addition to enjoying a full life at the University, he read Mechanical Sciences and joined REME in 1942. As a captain he serviced guns and vehicles on the second front. Forty years on, with glass in hand and arms waving exuberantly, he could tell yarns about the final advance to The Rhine that reduced his listeners to helpless laughter. He served his engineering apprenticeship with Vickers Armstrong, a company to which, after a decade of consultancy and business on his own, he returned in 1967 to command the hydraulic division. In this capacity he travelled the world, behind the iron curtain and elsewhere.

A neighbouring local doctor, a certain R A Andrews, invited Ratty to cruise extensively from Biscay to the Baltic. At the end of the 1950s, having also done much ocean racing, he bought from Gordon Gill RCC the beautiful Giles Brittany class 8-tonner *Droleen*. This coincided with his election to the Club and, at about the same time, his marriage to Elinor. Later, when his two daughters were old enough, the Club burgee was at the Rowson masthead again, with family cruising every year in the Arpège *Salanna* throughout Channel waters, in North Wales and later in the Mediterranean, particularly Greece.

Ratty's boats were orderly and shipshape. His engineering skills were applied and everything worked. There was endless chatter and laughter aboard and always an invitation to "stay for a toot" (see RCC Journal

Anti fouling in the 1950's, Ronnie on the left and Ratty on the right.

1983 p227). The kaleidoscopic range and applications of Ratty's talents and the unusual mix of gravitas and merriment which were his hallmarks will long be remembered by his many friends.

JHT

Dr Ronald Alford Andrews

> "Come, my friends,
> 'Tis not too late to seek a newer world,
> Push off, and sitting well in order smite
> The sounding furrows; for my purpose holds
> To sail beyond the sunset, and the baths
> Of all the western stars, until I die."

from Tennyson's Ulysses, oft quoted by Ronnie Andrews.

Retiring from general practice in Bexhill-on-Sea, Ronnie Andrews bought a cottage in Cargreen on the Cornish side of the Tamar and promptly set off to sail round the world in *Merlin*. When he returned three years later I greeted him as he stepped ashore in his home village. We walked up the narrow street together, he, unchanged, in short sea boots and a Breton smock. There was no flag-waving – simply one old resident who, leaning over his gate, recognised Ronnie and said, "Afternoon Doctor; had a nice time?" "Thank you. Yes. Now Bert, how's your wife?"

That typified Ronnie's sang-froid. He planned his circumnavigation over a long period and, as retirement approached, preparations became more detailed and intense. Ronnie was a seaman to the core and in the post war years he cruised the western seaboard of Europe extensively from Biscay to the Baltic. There was no surprise, no metaphorical jib-aback, when the English coast finally dipped as he set off to fulfil the ambition of his life. His departure was as unsung as his return. Although deep sea sailing at that time was beginning to attract some media attention, Ronnie was modest, austere, too refined to be drawn into the vortex of public relations.

Nevertheless, having retired earlier than he need, there was no money to spare. He wrote occasional articles for the yachting press to earn a fee, not to promote his name. And how admirably he wrote! Well read himself, and tending to a sensitive intellectualism, he could readily call on the experiences and words of a range of authors which gave his writing a special quality. It is a regret that Ronnie did not gather together and publish his seafaring reminiscences: they would have made better reading by far than some of the matter launched on the sailing bookstalls in recent years.

By today's standards, *Merlin* would be regarded as too heavy and cramped for a circumnavigation; for Ronnie she was just right. Strongly built of teak, her heavy displacement and long straight keel made for a comfortable ride at sea. Ronnie sold her only because he doubted his ability to finance and maintain her in his later years. This was a decision he regretted when elected Commodore of the Club at a time when he owned *Tetra*, a folkboat, a fact for which, quite unnecessarily, he always apologised. Somehow, with Rosemary, the latter usually swathed in voluminous woollen cloaks, he found space to cruise in *Tetra* for short periods and to fly the broad pennant at the joint Irish cruise in 1979.

Rosemary, a keen and accomplished dinghy helmswoman but not per-haps a natural deep sea sailor, gamely cruised many miles with Ronnie after their marriage in 1935. She was a graduate of Lady Margaret Hall,

an indomitable and captivating character who was a mine of interesting and entertaining information (see her delightful sketches in many Journals of the time), but the storms blew frequently between them. It was not altogether a surprise to his friends, but a bombshell to Rosemary, when Ronnie, after 45 years of marriage, walked out one fine morning from Cargreen never to return.

He hauled down his broad pennant in mid-term, fitted out his newly acquired Buchanan 8-tonner *Alceste* and in the autumn sailed quietly away bound downwind for the Panama Canal and beyond with Jill, a widow whom he had met in Australia during his circumnavigation, and her 14 year old son Matthew, as crew. Little is generally known about this voyage, but Ronnie's son Mike suggests it was perhaps his Father's greatest: the boat was small and the crew inexperienced; Ronnie was 70; he had no electronics; the petrol engine was so unreliable as to be useless and many of the passes through atoll reefs were made under sail alone.

In Australia he found a new life and, in Jill, a devoted and loving companion for the rest of his being. He continued to sail around Sydney, made friends and was much loved by Jill's young family. He absorbed with eager interest, in the words of his son Mike, "a new culture in a new continent", for, inspired by Tennyson, ". . . 'twas not too late to seek a newer world."

The RCC, to which Ronnie was elected in 1952, meant much to him. He served on the committee in the 1960s but was startled to be invited to stand for Commodore in 1977. He was uneasy in the role – his life as a doctor had not fitted him for it – but he nevertheless represented a core attribute of the Club and was true in every particular to its traditions. His "Message from the Commodore" in the 1979 Journal, as preparations began for the centenary year, recalled that the Club remained "a society of friends as our founders intended" and continued:

"It is only by preserving this heritage that we can hope to keep the joy and satisfaction we experience at times when cruising, moments when time for once becomes an ally, when realities are clear cut, when this spinning and tumultuous world of today sleeps on its axis, and when we too can still find that inner peace which is itself freedom."

JHT

Conrad Rawnsley

Born on 5th January 1907 in Sevenoaks, Conrad joined Osborne House as a naval cadet in 1920, followed by the Royal Naval College, Dartmouth, whence he graduated as general service officer. His first posting was to the Far East to serve in the Hydrographic Service, where he took part in the survey of the Malacca Straits.

Rawnsley met his wife, Elsin Little, in Shanghai in 1938. At the outbreak of war Rawnsley was seconded to the Polish Navy as liaison officer on North Sea convoy duties in the destroyer *Grom*. He was later promoted to Lieutenant Commander aboard the battleship HMS *Rodney*, from which he was invalided out in 1940.

Conrad's younger brother David had just been appointed Art Director for the film "In which we serve", a landmark in British cinematography. Conrad was able to supply technical advice for the construction of the set, which consisted of the upperworks of a J class destroyer. He went on to collaborate with his brother in the production of propaganda films for the Royal Navy and Ministry of Information.

In 1944, Conrad Rawnsley launched 'Common Ground', a company for the production of educational filmstrips. In the early 1960s, he became the National Trust's first Appeals Director, with a brief to raise funds for the purchase of unspoiled coastline throughout England, Wales and Northern Ireland. His 'Enterprise Neptune' was remarkably successful, but Rawnsley did not endear himself to what he considered an effete Establishment within the Trust. After attracting donations of £800,000 in the first year, Rawnsley was dismissed, provoking a debate about policy which reverberated within the National Trust for several years.

Conrad Rawnsley was elected to the RCC in 1934 and cruised regularly with other Club members.

PGC

Angela Sainsbury

I will never forget the wonderful cruises we enjoyed with Angela and Vernon in *Water Music* many years ago, when Ireland was our favourite destination. Later, aboard the smaller *Jemina*, the Sainsbury's gave us some memorable cruises in Brittany and my husband, Jack Lowis, used to crew for them in numerous RORC races. Angela not only kept everyone well fed but was also a stalwart member of the crew in those more traditional days of cruising and ocean racing.

Angela and Vernon had lived in Lymington for many years and were well known for their long sailing experience and very kind hospitality. Angela was a Senior Member of the Club, elected in 1950. She was 83 when she died and always remained cheerful. She will be missed by many friends.

JL

Charles Chatwin

After reading law at Birmingham University, Charles Chatwin joined his father's practice at Bennetts Hill. During the war, Charles escaped from the office into the Navy, where he had a distinguished career, first as a watch-keeping officer in the new Light Cruiser HMS *Euryalus*. After working up in Scotland, *Euryalus* was dispatched to protect the Malta convoys and joined the Eastern Fleet in Alexandria via the Cape of Good Hope. Having switched to small ships – minesweeping out of Valetta Harbour – Charles was sent to the United States with a Captain and crew to commission HMS *Cynthia*, a 'lease-lend' minesweeper under construction at Seattle. After passing through the Panama Canal, the Captain fell ill and had to be left ashore in Bermuda. So Charles assumed command and brought *Cynthia* home at the height of the U-boat war.

For his service in the Wavy Navy, Charles was awarded the Distinguished Service Cross, about which he never spoke except to say that it belonged to the whole ship's company. After the war, it was back to the ever expanding practice in the commercial life of Birmingham and the Midlands, making time for much voluntary service as trustee of local charities and hospitals.

Charles was elected to the Club in 1933 and cruised regularly with *Rakia 1* and *Rakia 2*, and later aboard his distinctive gaff-rigged ketch *Aireymouse*. He was 88 when he died on 27th December 1996.

HC

Terence Yates

In 1928, straight from school, Terence Yates joined the Training Ship at Plymouth as a Naval Cadet. There he was introduced to sailing in open boats, gigs and whalers from the R.N. Engineering College. A founder member of the RNSA, Terence sailed in the 1935 Fastnet Race aboard the old Bristol Channel Pilot Cutter *Amy*.

From 1936-39 he served in HMS *York* on the American station and had a good deal of sailing, including the spring racing at Bermuda where Sherman Hoyt – the America's Cup helmsman – was also racing. Sherman Hoyt later invited Terence to sail aboard *Endeavour I* and Terence well remembered Hoyt coming up from below with a tray of pink gins just as the helmsman let the boom start to lift on a dead run. In a rapid intervention by Hoyt, the gins landed on deck but the mast was saved.

Throughout his naval life, Terence enjoyed much cruising aboard RN windfall yachts and friends' boats. As Engineer Officer at Dartmouth, he spent a lot of time taking cadets cruising in the elegant 50 sq metre yachts the College had then. From Reserve Fleet Clyde, he often cruised the windfall 'cow' *Sigrid* up the west coast of Scotland. He sometimes sailed aboard the 33 ton *Seawolf* with the Miss Lawrences, of the chandlers Simpson Lawrence. They were often testing bits of equipment – including heads – which went wrong from time to time.

Terence was elected to the Royal Cruising Club in 1936. He leaves his wife Margaret, who usually sailed with him in Scottish waters.

PGC

BOOK REVIEWS

RCC Pilotage Foundation Desktop Publications

Cruising Notes on West Africa is the third title produced by RCCPF Desktop Publications. This part of the Pilotage Foundation is set up to publish pilotage information that is unlikely to be published commercially because of limited market appeal. We can undertake such projects because of voluntary effort. The books are produced in the style of an Imray pilot book and are marketed through Imray.

The other titles in print are:
Cruising Notes on the South Atlantic Coast of South America, compiled by Pete and Annie Hill, edited by Oz Robinson. The notes were compiled in 1993 during a voyage in *Badger* down the coast of South America from Recife in Brazil to Puerto Nuevo in Argentina. The book includes sketch plans of the numerous anchorages that they visited, and much practical advice on the logistics, delights and problems of cruising in this unfrequented area.

Supplement to Falkland Island Shores, by Pete and Annie Hill. This book was compiled during 1993/94, following the voyage chronicled above. It is specifically designed to be used in conjunction with Ewen Southby-Tailyour's original *Falkland Island Shores*, which is supplied with it, and mirrors the layout of the parent book for easy cross referencing. It expands on the original text and reflects the changes that have taken place in the Islands since the 1982 Conflict.

AJRW

Blondie – A Biography of Lieutenant Colonel H G Hasler DSO, OBE, Croix de Guerre, Royal Marines, by Ewen Southby-Tailyour (RCC) 1st Edn (Leo Cooper – £20)

The best biographies are perhaps those where author and subject are like-minded individuals. It's certainly true that Ewen and Blondie have more than a little in common and thus Ewen's empathy with his subject makes for a fascinating read. This is a well-balanced account of the life of a remarkable man who came to love the sea at an early age. He learnt the art of seamanship from a series of small craft before joining the Royal Marines in 1932, where he served with distinction during the war. Shortly after the war he raced with equal distinction in RORC races in the very wet *Tre Sang*. Possibly as a result of these experiences, his fertile and inventive mind concentrated on making life at sea more comfortable, initially with the Lapwing rig on *Jester*, followed by the renowned Chinese Lugs'l. He also developed his vane self-steering gear which many of us still use.

The 1950s were a hard time financially for Blondie and this, as his 'appreciations' describe, had a great effect on his love life. Some of his inventions failed to be accepted because of his lack of commercial experience. He tried his hand at play writing, with some success, and he wrote several books and articles that appeared in the yachting press and the Observer newspaper.

In 1956 he conceived the single-handed trans-Atlantic Race from which proliferated the now common short-handed races. It was during the search for 'X' in Loch Ness that Blondie met and in due course married Bridget. The final chapters are a delightful record of Blondie as a family man who takes up farming in Scotland. There is a wealth of detail and humour in this account of Blondie as a sailor, Royal Marine, inventor and family man.

RCC

From Duck Pond to Deep Ocean – a life of adventure, by Erroll Bruce (RCC)
1st Edn (Boldre Marine – £9.99)

This fascinating, light-hearted autobiography is an excellent read, in which the story of this remarkable seaman unfolds with modesty and great good humour. In a sense, this is also a biography of a particular era of sailing which many look back on with affection and nostalgia.

After a distinguished war service, Erroll Bruce raced four times across the Atlantic, completed 13 Fastnet races and four Bermuda races, earning a reputation as one of the most determined and successful yacht skippers of his time. His later collaboration with Adlard Coles in nautical publishing gave thousands of yachtsmen their first taste of the sea through the books of the highly successful Nautical Publishing Company.

RCC members will find a great deal of fun and some old friends within these pages.

PGC

The Pacific Crossing Guide, Edited by Michael Pocock (RCC)
1st Ed (Adlard Coles Nautical with the RCC Pilotage Foundation – £38)

This comprehensive book must be the starting point for anyone planning to explore the Pacific under sail. The accumulated experience of so many Club members and members of the OCC must add up to hundreds of thousands of miles of Pacific passage-making. The mouth-watering colour photographs in the centre show not only palm-fringed atolls and clear turquoise lagoons, but also snow and ice in Alaska and the towering mountains of Chile.

Divided into three sections, the book offers an encyclopaedic range of advice on weather patterns, radio communications, how to contend with cockroaches, and a fascinating chapter on the different peoples of the Pacific islands. The second section considers the various major passage routes and finally there is detailed information on individual harbours around the Pacific.

Space must be found for this book on every circumnavigator's bookshelf and it will equally be enjoyed by those many armchair sailors hoping, one day, to be able to visit the Pacific for real.

BJC

ROLLING INDEX OF CRUISES

This year the index covers the 1994, 1995, 1996 and 1997 editions.

ANTARCTIC, S ATLANTIC

1994 Hill 239, Shepton 185 **1995** Hill 134

AUSTRALIA, NEW ZEALAND

1997 Marriott 224, O'Grady 100

BALTIC, SCANDINAVIA

1994 Lomax 170, Price 27, Ridout 213, Wood 126 **1995** Lomax 182, Marsh 257, Power 169 **1996** Aish 159, Lewin-Harris 185 **1997** Ingram 163, Lewin-Harris 214, 265, Parkinson 186, Williams 286

BISCAY, ATLANTIC SPAIN AND PORTUGAL

1994 Clark 258, Thornhill 231 **1995** Lawrence-Jones 65, Nixon 37, O'Riordan 192, Sharp 264, Snow 106, Southby-Tailyour 242 **1997** Fenwick 20, Scott-Bayfield 251, Virden 55

BRITTANY

1994 Lawrence-Jones 71 **1995** Nodder 14, Watson 115 **1996** Gorer 74, Nockolds 252, Power 258 **1997** Clark 278, Franks 134, Lloyd 216, Straton 176

CANADA

1994 Ker 59, Smith 224 **1995** Stratton 48 **1997** Bonham Cozens 246, Hill 107, Smith 137

CARIBBEAN, CENTRAL AMERICA

1994 Bonham Cozens 145, Le Couteur 200, Marriott 3 **1995** du Plessis 239 **1996** du Plessis 144, Nockolds 14 **1997** Manzoni 256

CIRCUMNAVIGATION

1997 de Mowbray 271, Marshall 59

ICELAND, GREENLAND, FAEROES

1995 Clay 231, Ker 123, Wollen 90 **1996** Ker 82, Lomax 228, Thornhill 29 **1997** Southby-Tailyour 78, 86

INDIAN OCEAN

1994 Ford 138, Merewether 95, Woodhouse 112 **1995** Shepton 24

INLAND EUROPE

1994 Lloyd 21 **1995** Buckley 165, Cooper 214

IRELAND

1994 Marsh 103 **1996** Adam 100, Tew 218, Virden 262, Webster 23, Wiltshier 48 **1997** Gill 30, Thornhill 180

JAPAN, FAR EAST

1994 Winser 75 **1996** Fraser 249

MEDITERRANEAN

1994 Beiser 87, Trounson 160 **1995** Hunter 254, Millar 56, Raines 101, Trounson 207 **1996** Franks 194, O'Riordan 93, Roth 122, Wilkinson 35 **1997** Beiser 237, Butler 38, Lawrence-Jones 3, Raines 141

N ATLANTIC, AZORES

1994 Virden 48 **1995** Winser 76 **1996** Carr 3, Grindle 202, Richey 70 **1997** Mitchell 171, Morfey 202, Power 92, Richey 151

PACIFIC

1995 Finding 152 **1996** Finding 208, Kimber 52 **1997** Close-Smith 16, Hawkings 45, Power 292, Swetenham 117

SCOTLAND

1994 Sandberg 15 **1995** Fishwick 199 **1996** Taggart 61, Marsh 138, Lawrence 155 **1997** Bolton 8, Bruce 198, Bryer 154, Price 297, Quick 129

USA

1994 Bonham Cozens 150 **1995** Roth 3, Vasey 147 **1996** Coldrey 254, Hunter 39, McLaren 236, Vasey 106 **1997** Tew 26, Vasey 192

INDEX

330

Officers of the Club